1000   B.C. A.D.   1000   1900

...A CASSITE   NEO-ASSYRIAN   ACHAEMENIAN   PARTHIAN   EARLY ISLAMIC   ILKHANID   MODERN

...YLONIAN   MIDDLE BABYLONIAN   NEO-BABYLONIAN   SELEUCID   SASSANIAN   ᶜABBASID   OTTOMAN

Settlement:

...major ...return ...along

Hiatus in settlement?

Temporary decline of cities, towns?

Abandonment in south, growth of cities, towns and villages elsewhere

Virtual absence of permanent settlement in region

Region a desert. Villages encroaching on peripheries

Progressive abandonment of cities, larger towns. Shift toward dispersed small town–village pattern

Reemergence of towns, villages. Uruk again an important urban center

Population maximum? Many large towns, villages

Disappearance of cities, towns

Rare towns, shifting clusters of villages dominated by forts

Subsistence:

...e-scale, ...istered ...herding

Mixed large- and small-scale irrigation, date plantations, fishing

Limited pastoralism and/or fishing, buffalo breeding

Sparse pastoralism; irrigated zones encroaching

Limited pastoralism, small-scale cultivation

Planned, large-scale irrigation to north of growing swamps. Cultivation of rice?

Mixed pastoralism and shifting, small irrigation. Brigandage

Political:

Local effects of great urban-based empire not apparent; possibly speeded resettlement outside region

National state. Decline in strength, autonomy of tribes

...re stable, ...organized

Local resistance to Assyrian power

Military empire

Military empire with considerable regional autonomy in administration

Cycles of destructive conquest

...Declining state authority, ...ncreasing rural autonomy

Urban-based empire

Unstable, urban-based realms

Increasingly bureaucratic empire

Political fragmentation

Tribes and confederacies in flux. State control limited

The Uruk Countryside

The Uruk Countryside

The Natural Setting of Urban Societies

Robert McC. Adams and
Hans J. Nissen

The University of Chicago Press
Chicago and London

The University of Chicago Press, Chicago 60637
The University of Chicago Press, Ltd., London

© 1972 by The University of Chicago
All rights reserved. Published 1972

Printed in the United States of America
International Standard Book Number: 0–226–00500–3
Library of Congress Catalog Card Number: 78–179489

Contents

Illustrations

Preface

The archaeological reconnaissance furnishing the substantive data for this study was conducted over a four and one-half month period during the winter and spring of 1967. It had its inception in a discussion between Professor Heinrich Lenzen, then director of the Baghdad Abteilung of the Deutsche Archäologische Institut, and Dr. Henry T. Wright, who at that time was conducting a reconnaissance and soundings in the region around ancient Ur. Professor Lenzen expressed an interest in extending an archaeological survey approach into the desert lands around the great ruined mounds of ancient Uruk—modern Warka—where for many years the Deutsche Archäologische Institut has sponsored one of the most far-sighted and comprehensive programs of excavation yet developed in the Middle East. Other commitments led Dr. Wright to demur from conducting such a reconnaissance himself, whereupon the initiative fell to me.

Having previously conducted somewhat analogous operations over much of the northern portion of the Mesopotamian plain, I viewed the possibility of extending the same approach into the classic heartland of southern Sumer as a most welcome opportunity. Professor Benno Landsberger had once characterized the manuscript of my earlier study of changing systems of settlement and irrigation on the alluvial fan of the lower Diyala River as an attempt to describe a dialect before the paradigm of the heartland was known.[1] Although I do not fully share his view that the most significant developments of the past were encapsulated in a restricted region and span of time—I prefer to regard Mesopotamian civilization as a bundle of indefinitely ongoing dialects, an interacting system of regions and specializa-

tions whose paradigm shifted and is to a certain extent imposed only arbitrarily—it was undeniable that systematic study of the sustaining areas of the great cities of southern Sumer was long overdue.

From the outset, this study was conceived not as a repetition of survey approaches previously employed in other areas but as a further elaboration of them. Since Warka lay near the lower end of the alluvium, it was to be expected that the remains of early periods would be substantially less masked by later settlements and alluviation deposits than were similar remains farther north. Hence it seemed likely that settlement and irrigation patterns might be investigated in considerable detail even for as early a period as the late fourth and early third millennia, a time during which Uruk emerged as one of the oldest and largest of Mesopotamian urban centers. To this end, a program was envisioned that would extend over a considerable span of years. The first step was to have been a wide-ranging reconnaissance of the kind reported here, in which systematic coverage was sacrificed for knowledge of the larger geographic setting. From that point onward, plans were projected for detailed studies of the hydrology and ecology of portions of the ancient irrigation system. Also contemplated were further, more systematic resurveys aimed at small areas and particular problems, and ultimately test soundings in representative early sites.

It should be stressed that the field approach in 1967 was not only planned but executed on the assumption that it was only a part of this long-range framework. What has emerged with increasing clarity from all such studies is that archaeological surface reconnaissance is not a sharply bounded, independently justified, and more or less fixed body of techniques, but instead is a variable component within a wide and growing complex of ecologically oriented investigations of the kind sketched

---

1. R. McC. Adams, *Land behind Baghdad: A History of Settlement on the Diyala Plains* (Chicago, 1965), p. ix.

above. But in the sequel, political and other changes stemming initially from the June 1967 war made it impossible to pursue the other elements in this wider complex. Hence the findings reported here are less well supported and detailed than it was intended that they should be. Indeed, the exceptional quantity and quality of evidence awaiting the archaeologist directly on the surface in the Warka region demands further work at the earliest opportunity. The spirit of developing a many-sided ecological approach, however, is not consistent with the postponement of publication pending some indefinite final truth. Although we acknowledge the tantalizing incompleteness at many points of what it has been possible to learn thus far, the results nevertheless seem to significantly enhance our processual understanding of the growth of a major ancient civilization. Perhaps equally important, publication at this point serves to enlarge the empirical basis for settlement-pattern studies—and it provides a target for criticisms that can lead to future improvements in methods.

By far the greater part of the fieldwork in the Warka region was conducted jointly by Dr. Nissen and myself. There was a rough and informal division of labor in which I attended mainly to mapping problems, with the aid of aerial photographs, while he selected sherd samples for systematic discussion and illustration. In fact, however, the entire reconnaissance is better described as a time of fluid interchange of tasks as well as views. As a result many ideas originating with Dr. Nissen undoubtedly have been incorporated with my own in the first part of this volume, although during its actual writing the division of labor became formal. Similarly, some of my own observations probably are incorporated in the second part of the volume, for which he has taken the responsibility of authorship. In addition, he has prepared the supplement to chapter 3, dealing with textual sources on the historical topography of settlements and canals in the Warka region during the late third and early second millennia, and I am responsible for the appendix describing the surveyed sites. To a considerably larger degree than these complementary but separate sections suggest, this entire work should thus be regarded as a product of joint authorship.

It is a pleasure to acknowledge the personal and intellectual debts incurred in this undertaking. We are grateful, first, to Professor Lenzen for perceiving the need for it and for unstintingly lending the resources of the Deutsche Archäologische Institut toward its successful completion. Dr. Nissen was at that time a member of the staff of the Baghdad Abteilung, and in graciously agreeing to his full participation in the entire course of the reconnaissance Professor Lenzen took an essential step in making this jointly sponsored project possible. My own participation, originally planned as an exclusively Oriental Institute commitment, was made substantially more effective through my appointment as Annual Professor of the Baghdad School of the American Schools of Oriental Research for 1966–67. I also owe a more personal debt of gratitude to Professor George R. Hughes, who took over my duties at home as director of the Oriental Institute for the period of the fieldwork, and who then succeeded me in that post in July 1968.

As on so many previous occasions, the officers and staff of the Iraq Directorate General of Antiquities were unfailingly helpful not only in facilitating the execution of our plans but helping us to improve them. Thanks are due in particular to Dr. Faisal El-Waᶜilly, then director general, to Sayyid Fuad Safar, inspector general of excavations, and to Dr. Fawzi Rashid, who represented the directorate at the Warka excavations that season. As the aid and critical guidance we repeatedly received indicates, the directorate's own research now rests on a solid foundation of professional competence and intellectual strength. The gradually unfolding study of the ancient Mesopotamian landscape still awaits—and would richly repay—the diversion of some of that strength.

R. McC. A.

1| Configurations of Settlement
Robert McC. Adams

1 | Physiographic Characteristics and Problems

It would be well to begin an account of this reconnaissance with a systematic description of the Warka region. However, we lack both the data and the broad range of competences, ranging from geology to botany, that are necessary for this task. Nor can we merely draw on the conclusions of detailed studies by specialists in other fields, for there are none. Such indispensable preliminary aids as maps meeting minimal standards of completeness and accuracy are unavailable, and leveling traverses from which even generalized, largely conjectural contours might be drawn either have not been undertaken or remain unpublished and inaccessible.

The reasons for the apparent previous lack of interest in obtaining such data are not hard to adduce. No population centers in which economic development has been concentrated are close at hand. Nomadic and semi-nomadic groups for whom the region has been a haven currently are declining somewhat in importance, and the unsettled local conditions for which they have been only partly responsible remain as a deterrent to long-range investments in much of the southern part of the alluvial plain. Moreover, the reduced slope and drainage here, compared with regions farther north, exacerbates the problems of salinity and so retards the onset of market-oriented agriculture.

Of course, this does not mean that the region has been entirely isolated from and unaffected by the profound changes taking place elsewhere in Iraq, a point which will be elaborated presently. But the incongruous fact remains that a landscape from which came some of the earliest and most important impulses leading to Mesopotamian civilization, a landscape dotted with urban ruins testifying to past intensive settlement, prosperity, and even greatness, today is virtually empty and wholly neglected.

The main topographic features of the surveyed region nevertheless can be easily, if somewhat impressionis-tically, summarized. It is bounded on the south by the present main channel of the lower Euphrates, which pursues a meandering course of only moderate sinuosity between the present town of Samāwa and the more important provincial capital of Nasirīya. Smaller towns and villages, together with a continuous ribbon of date gardens and other forms of intensive cultivation, occupy the levee of the river for varying distances up to five kilometers northward from its present banks. Then commences a series of back-slope depressions subject to seasonal flooding. Under peak flood conditions these form an irregular series of shallow, open lagoons that are more or less interconnected, providing sluggishly moving drainage parallel to the main channel. However, most of the water which escapes into these depressions fails to find its way back into the river farther downstream and disappears from them only by penetrating downward to the subsurface water table or by evaporation.

Moving northward from the northern limits of these depressions until beyond the limits of this survey, the topography is that of an even, or at most very slightly undulating, plain that for the most part is devoid of vegetation. Save for the few ancient mounds that attain a significant elevation, its only irregularities are dunes. At least to macroscopic inspection, the dunes are composed of silt particles identical to those composing the plain itself, and they vary in morphology from stable, low, barely perceptible swellings that blend into the underlying land surface to loose, steep-sided accumulations up to six or eight meters in height.

Individual dunes clearly are responsive both to the prevailing northwest wind and to the less frequently occurring atmospheric depressions that periodically draw winds and storms across the area from the southeast. As little as a day of relatively strong winds may cause several meters of lateral movement and can alter their shape un-

1

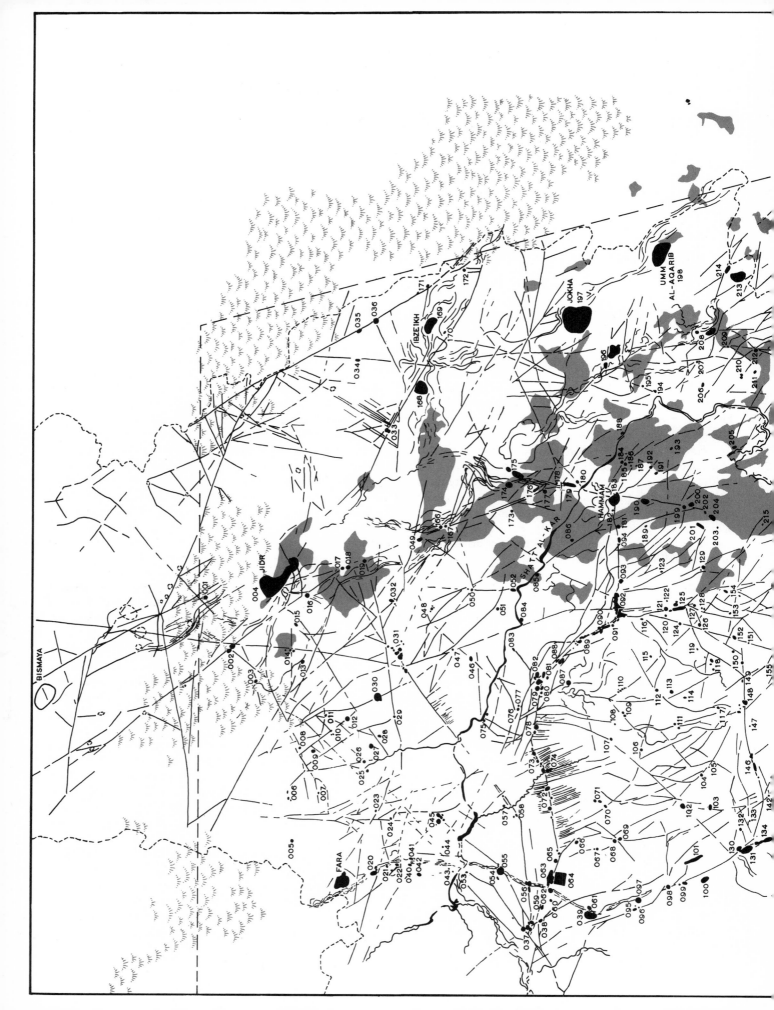

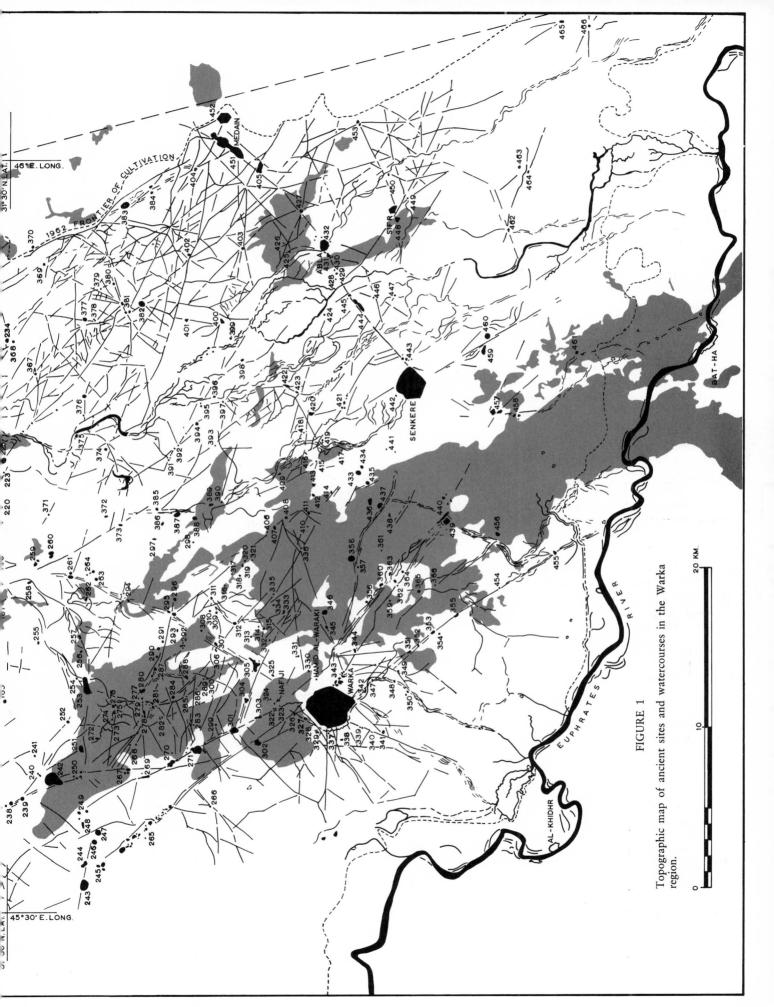

FIGURE 1

Topographic map of ancient sites and watercourses in the Warka
region.

recognizably. The general trend must be toward the southeast, particularly since winter rains tend to stabilize the dunes during the part of the year when southeast winds occur most frequently. It is unclear, however, how rapid and extensive are the movements of the great, irregular belts and clusters into which most of the dunes are grouped. According to one report, the very large formation of dunes now to be found in the district around the ruins of ancient Umma or Jokha first appeared late in the last century.[1] Closer to Warka, the excavators report a noticeable encroachment of the frontier dunes upon that site during the approximately four decades since modern excavations began.[2]

The principal areas now occupied by dunes are plotted on the base map of the region (fig. 1). In part, these areas are so thickly covered that the underlying land surface—and any small, low ancient sites that may occur on it—is rarely visible. To a much greater extent, the dunes are either isolated at considerable distances from one another or else are very loosely clustered, so that much of the adjoining land surface is unobstructed. On the other hand, it should be borne in mind that the areas shown in hachure do not encompass all aeolian deposits. The larger, more sharply contoured dunes are easily visible in the aerial photographs[3] from which the map was drawn; low-lying, sheetlike deposits of wind-laid silts often are not. If we assume that these two different kinds of formations occupy areas of roughly equal magnitudes, which was the subjective impression that emerged from the reconnaissance, then the area shown in the base map as continuously dune covered still may approximate that which is obstructed by recent wind-laid deposits of all types. Planimetric analysis indicates that this is about 19 percent of the total area of 2,800 square kilometers covered in the reconnaissance.

There is an important contrast between topographic features in this region and some that occur farther north. Canal levees are very prominent in Akkad and the Diyala region, culminating in spoil banks that often retain a height of several meters for more than a millennium after the canal has been abandoned, and that frequently run for many kilometers in multiple-stranded, diverging and intersecting chains. As was already noted by Andrae[4] many years ago, nothing of the kind occurs here. Only the largest trunk canals, like the one known locally as the Shatt al-Nil (a frequently recurring name for large, ancient canal remains), which persisted through Parthian times along the line of an earlier Euphrates course flowing southward to Warka, can be followed today as low, vaguely defined levees. What makes this difference still more significant is that average annual rainful in the northern part of the Mesopotamian alluvium is apparently slightly higher than around Warka,[5] surely indicating that the rate of sheet erosion of features like canal banks in the former also is slightly greater. Two factors probably account for the major part of the difference. One is the smaller load of silt carried by the lower Euphrates compared with rivers and canals farther north. The other, whose influence we will further analyze presently, is an increased rate of wind erosion through which old canal levees in the southern part of the plain presumably have been more rapidly and completely scoured away.

The eastern boundary of the survey is defined along virtually its entire length by the frontier of cultivation as it existed in 1967. This is naturally irregular and does not coincide with a historic frontier of any sort, since it is based on the configuration of right-bank branch canals from the Shatt al-Gharraf at a given moment in the long, slow, atomistic process of their extension that has continued since late in the last century. Two considerations led to the acceptance of the present margin of cultivation as a boundary in spite of these objections. First, disturbances associated with modern cultivation seriously impede the location of ancient sites—particularly the low, small prehistoric sites that were a major focus of our interest—and reduce the quantity of sherds available for surface inspection. Second, only sites in the uncultivated sector were easily accessible in a reconnaissance based at Warka. Routes to those sites in districts under cultivation could have been found only in a systematic survey of the entire right-bank Shatt al-Gharraf region (for which there

1. B. Moritz, "Zur Geographie und Ethnographie von Süd-Mesopotamien," Gesellschaft für Erdkunde zu Berlin, *Verhandlungen* 15 (1888): 188.

2. H. J. Lenzen, personal communication.

3. Aerial photography of this region was conducted by KLM from October 1961 to October 1962. The survey employed individual contact prints and stereoscopic pairs at an approximate scale of 1:35,000. We gratefully acknowledge the assistance of the Directorate General of Antiquities in securing copies of these prints, which now have been placed in the custody of the directorate.

4. W. Andrae, "Die Umgebung von Fara und Abu Hatab," Deutsche Orient-Gesellschaft, *Mitteilungen* 16 (1903): 26.

5. Although the span of years for which data from all stations is available is perhaps too short to be statistically significant, a comparison of reported precipitation from the three Directorate of Meteorology stations nearest the Warka region with precipitation in Baghdad is at least suggestive. For eighteen "water years" between October 1940 and the end of September 1958, the reported precipitation in millimeters was as follows:

	Minimum	Maximum	Mean
Baghdad	61.9	255.6	145.6
Hai	62.5	221.0	136.6
Nasirīya	33.5	249.3	120.9
Dīwanīya	57.6	179.5	112.1

SOURCE: Hydrological Survey of Iraq, Baghdad, 1959.

was insufficient time), since motorable roads in cultivated zones generally trace out a dendritic network radiating from the main towns and canals.

The western boundary of the survey is more regular but no less arbitrary. For the most part, it follows the north-south line of a particular series of aerial photographs chosen to cover an area to about fifteen kilometers west of Warka. This was extended farther west at one point to include the head reaches of a large, branching Sassanian canal system, while at the extreme north the western boundary was deflected eastward by advancing cultivation.

It was originally hoped that the survey would establish a northern boundary at about the latitude of Bismaya (ancient Adab). Dense dune formations, shortness of time, and the unavailability of all the necessary air photographs unfortunately made it impossible to attain this goal. The present boundary follows an irregular line from Fara (ancient Shuruppak) to Ibzaykh (ancient Zabalam), with a northward bulge in the vicinity of the important (but still unidentified) ancient site of Jidr or Imām Dhāhir.

One other physiographic feature of the region thus circumscribed needs brief mention. The former bed of the Shatt al-Kar pursues a meandering course across it, tending first in a southeasterly direction and then southward to a junction with the Euphrates. During Euphrates floods river water sometimes backs up in the old bed almost to Qalᶜa Falhīya (site 399), and in dry weather shallow wells are dug down to the level of groundwater by seminomads grazing their flocks in the vicinity. Elsewhere the bed has been infilled and virtually obliterated by dunes and drifts. In many of the early records of European travel in the region, however, the Shatt al-Kar takes a central place. Apparently it served as an outflow channel for swamps around ᶜAfak that were fed by the Dhaghara canal, as well as for swamps and irrigated lands southeast of Dīwanīya. Lacking a dependable source in the parent Euphrates, its water supply was always hazardous. Probably it was further affected by the shift of the main part of the Euphrates flow westward from the Hilla channel to the Hindīya channel in the latter part of the last century. Crumbling mud brick forts guarding once strategic weirs and canal offtakes along its course still punctuate the now barren horizon at wide intervals. We will return in chapter 5 to a fuller discussion of the little systems of settlement and cultivation they were designed to protect.

Having outlined the main features and limits of the region selected for study, it is essential to emphasize again their historical and geographic arbitrariness. Our unit of study was chosen mainly to frame an important, interacting set of early towns: proceeding in a clockwise direction, Zabalam (modern Ibzaykh), Umma (Jokha), Bad-Tibira (Medina), Larsa (Senkere), Uruk (Warka), and Shuruppak (Fara), as well as the area of the ancient Sumerian "high edin" enclosed by them. Since the bounds of the reconnaissance necessarily remain the same for all periods, this might be assumed to imply that the centrality, or at any rate the representativeness, of the region remained a constant. But as will be shown in detail later, one important outcome of the survey is the demonstration that it did not. Of the important early urban centers, only Uruk, Larsa, and Jidr survived as significant settlements until the first millennium B.C., and only the last was still occupied at the time of the Arab Conquest. In later periods, and possibly also in some intervening ones, historical initiative passed to other areas and centers so that this region was left marginal, backward, and at times almost abandoned.

It is also important to stress the arbitrariness of our unit of study from a geological and hydrographic standpoint. The Warka region is only a small portion of an alluvial plain that constitutes a geological continuum without sharp internal boundaries. Not only are its natural features in no way distinctive, but also they can be shown to be dependent in many ways on changes induced elsewhere. Periodic shifts in the distribution of the Euphrates flow among its various channels, for example, have repeatedly and decisively affected the fortunes of the peoples of this region; only the most recent illustration is the dessication of the lands formerly served by the Shatt al-Kar. Yet the explanation for these shifts is not localized here. Among the important contributory factors have been uneven processes of siltation in different channels, alternating repair and neglect of regulatory irrigation works farther upstream, and possibly even changes in the Tigris course that have secondarily influenced the regime of the lower Euphrates. From this viewpoint, no approach to explanation not embracing the whole alluvial plain can be really satisfactory. But granting the shortcomings of this or any similar region as a framework for full-scale analysis, it nevertheless sets convenient limits for the description of a meaningful segment of the historical development of Mesopotamian settlement patterns.

Any discussion of changing settlement patterns must take place against the background of regularities in landscape formation that are imposed by interacting factors of climate, water supply, and terrain. These formative processes have been summarized for the Diyala plains in terms generally applicable to the Mesopotamian alluvium,[6] and the reader may wish to refer also to a recent and very comprehensive review of research on alluvial

6. R. McC. Adams, *Land behind Baghdad: A History of Settlement on the Diyala Plains* (Chicago, 1965), pp. 4–12.

geomorphology in both empirical and theoretical terms.[7] With these studies available, discussion of the Warka region can be confined to distinctive aspects of the local topography which appear to exercise a crucial influence on our understanding of ancient settlement patterns.

Perhaps foremost among these is the question of the depth of the alluvial sediments that have been deposited here since the onset of an agricultural occupation. Unfortunately, the significance of observations made by archaeologists in many parts of the alluvium is much reduced by the casual way "plain level" has been recorded. Moreover, the depth undoubtedly is greatest along the levees of long-lived, major watercourses—near which, as it happens, most of the available measurements have been made. The problem is further complicated by the fact that over long periods waterlogged soil is not an entirely rigid material. Hence the initial occupation layers of at least the more massive ancient mounds must have been displaced downward in absolute level by the weight of overlying debris.[8] But in spite of these considerations, there seems little ground for doubt that in certain instances something approaching eight meters of sediments has been laid down in the upper alluvium since the late fourth millennium B.C.[9] Has the rate of alluviation in the Warka region been of the same order of magnitude?

At Warka itself, sterile soil in the deep Eanna sounding lay at an elevation of 0.99 meters above mean sea level, approximately six meters below the present level of the surrounding plain.[10] As was mentioned in the preceding paragraph, however, the great thickness and weight of overlying debris at Warka leaves the meaning of this depth open to doubt. What are badly needed, and currently unavailable, are measurements of the depth of initial occupation layers at several small, low sites located in different parts of the surrounding area. But although data permitting an unequivocal answer to this question currently are lacking, there are a number of converging lines of indirect evidence suggesting that the depth of alluvial sediments generally is much less than the measurement at Warka would indicate.

To begin with, it may be noted that the depth of virgin soil at Warka seemingly is inconsistent with that at Qalᶜa

Hajji Mohammed. Early occupation levels at the latter are even older than those encountered in the Eanna sounding, and probably may be assigned to the early fifth millennium B.C. The site occurs directly on the bank of a main branch of the Euphrates, where the depth of later alluvial sediments presumably is at its greatest. Yet the depth of sediment reported to have been found overlying a presumably single-period occupation, whose thickness was not ascertained but is unlikely to have exceeded one or two meters, is reported to have been only 2.5 meters.[11]

Second, attention may be drawn to the striking uniformity of all but a very few of the prehistoric sites recorded in the Warka survey. Most are low and small, and the character and sparseness of debris on many indicates that they were occupied only during a single relatively brief period. It is difficult to visualize more than a meter or two of cultural deposits accumulating in most of them under these circumstances, and yet numerous closely grouped, contemporary clusters of such sites still rise to or slightly above the present level of the plain. The inference is obvious, if not entirely incontrovertible, that in many areas not more than one or two meters of alluvial sediments overlie the land surface as it was known in early Sumerian times.

A third lead is provided by observations made at site 281 (cf. p. 25). Here, in a single-period site of Jemdet Nasr date, it was still possible to follow shallow surface depressions indicating a bifurcating network of watercourses that divided the site. Since the site lies on an otherwise even and undisturbed plain surface extending for many kilometers in all directions, no alternative explanation on the basis of localized factors seems possible, and the conclusion is reinforced that the depth of overlying sediments is relatively small. Elsewhere in the area are other apparent segments of pre- and protohistoric watercourses that still can be traced on the surface or in aerial photographs. Some unquestionably were already present in the Jemdet Nasr period or even earlier, providing a supporting argument for the prevailing thinness of alluviation, although in most cases they are of less significance since the possibility of persistence into later periods cannot be entirely excluded.

Still a fourth line of evidence arises from repeated observations of instances of very marked, rapid wind erosion. Perhaps the most clear-cut examples were Parthian cemeteries, which sometimes were placed on abandoned earlier mounds but which also were often located at some distance from the nearest occupational site. As is exemplified by sites 311–12, the striking feature of many of these cemeteries was the extent to which they had been denuded by wind erosion. Slipper coffins and

7. J. R. L. Allen, "A Review of the Origin and Characteristics of Recent Alluvial Sediments," *Sedimentology* 5 (1965): 89–191.

8. R. J. Russel, "Louisiana Stream Patterns," American Association of Petroleum Geologists, *Bulletin* 23 (1939): 1210; J. P. Morgan, "Ephemeral Estuaries of the Deltaic Environment," in *Estuaries*, ed. G. H. Lauff, American Association for the Advancement of Science Publication 83 (Washington, D.C., 1964), pp. 116 ff.

9. Adams, *Land behind Baghdad*, p. 9.

10. A. Nöldeke, in *Fünfter vorläufiger Bericht über die von der Notgemeinschaft der Deutschen Wissenschaft in Uruk unternommen Ausgrabungen* (Berlin, 1934), pp. 40–41.

11. E. Heinrich and A. Falkenstein, *Neunter vorläufiger Bericht . . . Uruk-Warka* (Berlin, 1938), p. 37.

urn burials which initially must have been placed at least a meter or so beneath the plain surface now are often found entirely exposed and with their upper portions irregularly scoured away by the wind's action. Similarly, there were instances in which recent movements of dunes had swept over archaeological sites, leaving behind on the surface badly scoured but otherwise nearly intact pottery vessels after the thick layer of cultural debris in which they must have been buried was carried away by the wind.

There is much additional evidence that wind erosion has been the decisive force in shaping the present terrain. Wind-carved butte formations, generally low but in some instances rising several meters, were found in many places; in all cases they were at least macroscopically indistinguishable from the horizontally stratified sediments composing the plain itself. A glance at the base map will indicate that major mounds or groups of mounds frequently are accompanied by clusters of dunes. The concentration of these dunes in the lee of such mounds is partly a reflection of prevailing patterns of wind movement, but it is hard to escape the impression that their presence also is to be partly explained by wind erosion of the upper mantle of material composing the mounds themselves. Finally, allusion has already been made to the flattening and virtual disappearance of ancient canal levees. Numerous canal lines that no longer could be traced as perceptibly raised levees nevertheless could be followed for considerable distances as dense lines of shell fragments. Apparently these fragments, once concentrated in canal beds and spoil banks, were too large to be transported by the wind and hence were left behind when the matrix in which they were originally embedded was eroded away.

It must be emphasized that wind action in the Warka region is not exclusively an agent of erosion rather than aggradation. As has been indicated, most of the immense volume of silts composing the dunes themselves is apparently of local origin. There are also large areas in which originally loose aeolian deposits have acquired a firm structure and crustlike surface and are no longer easily distinguishable from the presumed alluvial sediments on which they rest. This was especially true east of the Shatt al-Kar and north of Larsa, which perhaps helps explain the relative scarcity there of the small, low early sites that are so numerous elsewhere.

To summarize these disparate observations is not easy, at least in quantitative terms. All of them provide indirect leads at best to the relative importance of erosional and aggradational processes, underlining the need for a systematic program of stratigraphic soundings away from the major mounds like Warka. But at least the evidence does not support the widely prevailing impression that a massive, uniform, essentially constant addition of super-imposed sediments through alluviation is the dominant geomorphic process for the Mesopotamian plain as a whole. It is clear that nothing approaching the six meters of alluviation in six millennia that are reported for the immediate vicinity of Warka can apply as an average to the entire region of our survey, and that the increments resulting from alluviation vary substantially from place to place. It also seems likely that the increment of new sediments during the last two thousand years or so has been almost negligible. For at least this region and period, the primary geomorphic change must have consisted of an accelerating erosion not only of ancient tells and levees but even of portions of the plain surface, and of the complimentary formation of stable aeolian deposits and great belts of moving dunes.

This in turn underlines the uncertainties inherent in interpreting the survey's results. It is obvious that reconnaissance cannot be complete where there are dense belts of dunes. But in addition, if some wind-laid deposits have, over time, become unrecognizable as such, then even in areas without dunes the apparent paucity or absence of sites can be misleading. Something of the same kind occurs as a result of alluviation, to be sure, for mounds can be as effectively covered with alluvial deposits as with wind-blown silts. This is well illustrated at Ras al-ʿAmiya, where an early Ubaid mound almost three meters high was found entirely buried 1.2 meters beneath the present level of the plain.[12] Normally, however, alluviation is accompanied by (or is a direct result of) irrigation agriculture. Hence continuing disturbances of the soil such as plowing usually bring sherds from buried levels to the surface. In the case of Ras al-ʿAmiya, the presence of an underlying site can be known at once from the surface debris still to be found there. Wind deposition, on the other hand, generally occurs during periods when cultivation has been abandoned—as it was in much of the Warka region after Parthian times and before the advent of shifting, sparse, and superficial settlements during the last few centuries. Under these conditions, there may be many sites of which there are no surface vestiges at all.

Other lacunae or problems in the survey's coverage may be mentioned more briefly. Travel was difficult in the seasonally flooded depressions paralleling the Euphrates' course, and the effectiveness of reconnaissance there was further reduced by vegetation and irregularities of terrain. Moreover, alluviation there is surely continuing, and in the absence of ongoing cultivation many low sites in these depressions undoubtedly have been buried completely.

A limitation of a different character arises because the

12. D. Stronach, "The excavations at Ras al-ʿAmiya," *Iraq* 23 (1961): 95–137.

survey operated from a fixed base at Warka, so that coverage was naturally more complete in its vicinity. Does the large number of small, early sites around Warka testify to the special importance of this center in the Uruk and Jemdet Nasr periods? We believe it does, and that the contrast with the paucity of such sites around Senkere and Fara would be altered only in degree and not in kind if the survey's results could be corrected to provide for a uniform intensity of coverage. But admittedly this conclusion is partly impressionistic.[13]

All these problems and limitations underline the provisional character of most of the survey's results. Genuine uniformity of coverage, for example, would have required a uniformly spaced grid of search routes. But although this procedure would indeed permit more secure quantitative estimates of settlement distribution and population density, it would have been extremely difficult and time consuming to maintain in the almost featureless, largely dune-covered terrain around Warka. Greater systematization also might have been attained through reliance on large randomized sherd collections. This might well have led to some improvement in chronological control, as well as to an understanding of functional differentiation within and between sites. All such techniques, however, also multiply the time that is needed per unit area of reconnaissance coverage. The conscious choice in this survey was to cover a larger, historically more significant area, even though this made it necessary to rely on summarily recorded, rarely quantified assessments of sherd collections, and not to attempt absolute uniformity of coverage. In short, the decision here was to forego the employment of more intensive and sophisticated methods in order to provide a first approximation that would speak more comprehensively to major historical and anthropological problems.

One outcome of this decision is that broadly synthetic, qualitative statements about the region on the whole are more consistent with the existing empirical base than finely discriminating, analytic, quantitative ones. The former include, for example, characterizations of changes in overall settlement patterns during successive periods. Much of the account that follows consists of such characterizations, and the evidence for them is readily and economically summarized in the form of a sequence of maps. Ultimately, however, it is the task of the culture historian to deal *systematically* with questions like population change and distribution, settlement hierarchies, subsistence patterns, and intergroup relations, for only with an understanding of these variables can we hope ever to get at the socioeconomic roots of historic processes of change. Hence, in spite of the slenderness of the empirical base, it has seemed worthwhile to frame some aspects of this inquiry in quantitative terms drawn largely from recent advances in the field of locational geography.[14] This is particularly so in chapter 2, concerned with the pressing theoretical problem of the earliest formation of Mesopotamian cities and supported by a body of settlement data that is at least relatively large and secure. To be sure, there is no doubt that some of the analytical approaches followed there have severe limitations in their present application, stemming largely from inadequacies in the data with which to test them. But even with present uncertainties, they make possible an advance into interpretive realms that could not be attained on any other basis.

Intensification and systematization of survey methods is only one needed direction of future improvement. There is also a general need, although varying in urgency at different points in the sequence, for a substantial refinement in the chronological framework. Many of the time periods serving as the fundamental classificatory units for the survey's findings are excessively long, poorly tied to absolute chronology, and dependent in part on ceramic criteria that overlap them. Largely because of work at Warka itself, this is ironically less true for most late prehistoric periods than for the "better known" historic epochs that follow. And the dependence of the survey on the Warka sequence merely foreshadows a further, equally crucial trend toward the close articulation of reconnaissance programs with problem-oriented excavations of widely varying scale and intensity.

Even a casual scrutiny of the maps for successive periods will immediately make apparent a number of gross changes in settlement patterns. Those changes demand not only description but also such provisional explanation as we can offer without taking refuge behind the indefinite possibilities of expansion and refinement in the fund of available data. The aim of this study is to help turn research into new channels. If its comparatively primitive methods also provoke dissatisfaction, we welcome and encourage the subsequent efforts of others to improve them.

---

13. Some light is shed on the question by field books that were kept in the order that sites were visited. Of the forty-four prehistoric sites within fifteen kilometers of Warka, three were located during transit to more remote areas after the primary inspection of this district had been completed.

14. Cf. especially P. Haggett, *Locational Analysis in Human Geography* (New York, 1966).

2 | Spatial and Temporal Patterns of Early Urbanization

The earliest occupation of the plains around Uruk, at least in nucleated settlements of sufficient size and duration to be identified with the methods of the Warka Survey, is shown in figure 2. Without question, the dominant impression is one of sparseness of population, comparable only to a few later intervals of near abandonment. But the comparison is faulty in that during those later intervals population merely shifted from this region and concentrated elsewhere, whereas early concentrations are unknown anywhere in southern Iraq. Moreover, the map does not illustrate even an approximately contemporary grouping of sites, but instead combines data on a succession of time periods extending from the middle of the fourth millennium well back into the fifth millennium or even earlier.

Two arguments support the assumption that the observed low density is a genuine reflection of conditions at the time rather than an artifact of data that is heavily skewed toward overrepresentation of later periods. One, already adumbrated in the previous chapter, is that alluvial (and aeolian) deposition and wind erosion have been complementary geomorphic processes more nearly comparable in magnitude than is usually supposed. The supposition that early sites have been uniformly buried beneath deep overlying deposits of silt simply cannot be sustained with the available evidence. In this respect, it is also worth noting that the very numerous sites of the immediately succeeding periods are generally small and always of very modest elevation. Hence earlier occupations cannot be deeply buried within them, so that if an occupation during the periods included in figure 2 were indeed widespread, sherds representative of those periods ought to occur as a substantial component of our surface collections. Herein lies the second argument. Painted pottery, immediately recognizable from a distance, constitutes a very high relative proportion of the wares of those periods. If anything, painted wares are grossly overrepresented in our samples. Although an indeterminate number of sites from all periods must indeed have been overlooked, it follows that the relatively low density shown in the map must be essentially accurate.

Within this overall impression of sparseness, a slow but fairly steady increase also can be traced in the map. Only a single rather small site (298) may antedate the site of Eridu. This and an additional small site (267) were occupied during the Eridu subphase of the Ubaid period, and surface sherds at Uruk may testify to the earliest beginnings of the great center at about the same time. For the following subphases, seven, seven, and eleven sites are recorded respectively. This increases further, to eighteen sites, during the early phase of the Uruk period which concludes the time span covered by the map.[1] Unfortunately, in spite of this increase the number of coeval Early Uruk sites is still so small that most of the watercourse network they presumably adjoined cannot be even tentatively reconstructed.

It would appear that sites during this entire early time range were prevailingly rather small. To be sure, our information on many is inadequate in that their surface areas were obscured by later debris. But even when we add to those that can be measured directly (because they were later abandoned) the greater number of sites whose dimensions were taken from larger, later occupations, at least five of the fourteen Ubaid sites must have covered less than one hectare. It may be significant that the same applies to only three of the larger number of Early Uruk

---

1. Outside the area of the survey, and hence not included in these counts, are the sites of Hajji Mohammed and Raidau Sharqi (E. Heinrich and A. Falkenstein, in *Neunter vorläufiger Bericht . . . Uruk-Warka . . .* [Berlin, 1938] pp. 33–38). They are, however, shown in figure 2.

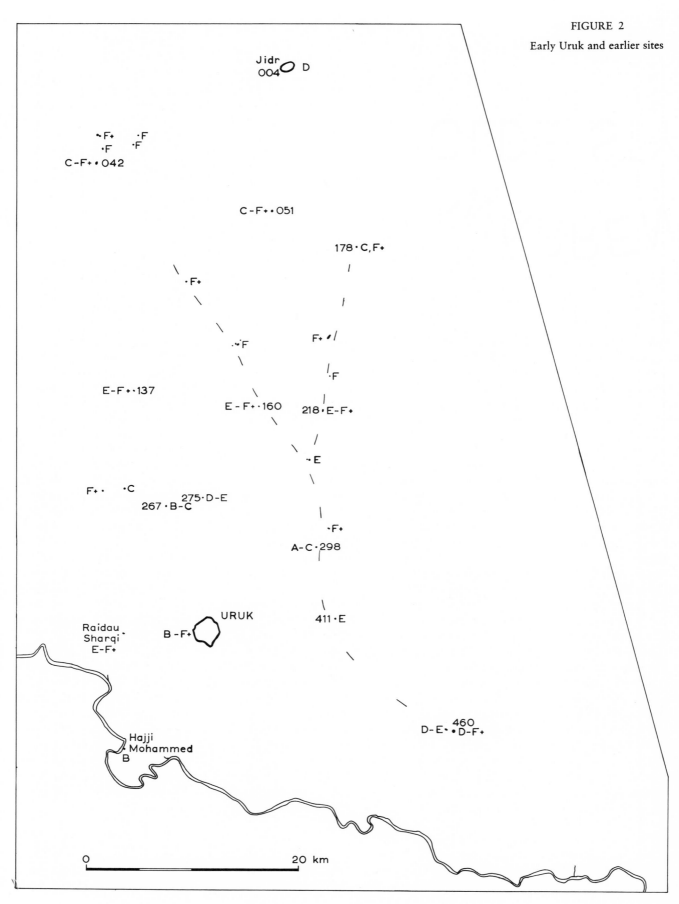

FIGURE 2
Early Uruk and earlier sites

Jidr
004 D

·F+   ·F
·F   ·F
C-F+·042

C-F+·051

178·C,F+

·F+

·"F

F+·/

/·F

E-F+·137

E-F+·160   218·E-F+

·E

F+·   ·C
275·D-E
267·B-C

·F+
A-C·298

Raidau
Sharqi·   URUK   411·E
E-F+   B-F+

Hajji
Mohammed
B

D-E·460
·D-F+

0   20 km

10

sites, although the aggregate numbers are not large enough to posit a decline in the proportion of extremely small sites on this basis alone.

Nevertheless, appearances are in some respects misleading. To begin with, the area covered by Uruk itself at this time is entirely unknown, but at least by the end of the Early Uruk period the construction of the Anu ziggurat and the ambitious program of temple building in the Eanna precinct suggest that it must have been approaching urban size. But even excluding Uruk, and considering only the six sites of the preceding Ubaid period whose size is known because they were subsequently abandoned, an average area of almost four hectares is indicated. Again, the problem of inadequate numbers makes comparison hazardous, but it may be noted that the average area of these six is about twice as large as that of the six sites abandoned after the Early Uruk period. Moreover, the latter figure is entirely consistent with the much more securely established average for the Late Uruk period (cf. fig. 7). Hence the possibility must be entertained that—excluding major centers like Uruk—average settlement size was in fact considerably larger during the Ubaid period than it was for a long time subsequently.

An essentially similar suggestion can be derived in a different way, independent of averages that admittedly have an inadequate numerical base. Individual settlements could exceed five hectares in area as early as the Hajji Mohammed period (042) and ten hectares by the end of the Ubaid period (460). These are no longer to be classified as mere agricultural villages. Together with others that were only on the order of one-hundredth of this size, they indicate that already by the Ubaid period there was a marked degree of social differentiation and complexity in spite of the sparseness with which the countryside was occupied.

A further noteworthy feature of the early settlement patterns shown in figure 2 involves the distribution of sites. With only one doubtful exception,[2] pre-Uruk sites are all isolated from one another at distances of four or more kilometers, on the whole remarkably evenly dispersed along the presumed watercourses of the time. This is in sharp contrast with the clustered distribution that is so characteristic of the Late Uruk period, although the Early Uruk data perhaps provide a bridge between the two distinctive configurations. One site (118) occurs during this Early Uruk transition which, although less clustered than its later counterparts (see fig. 11), is entirely without earlier precedent and may represent four closely related but separate communities. Also more similar to

later than to earlier patterns is a grouping of five small sites in the northwestern part of the region within an area where only one (042) had existed previously. But whether or not these sites document a genuine transitional phase, the broad change from the earlier to the later configuration is of such a magnitude as to suggest important shifts in underlying patterns of subsistence and land use. And the possibility must at least be recognized that major shifts of this kind coincided with the appearance in the region of new population elements.

New population elements, whether immigrant cultivators or formerly nonsedentary herdsmen and hunter-gatherers of local origin who now converted to agriculture, also may be suggested by the extraordinary jump in the number of occupied sites between the Early and Late Uruk periods. For the former, as mentioned above, only 18 sites are known, whereas for the latter 108 sites were recorded. An increase on this scale appears to offer a good prima facie case for population increments whose primary source did not lie in the natural fertility of villagers already resident in the region, particularly when it is contrasted with the relatively slow rate of growth over the preceding millennium or so. However, any explanation is obscured by uncertainties about time scale. If the Late Uruk period represents a span of not more than three or four generations (say, a century or even less), the arguments for immigration or conversion or both probably are compelling. If five times as long an interval were available, they may no longer be so. Both alternatives, unfortunately, lie well within the range of possibilities that present understandings of chronology do not permit us to exclude.

In virtually all respects we are on firmer ground when we turn to the subsequent span of time, for which figures 3–6 illustrate the Warka Survey's main findings. This period covers the course of general, decisive, irrevocable urbanization in the late fourth and early third millennia. To be sure, Warka itself may well have attained urban proportions by the outset of this transitional era. At that time, however, it appears to have been one of at most an extremely small number of such centers, and there is little doubt that it was organized along predominantly theocratic lines. The historic pattern, in which the great bulk of the population of southern Mesopotamia was persuaded or compelled to reside within the walls of many contending city-states, clearly had not yet made its appearance. In this sense, the sequence of maps by periods that these figures provide can be said to summarize the data that have been recovered on the redistribution of population accompanying the initial appearance of a genuinely urban way of life in a small but crucial part of the alluvial plain.

Certain gross trends can be posited simply from a comparison of these maps. To begin with, the pattern of

---

2. Sites 459 and 460. Early sherds at the former were sparse and may have been secondarily transported from 460 as inclusions in mud brick prepared there.

widespread rural settlement that reached its peak in the Late Uruk or Jemdet Nasr periods was progressively replaced by a smaller number of larger urban centers during the successive phases of the Early Dynastic period that followed. There are residual uncertainties in ascribing a date to the beginning of this shift, arising principally from difficulties in distinguishing Jemdet Nasr from Early Dynastic I surface collections that are adumbrated in chapter 7. But there can be no doubt of a cumulative shift of impressive proportions, at least over a longer time span.

A second, equally evident trend involves the reduction in the apparent number of watercourses. The earlier pattern was one of multiple, often meandering channels whose position relative to one another in a continuous network (or possibly in a succession of networks) is often unclear. Presumably they served a patchwork of relatively isolated enclaves of cultivation, save in the immediate vicinity of Uruk, the needs of whose relatively large population may already have dictated a more comprehensive approach to land use that left fewer adjacent tracts unutilized because of an absence of drainage or irrigation. But at least by the Early Dynastic II period (and possibly slightly earlier), this pattern had been replaced by one in which settlement was heavily concentrated along a small number of major Euphrates channels. The identification of these channels is discussed in chapter 3.

Further, it will be noted that two of the three channels in use at the end of the Early Dynastic period are marked for much of their length by a quite unprecedented degree of linearity. This must reflect the outcome of a process by which many watercourses were diked, straightened, and gradually subjected to artificial control, so that in the end they shifted decisively away from the regimes of natural stream branches in a floodplain, and along the continuum toward what can be identified as predominantly artificial canals.[3]

Lest all such trends be assumed to apply uniformly, simple inspection of the maps also indicates a number of local disparities in settlement and abandonment. For example, there is an obvious contrast between the relatively dense and continuous distribution of settlements north and northeast of Uruk during the Late Uruk period and the virtually unoccupied eastern and southeastern parts of the surveyed region during the same period. During the subsequent Jemdet Nasr period this is partly modified through the appearance of a new closely spaced, linear grouping of large towns south of the later city of Umma. This grouping, without contemporary parallel elsewhere in the region, suggests some form of federative activity that led to the construction of a canal more than fifteen

kilometers in length. Such was the form, it appears, of at least this instance of initial colonization of a formerly lightly occupied region. But it is also interesting to note that the example did not survive into the later Early Dynastic period. Although the area may have remained within the zone of cultivation upon which Umma depended, the population of the towns in question seems to have been drawn into the neighboring, larger center in much the same way as—and only slightly later than—the region surrounding Uruk was depopulated.

Descriptive statements like the above, as well as the sequence of maps from which they are derived, constitute one component of a "settlement pattern" approach. Where the available data are sufficient, as they are here, another component consists of spatial or locational analyses that seek to refine or penetrate within the grossly observable, descriptive regularities. Still a third focus of study involves detailed topographic plotting of former alluvial levees, depressions, and surface anomalies, as well as systematic exposure of soil profiles, in order to permit reconstruction of depositional history over wide areas. Finally, of course, some of the findings of traditional historiography and archaeology fall under the settlement pattern rubric. This is so at least insofar as they can be used to reconstruct subsistence, demographic, economic, and other aspects of man's changing relationship to a given landscape. Moreover, it is only from these disciplines that the crucial chronological framework for settlement pattern studies can be drawn.

Of the above four requisites if settlement pattern studies are to be used as a secure basis for interpretation, it has already been noted that one, systematic exposure of soil profiles and topographic leveling, is wholly lacking in the Warka region. A second indispensable requirement, relevant archaeological and historical studies, is at best very inadequately met for the periods in question. Archaeological excavations in the region have been virtually confined to ceremonial precincts at Warka and to somewhat enigmatic trenches at Fara. These sites (and others outside the immediate region) currently provide a fairly secure chronological basis for the analysis of surface collections, but are of little assistance in establishing a basis for demographic, ecological, and socioeconomic inference that is independent of our settlement pattern data. Then too, texts that were contemporaneous with the initial onset of urban life are of very circumscribed utility at best until there have been further advances toward even an approximate assignment of meaning (let alone translation). Even then, it may be found that their subject matter is too limited to provide an independent, converging line of evidence against which deductions from settlement pattern data can be checked.

The outcome is that an ecologically oriented interpretation of the onset of urban life in the Warka region at

---

3. R. McC. Adams, *Land behind Baghdad* (Chicago, 1965), pp. 8–9.

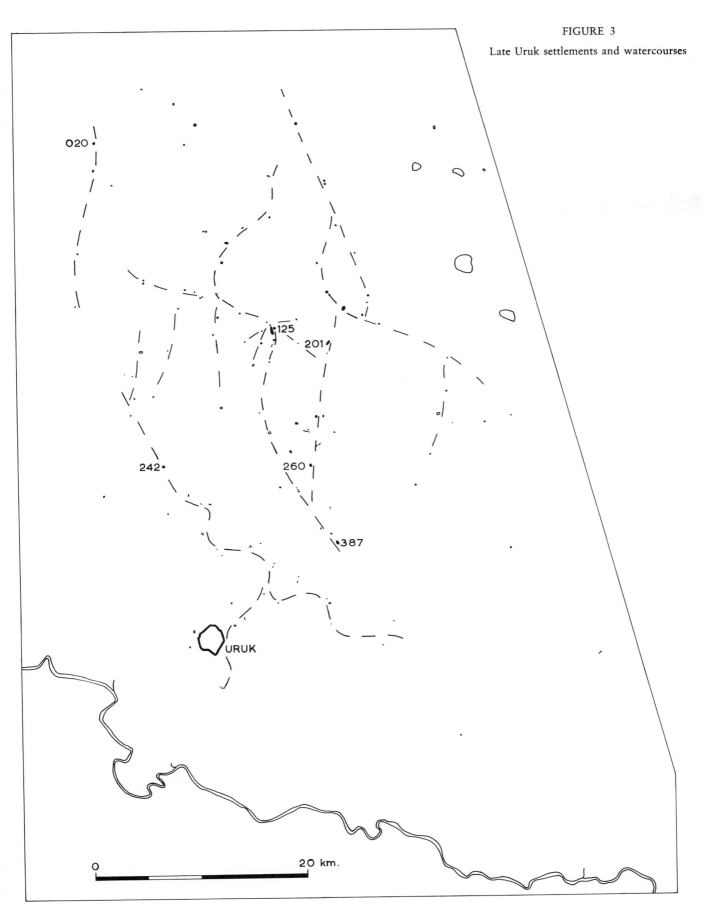

Late Uruk settlements and watercourses

020

125
201

242

260

387

URUK

0   20 km.

13

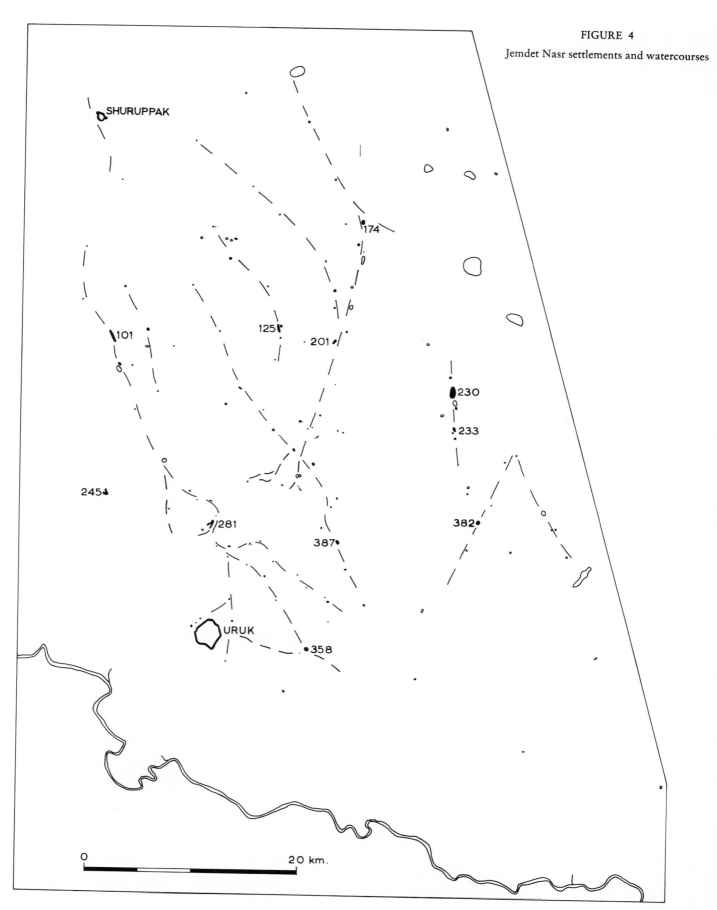

FIGURE 4
Jemdet Nasr settlements and watercourses

SHURUPPAK

174

101

125

201

230

233

245

281

382

387

URUK

358

0   20 km.

14

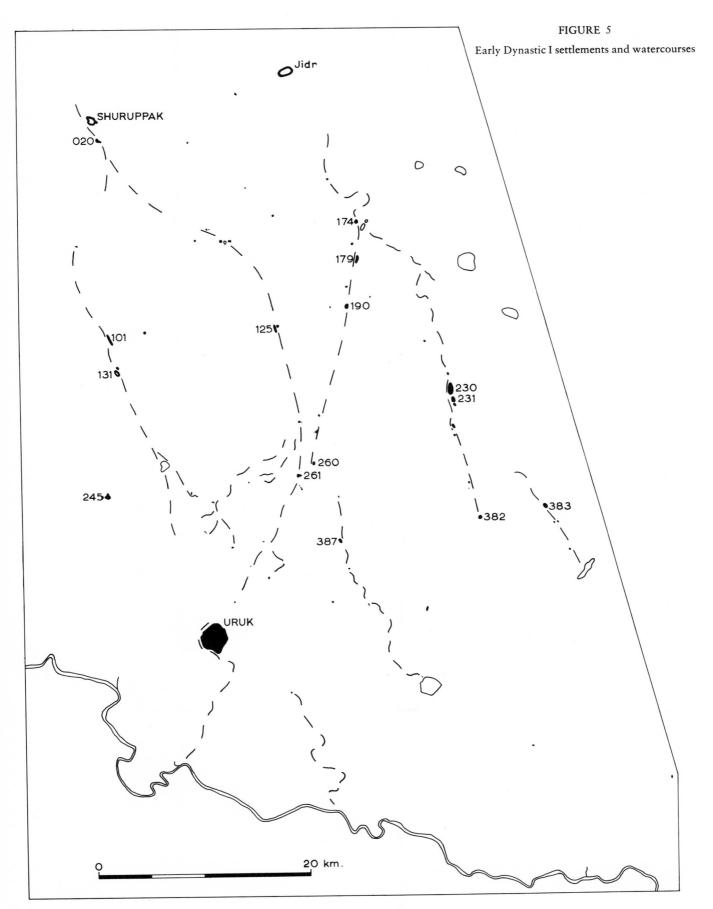

FIGURE 5

Early Dynastic I settlements and watercourses

Jidr

SHURUPPAK

020

174

179

190

125

101

131

230
231

260

261

245

382

383

387

URUK

O   20 km.

15

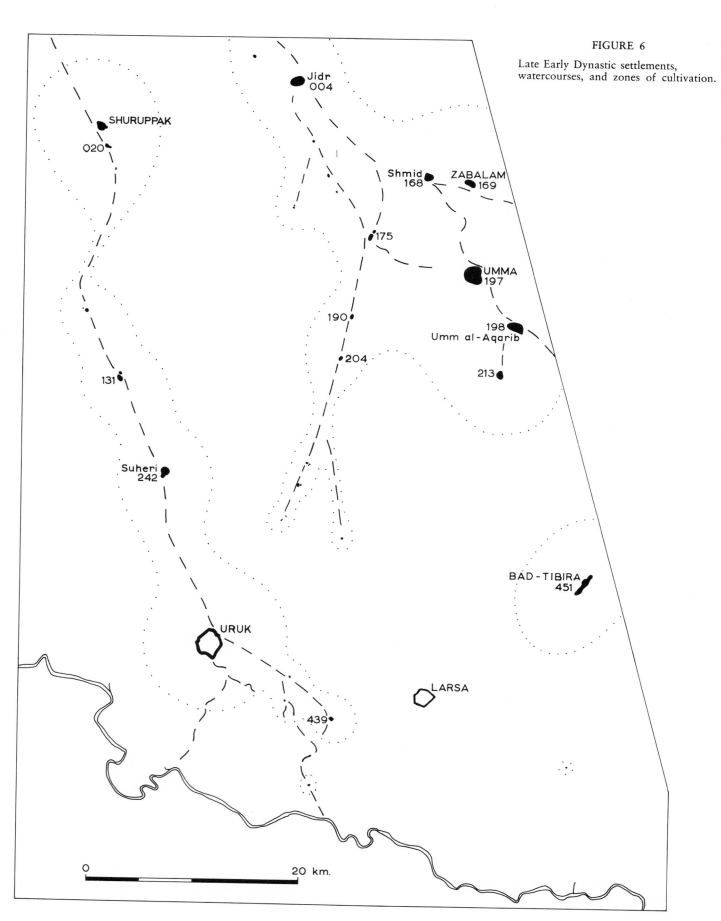

FIGURE 6

Late Early Dynastic settlements, watercourses, and zones of cultivation.

Jidr
004

SHURUPPAK

020

Shmid
168

ZABALAM
169

175

UMMA
197

190

198
Umm al-Aqarib

204

213

131

Suheri
242

BAD-TIBIRA
451

URUK

LARSA

439

0   20 km.

16

present must rest virtually exclusively on settlement pattern data. Some will accordingly reject any attempt here to place our findings in an interpretative framework, beyond that implicit in the periodization and display of those findings in a series of maps, as poorly founded—at best probabilistic, at worst, barely more than speculative. Perhaps they are right, but the subject of the rise of urban civilization in Mesopotamia is altogether too important to be abandoned until the uncertain future day when "sufficient" data are at hand. Moreover, it is quite unlikely that certainties will generally be substituted for probabilities in any reasonable future; our task, in fact, is not to avoid probabilistic statements, but to make explicit the evidence and assumptions on which they are based. In this spirit, it seems important to carry an analysis of the settlement pattern data well beyond the descriptive statements made above. Not all of the specific approaches hereinafter attempted ultimately may prove fruitful, but as a group they may at least suggest a range of propositions which can and should be independently assessed by reference to our own or other data.

Taking the Warka region as a whole, the changing distribution of sites according to size (fig. 7) provides one approach to an understanding of urbanization. To be sure, there are important difficulties in plotting such changes in the case of multiperiod sites. Since there is some tendency for larger sites to be occupied for longer periods, the results shown in the chart probably are somewhat skewed in that they give disproportionate emphasis to sites occupying only a few hectares or less. Clearly the chart should be read and interpreted with full attention to the figures shown in the "uncertain" column, and it may be noted that these figures are particularly large (in relation to the total number of sites known to have been occupied) for the Jemdet Nasr and Early Dynastic I periods that constitute the crucial intermediate phases in the urban transformation. On the other hand, sites which can be assigned to one or another of the size shown constitute a definite majority for all periods. Hence with all its limitations the chart does furnish a basis for the analysis of certain regional trends in settlement size.

A first such trend involves a progressive increase in average size, from between one and two hectares in the Late Uruk period to between six and ten hectares in the late Early Dynastic period. This trend continues regularly through the intervening periods as well, although there is a temporary reversal in the corresponding increase of the mode (perhaps to be explained by the large "uncertain" category) during the Early Dynastic I period.

A second trend, related to the first, involves increasing irregularities in the curves of settlement size. In the Late Uruk period, save for Uruk itself, all sites whose size can be determined seem to fall within a unimodal distribution. The picture is less clear for the Jemdet Nasr and Early

Dynastic I periods, again partly as a consequence of the larger "uncertain" categories. However, there is a steady growth in the number of settlements occupying more than fifty hectares, surely to be classified as "urban" by any definition, and by the Early Dynastic period this indicates that the distribution has become at least a bimodal one. Probably there is even a third, intermediate mode during and after the Jemdet Nasr period, its magnitude obscured by the special relevance of the "uncertain" category to sites occupying the broad intermediate range between the small villages or hamlets and the major urban centers.

In a sense, these trends constitute only an alternative representation of a point that can be established directly from the period maps: that the great Mesopotamian cities grew at the expense of smaller rural settlements in their hinterlands. A statistical representation does, however, permit clearer understanding of the changing ranges of actual variation in size that accompanied this process. Moreover, it makes possible a description of the process of urbanization in terms of a tiered hierarchy of site sizes.

For the Late Uruk period, close examination of the survey data makes it reasonable to assume that all settlements except Uruk itself fell within the broad curve at the lower end of the areal distribution shown in figure 7. Some uncertainty may be felt as to what underlies the handful of major Early Dynastic (and later) centers along the eastern margins of the surveyed region (sites 168, 169, 197, 198, 451). The heavy overburden of later occupational debris at these sites may tend to minimize the areal

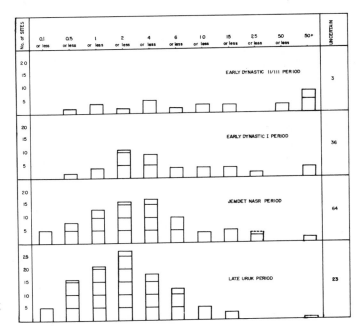

FIGURE 7

Classification of early sites by period and area (hectares)

extent of earlier remains. However Uruk continued to be occupied on an urban scale long after all of these communities had been abandoned, and yet even casual, unsystematic inspection there makes it clear that pottery of the Uruk period is an important constituent in the surface ceramics over much of the central area of the site. Hence the extremely small amount of Uruk pottery noted during the survey at the more easterly centers almost certainly indicates that they did not approach the size of Uruk during this period and may have been only very minor settlements.

We can generalize, then, that the settlement hierarchy of Late Uruk times included only one small urban center, whose public buildings all suggest that it was largely or wholly integrated by institutions of a theocratic character. Below this single apex of the settlement hierarchy lay the surprisingly large number of 107 much smaller sites that were located during the course of the survey. Equally striking is the apparently unimodal character of settlement size distributions within this very large, little differentiated group of smaller sites. A hierarchy of settlement sizes, presumably linked to the emergence of specialized economic, religious, military, or administrative functions that required some centers with larger residential populations, thus had only just begun to make its appearance in the Late Uruk period.

The character and extent of the subsequent shift is best ascertained by aggregating the available data in order to reduce the large "uncertain" category shown in figure 7. One difficulty, already adumbrated earlier, is that a Jemdet Nasr component is often difficult to distinguish on sites that continued into the Early Dynastic I period. For purposes of establishing a contrast with the Late Uruk period, this can be eliminated by grouping Jemdet Nasr and Early Dynastic I sites together. The other major difficulty involves estimations of size where there were significant, or even larger, occupations in later periods. Continuing the procedure followed for the Late Uruk period, we can largely overcome this problem by assigning sites to approximate categories of size rather than seeking to fix their exact areal limits. Inspection of Jemdet Nasr and Early Dynastic I curves in figure 7 suggests a three-tiered hierarchy of settlement sizes: "villages" 0.1–6.0 hectares, "towns" 6.1–25 hectares, and "urban centers" more than 50 hectares. Uruk, whose major growth apparently occurred in the Early Dynastic I period, probably should be listed alone as a "city" in an uppermost, fourth tier, with an occupied area at that time of about 400 hectares.

If this procedure is followed, only the Jemdet Nasr–Early Dynastic I areas of the later cities along the major, eastern branch of the Euphrates are impossible to assign with reasonable confidence to one or another of these categories. For the rest, there is unequivocal evidence of

a well-developed hierarchy: one city, two small urban centers (Shuruppak and site 230), 21 towns (004, 079, 087, 101, 125, 130, 174, 179, 212, 231, 232, 233, 242, 245, 260, 261, 281, 358, 382, 383, 387), and 124 villages or hamlets.

These sites are shown by symbols differentiated according to the above categories in figure 8. Probably it may be assumed that the eastern settlements, in Jemdet Nasr–Early Dynastic I times, fell in the range of towns or minor cities rather than into either the largest or smallest category. If so, the overall ratio for city : small urban center : town may have been on the order of 1 : 4 : 24. Since the village category must include essentially all the undiscovered sites, the final term in this ratio probably represents more than 140 settlements.

The same analysis can be extended to the Early Dynastic II/III periods, by which time uncertainties arising from later overburdens are no longer a significant factor. Both Uruk and Umma probably are best described as cities. Shuruppak, Zabalam, Bad-Tibira, possibly Larsa, and four others (004, 168, 198, 242) may be listed as small urban centers. To this last group also may be added three sites appearing for the first time in the 25–50 hectare range of size (131, 175, 213). Then in addition there are six towns and only seventeen villages. Excluding the very few sites of uncertain size and acknowledging the disproportionate omission of the smallest category of sites from the survey's findings, the set of ratios in successive periods thus may be summarized:

	Villages	Towns	Small Urban Centers	Cities
Early Dynastic II/III	17	6	8	2
Early Dynastic I / Jemdet Nasr	124	20	2	1
Late Uruk	112	10	1	–
Early Uruk	17	3	1?	–

These figures reflect in tabular form some of the most salient features of the urban revolution in the region around Uruk. The initial step, probably around the beginning of the Late Uruk period, was a massive increase in rural settlement. Whereas Uruk itself was already a flourishing theocratic center, the small average size and absence of a well developed hierarchy among outlying settlements implies only a minimal development of the economic or administrative structures that are concomitants of centralized control. The appearance of a tiered hierarchy of site sizes in the Jemdet Nasr and Early Dynastic I periods, on the other hand, clearly reflects the elaboration and wide extension of these structures. However, a countervailing trend also became manifest during the Early Dynastic I period, as is seen in the wholesale abandonment of smaller settlements in many parts of the region. Uruk probably attained its largest urbanized area during the Early Dynastic I period, but thereafter its ascendancy was increasingly challenged by the growth of a number of other city-states of rival size. This trend continued through the end of the Early Dynastic period, leading to the aggregation of the great majority of the region's population within walled centers of unquestionably urban proportions.

The distribution of sites of different categories shown in figure 8 encourages an attempt to delineate local ethnic, administrative or economic units immediately before the collapse of rural settlement in Early Dynastic I times. It is reasonable to assume that small villages and hamlets generally were closer to the town to which they were subordinated in varying ways and degrees than to any other town or city. On this basis, minimal territorial units can be defined as shown, although obviously very tentatively and roughly.[4]

The pattern which emerges is somewhat variable but also exhibits a number of important regularities. There is one town for which the survey failed to find any outlying dependent settlement at all, whereas at the other extreme one grouping contains no less than twelve such dependencies. However, all but one of the groupings with two or fewer dependencies lie along the outer limits of the surveyed area, so that almost certainly there were more small sites around them than those currently plotted. Hence it seems reasonable to conclude that a normal grouping comprised from three to eight or nine small settlements, as well as the one or more centers to which they were related.

In most of the region there was, as a rule, only one central town in each grouping. In two of the apparent exceptions, rival centers are found on closer inspection to result from a shift in the position of a single town during the Jemdet Nasr or Early Dynastic I periods. Quite possibly this single-center pattern was a special characteristic in the domain of Uruk, within which a number of such groupings can be defined. Farther to the east, on the other hand, closely spaced groups of towns accompanied by relatively few smaller sites suggest that configurations of settlement were based on different principles. Unfortunately, that area is not sufficiently known from the survey data for its internal structure to be analyzed in greater detail.

For the central and western parts of the surveyed region, then, we can define a three-tiered hierarchy of sites in which variable groupings of the smallest class of settlements seem to depend on larger, centrally located towns. The towns in turn then tend to be grouped around the city of Uruk. This pattern immediately makes relevant the formal propositions of central place theory about the distribution of cities and towns and their relation to their hinterlands. At the core of the rapidly growing body of research in locational geography that is ordered by central place theory is the proposition that "settlements arranged in a triangular lattice, with a separate hexagonal field about each center, represent the optimum spatial division of an undifferentiated landscape."[5] Striking empirical confirmation has been obtained in a number of widely separated modern areas, but a regular hexagonal pattern is not readily apparent in the available data of the survey in the region around Uruk.

Several explanations may be offered for the failure of sites in figure 8 to correspond with a uniform, superimposed grid of hexagons. There may be omissions in the data, particularly among the smaller sites, that make the distribution seem more irregular than it is. Moreover, the surveyed region has neither a natural center nor natural boundaries; had the survey extended farther west so as to cover all the terrain around Uruk, patterns might have emerged that are not now apparent. In any case, a number of assumed conditions on which central place theory is explicitly founded do not apply in southern Iraq at this period. Lines of communication, rather than following the shortest, most economical path across the ideally uniform plain presupposed by the theory, must have been subject to severe warping or distortion by the numerous navigable channels of the Euphrates. Likewise, population, rather than being uniformly distributed over a land surface of constant agricultural potentiality, was concentrated in enclaves interspersed with swamps or arid steppes. Under all these conditions, lack of uniformity is only to be expected.

Although it is irregular and discontinuous, there nevertheless remains a widespread latticework pattern of central towns and outlying, smaller villages. The addition of a time dimension to figure 8 possibly offers some understanding of its social basis. This has been provided by arrows leading from sites largely or wholly abandoned in Jemdet Nasr times or at the beginning of the Early Dynastic I period toward other, nearby sites that continued longer. As the distribution of arrows demonstrates, several formerly extensive groupings collapse during this interval except for their largest center. In these cases part of the population of outlying settlements may then have

---

4. Only three village sites, 267, 310, and 372, are shown included within the terrain of a town or city other than the one nearest them. These exceptions are based on the assumption that common affinity is even more likely for closely neighboring groups of villages, or they take into account shifts in the settlement pattern over time that are discussed below. In any case, the resulting increase in distance for each of them is relatively slight.

5. P. Haggett, *Locational Analysis in Human Geography* (New York, 1966), pp. 118–19.

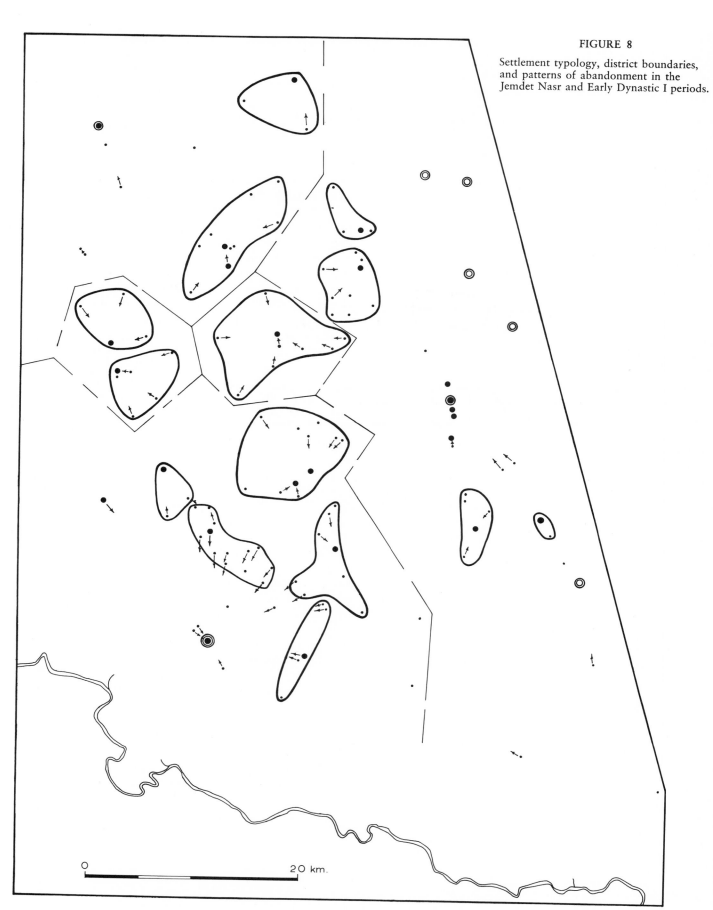

FIGURE 8

Settlement typology, district boundaries, and patterns of abandonment in the Jemdet Nasr and Early Dynastic I periods.

O ⊢━━━━━━━━━━━━━━━━━┥ 20 km.

aggregated in the central town, although it is not unlikely that a larger part emigrated from the immediate district altogether and was drawn into Uruk, Shuruppak, or their emerging urban counterparts farther east. At the same time, the towns as well as the villages virtually disappeared in several other groupings close to Uruk, all the former inhabitants almost certainly taking up residence within the Uruk city wall.

The hypothesis most economically explaining these population shifts is that the settlement pattern was radically reoriented in response to military-political pressures. Smaller units were proving less viable than large ones, and there is much historical and archaeological evidence that the latter were increasingly engaged in the construction of major defensive works, in the support of bodies of at least semiprofessional soldiery, and in periodic struggles for supremacy. To a considerable degree, the ambitions of city rulers and the fears of rural peasantry would have converged to persuade or compel the latter into a piecemeal flight from their dispersed agricultural enclaves into the larger centers. And among the larger centers, preference would have been given over time to those enjoying the convenience and security of positions along major waterways.

The population movements indicated by arrows perhaps also imply the existence of somewhat more extensive social or administrative units composed of one or more of the settlement groupings. In many cases neighboring settlements were abandoned at about the same time, their occupants falling back in opposite directions upon larger, presumably better fortified towns. The overall pattern of these abandonments suggests the more inclusive ethnic or political boundaries that are very tentatively delineated in figure 8. Among the more inclusive units, it is noteworthy that most of the smaller ones disappeared soon after the end of the Early Dynastic I period. Probably they were swept away as a result of military or other pressures emanating from their more powerful, urbanized competitors.

An analysis of site distribution within uniform areal units forms a third probabilistic approach that can usefully be applied to the available data. For this purpose, the surveyed region is divided into a regular checkerboard of squares that are five kilometers along each side. Squares not preponderantly enclosed by the survey boundaries then are eliminated in order to assure conditions of comparability, and in the remaining squares the number of sites during each relevant period is plotted (fig. 9). This provides at least a schematic representation of contrastive trends in different parts of the surveyed region.

Considering first the charts for individual periods, it is interesting to note that the maximum number of sites in the unexcluded squares appears in the Jemdet Nasr period:

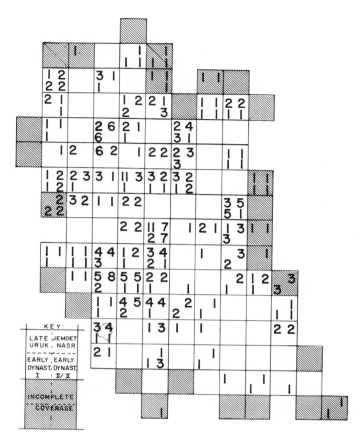

FIGURE 9

Distribution of early sites by period and five-kilometer square

Late Uruk	125
Jemdet Nasr	132
Early Dynastic I	66
Early Dynastic II/III	33

The reduction during the Early Dynastic period is simply another form of expression of the trend toward concentration in urban centers that has been adumbrated earlier. But although the difference in the absolute number of Late Uruk and Jemdet Nasr sites is rather small, the difference in their degree of dispersion is substantial. Given the general extent and density of settlement, it seems reasonable to assume that the squares not occupied by sites during the entire time period (numbering thirty-two of the ninety-seven squares after the marginal ones were eliminated) were covered with swamps or were otherwise of limited utility for sedentary groups. On this basis, the totals of unoccupied but potentially occupiable squares for each period are as follows:

Late Uruk	14
Jemdet Nasr	7
Early Dynastic I	24
Early Dynastic II/III	44

21

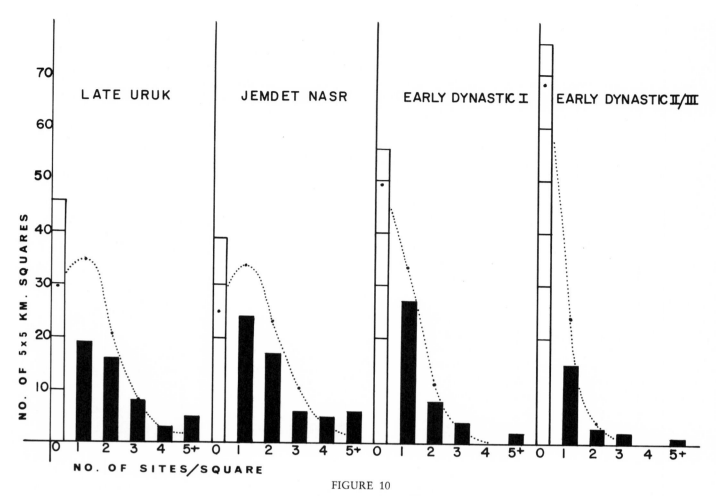

FIGURE 10

Actual and random dispersion of early sites by period

It would appear from this that the degree of dispersion of the Jemdet Nasr sites (vis à vis Late Uruk) over the available land surface is considerably greater than can be accounted for merely on the basis of the slight increase in total number. Similarly, it would appear that the reduction by almost half in the number of sites occupied during the Early Dynastic I period (again vis à vis Late Uruk) ought to induce more than a 20 percent reduction (from fifty-one to forty-one out of sixty-five occupiable squares) in the number of tracts where settlements occurred. To phrase this differently, there is an obvious suggestion here that sites in the Late Uruk period tended to be not only smaller than they subsequently were, but also more clustered. We will return to this theme presently with additional evidence.

When these data are summarized in graphic form (fig. 10), additional aspects of the changing settlement pattern come into focus. On a purely random basis, the numbers of square tracts occupied by the given numbers of sites during successive periods should coincide with the Poisson curves that are shown in dotted lines.[6] Al-

though differing in degree at different periods, they generally fail to do so. The deviation is most significant during the Late Uruk and Jemdet Nasr periods, taking the form of a clumping or aggregating of sites within fewer squares than would normally be occupied on a purely random basis. This "contagious" distribution reflects the presence of multiple prevailing small, closely spaced, presumably interrelated settlements as a significant component of the settlement pattern as a whole. As many as eleven such sites are contained within each of two tracts during the Late Uruk period. Although the Early Dynastic distribution is considerably more random, even in late Early Dynastic times there is one tract which contains seven sites. This is a phenomenon which invites closer scrutiny through comparative study and excavation—and whose explanation might provide insights into the structure of larger, urban components of Mesopotamian society as well.

To be sure, not all aggregations of seemingly contemporary sites necessarily imply coexisting, distinct communities. For example, closely spaced site pairs of more or less equivalent size constitute one of several significant subtypes into which all the clustered sites may be divided (fig. 11). On the basis of close parallels with

6. P. Greig-Smith, *Quantitative Plant Ecology* (New York, 1964), pp. 61–62.

some modern Maᶜdān, or Marsh Arab, communities, binary settlements of this kind may involve alternating seasonal occupance by a single social group. To illustrate with a modern case, winter quarters were located on the west bank of a watercourse and there was an annual movement to the opposite bank during the summer months. Local inhabitants said that the move was motivated by greater summer coolness and fewer insect pests. Even a very slight increase in the elevation of the eastern bank may have significantly increased exposure to cooling winds, the investigators point out, and the community's palm groves on that side also would have provided cooling shade. Moreover, an annual alternation of this kind just before the advent of summer heat was thought to improve materially not only the insect problem but the sanitation problem.[7]

It is obvious that an appeal to unchanging conditions like these fails to account for the gradual disappearance of the binary pattern, for the latter is encountered only in the early stages of settlement in the Warka region. Without excavation, the observed binary pattern alternatively might be supposed to reflect not seasonal movement but instead the sedentary coexistence of presumably related groups. The latter alternative, however, would be of even greater interest in that it might contribute to an understanding of the social organization of the time. And it is within the range of archaeological techniques that have already been tested not only to discriminate permanent from seasonal occupance[8] but to deal with patterned local variation between neighboring subgroups in terms of the organizing principles of residence on which they were based.[9]

Several of the approaches taken heretofore share a common limitation. Essentially, they group all parts of the surveyed region into single tabulations, whereas a glance at the period maps shows that developments throughout the region were by no means uniform in rate

or even in direction. Accordingly, there is a need for some form of analytical breakdown of the region that potentially can be linked with ecological or demographic variations within it. Were data available, one important basis for such a breakdown would consist of different combinations of subsistence resources. At present, however, arid steppeland and swamp are equally valid as alternative characterizations of localities where settlements were absent. Other ecological configurations, equally indistinguishable at present, involve differences in the quantity and reliability of the available water supply. We may turn once more to the contemporary Maᶜdān for an illustration of the widely ramifying effects this may have.

Two broadly contrastive patterns of settlement and social organization have been distiguished among the Marsh Arabs occupying different parts of the Haur al-Hammar and the great lacustrine depressions above the confluence of the Tigris and Euphrates rivers. Along the western edge of this area, ample supplies of year-round water apparently are better assured; the decisive consideration reportedly is not its sufficiency for irrigation during the growing season but rather that adequate fodder for the herds of buffalo is continually available locally. Permanent settlements of several hundred houses are the rule under these conditions. They tend to be relatively nucleated, although component groups of reed houses are divided from one another by numerous waterway branches of varying size. These internal units tend to consist of descent groups under the informal, and somewhat unstable, leadership of a headman or chief spokesman, and apparently they are not of primary structural importance. More significantly, the larger settlements usually house a local shaykh or at least a wakīl, his representative, and the presence of these individuals leads to greater diversity in the materials, size, and complexity of the architecture within the settlement through the construction of buildings formally devoted to their social and administrative duties. Increased settlement size and internal diversity also are linked in the presence of small numbers of specialists in cottage industries like weaving and boat repair, as well as a handful of traders. Suzerainty over the lands and activities of smaller communities deeper into the swamp is exercised, and the tributary payments stemming from it perhaps help to account for a considerable net flow of population in the same direction.[10]

It is the smaller grouping of thirty to fifty houses, under the leadership only of a mukhtar or headman, that emerges as the decisive component of settlement along

7. S. Westphal-Hellbusch and H. Westphal, "Die Maᶜdān: Kultur und Geschichte der Marschenbewohner im Süd-Iraq," *Forschungen zur Ethnologie und Sozialpsychologie* 4 (Berlin, 1962): 151.

8. Cf. R. S. MacNeish, "Ancient Mesoamerican Civilization," *Science* 143 (1964): 531–45; M. D. Coe and K. V. Flannery, "Microenvironments and Mesoamerican Prehistory," *Science* 143 (1964): 650–54; K. V. Flannery, "Archeological Systems Theory and Early Mesoamerica," in *Anthropological Archeology in the Americas,* ed. B. J. Meggers, pp. 67–87 (Washington, D.C., 1968); P. J. Munson, P. W. Parmalee, and R. A. Yarnell, "Subsistence Ecology of Scovill, a Terminal Middle Woodland Village," *American Antiquity* 36 (1971): 410–31.

9. Cf. W. A. Longacre, "Changing Patterns of Social Integration: A Prehistoric Example from the American Southwest," *American Anthropologist* 68 (1966): 94–102; J. N. Hill, "A Prehistoric Community in Eastern Arizona," *Southwestern Journal of Anthropology* 22 (1966): 9–30.

10. Westphal-Hellbusch and Westphal, "Die Maᶜdān," pp. 101–3.

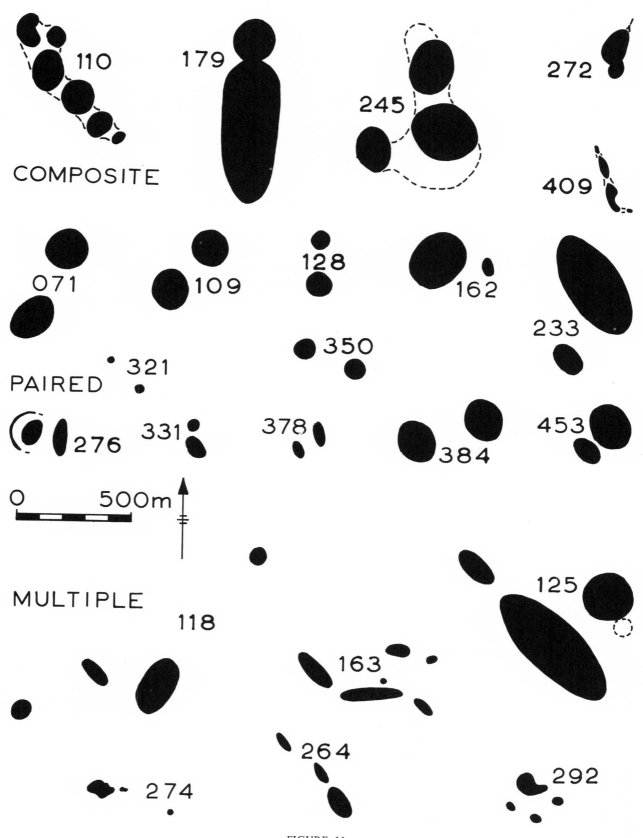

FIGURE 11

Early composite sites and site clusters

the eastern margins of the marshes. Because it is shallower in that area, the surface water upon which much of the swamp vegetation depends often recedes several kilometers from these more egalitarian villages; at such times the community must rely on shallow wells. As a result, the permanent core of the settlement (often located on an ancient mound or ishān) is merely the center of a cluster including numerous outlying stations where individuals or entire families may settle with their herds for varying portions of the year. Very small, less distant groups of outlying houses also are reported to be occupied on a year-round basis by families awaiting the general approval of the tribal section or ᶜashīra before formally joining the group. Although cultivation tends to be localized around the parent settlement, individual families thus follow markedly different itineraries for at least part of the year. The picture is further complicated by the availability of the outlying, temporary stations to all members of a number of such communities that are thought to form a larger, related unit.[11] There is, in short, a marked degree of spatial and temporal fragmentation associated with this geographic variant, persuasively recalling the unusual number of square five-kilometer tracts reported earlier in which five or more roughly contemporaneous sites are located during the urbanization of the Warka region.

To be sure, this striking contrast in contemporary patterns is closely tied to the important place in Maᶜdān subsistence now occupied by the water buffalo, a domestic animal whose presence in Mesopotamia before the latter half of the third millennium cannot yet be documented.[12] However, roughly similar differences in pattern may well have been occasioned as early as prehistoric times by the needs of the domesticates of that period—perhaps focusing on the availability of lush grass in seasonally filled depressions rather than on swamp vegetation proper. Settlement pattern data from the Warka region lend some support to this parallelism. On the one hand, reference has already been made to clusters of small sites recalling the groupings of several dozen households under a mukhtar that occur along the eastern perimeter of the contemporary marshes. On the other hand, a Jemdet Nasr site like 281 (fig. 12) has many persuasive similarities with the larger, more differentiated sites farther west. Not only does it contain detached areas of debris interspersed with canals, similar to those of the modern descent groups that compose the settlements of several hundred households, but also the small shrine or temple at its center perhaps can be thought to correspond with the modern baked-brick house of the shaykh or his sirkal. In any case, this serves to illustrate important relationships between subsistence and settlement patterns that can lead to discontinuities in the latter, even on an alluvial plain where differences in topography and vegetation at first glance seem quite minor.

Another basis for analytical breakdown, more consonant with the data of the Warka Survey, involves the proximity of major population concentrations and cultural centers as a determinant of settlement patterns. In pursuing this approach, one subunit ought to consist of the district around, and hence presumably dependent upon, the uniquely large and early center of Uruk. An-

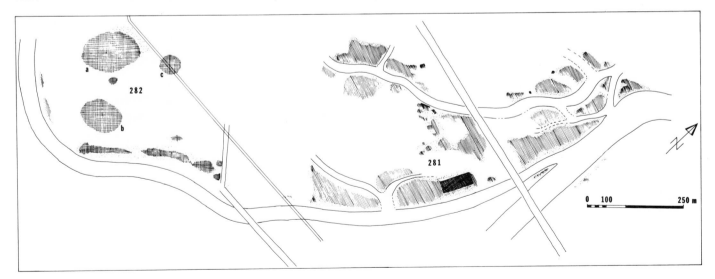

FIGURE 12

A Jemdet Nasr marsh settlement (sites 281, 282)

11. Ibid., pp. 152–55.

12. B. Brentjes, "Wasserbüffel in den Kulturen des Alten Orients," *Zeitschrift für Säugetierkunde* 34 (1969): 189.

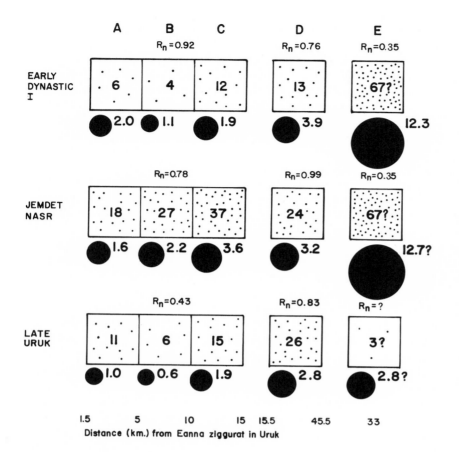

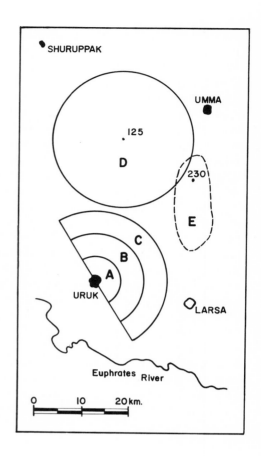

FIGURE 13

Nonurban population density (per square kilometer), average settlement
size (hectares), and nearest neighbor coefficients (R_n) in early periods.

other should lie in the great central region north and northeast of Uruk, framed to the east and west by what were then major Euphrates branches. This was a densely settled region at some distance from any contemporary urban center during the Late Uruk and Jemdet Nasr periods, and its divergence from the Uruk area is also shown by the fact that it was almost abandoned by late Early Dynastic times. Still a third subunit should correspond with the district south of Umma, where a number of large towns suddenly appeared along an apparently artificial canal during the Jemdet Nasr period (see above, p. 12). Ideally, a fourth subunit might consist of the hinterlands of Umma, in order to contrast patterns of urbanization there with similar patterns, apparently at a considerably earlier time, around Uruk. In this last instance, however, exceptionally heavy and widespread dune deposits severely reduce the data available at this time and hence make the designation of an additional subunit unproductive.

The three subunits selected for study are illustrated in figure 13. Since relationship to Uruk was a guiding consideration in the first, ideally it should be constructed in the form of a circle around that center. Problems of completeness of coverage in the depressions paralleling the present Euphrates course make this impossible, so that instead it has been drawn in the form of three concentric semicircular rings, each adding five kilometers' radius. In order of proximity to Uruk, these three rings are labeled A, B, and C. The second subunit, labeled D, also has been drawn with a radius of fifteen kilometers. Problems of completeness of coverage do not obtrude in this case, and so a full circle is included. Its center has been placed on the largest mound in the immediate area during this time period, and this choice is perhaps additionally justified because the site in question dominates a cluster of smaller neighboring sites as well. On the other hand, the choice is also to a large degree an arbitrary one in that, unlike Uruk, the site failed to survive throughout the time period and surely was never of more than very local importance. Hence in this case there is no basis for additional subclassification into three concentric parts. The third subunit, E, unlike the others, does not consist of a fairly dispersed array of settlements. Instead it takes the form of a closely adjoining string of substantial towns and villages, with only a very few outliers. In this case, the boundaries of cultivation and influence maintained by the settlements within the subunit are indeterminate, so that its outline has been shown only as an irregular broken line. Clearly this is an entirely different pattern of settlement than occurs during the period of initial urbanization in either of the other subunits. Perhaps it suggests comparison with the enlarged, nucleated form of Maᶜdān settlement mentioned earlier.

Before turning to a comparison of developments in these subunits in more analytical terms, a brief descriptive résumé may highlight their divergent patterns. Uruk probably attained its maximum size in the Early Dynastic I period. Study of the effects of urban growth upon its hinterlands accordingly must focus on the Late Uruk, Jemdet Nasr, and Early Dynastic I periods. Subunit D also underwent profound changes during this interval, probably having been most densely occupied during the Late Uruk period, whereas after the Early Dynastic I period it was only very sparsely settled. Subunit E underwent an even briefer floruit. Probably it was first colonized on an extensive scale in Jemdet Nasr times, and after the Early Dynastic I period all settlement seems to have been abandoned. As these capsule summaries suggest, our attention must now focus on the Late Uruk, Jemdet Nasr, and Early Dynastic I periods. By late Early Dynastic times population had been so concentrated in the major city-states that a contrast of urban hinterlands and rural subunits within the Warka region is no longer helpful.

Figure 13 graphically tabulates similarities and differences between our subunits with respect to a number of key variables. Let us first consider progressive changes in average settlement size. It will be observed at once that this differs substantially from one column to another, both at particular time levels and in directional changes spanning all three periods. Leaving aside the major city-states, by all odds the greatest average size occurs in the rapidly colonized, newly irrigated area south of Umma. On the assumption that this precedes the growth of Umma (and was, in fact, later abandoned as a result of the latter), there is a continuous, fairly close correlation at all periods shown between average size of settlement and distance from Uruk. This suggests that the relationship between Uruk and its hinterlands was one in which the main center strongly inhibited tendencies toward urban growth among its dependencies, either through monopolizing the production of specialized goods and services within its walls or through direct economic and political exploitation.

Already in the Late Uruk period, at the outset of the time span covered by the chart, it is interesting to note that there were marked differences between average settlement size in the area within fifteen kilometers of Uruk and in the area beyond. Possibly this provides a clue to the range of primary influence of Uruk at that time. At any rate, it suggests the possibility that there were somewhat different forms or emphases in social organization among the small settlements closely dependent upon Uruk. This hypothesis is supported by differences in "nearest neighbor" coefficients, to which we will turn presently.

In the Jemdet Nasr period it will be observed that there is a uniform trend toward increased settlement size throughout the surveyed region, even though there are large differences in absolute values from subunit to subunit. This may imply a temporary attenuation in Uruk's integrative functions or authority, or alternatively only a general increase in population density and economic well-being. In any event, the Early Dynastic I period saw a reversal of this trend in the greater part of the Uruk district. Only the zone most closely adjacent to Uruk itself continued to show a slight increase in average size. Why this was so is extremely difficult even to conjecture, but that there was a genuine bifurcation in directional trends within the Uruk district will be confirmed below with other data.

We turn next to a comparison of nearest neighbor coefficients for the three subunits. This statistic (R_n in the chart) provides a measure of relative degrees of settlement clustering in which values near zero reflect maximum clustering around a central point, a value of 1.0 indicates a random distribution, and a value of 2.15 reflects a maximally dispersed (hexagonal) distribution.[13]

During the Late Uruk period we must deal essentially with a comparison of two subunits, A–C and D. Subunit E was too lightly occupied at that time for the use of the statistic to be meaningful. Both subunits indicate a degree of clustering, although this is much more marked for the Uruk district than for the area to the north ($R_n = 0.43$ in the former, 0.83 in the latter). In other words, the small average settlement size around Uruk is accompanied by a much stronger tendency for sites to occur in closely grouped enclaves or clusters. To be sure, spacing of sites within what can be termed clusters or enclaves is highly variable. These terms can be employed for groups of sister-sites that are almost immediately adjacent to one another (fig. 11) and whose relations hardly seem to imply any sort of local dominance hierarchy. They can

---

13. Haggett, *Locational Analysis,* pp. 231–33, citing P. J. Clark and F. C. Evans, "Distance to Nearest Neighbour as a Measure of Spatial Relationships in Populations," *Ecology* 35 (1954): 445–53, and P. J. Clark, "Grouping in Spatial Distributions," *Science* 123 (1956): 373–74. E. N. Thomas ("Towards an Expanded Central Place Model," *Geographical Review* 51 [1956]:400–411) has pointed out that calculation of the statistic should be based on measurement to nearest neighboring settlement of equivalent or larger size for optimal results. I have been unable to follow this stricture because of the large number of sites during each period whose areas cannot be plotted accurately from surface data.

also be employed for a much larger, more complex grouping like that shown in figure 14. In this case the central site, thirty kilometers from Uruk, is so very much larger that its local predominance seems assured—and this supposition receives further support, incidentally, from the concentrations of costly metal objects found there exclusively (cf. chapter 8). Perhaps the conclusion to be drawn is that, even as early as the Late Uruk period, minor local power centers of this type simply could not be maintained in close proximity to the much more impressive center at Uruk. It is all the more interesting, then, that settlement within the Uruk district nevertheless often took the form of still more closely grouped clusters of tiny hamlets.

The Jemdet Nasr period witnessed, for the most part, a shift toward increasing randomness of distribution, with coefficients of 0.78 for the Uruk district and of 0.99 for subunit D to the north. It is tempting to conclude that this

is somehow related to a partial breakup of the clustered-hamlet pattern that may have been occasioned in turn by increasing average settlement size. On the other hand, it has already been observed that some clusters of this kind persist, even if only as a minor constituent in an increasingly urban settlement pattern, until the late Early Dynastic period or even longer. With regard to clustering, subunit E again exhibits its distinctively different character. The very low coefficient of 0.35 reflects the fact that in this area settlements were concentrated almost exclusively along the newly constructed arterial waterway that presumably made them possible.[14]

The dispersal of settlements in the district around Uruk became increasingly random with the Early Dynastic I period ($R_n = 0.92$). In subunit D to the north, however, the randomizing trend of the previous period reversed itself slightly (from 0.99 to 0.76). This presumably reflects the process of abandonment that was already under way there, with the remaining settlements increasingly confined to a relatively small number of surviving watercourses along which cultivation still was possible. No change can be observed in subunit E from the available data. The pattern there was one that was abruptly imposed in the Jemdet Nasr period, that was maintained intact during the following period, and that then seems to have vanished equally abruptly.

Still a third basis for comparative analysis of the regional subunits involves population density. Any attempt to calculate this with the data of a surface reconnaissance alone faces very serious pitfalls. Only by making such an attempt, however, can we come to grips with crucial questions like urban population size or the intensity of land use. Hence it seems worthwhile to freely concede the possibility that major future modifications may be required —and still to press forward with the attempt.

The central assumption on which any such attempt has to be founded is that population covaries with settlement area. Within what limits, and with how great a range of variability, is this true? Unfortunately, data from the Mesopotamian plains that is pertinent to these questions, not only from ancient times but even under modern conditions, is either very scarce or inaccessible. A review of the available evidence some years ago led to the estimate

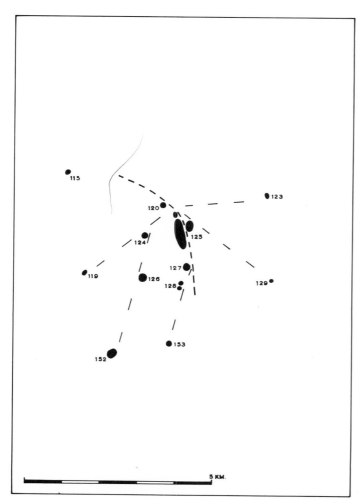

FIGURE 14

A Late Uruk settlement cluster or enclave

14. Direct comparison of this coefficient with the others is obscured, in any case, by the different basis for its calculation. The coefficient varies inversely with the square root of the area considered, and it has been pointed out that the limits of subunit E cannot be enclosed within an arbitrary circle or semicircle. The procedure followed here was to calculate the population of the settlements within the subunit on the basis of an assumed average of 100 persons per hectare, and then to calculate the cultivable area on which they depended with an assumed average of 1.5 hectares per person. Cf. Adams, *Land behind Baghdad*, pp. 23–25, 123–25, and discussion below.

of two hundred persons per hectare as a reasonably constant figure both through time and in settlements of widely varying gross size. One implication of the present study is that the application of this figure to estimates for whole regions or systems of settlement needs to be sharply qualified, even if there is no sound empirical basis for modifying it with respect to individual sites at particular moments in time.

Some light may be shed on the problem by a closer inspection of data on 53 villages in Khuzestan, the largest body of carefully and systematically collected evidence yet published that is relevant to the Mesopotamian plain.[15] The median density for this series is 223 persons per hectare and the mean density 231 persons per hectare, and the extremely wide range of variation is at least equally significant. The latter is plotted graphically in figure 15. For a group of contemporary agricultural villages, all small to moderate in size and all located within a very small region, this is not a particularly impressive demonstration of the covariance of settlement size and population without important intervening variables.

Additional complications arise from the examples of Maᶜdān or Marsh Arab settlement that were adduced earlier. The large, nucleated villages or small towns are only slightly elevated above the plain, and their component groups of houses are interspersed with numerous watercourses. In such settlements, paralleled by at least one (281) recorded in the Warka Survey, density is correspondingly much lower if it is calculated only from the gross outer limits within which the occupation occurs. That consideration may not arise for the smaller communities located on more elevated ancient ishāns to the east of the main swamps, but there the importance of seasonal movements produces an even greater effect of the same kind. Although no basis for an accurate estimate exists at present, the available accounts make it reasonable to suppose that at least twice as large a living area is occupied by these groups on a seasonal basis as their members occupy in scattered locations at any one time. Further, we must bear in mind that mobility and spatial fragmentation in the Maᶜdān communities are associated with low population densities, poorly drained terrain, and relatively limited governmental or landlord-imposed restraints—all conditions that surely were paralleled during early periods around Uruk. In short, one hundred persons per hectare of built-up area probably represents a better approximation of the density within modern systems of settlement that are comparable to those with which we must deal around ancient Uruk.

15. F. G. L. Gremliza, *Ecology of Endemic Diseases in the Dez Irrigation Pilot Area: A Report to the Khuzestan Water and Power Authority and Plan Organization, Government of Iran* (New York: Development and Resources Corp., 1962).

The problem is more difficult if we turn from the assured contemporaneity of modern villages (even if modified by seasonal alternation) to a group of archaeological sites that can be ascribed only to a fairly broad and somewhat indefinite time interval. Consider, for example, the little enclave of fifteen Late Uruk settlements centering on site 125 (fig. 14) that has been dealt with earlier in another context. If all these settlements are assumed to have been concurrently occupied at their maximal extent with densities of two hundred per hectare, a simple calculation on the fairly well attested basis of 1.5 hectares of cultivable land needed per person shows that even the entire surrounding area included in the figure would have been inadequate. This is extremely difficult to reconcile with a clustered distribution that seems to argue for boundaries of cultivation reasonably close to the outermost inhabited sites.

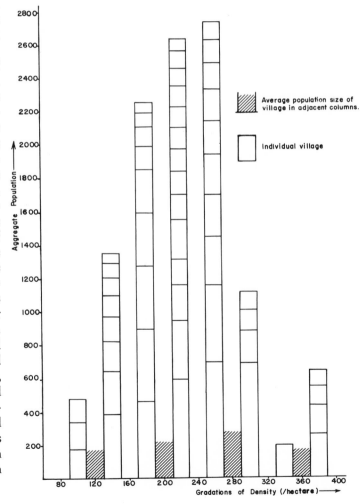

FIGURE 15

Relationship between population size and density in fifty-three Khuzestan villages.

Part of the solution, of course, is to assume the lower average of around one hundred persons per hectare that the Maᶜdān villages imply. But in addition, it must be recalled that a map of ancient settlements may summarize several stages of an ongoing historical process. To take the enclave or cluster in question, only the main mound and four others (two components of 125; also 127, 129, and 153) continued into the Jemdet Nasr period. This at least suggests a partial shift and consolidation of settlement rather than a static pattern. If so, it would be a mistake to calculate the total population of the enclave from mere addition of the maximal population of each site. As an alternative, a relatively instantaneous set of conditions might be defined by counting only those sites where the presence of both the Late Uruk and Jemdet Nasr surface pottery suggests that they were occupied during the transition between the two periods. But this ignores the possibility of cyclical reoccupation, interrupted by abandonment during the actual transition.[16] More important, it ignores the evidence that this area declined after the Late Uruk period, so that to count only sites continuing into the following period may unreasonably reduce our population estimate. What all these considerations tend to show, in any case, is that applying densities recorded at a given time to whole archaeological periods can be both uncertain and misleading.

Many of the basic considerations in the foregoing discussion will no longer apply uniformly if we consider not merely small, presumably agricultural settlements but also urban centers. On the one hand, it might be argued that tactical considerations and high construction costs would reduce the length of urban fortification walls, leading to a congestion of population within them. But at the same time, major portions of urban areas unquestionably were devoted to public buildings housing only a very limited resident population. Moreover, although densely built up areas of private houses have been unearthed by archaeologists, the crucial unanswered question is: what proportion of early urban areas actually were devoted to residential use at any one time? Dumps and abandoned areas, used only as sources of mud for construction, are archaeologically attested. Intensively cultivated orchards

and garden plots seem likely to have occurred in places even within city walls. Finally, the walls had to enclose substantial areas where herds from the surrounding rural districts could be sheltered during times of trouble.[17] Taking all these considerations into account, the possibility is very real that average urban population densities were only a fraction of contemporary densities in villages and small towns. In any event, it is clearly an oversimplification to assume that the same proportional relationship between settled area and population that may be reasonably accurate for the latter can be uniformly applied in the major cities of ancient Mesopotamia as well.

The population densities recorded in figure 13 make no reference to the major cities. They are expressed in number per square kilometer, derived by adding the populations of all settlements within a particular subunit that were occupied during a given period and then dividing this figure by the gross area of the subunit. Settlement populations have been calculated on the basis of one hundred persons per hectare of built-up area; hence they, and to an even greater degree the subunit totals, are unquestionably subject to the reservations outlined earlier. This is likely to mean that the figures given are somewhat too high rather than too low. On the other hand, it is interesting to note that, except for subunit E, the highest densities given in the chart amount to less than 50 percent of the sustaining capacity of a completely cultivable land surface as calculated on a basis of 1.5 cultivable hectares per person.

Since the area associated with settlements in column E is by definition undefined, no calculation of population density on the same basis is possible. However, the close grouping of large settlements along a single watercourse suggests that the cultivated zone on which they depended was an immediately adjoining, continuous strip rather than a series of detached enclaves interspersed with swamps or unirrigated land. If so, an average density of 1.5 hectares per person seems entirely reasonable, and the figure of sixty-seven persons per square kilometer that is given in the column for the Jemdet Nasr and Early Dynastic I periods is based on this assumption. The late Uruk density of three persons per square kilometer is in the same ratio to this figure of sixty-seven as the ratio of site areas between this and the subsequent periods. Naturally, the different, and much more problematical, methods of calculating densities for subunit E imply that comparison with the other columns can only be suggestive and not conclusive.

The omission of major urban centers from all of the

---

16. Cf. discussion in chapter 5 on the general instability of occupation during the late Ottoman period. It is to be regretted that modern instances of short, repeated resettlement have been brought to notice only rarely. But in the Warka region the village of Khanazirīya was occupied during the German excavations at nearby Fara at the beginning of this century, was found deserted in 1926 (R. P. Dougherty, "Searching for Ancient Remains in Lower ᶜIrāq," American Schools of Oriental Research, *Annual* 7 [1927]: 35), and was found by us in 1967 to have been again recently deserted after a reoccupation (H. J. Nissen, "Survey of an Abandoned Modern Village in Southern Iraq," *Sumer* 24 [1968]: 107–14).

17. I am indebted to M. B. Rowton for reference to an Agade-period letter attesting to this practice: S. Smith, "Notes on the Gutian period," Royal Asiatic Society, *Journal* (1932), p. 297.

subunits has differentiating effects which also must be borne in mind. Subunits D and E were at a considerable distance from any city until after the emergence of Umma as a major center, an event we believe took place only toward the end of Early Dynastic I or even later. Hence densities given for those districts ought to approximate the actual intensity of land use. The area around Uruk is another matter, for Early Dynastic textual evidence from Lagash, Shuruppak, and similar centers demonstrates that by far the larger part of the urban population also was engaged in agriculture and other subsistence pursuits. To the densities given for the concentric zones around Uruk, then, must be added that proportion of Uruk's population that went out to cultivate fields within these zones. Therefore, the apparent decline in density in this district during the Early Dynastic I period, probably the time in which Uruk attained its maximum size, is more apparent than real. The actual intensity of land use may even have increased, but those who were responsible for it now had moved (or been forced to move) to the city.

Even for earlier periods, Uruk's already substantial size tends to obscure comparisons between the subunits. If the needs of Uruk's population are not taken into account, for example, it would appear that the greatest intensity of land use during the Late Uruk period lay in subunit D, well to the north, rather than in its immediate hinterlands. This situation was reversed, to be sure, in the following Jemdet Nasr period, and the striking growth in settled rural population of the district around Uruk may reflect some net movement in the direction of the city out of subunit D. The real decline in the latter, however, seems to have come too late to explain the changes in the Uruk hinterlands. Moreover, subunit D probably also served as a reserve not only for the colonization of subunit E but also for the later growth of Umma and for the formation or expansion of a number of towns along the line of the Euphrates branch immediately to the west.[18] Hence the surge in rural settlement around Uruk during the Jemdet Nasr period remains an unexplained anomaly. The possibility must at least be considered that there was at this time a temporary devolution in Uruk's former size and complexity, a remote predecessor of what now might be termed a "flight to the suburbs." But in the absence of further evidence a contrary hypothesis is almost equally satisfactory. The precocious importance of Uruk as a ceremonial and political nucleus might have generated

---

18. It would also have been instructive to examine population and settlement trends along the Euphrates course between Shuruppak and Uruk, through the designation of another subunit comparable to E. Most of the important towns there, however, were continuously occupied until well into the second millennium. Hence surface data on their areas of occupation during the late fourth and early third millennia seems insufficient to justify the attempt.

improvements in drainage or irrigation in its immediate environs, leading to a quite unprecedented growth of rural settlement around it.

The problem of Uruk's relations with its immediate hinterlands is sufficiently perplexing, and important, that a finer-grained analysis seems justified. Whereas subunits A–C consisted of only three concentric rings, figure 16 presents the same data on density by fourteen one-kilometer increments. Obviously, the density figures in this chart are not to be taken entirely literally, since at least the larger individual settlements must have cultivated lands in several of the narrow semicircular bands that provide the areal component for the calculation. But even if it is too abstract to deal adequately with individual cases, the chart does suggest several new features of the relationship that are worthy of mention.

The distribution of the bands in which sites are concentrated is of particular interest. One clearly demarcated zone, in all periods, lies within four kilometers of the Eanna ziggurat. Since this is separated from the remaining groups of sites by a two- to three-kilometer interval in which settlements never occurred until a much

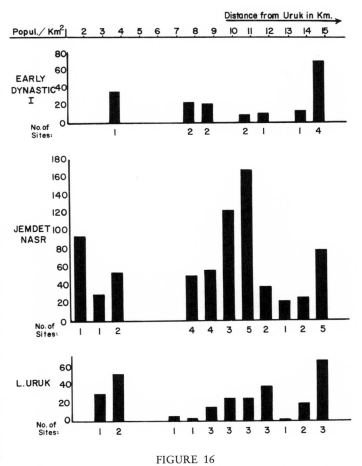

FIGURE 16

Population density in Uruk sustaining area

later time period, it suggests that the inner zone was composed of sites maintaining some special relationship with the city. Rather than being regarded as merely the closest of the outlying agricultural villages, perhaps these sites served as depots or specialized processing centers of some kind. A second discontinuity in distribution seems to occur in the band from twelve to thirteen kilometers, although inspection of the graph will show that this is narrower, less uniform, and hence possibly of less significance.

The densities recorded for the Jemdet Nasr period suggest a different possibility that is worthy of mention. Beginning with the band that commences seven kilometers from the center of the city, the figures rise sharply in successive bands to a very high level. This seems to indicate that by far the greater bulk of the subsistence pursuits carried on by the population of Uruk itself were concentrated in an inner zone, since most or all of the land at distances greater than seven or eight kilometers would have been required to meet the needs of the resident population there. On this basis, in turn, we can indirectly derive a population estimate for Uruk—again assuming that a gross average of 1.5 hectares of cultivable land was needed for each inhabitant. The calculation indicates that about ten thousand persons could have been supported by the available land. To this must be added, of course, the presumably rather small proportion of the population who may have been supported by offerings or tribute from more distant regions.

Unfortunately, the lower rural density bars in the graphs for other periods do not allow the same procedure to be followed with equal confidence. In Late Uruk times, the low figures may reflect the persistence of fairly large areas close to the city that were still undrained or, at any rate, uncultivated. The existence of a major swamp settlement within eleven kilometers of Uruk as late as the Jemdet Nasr period certainly supports this explanation. Even later testimony to the same effect is provided by the Lugalbanda Epic, although the weight of a stylized literary account as evidence is admittedly uncertain. Enmerkar, credited in the Sumerian King List with having "built" Uruk, therein describes the setting of the city as a swampy, reed-filled wasteland upon his accession to rulership.[19] For the Early Dynastic I period, contemporary with the major expansion of Uruk and the construction of its wall, rural settlement as graphed in figure 16 is sparse until the ring beginning fourteen kilometers away from the city. Although the evidence is entirely too scanty to be conclusive, this does at least hint at an urban population roughly four times what it had been in the Jemdet Nasr period.

This lengthy comparative discussion of different regional subunits has rested on calculations of average settlement size, nearest neighbor coefficients, and population density. It was pointed out at the outset that, for different reasons, none of these measures were applicable to the culmination of the urbanization process in the Early Dynastic II/III period. With the increasing concentration of the great bulk of the population in a drastically reduced number of major centers, the declining numerical base for the nearest neighbor statistic undermines its reliability. Moreover, there are boundary problems under the new conditions that may make the previously chosen areal subunits no longer suitable. At the same time, plotting occupied areas for specific periods in the long-lived major cities is at best a complex, somewhat problematical undertaking that demands special studies of its own. No such effort was included within the program of the Warka Survey. Even the extensive excavations carried out at Uruk, having been focused on different problems, do not permit settlement areas for various periods to be plotted. Finally, as was explained more fully above, estimates of population density within the urban centers seemingly are subject to major imponderables that have little or no effect on sites of lesser size. For all these reasons, then, we are left with a far less complete and satisfactory picture of overall settlement patterns in late Early Dynastic times than in earlier periods. And what makes this especially unfortunate is that it is precisely in late Early Dynastic times that the Warka region emerges into the light of history.

Short of further extensive excavations and the programs of specialized reconnaissance that have been referred to, we know of no way to rectify this shortcoming. Figure 6 provides a frankly impressionistic reconstruction of where the frontiers of cultivation around all of the major centers and their dependencies may have been situated. It reflects what we assume to be the historical reality of a now virtually abandoned "high edin" between the eastern and western branches of the Euphrates.[20] This formerly densely settled area seems to have become only a buffer region between hostile, contending city-states which had consolidated their own domains of cultivation and settlement along the major watercourses. Aside from a string of small towns along a single branch canal, its only inhabitants were small groups of wary nomads or semisedentary folk, moving with their flocks. To be sure, the shift into the cities must have led to some intensification of agriculture and a corresponding increase in the

19. C. Wilcke, *Das Lugalbandaepos* (Wiesbaden, 1969), p. 119.

20. T. Jacobsen, "La géographie et les voies de communication du pays de Sumer," *Revue Assyriologique* 52 (1958): 129; H. Sauren, *Topographie der Provinz Umma nach den Urkunden der Zeit der III. Dynastie von Ur: Teil 1, Kanäle und Bewässerungsanlagen* (Heidelberg, 1966), p. 14.

extent and complexity of the requisite irrigation systems. In the "high edin," on the other hand, the influence of these newly consolidated domains was an almost wholly disruptive one. This had become a dangerously unsettled district where "fate is a cloth which hangs over one," in the words of a Sumerian proverb.[21] One of the unan-

ticipated by-products of the growth of cities, in other words, seems to have been an intensification of the contrast between the steppe and the town, perhaps helping to explain an antagonism that has remained with us ever since.

21. E. I. Gordon, "Sumerian Proverbs: Glimpses of Every-day Life in Ancient Mesopotamia," *Museum Monograph* (Philadelphia, 1959), p. 186.

3 | Continuity and Change in Early Historic Settlements and Watercourses

The Warka region was an early innovative center—perhaps as early as any—in the transition to an urban way of life. We have followed the course of that transition in the previous chapter, primarily with regard to the changes in geographic patterning that an archaeological reconnaissance makes available. From the same standpoint, it remains to trace out the sequel to those changes through the millennia that followed.

For several reasons, this requires a somewhat altered focus. The region has witnessed no subsequent transformation of comparable irreversibility and magnitude—at any rate, of a kind on which an analysis of sequent settlement patterns can shed a comparable degree of light. The crucial data for later periods come from texts, so that interpretations derived from a reconnaissance become ancillary to interpretations of a more traditional historiographic character. To be sure, this does not mean that surveys are redundant for historical periods. One useful contribution, under the altered circumstances, is to help place the records of literate, urban-oriented scribes and administrators in the wider context of the predominantly nonliterate, agriculturally oriented society that supported them. Another is to provide a systematic basis for the study of cumulative change and development through successive periods, for which the written sources alone often are misleading in that they change radically over time both in quantity and in subject matter. Neither contribution necessarily involves as detailed or quantitative an approach as that to which the initial urban transformation has been subjected.

There are, in addition, two methodological limitations that combine to restrict the possibilities of a detailed spatial and temporal analysis of later settlement patterns. Continuity rather than change became the dominant theme for long periods after the achievement of urbanism, so that the principal part of the account must be derived from overlying layers of debris in a handful of major centers. It has been shown elsewhere that the methods of surface reconnaissance also can be applied with considerable precision to tracing changes in the extent and character of occupation within such centers,[1] but only with an intensity of fieldwork for which the limited duration of the Warka Survey did not permit even a beginning. Our approach was more appropriate for the relatively short durations of most settlements in late prehistoric times, for this permits surface areas of many small, shallow sites to be quickly and more accurately recorded.

In addition, knowledge of the ceramic indicators on which this survey depended is considerably more refined and precise for late prehistoric times than for any subsequent epoch. From the Ubaid through the Early Dynastic periods we can deal with sharply defined changes affecting a relatively high proportion of the whole ceramic inventory at relatively short intervals. For later periods, on the other hand, we generally must depend instead on a small handful of "index fossils" whose beginning and terminal points often are insecurely fixed in time (cf. chap. 7). As a result, pending further progress in the excavation—and publication—of properly controlled stratigraphic sequences, only a less detailed approach to later periods seems justified by the available evidence.

AKKADIAN–OLD BABYLONIAN PERIODS
(ca. 2400–1600 B.C.)

The distribution of settlements and watercourses illustrated in figure 17 conflates a number of periods which, primarily on political but to a lesser degree on other

---

1. Cf. R. F. Millon, "Extensión y población de la ciudad de Teotihuacán en sus diferentes periodes: Un cálculo provisional," in *Teotihuacán*, pp. 57–58. Sociadad Mexicana de Antropología, XI Mesa Redonda (México, D.F., 1967).

FIGURE 17
Akkadian–Old Babylonian settlements and watercourses

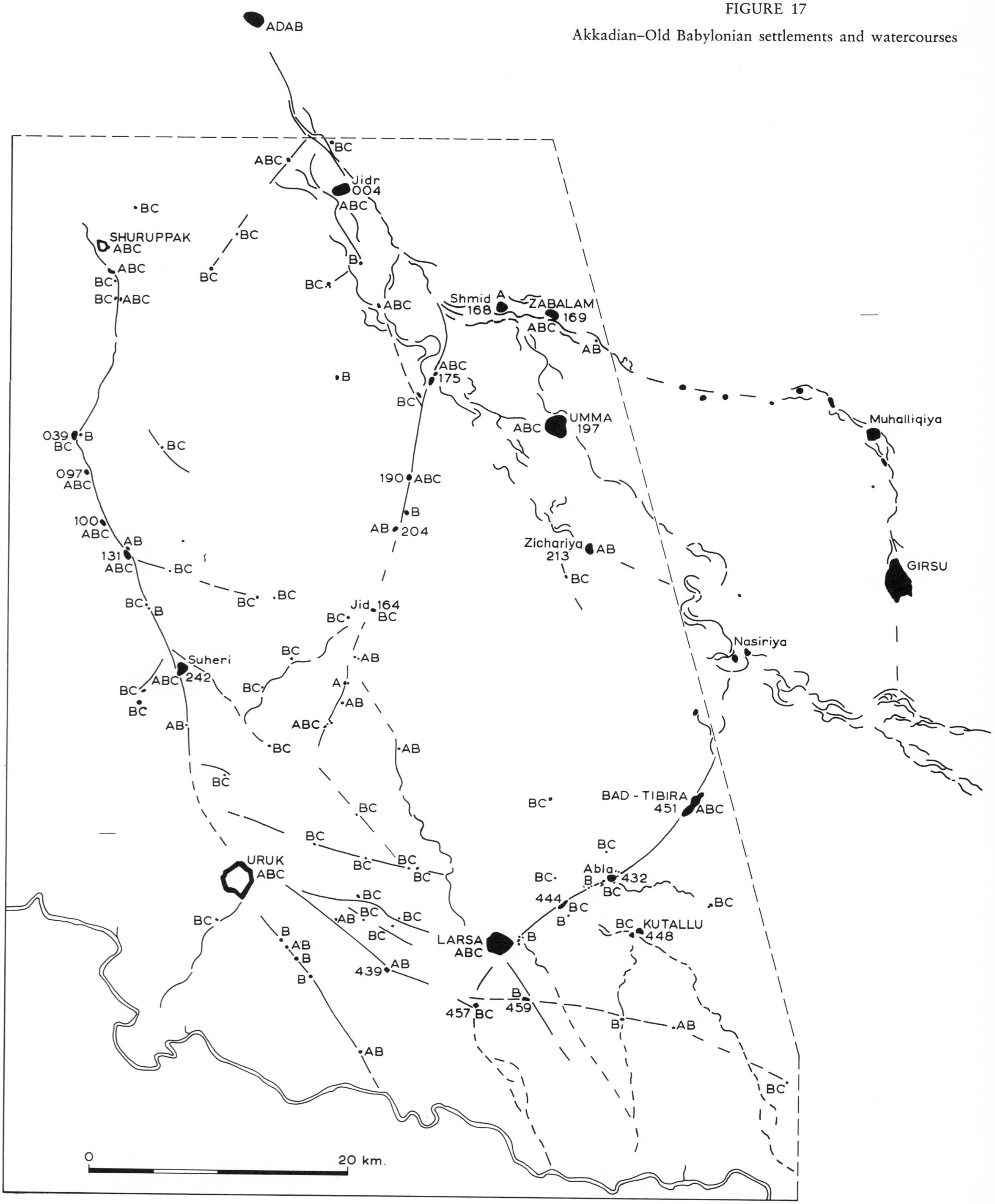

ADAB

•BC

ABC

Jidr
OO4
ABC

•BC

•BC

SHURUPPAK
ABC

•ABC

BC•
BC •ABC

•B

•BC

Shmid A
168 • ZABALAM
169
ABC

AB

ABC
175

BC•

Muhalliqiya

O39 •B
BC

•BC

ABC
UMMA
197

O97•
ABC

190 •ABC

Zichariya
213 •AB

•BC

GIRSU

100•
ABC

AB

B

131•
ABC

AB• 204

•BC

BC•

•BC •BC

Jid•164
BC

Nasiriya

BC •B

•BC

BC• •AB

Suheri
ABC 242

BC• A•

•AB

BC•

ABC•

•BC

•AB

BC•

•AB

BC•

•BC

BAD - TIBIRA
451 •ABC

BC•

URUK
ABC

BC

BC

BC•

BC•

BC•

Abla •432
BC

BC•
444

BC

BC •AB

•BC

•BC

B

BC KUTALLU
•448

BC•

B•

AB
B

B

439 •AB

LARSA
ABC

•B

B

457 BC •459

B•

•AB

•AB

•BC

grounds, historians of ancient Mesopotamia have traditionally distinguished. Some of the reasons for treating them together here have already been adumbrated. In particular, the dominant feature of the whole settlement configuration over this eight-century interval is its continuity; individual centers rise, decline, and disappear, but the geographic pattern they define seems to remain essentially unchanged. Then too, there is a not inconsiderable subjective element in the dates that have been assigned within this range to individual sites that are listed in the site catalogue (appendix). Akkadian and Old Babylonian ceramics can be unambiguously distinguished from one another, but because of overlapping criteria both in turn are difficult to differentiate from the ceramics of an archaeologically ill-defined span corresponding to the Third Dynasty of Ur and the Isin-Larsa period. The most useful distinction in the Warka region would be precisely that which is most uncertain, intended to illuminate with settlement pattern data the political and institutional changes accompanying the rise of the kingdom of Larsa.

The letter designations for individual periods that are given in figure 17 reflect these drawbacks. Separate letters are assigned to the Akkadian and Old Babylonian periods, whereas the Third Dynasty of Ur and the Isin-Larsa period are grouped together. In many instances the latter have been kept separate in the site catalog, primarily on the basis of preliminary field assessments whose validity is more open to doubt.

It is tempting to consider that gross numbers of sites in different periods convey a useful impression of changes in the extent or intensity of settlement. The Akkadian period is least well represented, with thirty-three sites. The maximum of eighty-nine sites occurs in the combined Ur III and Isin-Larsa periods, whereas for the Old Babylonian period the number drops to sixty. In many respects these totals accord well with known political and economic features of the time—the firm rule, prosperity, and stability of the Third Dynasty of Ur in contrast with more fluid, unsettled conditions in the Akkadian period; the subsequent, presumably favorable influence of Larsa over a region encompassing most of its immediate hinterlands; and then finally, the northward shift of power and prosperity away from this region as a result of the conquests of Hammurabi.

However, there are also reasons to treat this apparently independent "confirmation" of expected patterns with some reserve. The combination of the Ur III and Isin-Larsa periods in a single category could overstate the number of sites inhabited at any one time, at least in comparison with figures for politically more homogeneous periods. If certain Isin-Larsa ceramic types continued into Old Babylonian times, as is not unlikely, the apparent number would be further inflated by sites that in fact were occupied only during the latter period. Although many

Isin-Larsa sites were recorded that did not continue later, it will be noted in the map that no Old Babylonian site was found without what were assumed to be traces of an underlying Isin-Larsa occupation. Such a pattern is by no means inconsistent with known historical trends, but at the very least it justifies a certain skepticism. In short, the statement of these doubts leads to what is almost a platitude: comparisons of gross numbers of sites in successive periods probably are little if any more valid than the criteria that were used initially in assigning spans of occupation to individual sites. Having indicated the debatable basis of many of the former, we can only express reservations also about using the latter as a basis for wide-ranging historical interpretations.

Gross numbers of sites are not the only index of changes that went on during this interval, in spite of its overall continuity. Almost all of the urban centers that constitute the most important individual components of the pattern did not remain unaltered. Unfortunately, the very limited extent of excavations outside of Warka—and the limitations of our survey—do not permit this theme to be dealt with yet other than very superficially. Larsa surely must have reached its maximum size during the period identified with its name. Uruk probably never approached its Early Dynastic I apogee at any point during this entire eight-century span, although within the giant shell of its ancient wall the city that remained undoubtedly experienced successive cycles of prosperity and retraction. Umma, Zabalam, and Bad-Tibira are entirely unknown from the reports of scientific excavations. All three continued well into the Old Babylonian period as very substantial towns, but the areal extent of their occupations in earlier periods is only inadequately hinted at in texts and cannot be more than guessed at from our limited surface observations.

Other centers, apparently of a slightly lesser order, for the most part still cannot be identified by their ancient names. Umm al-Aqarib dropped from sight before the end of Early Dynastic times, its population perhaps having been incorporated into an expanding Umma. Tell Shmīd continued on a slightly diminished scale into or through the Akkadian period, its inhabitants perhaps then similarly moving to nearby Zabalam. Fara, ancient Shuruppak, probably never regained its earlier size after it was destroyed by fire in Early Dynastic III times. Continuing to dwindle, it was finally abandoned during the Isin-Larsa period, if not earlier. Suheri continued into Old Babylonian times, but only much reduced in size. Jidr is difficult to judge beneath an immense later overburden, but a fairly intensive scrutiny of its surface provided evidence of continuous occupation throughout this entire time span and failed to hint at any intervening phase of decline or abandonment. As even these inadequate sketches suggest, developments in individual towns were anything but static. On the other hand, a consistent, common pattern subsuming them all is not immediately in evidence.

The watercourse system exhibits most clearly the unchanging character of the basic pattern. With rare exceptions, new towns make their appearance in positions defined by the same streams or canals along which other towns had expired many centuries earlier. The multiple small, shifting channels reflected in the Late Uruk, Jemdet Nasr, and Early Dynastic I maps (figs. 3–5)—surely constituting together a span of time considerably shorter than that included in figure 17 alone—by now had been consolidated into a much reduced number of larger and more permanent courses. Also transformed were the little enclaves along short, discontinuous segments of watercourses that characterized much of the prehistoric settlement pattern. Now the prevailing pattern consisted instead of a more or less evenly spaced series of larger towns, suggesting that the major streams were accompanied by an essentially uninterrupted ribbon of cultivation along their banks. Of course, in retrospect this new aspect of the landscape already had made at least a partial appearance in late Early Dynastic times. But figure 17 both extends the pattern then introduced and confirms its durability.

It would be difficult to avoid the conclusion that the hand of man was dominant in this substantial alteration. The numerous branch canals stemming from the main arteries cannot be directly observed beneath their later overburden, at least in the available small-scale air photographs, but their existence at this time also cannot be doubted. From the Ur III period onward, outlying small settlements and the accompanying lines of canal levees that were followed again in later periods confirm at least their approximate disposition in the region north and east of Uruk. Elsewhere the newly emerging pattern may have been similar but less extensive, although, as in the vicinity of Umma, it is difficult to detect beneath dense clusters of modern dunes.

Hence the *anastomosing* network of bifurcating and rejoining watercourses that is natural in an alluvium was well on its way to replacement by a more artificial, *dendritic* system in which only the main channels carried a sufficient flow to scour their beds and retain an approximate equilibrium, whereas the grids of successively smaller canals branching away from them required annual desilting and other maintenance. Moreover, the striking longevity of the main courses surely argues for at least periodic human intervention there also—measures such as diking, straightening, and even reexcavating in order to avoid disastrous shifts that would deprive important towns of their communications and water supply.

These generalizations should not be taken to imply strict uniformity throughout the area, for there are also substantial differences between the regimes of even the major watercourses. In particular, the route followed by the Euphrates branch north of Uruk is singularly direct and free of traces of meanders, whereas the eastern branch in the vicinity of Jidr, Zabalam, and Umma seems to have followed an almost continuously meandering course. To be sure, this apparent difference may be accentuated by the accidents of later occupation. The line north of Uruk was reused later for an extensive dendritic canal system, particularly during the long interval from Neo-Babylonian through Parthian times. Hence its observed straightness may derive in part from the distribution of sediments in the later, overlying levee. No similar reuse was made, at least on so intensive and long-lived a basis, of the old eastern channel leading through Umma.

Later occupations surely cannot account, however, for more than a minor proportion of the very striking differences between these courses. Given the extent of wind scour of the entire plain, the almost total absence of old meander traces along the western branch indicates that the course remained at all times within the limits of a relatively straight and narrow meander belt levee. This is confirmed by the straight alignment of sites spaced at relatively short intervals along the old course, as well as by what clearly must be surface traces of the old bed adjoining sites that were permanently abandoned after the Old Babylonian period. In the Umma area, on the other hand, obvious traces of numerous, powerfully developed meanders form wide belts adjoining and connecting most of the ancient sites—and this in spite of the heavy concentration of overlying dunes which severly limits study of the aerial photographs.

The decisive factor behind this gross difference in regime must have been differences of flow in the two channels. It would appear that, at any rate from late Early Dynastic times onward through the Old Babylonian period, the eastern channel carried a very much larger volume of water than the western one. Further evidence in support of this conclusion is found in pairs of contemporary sites on opposite sides of the western course (039 and 061, 130 and 131), indicating that even the exigencies of periodic flooding and desilting could be met within a bed-and-bank width of only one hundred meters or so. Along the eastern course, by contrast, both the direct traces of the bed and the absence of similar site pairs argue that the stream was several times wider, shifted back and forth between several alternative channels, and in general was less readily subjected to human control.

Perhaps, then, the early development of the dendritic canal system north and east of Uruk was a consequence of the relatively smaller flow and more docile character of this system. It would also follow that much of the water this branch carried was consumed by the irrigation grid around Uruk, so that the main flow of the Euphrates that reached the sea did so via other channels. The regular movement during this period of fifteen-metric-ton consignments of cargo by ship along more easterly watercourses in the vicinity of Umma,[2] accordingly may have had no parallel on the Uruk branch.

Finally, two lesser watercourses in use during this period also deserve mention. One follows a line from above Bad-Tibira to Larsa. To judge from ceramic surface collections, its extension below the former town began only at about the time of the Third Dynasty of Ur. The other follows a south-southwesterly line from near Tell Shmīd past Tell Jīd and in the direction of Uruk. Its course is indicated by unambiguous traces of an ancient levee, and it is adjoined by the remains of a number of substantial towns. Nevertheless, this canal poses a problem in that the extensive sources on Umma watercourses during the Ur III period apparently are silent concerning it. Since stamped bricks of Amarsuena were found in most towns of comparable size along the branch of the Euphrates above Uruk but were entirely absent along this line, independently converging lines of evidence suggest that it was largely abandoned during the Third Dynasty of Ur. Perhaps, we may speculate, Amarsuena preferred to reserve the available water supply for other projects closer to the capital and hence farther downstream. In any case, it reveals something of the limitations of reconnaissance methods that this apparent hiatus could not be directly detected from ceramic surface collections.

CASSITE–MIDDLE BABYLONIAN PERIODS
(*ca.* 1600–800 B.C.)

As elsewhere on the Mesopotamian plain, the relatively stable configurations of settlement that had first crystallized in Early Dynastic times drew to a close in the Warka region with the Old Babylonian period. Of the widespread series of abandonments that followed there can be no doubt, although surface collections (and the very modest excavations heretofore undertaken in this time range) provide little basis for deciding whether this was a relatively sudden, catastrophic collapse or the outcome of a slow, protracted process.

Such evidence as there is seems to favor the latter alternative. As was noted earlier, the dating criteria employed in the survey suggest an overall reduction of about one-third in the number of sites occupied during the Old Babylonian period as compared with previous periods. To this abandonment of twenty-nine sites already by the outset of Old Babylonian times may be added an additional six sites, some of them fairly large (175 and 242) whose terminal occupations during the Old Babylonian period

were on a significantly reduced scale. On the other hand, a number of major centers, including in particular Umma, Bad-Tibira, and Zabalam, were observed not only to have been very extensively occupied during the Old Babylonian period but also to give every indication of containing thick layers of debris of that date. For them, as for about two-fifths of all Old Babylonian sites (twenty-three out of sixty), the events leading to their abandonment must have taken place only after a considerable portion of the period had elapsed.

The reduction in the total number of sites in Cassite time, from sixty to fifty-seven, at first glance is fairly insignificant. Moreover, although the proportion of Old Babylonian sites that failed to continue into Cassite times (twenty-nine out of sixty) is somewhat higher than after previous periods, the increase again appears initially to be of no great importance. But a better indication of the real decline in settlement is given by taking into account not only numbers but areas. The twenty-nine settlements abandoned during the Old Babylonian period aggregated about 750 hectares, whereas the twenty-six newly founded Cassite sites—averaging only slightly more than five hectares in size—replaced less than one-fifth of this loss. In addition, it is not unlikely that there were substantial reductions in the occupied areas of the remaining major centers like Uruk and Larsa.

Additional evidence of a disruptive break associated with the onset of the Cassite period is provided by the watercourse system outlined in figure 18. Both of the principal streams of Old Babylonian and earlier times, together with many of the principal branches, no longer can be traced in the alignments of Cassite settlements. To judge from both settlement areas and levee widths, none of the channels attributable to this period was comparable in volume of flow to the eastern and western branches of the Euphrates that were traceable in earlier periods. Their limited length and dendritic patterns instead suggest that they form only the "tails" of more extensive watercourse systems that now had developed farther to the northwest. And with these changes also went a substantial reorientation in the prevailing direction of drainage, roughly from north-northwest to west-northwest.

In short, the Warka region provides evidence of a decisive westward shift of the center of gravity of the Euphrates system as a whole, comparable to the ascendancy of the Hindīya channel over the Hilla channel in the nineteenth century A.D. (cf. chapter 5). That this was a widespread phenomenon and not a purely local one is indicated by independent identifications of a comparable shift in the region of Ur, across the Euphrates to the south, and in the environs of Kish, far to the northwest.[3] Clearly

---

2. H. Sauren, *Topographie der Provinz Umma nach den Urkunden der Zeit der III Dynastie von Ur* (Heidelberg, 1966), p. 37.

3. H. T. Wright and McG. Gibson, personal communications.

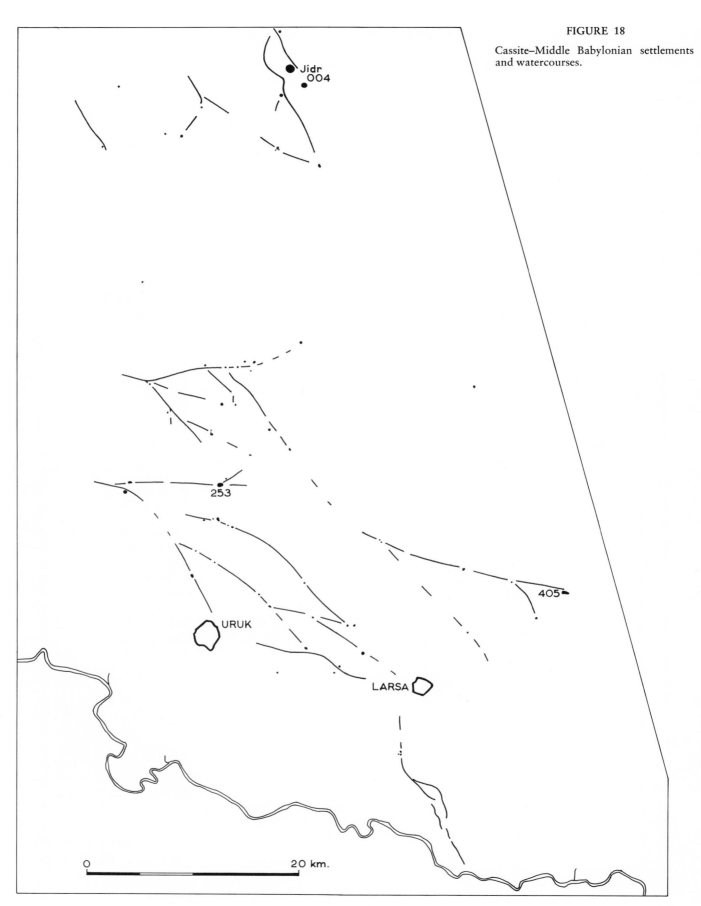

FIGURE 18

Cassite–Middle Babylonian settlements
and watercourses.

Jidr
OO4

253

405

URUK

LARSA

O   20 km.

then, we are dealing with varied, but generically similar and probably simultaneous, manifestations of a major alteration of the Euphrates course. Any such change would have had potentially dangerous consequences for townsmen and cultivators alike in any period. As the culminating episode to what seems to have been a long prior process of attrition and abandonment, however, this alteration occurred at a time when capacities to adjust patterns of settlement and cultivation to it had been progressively weakened. Hence it is not surprising that whatever Cassite recovery ensued was at most rather limited and localized, as is suggested by the fact that more than half of the newly founded Cassite sites in the Warka region were located along the branches of a single watercourse some twenty-five kilometers north of Uruk. Interacting historical and natural factors, in other words, underlay the sharp drop in population and the trend toward smaller, more rural settlements that are characteristic of the Cassite period as a whole.

The immediate sequel to the Cassite period was, if anything, even more small-scale and obscure. In part, to be sure, sites of this time may be difficult to identify because the stratigraphic exposures that would provide a ceramic sequence for the late second and early first millennia have not been undertaken. Moreover, it is not unlikely that some of the major Cassite ceramic types continued with little alteration. But at any rate, no pattern of sites and watercourses, or even individual sites, can be discerned that seems to represent a Middle Babylonian innovation after the end of the Cassite period. Here as elsewhere, the scattered vestiges doubtfully attributable to the early centuries of the first millennium instead suggest that the conditions of settled life must have approached their nadir.

HISTORICAL AND TOPOGRAPHICAL NOTES: UR III–OLD BABYLONIAN PERIODS
Hans J. Nissen

Fuller textual information is available for the Warka region during the span of the Third Dynasty of Ur through the Old Babylonian periods than for any other comparable interval. To be sure, information from both earlier and later periods is also available, but with rare exceptions it is not of a kind which can enable us archaeologically to identify features like ancient sites or canals. Hence a fuller discussion is justified of those texts which, of the thousands of economic and other texts that fall within this interval, refer to conditions within our area. They come mainly from sites within the Warka survey region, including especially Uruk and Umma, but also from elsewhere.[4]

Unfortunately, this span of time, which is perhaps the best documented historically of any, does not correspond to the time during the late fourth and early third millenia when the most dramatic developments in settlements and social organization were taking place. Written sources stemming from the Late Uruk, Jemdet Nasr, and Early Dynastic I periods are, of course, available in considerable numbers.[5] As yet, however, they are only rarely and partially intelligible, so that a discussion here would not aid in their evaluation. Similarly, archaeological evidence for the early periods, principally from Uruk, still awaits systematic analysis and summarization. Any such study would be far beyond the scope of what can be attempted here.

It is particularly unfortunate that little can be said with regard to the role of Uruk in the earlier periods from either a textual or an archaeological viewpoint. There is no doubt that Uruk is the pivot about which much of this study turns. But since excavations there have been focused almost exclusively on architectural clearance of the two main temple areas, little can be said about the overall size of the city in different periods. We are also largely ignorant of other components of its social structure, although it seems clear that the religious sector played a major role.

Even within the relatively narrow framework of their subject matter, the preliminary reports so far available on excavations in Uruk present certain unresolved prob-

umes of *The Assyrian Dictionary* (Oriental Institute of the University of Chicago, 1956–). The following (cited with the special abbreviations shown) provided the major sources of information:

AnOr 30	A. Falkenstein, *Die Inschriften Gudeas von Lagaš I* (Rome, 1966).
AOS 32	A. L. Oppenheim, *Catalogue of the Cuneiform Tablets . . . Wilberforce Eames Babylonian Collection* (New Haven, 1948).
Bagh. Mitt. 2	A. Falkenstein, *Zu den Inschriftenfunden der Grabung von Uruk/Warka 1960/61* (Berlin, 1963).
OIP 14	D. D. Luckenbill, *Inscriptions from Adab* (Chicago, 1930).
Snyder/Jones	*Sumerian Economic Tablets from the Third Ur Dynasty* (Minneapolis, 1961).
TUU	H. Sauren, *Topographie der Provinz Umma nach den Urkunden der III. Dynastie von Ur* (Heidelberg, 1966).
UET 3	L. Legrain, *Ur: Business Documents of the Third Dynasty* (London, 1947).
UNL	G. Pettinato, *Untersuchungen zur Neusumerischen Landwirtschaft*, vol. 1 (Naples, 1967).
ZZB	D. O. Edzard, *Die Zweite Zwischenzeit Babyloniens* (Wiesbaden, 1957).

5. S. Langdon, *Pictographic Texts from Jemdet Nasr. Oxford Ed. Cun. Texts VII* (1928); A. Falkenstein, *Archaische Texte aus Uruk* (1936); E. Burrows, *Archaic Texts from Ur* (1936).

4. Bibliographic abbreviations used in the footnotes to this section follow the style set forward in the prefaces to the vol-

lems. For any discussion of the early development of Uruk as a city, for example, it would be vital to know the exact temporal relationships of structures in its two main temple areas. Equally crucial would be a clear definition of the time of the first construction of the city wall in relation to the temple sequence at the core of the city. Both of these problems remain obscure, and in fact, even the Early Dynastic I dating of the city wall still must be considered only provisional.[6] Thus any attempt to complement the analysis of changing settlement patterns in the surrounding countryside with a discussion of changes in the urban structure of Uruk itself would presuppose a detailed reworking of the basic evidence, again an undertaking beyond the scope of the present study.

The available documentation for the Ur III–Old Babylonian interval conceivably would permit us to deal with a wide number of themes. It seems appropriate, however, to consider only those that are closely related to the findings of the survey. Of particular concern, as a basis for further historical work, is an attempt to identify ancient place names with topographic features recorded during the reconnaissance. The first part of what follows deals with the system of canals and watercourses, and the second is concerned with the ruins of ancient towns.

The Main System of Watercourses in the Survey Area

The Warka region in every period has received virtually its entire water supply from the Euphrates. Only occasionally were supplies from the Tigris introduced into the eastern part of the surveyed area,[7] as is the case today as the tails of the Shatt al-Gharraf are gradually extended along its eastern borders. Maintenance of flow in the modern Gharraf depends, however, upon a barrage and regulator at Kūt. Predecessors of this contemporary diversion from the Tigris apparently never were a long-lasting success.

It is evident from the geographical distribution of Babylonian sites, as well as from the classical and post-Hellenistic sources, that the ancient regime of the Euphrates never consisted of only one channel. Shortly after its entry into the Babylonian plain the river divided into several roughly equal branches. Below that point the overall picture was that of a changing configuration of channels, with new branches forming as others silted up and were cut off. As an aid to the reconstruction of settlement patterns and the identification of ancient topographic names, it would be of great importance to know what branches of the Euphrates existed in particular areas

at particular periods and what their relative importance was. On one assumption, the different branches could have been considered essentially as separate rivers and then might be expected to have borne separate names. An alternative, however, is that the Euphrates system as a whole could have been regarded as a unit, with little or no identifying nomenclature for its individual branches. In this case ancient texts would provide us with very little information on the configuration of the Euphrates system.

The need for clarification of this point emerged very early in our study. Following established custom,[8] we began by identifying the eastern branch of the Euphrates, whose bed may be traced on the air photographs in the vicinity of Zabalam and Umma, as the "Iturungal." Serious doubts soon arose, however, whether this name can be applied to all parts of the course in question. Since the main western (Uruk) and eastern (Umma) branches of the Euphrates serve as the outer frame for the discussion to follow, a consideration of the distribution and use of the names "Euphrates" and "Iturungal" must be undertaken first.

As one would expect, there is very little textual material at our disposal. This is limited still further if a distinction is made between various kinds of sources, dividing them according to date and significance. A major difficulty is provided by the very nature of the economic texts which mention canal or river names. For obvious reasons, scribes sought to identify a locality with as few words as possible. Hence where an important, widely known town is mentioned no need was felt to identify its accompanying canal by name. In such cases even a major watercourse frequently is referred to only as "the canal."[9]

Another group of texts, including building inscriptions and year formulas, normally is more explicit when mention is made of the construction or maintenance of canals. But, unfortunately, only a few of the canal names given in these cases can be connected with canals known otherwise. Instead they are often "propaganda names," like "Apilsin (a king of Babylon) is abundance" (Apilsin year 8), or names given to propitiate a certain god.[10] Such names may not have lasted longer than the lifetime of the sponsor.

Again, conflicting interpretations are possible. The absence of other references to names of this kind might indicate that they were applied only to unimportant, minor watercourses, whereas the necessary construction and maintenance work on the major ones was regarded as routine and therefore left unmentioned. A different

6. For a summary see H. J. Nissen, "The City Wall of Uruk," in *Man, Settlement, and Urbanism*, ed. P. J. Ucko, R. E. Tringham, G. W. Dimbleby (in press).

7. J. Renger, "Die Lokalisierung von Karkar," *AfO* 23: 73–78.

8. Th. Jacobsen, "The Waters of Ur," *Iraq* 22:174; H. Sauren, *TUU* 11; A. Falkenstein, *ZANF* 21:19[45].

9. *UNL* 1. 429, 430. *TUU* 128.

10. See the compilation of year formulas containing canal names in *ZZB*, p. 112.

LAGASH

This chart is based on the Middle Chronology (Hammurabi 1792–1750).

——

URBABA

——

GUDEA   UR

——

FOUR MORE KINGS

——   UTUHENGAL

2100   ——

URNAMMU

——

Third Dynasty of Ur   SHULGI

——

AMARSUENA

SHUSIN   ISIN

IBBISIN

——

2000   ISHBIERRA   LARSA

SHUILISHU

IDDINDAGAN   ——

SAMIUM

ISHMEDAGAN

——   ——

LIPITESHTAR   ZABAYA

BABYLON   GUNGUNUM

URNINURTA

1900   ——   ——   ABISARE

SUMUABUM   BURSIN   SUMUEL

——

SUMULAEL   LIPITENLIL

First Dynasty of Babylon   ——   NURADAD

——   ENLILBANI   SINIDDINAM

SABIUM   SINERIBAM

——   ——   SINIQISHAM

APILSIN   WARADSIN

SINMUBALLIT

1800   ——

RIMSIN

HAMMURABI

——   ——

Ur III–Old Babylonian Chronology in Lower Mesopotamia

43

explanation is suggested by the thirty-third year formula of Hammurabi, identifying a canal by the name "Hammurabi is the wealth of the people."[11] The watercourse referred to must have been identical with a part of the course of the Euphrates above the bifurcation of the Isin and Nippur branches, since its reopening served to provide water to Nippur, Eridu, Ur, Larsa, Uruk, and Isin. From this it appears that propaganda names in fact may have been assigned to existing rivers or canals, and even to sections thereof.[12] If so, the problem of identifying by name the ancient watercourses that served particular towns and regions becomes vastly more complicated.

Finally it must be mentioned that a study of the changing configurations of Euphrates branches through a succession of periods seldom involves textual sources from the same cities or towns. Only rarely is an individual site represented by texts of all periods. Much more commonly, sites have yielded texts of only one or two periods, so that topographic study is made more difficult by fluctuations in the character and provenance of its sources.

Use of the Name "Euphrates"

In the form [i.]UD.KIB.NUN[ki] "Sippar River" the name occurs for the first time in texts from the beginning of the Early Dynastic III period from Abū Salabikh.[13] This form is the usual one for later times and is given the pronunciation "buranunu" or "purattu" in later vocabularies.[14] In the Salabikh texts, the name unfortunately cannot be related to any place names, or even to the find-spot, since it occurs only in literary texts and there mostly in the general phrase "Tigris and Euphrates." Only a very few texts dating to the following Akkad period mention the name[15] and in these the river Euphrates is called the "Sippar River" in the area of today's Syria, which is well above Sippar; one might infer that the entire river system was called by this name.

Strangely enough, the name is not found once in the more than 20,000 economic texts of the Ur III period,[16] not even in the various official documents such as building inscriptions or year formulas. Conspicuously, the one inscription of Urnammu's which reports the construction or reconstruction of the main canal of Ur does not mention the Euphrates but calls the canal the "Ur canal," probably a local name for this part of the Euphrates.[17]

Of course the name of the Euphrates as such was known, but was used only in literary texts, with a general meaning, as for instance in Gudea Cyl. B X 20 where the Euphrates is given as an example of pure water. In these cases the name is used in an abstract form, and refers to the entire system, never to special parts. In the latter cases the designation "the river" was apparently always used, as can be shown from the numerous instances where the reference is obviously to the main canal.[18]

This situation changes with the following Isin/Larsa–Old Babylonian period. The name, always given as the "Sippar River," appears more frequently in year formulas, in letters, and now also in economic texts. It occurs in connection with the following places:

Sippar	passim (R. Harris, personal communication)
Kish	Samsuiluna year 24: "he built the city wall of Kish . . . on the 'Sippar River'"
Nippur	no direct texts; but cf. Rimsin year 23 (Ur)
Uruk	no direct texts: but cf. Rimsin year 23 (Ur)
Larsa	no direct texts; but cf. Vorderas. *Bibl.* VI, 43, 27 ff. (letter): "the 'Sippar River' flowing from Larsa to Ur"; cf. also Rimsin year 23 (Ur)
Ur	mentioned three times in documents from Ur (cf. *UET 5* index); Rimsin year 23: "he dug the 'Sippar River' which brings life to Ekur, from Uruk (var. Larsa) down to the coast of the sea . . . and thus made Ur continuously watered" (*ZZB*, p. 114 f.).

Taking into account the rather large number of texts from this period, we have relatively few references to the Euphrates. There are conspicuously few occurrences in economic texts and letters, which may explain the total absence of the name in the texts from Larsa.[19] In literary texts the name again occurs only in general references. From the occurrences at Ur we learn however, that there at least the river was called the "Sippar River." The use of this name at the "other end" of the river certainly indicates that "Sippar River" was meant to designate the entire system.

We find the Euphrates mentioned relatively frequently in the texts of the Neo Babylonian–Achaemenid period. The name is usually written as "Sippar River," but sometimes writings like pu-rat-ti, etc., also occur.

11. Cf. *ZZB*, p. 115.

12. Rimsin year 26 (*ZZB*, p. 115): "Rimsin deepened the long since abandoned canal which brings abundance to Larsa, named it the canal of justice, and made its name great." If the main feeder of Larsa is meant, this canal should be identical in part with the Bad-Tibira–Larsa canal.

13. R. D. Biggs, personal communication.

14. *Sum. Lexikon* 27Ob.

15. Hirsch, *AfO* 20, 22, c7; 74, b5II.

16. At least not in the comprehensive and easily accessible editions and studies: Snyder-Jones; *UET 3*; *TUU*; *UNL*; *AOS* 32; *OIP* 14.

17. *UET* 1. 45. Cf., however, Jacobsen, "Waters of Ur," p. 82, who would make this a small branch canal.

18. Cf. the indexes of *TUU* and *UNL* s.v. "e" and "i₇."

19. E. Ebeling, *Mitt. Altorient. Ges. XV and XVI*; W. F. Leemans, *SLB* 1².

Babylon	normally given as "Sippar River" or just "the river" (Unger, *Babylon,* p. 100). Within the city limits, particularly in official inscriptions given as "arahtu," which in Sennacherib's account of the destruction of Babylon is used interchangeably with pu-rat-ti (Unger, *Babylon,* p. 95).
Borsippa	the river nearby called "Sippar River" (*Reallex. Ass.* 'Borsippa' #6)
Dilbat	spelling pu-rat-ti is common (Unger, *Archiv Or.,* 3. 21, 8)
Kish	no texts
Nippur	main canal called "Sippar River" (*PBS* II/1 ind.; *BE* 10. 26, 9)
Uruk	"Sippar River" mentioned only very rarely (*YOS* 6 and 7), whereas the "king's canal" appears more frequently. This led Cocquerillat, *Palmeraies,* p. 16 to assume that the king's canal was the canal right near the city, whereas the "Sippar River" would have been a canal or river flowing farther west, identical with the course of the modern Euphrates. Aerial photographs suggest that a major river passed by Uruk in the west, a smaller canal in the east. As we know from textual evidence (Falkenstein, *Topogr. Uruk* 43) the king's canal has to be located in the east, so the "Sippar River" may be the one to the west.
Ur	at the only occurrence of the Euphrates it is called the "Sippar River" (*UET* 6)

These few occurrences at least show that the various branches of the Euphrates passing through Babylon, Borsippa, and Dilbat on the one hand and through Nippur and Uruk on the other hand were indiscriminately called the "Sippar River." This name thus was obviously used for the entire system, and recalling our discussion of the use in earlier periods, we can say that this seems to have been true even from the first occurrences.

"Iturungal"

The above discussion shows that the name "Sippar River" was used indiscriminately for the entire system, contradicting attempts in recent years to call the eastern branch of the Euphrates by a separate name, the "Iturungal." Jacobsen proposed that the canal which connected Kasahara, Adab, Umma, and Larsa was the Iturungal,[20] an interpretation which has found wide acceptance but is not supported by the original sources.

The main difficulties are the unusual writings of the name,[21] and the fact that in texts from places which are supposed to lie on this canal, the main canal is always called only "the river."[22]

If we reject the writing ^{i7}e-eren-na[23] as a further variant of the name Iturungal, our earliest occurrence is in the so-called victory inscription of Utuhengal,[24] where the two main texts give the variants ^{i7}EN.URÌ.gal and ^{i7}UD.NUN.NA[25] (= Adab River). In a later vocabulary[26] ^{i7}UD.NUN is equated with i-su-ru(en)-gal, which, if inserted in the equation of the Utuhengal inscription, gives ^{i7}EN.URÌ.gal = Iturungal.

In the Utuhengal inscription the Adab river is used to define more closely the location of a small town, Nagsu, which according to other texts must be located south of Umma (cf. s.v. NAGSU). The designation "Adab river" and the occurrence together with a town south of Umma seem to identify the Iturungal with the canal Adab-Umma, the main watercourse in that area. However, although we should expect the name of the main trade route to occur often in texts concerned with trade, the writing ^{i7}EN.URÌ.gal is found in only one economic text,[27] and the writing ^{i7}UD.NUN in none. Except for this one occurrence, the Iturungal is mentioned only in literary and lexical texts, the only dated one being an inscription by Anam, a ruler of Uruk,[28] who reports the erection of a temple for the goddess Ganisurra, "the lady of the ^{i7}UD.NUN." As the territory of Anam was probably not very extensive,[29] this temple should have been quite close to Uruk, which would also place the Iturungal close to Uruk. There is another text *SRT* 3, 1. 133 f.,[30] which, depending on the interpretation, could be adduced to show a close relationship between Uruk and the Iturungal: "On the splendid fields of Uruk your sheep shall eat barley, your small ones shall drink water from the ^{i7}UD.NUN.gal." Unfortunately, the group of signs in question can be read either as "the splendid fields of Uruk" or as the place name "Zabalam," a town north of Umma on the main canal from Adab. A reading as Zabalam would conform

20. Jacobsen, "Waters of Ur," p. 177 with note 9.

21. Collected by H. Sauren, *TUU* 127⁶⁷.
22. *TUU* 129.
23. Cf. a year formula of Naramsin of Akkad: Hirsch, *AfO* 20, 22, c2.
24. Now H. Sauren, *RA* 61. 75.
25. Because of the prolongation -na ^{i7}UD.NUN-a must have had a pronounciation ending in -n-, which thus was different from either edaba or isurungal.
26. *Diri* 4. 182.
27. *Nik.* 2. 162 (discussed in *TUU* 129). I was not able to verify the citation of Jacobsen, "Waters of Ur," p. 177⁹⁽³⁾, as *Nik.* 2. 153 presents a different text.
28. *TUU* 136.
29. A. Falkenstein, *Bagh. Mitt.* 2, 35.
30. J. J. A. van Dijk, *La sagesse sumero-accadienne* 65.

with Jacobsen's theory,[31] but because of the Anam inscription, the other interpretation also seems possible.

However this is to be resolved, two later literary texts contradict the assumption of a Kasahara-Larsa Iturungal, since they call Iturungal the part of the Euphrates below Uruk. In the composition "Inanna's journey to Eridu," the Iturungal (or a toponym composed with that name) seems to be the sixth station, shortly before the arrival in Eridu,[32] and in "Nanna's journey to Nippur," the Iturungal is mentioned in the prologue, before Nanna has boarded the ship. There cattle are mentioned grazing on the banks of the Iturungal.[33] I would like to assume that this alludes to a part of the area through which Nanna will travel. Since Nanna's journey leads him up through Uruk and Shuruppak to Nippur, this would mean that the western branch of the Euphrates could also be called Iturungal.

There is clearly not yet enough material for a convincing interpretation, yet certain observations may be worth noting. The main point is that the complete equation of the ^{ir}EN.URÌ.gal and the ^{ir}UD.NUN should not be taken for granted. It seems quite posssible, and even likely, that these are not merely two spellings for the same name, but render two different names which could be used for the same watercourse. This assumption might then imply that the two names also had different meanings, since, for instance, the name Adab River may have been a local name for a part of the river and the ^{ir}EN.URÌ.gal a surname. Unfortunately, nothing further can be learned from the etymology of the latter name, as we cannot interpret it. Yet, taking into account the above mentioned literary texts, one might speculate that ^{ir}EN.URÌ.gal, with an original pronunciation of Iturungal, originally meant the procession road of the gods from Ur or Eridu to Nippur. That ^{ir}UD.NUN and ^{ir}EN.URÌ.gal mean the same in the Ur III period may result from the fact that during this period the eastern branch of the Euphrates was the main trade connection, and thus probably also the procession road.

The western branch of the Euphrates is known to have regained some of its importance during the following period, perhaps loosening the connection between the procession road and the eastern branch of the Euphrates. Thus we find that after the Ur III period the Iturungal—now written as ^{ir}UD.NUN as a result of the contamination during the Ur III period—again has its original meaning of procession road. One can easily explain in this way

its occurrence in the god's journeys and in the Anam inscription.

The above discussion indicates that the eastern branch of the Euphrates cannot be simply identified as the Iturungal, since it seems to be called that only for a short time and in a limited sense. The term should therefore be dropped entirely as a geographical designation. Whenever the Euphrates is mentioned in this study, this will mean the entire system with all branches. Parts of the system are referred to by combining the name Euphrates with the names of major towns along its banks.

The Course of the Eastern Branch of the Euphrates

The course of this main water artery is by no means as well established as Jacobsen and, following him, Falkenstein and Sauren[34] assume, especially in the area south of Umma. On the basis of a brief surface reconnaissance, Jacobsen proposed that the watercourse went straight south from Umma to Tell al-Madain. Traces of an old canal were indeed observed on the surface in this area, but the ruins along its banks are dated without exception to the Jemdet Nasr or Early Dynastic I periods. Hence that course may be regarded as having been abandoned, or at least of having no great importance, in the Ur III period when the eastern branch of the Euphrates is known to have been important. Furthermore, the long northeast-southwest extension of Bad-Tibira suggests that it was located at a straight canal, not at a sharp bend in the stream, as Jacobsen suggested.

Unfortunately, both Umma and Bad-Tibira were located on the eastern margins of our reconnaissance area, in a locality densely covered by dunes. It was therefore not possible to locate the entire course of the main canal. Aerial photos of the area southeast of Umma, now partly under cultivation, show traces of watercourses which lead directly southeast of Umma toward Tell al-Nasirīya and then divide. One branch continues southeast, and another flows southwest toward Bad-Tibira. The latter seems to be the watercourse on whose banks Bad-Tibira lay (cf. fig. 17).

Although the general course is thus fixed, we are faced with several difficulties about specific points. One of these is the location of the watercourse between Umma and Tell al-Nasirīya, an area which is heavily covered with dunes. There are two major sites, each of which must be supposed to have been situated on the main canal: Umm al-Aqarib (WS 198) and Tell Zichariya (WS 213). Umm al-Aqarib was abandoned after Early Dynastic III, and Tell Zichariya had its peak during Akkad–Old Babylonian times. This strongly suggests a shift of the position of the beginning of the main course from the area near

31. Jacobsen, "Waters of Ur," p. 177[9 (2)].

32. M. Civil, personal communication. This text is adduced by Jacobsen, "Waters of Ur," p. 177[9 (5)] for the location of the Iturungal.

33. M. Civil, personal communication.

34. cf. note 8 above.

Umm al-Aqarib to the area five kilometers farther south near Tell Zicharīya, during or shortly after the Early Dynastic III period and may, incidentally, explain the abandonment of Umm al-Aqarib.

Another difficult point is the location of the junction of the eastern branch of the Euphrates coming from Bad-Tibira and the western branch coming from Uruk. Jacobsen considers that this point was in the area immediately around Larsa.[35] Unfortunately, the area around Larsa also presents difficulties for reconnaissance, since wide stretches are covered by dunes, and the area to the south is a regularly flooded back-levee depression of the modern Euphrates. The distribution of settlements and the few surviving traces of watercourses show clearly, however, that the junction must have been located between Uruk and Larsa, probably nearer to Larsa.

From here to the southeast some traces of the watercourse may be lost in the flooded depressions paralleling the modern Euphrates, and the ancient course becomes unambiguous again only some distance to the southeast, in a line suggesting a more or less straight course between the Uruk-Larsa junction and Ur.[36]

The Main Canals under Amarsuena

The following remarks take as their starting point the finds of stamped bricks of Amarsuena in all major places along the Uruk-Euphrates.[37] These bricks are evidence of public buildings along this branch of the Euphrates, possibly constructed as part of attempts to revive the western course. Since they were found in places fifteen to twenty kilometers apart, it is possible that the buildings were associated with way stations along a major artery for barge movement.

Earlier in this chapter the difference in the formation of meanders between the two branches of the river has been taken to suggest that the Uruk branch contained much less water than the Adab branch. Adjoining settlements on opposite banks of the Uruk course also point to this branch's being rather stable, tending neither to widespread, uncontrolled flooding nor to shifts in course. General observations of this kind do not necessarily apply specifically to the situation in the Ur III period, although it may be assumed that the Uruk branch was also of lesser importance during that period.

There is unfortunately little that can be learned about the western branch from the numerous Ur III transportation texts. This in part reflects the fact that no texts of this kind have yet been found in Uruk, surely the most likely

source of information about the amount of water in, and the navigability of, the Uruk branch. From the available information it would appear that the heavy trade from Ur to Nippur used the Adab branch exclusively, in spite of the Uruk branch's being about forty kilometers or two days shorter. Possibly there was more than pure chance involved in the only two texts that mention round trips from Umma to Ur and through Nippur back to Umma, dating from the early years of Shusin, for this was after the alleged revival of the Uruk branch by Amarsuena.[38] Unfortunately, nothing is said in these texts about the size of the ships used, from which we could get an idea of the minimal size of the canal. Although the Ur III sources provide no further information, a later text reports that during the time of Nuradad of Larsa Ur got its entire water supply from the Adab branch (see below), suggesting that no water came down the Uruk branch, at least not past Uruk. Perhaps this was also the situation in preceding periods.

We know from a number of texts that Amarsuena was engaged in the expansion of the canal system. To be mentioned here is an otherwise rather unimportant "Amarsuena canal," two days' travel long, which branched off the Adab course shortly south of Umma, flowed in southwesterly direction and then joined another canal.[39] It was dug in the first years of Amarsuena; yet ship movements are mentioned very rarely and only in the first years of Shusin. Unfortunately, we are not able to identify this canal clearly with any of the watercourses found during the Warka Survey; however, the possibility should be mentioned that this canal may be identical with a canal found in the proposed area south of Umma, but without remains of Ur III occupation along its banks. This may be due to its short life or its low importance. The Amarsuena would then have joined the main course somewhere between Bad-Tibira and Larsa.[40]

Both the revival of the Uruk branch and the construction of a new canal may have been merely a part of a general effort to enlarge the cultivated area or to facilitate

35. Jacobsen, "Waters of Ur," p. 179.

36. H. T. Wright, *The Administration of Rural Production in an Early Mesopotamian Town* (Ann Arbor, 1969), fig. 3.

37. See the discussion in chapter 8.

38. *AOS* 32, Text G 20 dated to Shusin year 1; *Nik* 2. 116 dated to Shusin year 4.

39. *TUU* 97.

40. The main reason for this assumption is that the point where the Amarsuena branches off the main course is said to be south of Umma, but cannot be far from this city, as the branching off is said to be near the Endudu field in the immediate neighborhood of Umma. It is therefore neither possible to identify the Amarsuena canal with the Tell al-Nasirīya–Larsa watercourse (one also would wonder why only small and seemingly unimportant places like Dukiriabba and Ituma are mentioned to lie on the Amarseuna canal and not major towns like Bad-Tibira and Larsa), nor with a watercourse branching off from the Adab course near Tell Jidr, flowing past Tell Jīd in the direction of Uruk.

trade connections; but in the case of the Amarsuena canal additional reasons may have been involved, assuming the above-mentioned location. As we have seen, the main Adab course bifurcates in the area of Tell al-Nasirīya, with the major stream leading off in a southeasterly direction and a smaller, but apparently more important branch turning back to Bad-Tibira, Larsa, and finally Ur. Since the branch which went on to the southeast continued the direction of the upper course and followed the natural slope of the plain, strong measures probably were needed at that point to maintain flow in the branch to Bad-Tibira.[41] This diversion or bifurcation may have been a constant source of difficulty and concern, particularly for Ur, which depended on water from this branch. One way of dealing with the problems was to erect a weir in the branch flowing to the southeast. However, only temporary relief could be afforded in this manner, since a major flood would destroy even baked brick construction at once. A more radical solution might have consisted of constructing a canal which would circumvent the dangerous point by cutting off the entire bend to the east between Umma and Bad-Tibira.

There is still another aspect to this problem, centering on the possibility that part of the area crossed by the eastward bend of the canal belonged to the territory of Lagash, whereas a shorter canal farther to the west would have led directly from the province of Umma into the province of Ur.[42] The implication that Ur and Lagash were not always on good terms is, to be sure, in contrast to our usual picture of the political situation in the Ur III period, usually characterized as having a highly centralized government. There are, however, certain indications that the relationship between Lagash and the central government was not always smooth. Apparently Ur treated Lagash differently from the other provinces. This is most

conspicuously shown by the fact that the ruler of Lagash apparently also had the hereditary title of sukkal-mah of the empire, a title which is somewhat ambiguous but apparently ranked second in the empire.[43] Under Amarsuena's successor Shusin a certain Irnanna held this position. He had an unusual accumulation of offices and titles, for he was not only ensi of Lagash and sukkal-mah but also the prestigious sanga priest of Eridu, and governor of all the more or less loosely associated territories from Assyria to the head of the gulf.[44] We have no information on the relationship of Irnanna to the king in Ur, but it is clear that Lagash was more independent than the other provinces. Since Lagash and Ur were, in any case, natural competitors because of their rivalry to control shipping at the head of the gulf, it would be surprising if the relationship between the central government and the sub-empire of the sukkal-mahs were not at times tense. Thus a further reason for the construction of the new canal may have been Ur's desire that the inland trade which was essential for its role as a port should pass only through directly controlled areas.[45]

The main reason for the suggested revival of the western branch of the Euphrates was to secure the water supply, but admittedly this alone would not explain the presence of the many inscribed bricks. If we assume that the western branch was intended to be a trade route with way stations at certain intervals we may come closer to a solution. The bricks could be an indication of the existence of something like royal rest stops and provisioning points.[46]

Events in the Reign of Nuradad of Larsa

J. J. A. van Dijk has recently published a text which reports the activities surrounding the erection of a stela of Nuradad by his son Siniddinam.[47] The speeches given on that occasion constitute almost the entire text, and deal with events shortly before the accession of Nuradad and

---

41. See below s.v. Nagsu the mention of a weir, which possibly is such a regulation device, and the part "Events in the Reign of Nuradad."

42. Unfortunately we have little evidence for the borders of the provinces in our area. Especially interesting would be the extension of the province of Ur, which probably included Uruk and Larsa. Along the western branch of the Euphrates the province of Ur seems to have had a direct border with Nippur, along a line running south of Shuruppak, which probably belonged to Nippur. On the eastern branch of the Euphrates the province of Ur bordered Umma and Lagash; however, the exact borders are difficult to establish, since in the area between Umma-Lagash and Larsa there are few identified places. In particular there is no information on where Bad-Tibira belonged. Sauren thinks that Nagsu was in the province of Umma, but can base his argument only on the fact that transports through Nagsu to Umma are reported. However, as pointed out below s.v. Nagsu, these references may be a result of the favorable location of Nagsu at the confluence of two important canals. If Nagsu indeed should be sought in Tell al-Nasirīya, then it would have been much nearer to Lagash than to Umma.

43. D. O. Edzard, *Fischer Weltgesch,* 2: 138.

44. Ibid., p. 149. For the location of the various parts of the area of Ir-nanna see C. J. Gadd, *CAH*[2] I chap. 22, p. 13.

45. The construction of this new canal probably did not interfere with the water situation of Lagash, since this area secured most of its water from the Tigris canal, and since it is most likely that the water flowing through these southeast-bound canals was not used for irrigation in any case, as the area probably was too marshy.

46. In a paper read before the German Orientalist Congress in Wuerzburg, 1968, Sauren thought of the possibility of "pilgrimage stations" along the main pilgrimage ways to Nippur. This would also touch on the problem of "Gottesfrieden" (H. Sauren, *Or NS* 38: 234). Now cf. *ZDMG*, suppl. 1, 1: 125 (2.2.3).

47. J. J. A. van Dijk, "Une insurrection generale au pays de Larsa avant l'avenement de Nuradad," *JCS* 19: 1–25.

during the first years of his reign. Since these events are closely related to the water supply of Larsa, this text will be discussed here with regard to possible topographical identifications.

An unknown enemy had cut Larsa off from its water supply by damming the main canal. Intimidated by the resulting famine, the inhabitants of Larsa surrendered. Thereupon Utu, the city god of Larsa, chose Nuradad, "one of the multitude," to regain Larsa for Utu. With the help of Utu of Larsa, Ningirsu (of Lagash), Inanna of Zabalam, and Ishkur (of Karkar),[48] Nuradad expelled the enemy, ripped out the dam, and made the water flow again. He deepened the Euphrates, which had silted up because of the dam, enabling Nanna of Ur to receive water again.[49]

The identity of the enemy is an important question already discussed by van Dijk on the basis of the textual evidence and the year formulas.[50] The attack seems to have been against the eastern Euphrates, the main canal of Larsa above Larsa but below Zabalam, since the latter city seems to have been unaffected and is listed among the allies of Nuradad. Had the attack come from the north, both Karkar and Zabalam should have been conquered before Larsa. An approach from the south is ruled out by the fact that Ur itself is reported to have suffered from the damming. An attack from the west or northwest, that is from Uruk or Isin, is rather unlikely as we would expect to have knowledge of hostilities involving those towns from other sources. There remains the east, through the area south of Lagash since it was not affected. This points to Elam as the aggressor.

The problem of the specific point at which the eastern branch of the Euphrates was dammed also makes an attack from the east probable. In a flat country like the area north and northeast of Larsa the only effective way of drying up a river is to divert it—that is, to put a dam at a point where the water can be diverted into an already existing channel. There are three possible spots where this can be done between Zabalam and Larsa:

1. Near Zabalam, where the Gibil canal flows from the eastern Euphrates in the direction of the Tigris canal.
2. Near Tell al-Nasirīya (Nagsu?), where a big watercourse goes off in a southeasterly direction.
3. To the southwest of Bad-Tibira, where a canal must have branched off toward Tell Sifr (Kutallu).

The last possibility probably may be ruled out, since it is very difficult to divert a river to a course perpendicular to its natural flow. To dam the main course and divert the water at the other two points could be very easy. Of the two possibilities, however, the nearness of the first one to Zabalam seems to make it very unlikely since, as we have seen, Zabalam was not affected by the attack. The spot near Tell al-Nasirīya remains as the most likely.

In this respect the possible identification of Tell al-Nasirīya with Nagsu is important because of the weir reportedly built near Nagsu. We may assume that this weir was placed across the branch of the watercourse running east and by damming this the water level in the other branch could be kept at a constant height. If so, then all that was necessary to dam the branch to the southwest would have been to block it partially with brushwork while completely opening the weir. What would appear at first glance to have been a substantial undertaking in order to cut off the water from Larsa and Ur may in fact have been accomplished with little effort.

This discussion also demonstrates the inherent instability in the watercourse system near Tell al-Nasirīya, as similar effects could have been produced by a major flood. One purpose of the construction of the Amarsuena canal may, in fact, have been to reduce the dangers of a disastrous shift in course farther downstream.

Identification of Sites

Only at one site was inscribed material found mentioning the ancient name of its find-spot, and in that case the identification had already been made previously. The Survey of Central Sumer reported finding a brick on the surface of Tell Ibzaykh in 1953–54, inscribed with a building inscription of Hammurabi for a temple of Inanna of Zabalam. There can be no doubt that the inscription identifies the place, as numerous bricks with the same inscription still occur in situ in the walls of a large building which easily can be identified from its plan as a temple.[51]

To be sure, inscribed bricks also were observed on the surface of other mounds, but they mentioned only building activities in the capital of the ruler and in no case gave more specific information about their immediate locality (cf. chapter 8).

Just before our survey, Herbert Sauren's *Topographie der Provinz Umma* appeared. Sauren attempts to reconstruct the topography from the economic texts from

---

48. For Karkar as the cult-center of Ishkur see J. Renger, *AfO* 23: 74.

49. Van Dijk, "Insurrection," p. 9 to lines 209 ff. and the commentary to these lines.

50. Ibid., p. 12 to lines 48–60 and "note additionelle" p. 24 f.

51. Since on that occasion only the consequences of this find were reported, the text of the inscription is published here in full (chap. 8).

Umma of the Ur III period. Since the eastern branch of the Euphrates was the main water and trade route of the province of Umma, and since this watercourse was also a main focus of our studies, there were many points on which we initially hoped to make use of the information and results of Sauren's study. This was particularly true with regard to the identification of sites along the banks of the eastern branch of the Euphrates, with the help of the information on the traveling time, and therefore presumably distance, between major places. However, the definition of the "day's journey" as a measure of distance presented a major difficulty. From the various transportation texts, especially from Umma, there is information on the number of days' travel between named places. It is tempting to apply a fixed unit of the number of kilometers which could be covered in a day in order to convert this information into exact distance measurements.[52] Sauren thus posits 15–20 kilometers as a day's journey, referring to texts which give ten to eleven days from Ur to Nippur and estimating this distance to have been 150 kilometers.[53] However, 150 kilometers is only the direct distance between these two cities, whereas the distance on the eastern Euphrates with the detour over Kasahara must have been about 220 kilometers. This would mean an average day's coverage of 20 kilometers. Still other figures are known, sometimes differing completely with one another.[54] In part, the differences may be explained from additional information in texts. In some cases, for instance, there may be fewer towing personnel mentioned than is usual. This explanation does not cover all cases, however, and it is unfortunate that other variables, such as the size of the ships, are rarely mentioned.

Thus one must question whether a day's journey can be considered a fixed unit at all. Variables about which we hear nothing, although surely they influenced the length of a trip, include the strength of the current, the height of the water, the wind velocity and direction, and the varying length of the day in summer and winter. In short, it seems unjustified to convert day's journeys into distances unless we take the range of from 10 to 25 kilometers for a day's journey. And since such a wide range is of little use we must conclude that the textual information is not of much value in the reconstruction of an exact topography.[55]

In spite of these limitations, some attempt shall be made to identify some of the mounds found during our survey with their ancient names. In no instance can these identifications claim to be more than tentative, but the material is presented in full so that the reader can decide for himself whether to accept the identifications as working hypotheses.

In the first section below, textual evidence is cited indicating that a particular place was located within our survey area. However, only those places are discussed (in alphabetical order) for which we have textual material allowing us to relate them to known archaeological sites. In the second section those ruins which are likely to be identifiable are listed by survey site numbers. In each case the number is equated with the site in the first section with which it seems most likely to be identified.

The Textual Evidence

Apisala

Apisala was situated on the Tigris canal (TUU 120), the course of which seems to have been approximately the same as the modern Shatt al-Gharraf (TUU 119f.). Near Apisala the Edena canal seems to branch off to the east (TUU 108), and in the area of Apisala the Gibil canal joins the Tigris canal coming from the west (TUU 114). Sometimes transports from Apisala to Zabalam are mentioned, always, however, without the name of the canal being given (TUU 165f.). It is likely that the Gibil canal is meant, since the Gibil canal is said to leave the eastern branch of the Euphrates near the Endudu field and very close to Umma; the canal connecting Zabalam and the Tigris canal also branches off in that area from the eastern Euphrates (TUU 85). The distance from Apisala to Umma is covered in one to three days (TUU 92 with note 6), but nothing is known about the distance from Apisala to Zabalam. Apparently Apisala was located on the border between Umma and Lagash (TUU 13), and was thus certainly outside our survey area. We therefore cannot propose a specific mound to be identified with Apisala. The important point, however, is that Apisala may have been considerably south of the spot on the Tigris canal where Sauren has located it, since the Gibil canal did not join the Tigris canal at Apisala but only in the area of Apisala (TUU 93).

Dabrum

Dabrum[56] must have been a "relay station" between Umma and Nippur on the eastern branch of the Euphrates

52. For one attempt see A. Salonen, *Stud. Orient.* 11:45, who postulates a day's work of 9–10 kilometers. This was rejected as too short by A. Falkenstein, *AnOr* 30.29[9].
53. *TUU* 10 with note 31. Cf. also a normal day's march of the Roman legions was 15–17 kilometers (*R.E. s.v. Marsch*).
54. *TUU* 131[78]; 132[80]
55. Possibly thorough study of this problem would give us more information. It would be interesting to know, for instance, how the ships' crews were fed, whether they took along

food for the entire journey or relied on depots along the way. There is not enough material at present to answer this question.
56. For an attempt to localize this place see H. Sauren, *RA* 61: 77.

(TUU 7[18]). Sauren suggests, without citing evidence, that it may have been not more than two days' journey from Umma. Dabrum had an ensi in the Ur III period but was not the center of a province. No information is available from economic texts. The only text providing some evidence as to location is a campaign report of Utuhengal discussed by Sauren.[57] This text mentions other place names that may help to localize Dabrum.

All place names mentioned in the text apparently lie in our survey area, but unfortunately all are unidentified except Uruk. Of particular interest are the places mentioned after the fourth day: Nagsu, Ilitappe, Karkar, and Dabrum. Nagsu is said to have been located on the Iturungal four days from Uruk, on a journey on which the army probably marched upstream along the eastern Euphrates. Nagsu, therefore, should be a considerable distance above Larsa (for a detailed discussion cf. Nagsu and Tell al-Nasirīya). The name of the next station, Ilitappe, is never mentioned again and is thus of little use. The location of Karkar also cannot be precisely fixed from the available sources,[58] although it seems to have been west or northwest of Umma.[59] Utuhengal reached this place two days after Nagsu, and it is near Karkar that the decisive battle was fought with the forces of Tirigan of Gutium coming from Dabrum. No direct evidence is available for the distance from Karkar to Dabrum, but we can now refer to what was said earlier about the location of Dabrum. Since it is on the banks of the eastern branch of the Euphrates and not too far upstream from Umma, we should look for it northwest of Umma and west of Zabalam, that is, north of the area we just proposed for Karkar. This assumption agrees closely with the topographical scheme proposed by Sauren and limits the choice of ruins which may be identified with Dabrum: only Tell Shmīd can be eliminated because it dates to the Early Dynastic III period with a terminal Akkadian occupation.

If we accept Dabrum as Tell Jidr and Nagsu as Tell al-Nasirīya then everything that happened during Utuhengal's campaign between Nagsu and Dabrum can be placed in the area between Tell Jidr and Tell al-Nasirīya, west of Umma. Assuming that Karkar was rather close to Dabrum, on a purely mechanical basis we may divide the distance of about fifty kilometers into two and a half days of travel, assuming a day's journey to have been approximately twenty kilometers long. Unfortunately, the area around Tell Jidr, especially to the southeast, is densely covered by dunes. The only ruin of some size located in this area was WS 175, which is highly unlikely to have been an important religious center like Karkar.

Dukiriabba

Dukiriabba is situated on the Amarsuena canal (TUU 97) near a weir (TUU 52) and a bar-la pool (TUU 61). Only once is the place given, without further details, as the destination of a shipment from Umma (TUU 61). Together with the Amarsuena canal, it must be located south of Umma, and because of the weir and the pool it may have been very near the offtake of that canal from the eastern Euphrates.

Eduru Amarsuena

Eduru Amarsuena is situated at the point where the Amarsuena canal joined another canal (TUU 98), which is not named. Sauren thinks the Uruk-Euphrates is meant (TUU 99f.), but the lower part of the eastern Euphrates between Bad-Tibira and Larsa seems more likely. The distance from here to Apisala was covered in six days, but this information is not very useful.

The place was probably rather small. It may in fact have been founded at the same time as the construction of the canal, to guard the pool at its mouth (TUU 98 to TCS 5c). There must have been a larger settlement, Ituma, nearby, unless we assume with Sauren that the two places are identical (TUU 167[142]). The likelihood of providing a more exact location on the basis of present evidence is very low (cf., however, Tell Abla).

Enegi

There are no direct references which place Enegi on the banks of a canal. However the list Enegi, Larsa, Uruk, and Shuruppak, in the literary composition "Nanna's journey to Nippur,"[60] suggests that Enegi was on a branch of the Euphrates. Distances to other places are not known but the above list and another in the "Temple hymns,"[61] Larsa, Enegi, Gishbanda, and Uruk, suggest a location not far from Uruk and Larsa. The lists seem to contradict one another as one puts Enegi between Ur and Larsa, whereas the other places it between Larsa and Uruk. This could be explained if the point where the two branches of the Euphrates joined is placed not near Larsa but in the area between Larsa and Uruk (cf. above). Since Enegi is reached before Larsa on the way upstream from Ur, and since it is at the same time between Larsa and Uruk, it then may have been located right at the confluence of the two branches of the Euphrates.

Ituma

Ituma lies two days downstream from the beginning

---

57. H. Sauren, *RA* 61:75.
58. J. Renger, *AfO* 23.
59. See s.v. Karkar.

60. Sauren, *OrNS* 28:215.
61. A. Sjöberg and E. Bergmann, "The Collection of the Sumerian Temple Hymns," *TCS* 3 (1969).

of the Amarsuena canal and thus at its mouth (TUU 99). Nothing more is known.

Karkar

Rarely mentioned in economic texts, and never in connection with a canal, Karkar[62] occurs between Zabalam and Adab in two lists of gods and their cult centers; since the other two towns are on the eastern Euphrates, the location of Karkar on the eastern Euphrates seems possible. There is, however, a text which mentions a land shipment from Umma to Karkar, suggesting that both places did not lie on the same canal. The distance was covered in one day. Since canals radiated out from Umma in nearly all directions except to the west, so that Umma could be reached by ship from all directions except the west, Karkar should be located in the area west of Umma and rather close. This would corroborate the suggestions made above concerning Dabrum.

Karkar was important as the cult center of Adad. It seems to have had little or no economic importance, since, in spite of its proximity to Umma, the name appears only once in the numerous economic texts from Umma.

Keši

Keši[63] is almost certainly outside of our survey area, but a discussion is nevertheless included here because an attempt has been made to identify this place with modern Tell Jidr.[64] This identification was based on the information that Keši was near Adab and that it was built near the an-edena, which was assumed to be the name of an area near Zabalam. However, an-edena seems to designate not just an area near Zabalam, but the entire "steppe" area, difficult to irrigate, between the two branches of the Euphrates.[65] Moreover, the list of place names in the "Lamentation over the Destruction of Ur," Nippur, Keši, Isin, Uruk, Ur, Larak, Umma, Urukuga, seems to imply a geographic order. The author first followed the Uruk branch downstream, then shifted west to the Isinnitum beyond its confluence with the Uruk branch, and then continued down to Uruk and Ur. Then beginning again, followed the eastern branch of the Euphrates. According to this interpretation, Keši would have been on the Uruk branch south of Nippur or on the Isinnitum north of Isin. Because of the evidence regarding the proximity of the place to Adab, a location on the Uruk branch south of Nippur is preferable. This would put it either on the same latitude with or slightly south of Adab,

but on the western branch of the Euphrates. As this area was not surveyed, no mound can yet be suggested for the site.

KI.AN (reading unknown)

On the banks of the eastern branch of the Euphrates,[66] KI.AN is the next station after Zabalam in the report of the journey of Dumuzi of URUxA to Nippur. Thus the place was near or above the point where the canal flowing through Zabalam leaves the eastern Euphrates. No distances to other places are ever given, but from the general composition of this text Sauren believes that the distances covered in one day were very small, and that therefore KI.AN was very near to Zabalam.[67] KI.AN was not the center of a province,[68] but did have an ensi, probably because of its cultic importance.[69]

Nagsu

According to the Utuhengal inscription, the place lay on the banks of the "Iturungal"; according to economic texts, it lay on "the canal," specifically at the point where the Nanatuma canal branched off.[70] Near Nagsu there was a weir, probably at the entrance of the Nanatuma canal (TUU 52; 85). The place was reached in one day's journey from Umma (TUU 134 f.) and in four days from Uruk (Utuhengal inscription). The place is mentioned only very rarely as the destination of shipments. The relatively frequent references to it in transportation texts may be due not to its economic importance but to its favorable location at the branching point of a major canal leading into the Tigris canal from the eastern Euphrates. This

62. Renger, AfO 23.
63. See the discussion by G. Gragg, "The Keš Temple Hymn," in TCS 3: 164.
64. A. Falkenstein, ZANF 21: 19[45].
65. For the an-edena in the vicinity of Larsa cf. J. J. A. van Dijk, JCS 19: 6 to line 79.

66. H. Sauren, OrNS 38: 221.
67. H. Sauren, personal communication.
68. TUU, p. 6[17]. An ensi of the Ur III period of KI.AN is attested in YOR IV/2, 17 to RA 12.155, 13.5–7. (Sauren, personal communication).
69. The religious importance of the place seems to have been considerable during the Ur III period. AnOr 1. 88.233–83 lists 48½ gurus workers under the gudu4 priest of Šara of KI.AN as opposed to only 42 gurus workers of the Šara temple of Umma (ll. 198–232). Already in the fortieth year of Šulgi a temple for Šulgi was founded in KI.AN (TCL 5. 5672, 5.9 "e-dšulgi-ra"). Besides the temples of Šara, Ninurra, and Šulgi, temples are mentioned for Amarsuena, Geštinanna, Dumuzi, Gula, Ninlagaša, and Nine'e in KI.AN (for all these buildings see N. Schneider, AnOr 19, under the names of the gods). (H. Sauren, personal communication.)
70. TUU 148 f. Sauren interprets the text Nik. 2. 141, as meaning that this canal brought water into the eastern branch of the Euphrates. However, if one takes the five days of line 13 not as a total of the previously mentioned days but as a further entry in the list, then the line means that the ship had to be towed for five days against the current to Nagsu. In other words, Nagsu was not at the mouth of that canal but on the outlet.

location could take into account the fact that shipments from the area of Apisala apparently were routed to Umma by way of the Nanatuma canal and Nagsu (TUU 148).

The Archaeological Evidence

WS 004 Tell Jidr

Tell Jidr is one of the largest ruins in the survey area, with thick layers of Parthian and Sassanian material covering almost the entire surface, and burying most of the older material. Early sherds and inscribed bricks of Gudea on the northern part of the site (cf. chap. 8) show that the settlement goes back as far as the Ubaid period. One may doubtless assume that a large settlement of the Ur III–Old Babylonian period existed here.

The site is approximately halfway between Ibzaykh (= Zabalam) and Bismaya (= Adab), and lies on the eastern branch of the Euphrates. One should expect a site of this size to be mentioned as a station on the way between Umma and Nippur, but no identification can be proposed with any certainty. Three ancient places are to be located in this general area—Dabrum, KI.AN and Karkar—and the discussion above has shown that an identification with either KI.AN or Karkar is highly unlikely. The earlier identification with Keši has also to be refuted. Although it is not entirely convincing, Dabrum is here proposed as the ancient name of Tell Jidr.

WS 168 Tell Shmīd

Tell Shmīd was last extensively settled in the Early Dynastic III period, with the beginnings of occupation going back at least into the Late Uruk period. Post-Early Dynastic remains date mainly to the Akkadian period. The site appears to have been a rather important center in the Early Dynastic period, and was afterward reduced in size and importance, possibly to an isolated citadel or a holy district.

The site lies about twelve kilometers northwest of Umma, on the banks of the eastern branch of the Euphrates slightly above the offtake of the canal flowing through Zabalam into the Tigris canal. From its location it would seem to have been the first station on the main branch when coming up from Lagash to Zabalam, and to have been the next station after Umma when coming up the eastern Euphrates. We should thus expect to find its name in numerous transportation texts. We find, however, no name which exactly fits the evidence. The most likely candidate is KI.AN, and the impression given by the texts of the considerably reduced importance of that site in the Ur III period partly corresponds with the findings of the survey. But KI.AN remained an important religious center during the Ur III period, while a significant occupation of the site as late as the Ur III period is at best questionable.

We cannot propose an alternative suggestion to the identification with KI.AN, except for the almost unknown Tumtur, which seems very unlikely (TUU 167). It may be that the site was already so minor by Ur III times that one should not expect to find its name in the texts.[71]

WS 175 (no modern name)

This ruin consists of a long southern mound and a small, seemingly older northern one. The latter began in Early Dynastic I times, but the principal occupation of the site was in the Akkadian–Ur III periods; it continued on a smaller scale into the Isin-Larsa period. The site was situated on a canal of unknown name, which branched off from the eastern Euphrates southeast of Tell Jidr and flowed in an almost straight line past Tell Jīd toward Uruk. Since this was certainly not a main transport route, there is little hope of finding much information in the transportation texts. The only ancient place known to have been located somewhere in this area is Karkar, but the distance of sixteen kilometers from Tell Jidr (Dabrum ?) makes this identification rather unlikely in the light of the information of the Utuhengal inscription (cf. s.v. Dabrum).

WS 213 Tell Zichariya

Settled from Early Dynastic times, the main occupation at Tell Zichariya seems to have been during the Ur III–Isin-Larsa periods. The site seems not to have been directly on the eastern Euphrates but on, or more probably near, the offtake of a canal which we have tentatively identified with the Amarsuena canal (cf. above). Because of its proximity to Umma, its possible location on the Amarsuena canal should permit us to identify the site. Unfortunately, shipments on the Amarsuena canal are attested only rather late and are very infrequent. The place which best seems to fit the material for Tell Zichariya is Dukiriabba.

WS 432 Tell Abla wa Assam

Tell Abla wa Assam consists of a group of small mounds around a larger mound. All seem to date to the Ur III period and were largely abandoned during Old Babylonian times; a few areas were resettled in the Parthian and Sassanian periods. The main mound lies on the canal between Bad-Tibira and Larsa. If, as we have suggested, the Amarsuena canal left the eastern branch of the Euphrates near Zichariya, it might have joined the

---

71. See *TUU* 11, where Sauren enumerates the names of several small settlements in the general area, one of which could very well have been the name of a nearby abandoned settlement.

lower course of this eastern branch again in the area of WS 432. In this case, the main site might be identified with Ituma, which was near the mouth of the Amarsuena canal, and one of the small mounds could represent the remains of Eduru Amarsuena, which was directly at the confluence. These identifications, however, cannot be more than speculations.

Ws 439 Umm al-Wawīya

The almost rectangular mound at Umm al-Wawīya rises to a long ridge in the northeast, and much of the remainder is low and flat. It seems possible that the entire site was surrounded by a moat. Baked planoconvex bricks and Early Dynastic III–Isin-Larsa sherds on the surface suggest that the place was settled in the Early Dynastic period and occupied through the Isin-Larsa period. The site is situated on the banks of a major canal coming from Uruk, probably the western branch of the Euphrates. This is corroborated by the find of inscribed bricks of Amarsuena, which elsewhere were found only on sites along the western branch of the Euphrates. Since traces of defense systems are rather rare in connection with settlements of this size, and since the site is located between Uruk and Larsa, we feel that it may be a town on the border between the two city-states.

The flood plain of the modern Euphrates begins slightly south of this site, whereas the area in the direction of Larsa is largely covered by dunes. Smaller settlements and ancient watercourses in this area thus may have been lost almost completely. What makes this particularly unfortunate is that the confluence of the two main branches of the Euphrates must be located in the vicinity. We have speculated that WS 439 might mark the confluence or at least be near it. Since a similar conclusion was reached from the textual evidence for Enegi, we propose to identify Umm al-Wawiya with Enegi.

WS 457 Tell Mīzan

Like WS 439, Tell Mīzan lies just north of the modern flood plain of the Euphrates, and like WS 439 again, the perimeter of the mound is almost rectangular. The lower, inner area is surrounded by a wall-like ridge, and thus also resembles WS 439 in the apparent presence of a defense system. The place, however, seems to have been occupied only during the Isin-Larsa period, with sparse later remains of the Seleucid period. Although the location seems a more likely one for the confluence of the two branches of the Euphrates than Umm al-Wawiya, an identification with Enegi seems to be excluded by the limited period of occupation.

Tell al-Nasirīya

The two mounds which constitute Tell al-Nasirīya lie in the irrigation zone of the Shatt al-Gharraf, east of the survey area and beyond our reach. Information about their size and location on the ancient eastern branch of the Euphrates was taken from the aerial photographs. These also provided the evidence for the mounds being at the point where the canal leading toward Bad-Tibira and Larsa left the eastern, Umma branch of the Euphrates. The site was dated by the Survey of Central Sumer to the period from Early Dynastic to Old Babylonian times. In spite of this rather fragmentary evidence, the location seems to fit Nagsu best.

4 | Resettlement and Abandonment in Later Antiquity

NEO-BABYLONIAN–SELEUCID PERIODS
(ca. 800–120 B.C.)

The progressive abandonments that characterized Cassite and Middle Babylonian times came to an end before the middle of the first millennium. Neo-Babylonian stamped bricks, ubiquitous in northern Babylonia, are distinguished here by their absence. On the other hand, pottery attributable to that approximate period is found on 102 sites in the survey region—more than for any period since Jemdet Nasr times. And although many Neo-Babylonian settlements were small and widely scattered, it is not unlikely that the pattern as a whole was distinctly more urban than its late prehistoric counterpart.

Thus the settled population of the region must have multiplied at least severalfold over what it was in Middle Babylonian times. Part of this massive increase undoubtedly came abruptly, from the systematic resettlement of conquered populations that was practiced by the Neo-Babylonian monarchs. However, it is likely that districts closer to the capital in Babylon received the bulk of the increment from this source. Hence slower, natural increases resulting from improved local conditions for agriculture and settlement probably were also an important factor here, and there is no reason for believing that the presence of such conditions coincided exactly with the dynasty's rise to power. An earlier onset to the process of resettlement and population growth, presumably in Neo-Assyrian times, is at any rate not inconsistent with the ceramic surface collections and the limited body of excavated material with which they can be compared. Herein lies the archaeological justification for tentatively including the final two centuries of Neo-Assyrian hegemony within the span illustrated in figure 19.

Perhaps even more important, the Assyrian annals directly attest the existence of populous districts extending in almost all directions from the walls of Uruk. Bīt Dakkuru apparently lay immediately to the northwest, already with 33 strong, walled cities or towns and 250 hamlets by the close of the eighth century. Similarly, Neo-Babylonian documents place lands of Bīt Awakkanu immediately east and northeast, with 39 towns and 350 hamlets if credence is given to Sennacherib's claims of victory over them, while Uruk (Kullab) and Larsa were counted among the eight towns and 100 hamlets of Bīt Yakin.[1] To be sure, the urban categories forming the basis for these claims are likely to have been fairly elastic. Moreover, the included territories extended more than half the length of the alluvium, from Marad to the Persian Gulf. But the implication of a widespread resurgence of settled life by the eighth century or so is nonetheless unmistakeable.

Unfortunately, while the finding of ceramic types primarily associated with the Neo-Babylonian and Achaemenian periods confirms widespread settlement within the region at the time, it does little to illuminate the areas occupied in individual sites. Since the pattern initiated in the Neo-Babylonian period persisted with little change into Parthian times, in most cases there are deep overlying layers of later debris which make assessments of surface areas difficult. Our subjective impression during fieldwork, with rare exceptions noted in the site catalog, was that Parthian remains generally represented by far the most extensive occupation on sites that were also occupied earlier. However, it must be borne in mind that

---

1. D. Cocquerillat, "Palmeraies et cultures de l'Eanna d'Uruk (559–520)," Deutsche Forschungsgemeinschaft in Uruk-Warka, *Ausgrabungen* 8 (Berlin, 1968): 19–20; D. D. Luckenbill, "The annals of Sennacherib," *Oriental Institute Publications* 2 (Chicago, 1924): 52–53.

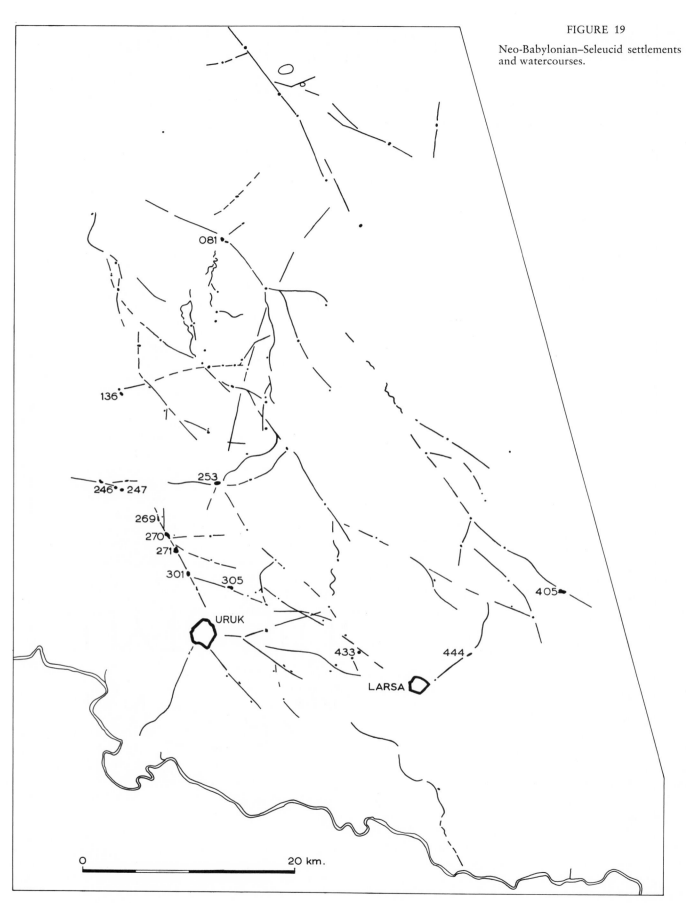

FIGURE 19

Neo-Babylonian–Seleucid settlements and watercourses.

081

136

253

246 • 247

269

270

271

301 305

405

URUK

433 444

LARSA

0   20 km.

the Parthian occupation tended to be the terminal one at most sites, especially in the southern part of the region, often leading to an exaggeration of its relative extent.

The watercourse pattern outlined in figure 19 suffers from the same defect as computations of settlement size: later levee deposits obscure those of the Neo-Babylonian and Achaemenian periods. However, the basic continuity in site locations assures general similarity with later patterns. Hence the essential characteristic must have been the same in both cases—a very extensive, but also increasingly artificial, distribution of irrigation water. The meandering, anastomosing channels of earlier times have almost wholly disappeared, and instead we are faced—particularly in the vicinity of Uruk, but also elsewhere—with a largely dendritic system in which a few straight, main canals supplied many lateral offtakes. Quite possibly the introduction of this new pattern implies a considerable element of centralized planning and labor management. It may also be related to the devotion of extensive areas around Uruk to centrally managed date plantations, for the latter are well attested in Neo-Babylonian textual sources.

A much fuller and more meaningful picture emerges from these sources than from the reconnaissance, even though most of the numerous geographical references are very difficult to localize with any precision. The main course of the Euphrates had shifted to the west, as indicated earlier, and the important waterway approaching Uruk from the northwest along its former bed was known as the Royal Canal. The latter's essentially artificial character under the new regime is confirmed by references to sluice gates controlling the intake of at least some of its branches. Another important and well-documented canal system, the Takkiru, apparently approached Uruk from the west or southwest. Since the survey's coverage in this direction was limited by the presence of cultivated land and seasonal swamps, there is a regrettable lack of overlap between its findings and the fairly detailed reconstruction that the texts permit. In all directions from the city, however, perhaps the most striking impression furnished by the texts is of the presence of very extensive swampy areas. In many cases these were sufficiently permanent and well defined to justify the careful cadastral records that have come down to us, and the year-round character of at least the larger of them is indicated by the presence of quantities of fish. Fully consistent with this picture are references to villages and plantations entirely surrounded by swamps.

Branches of both the Royal Canal and the Takkiru are described as having extended through the ancient walls of the city. Presumably they served in part to meet domestic needs, and references to quays indicate that these more minor waterways also met the needs of extensive long-distance commerce that may have been partly in Phoenecian hands,[2] as well as the local movement of agricultural produce. More surprising are references within Uruk itself to considerable irrigated farmland, as well as to the presence of several named areas of permanent swamp.[3] Quite appropriately, the representation of Uruk in figure 19 is a hollow shell. These conditions suggest a population far below that which first aggregated within its walls two millenia earlier.

Grouped with Neo-Babylonian and Achaemenian sites in figure 19 are sites of the Seleucid period. Whether this is preferable to including Seleucid sites in the map of the Parthian period is, in the present state of our knowledge, little more than a matter of arbitrary choice. In spite of the many political and cultural innovations that followed in the wake of the conquests of Alexander, few ceramic features can be identified that are distinctive of the Seleucid period alone. Most were already present in Achaemenian times; somewhat fewer seem to have continued into the Parthian period, and others remained in use throughout. Hence the identification of individual surface collections as specifically Seleucid, rather than Achaemenian-Seleucid or Seleucid-Parthian, can only be largely subjective. Except where there are bricks with Seleucid geometric stamp impressions, we have accordingly avoided identifying sites with the period at all. Because of the continuity of basic configurations of settlement throughout this entire time range, however, the evaluation of trends affecting Seleucid settlements is little influenced by whichever grouping it is placed with.

PARTHIAN PERIOD (ca. 120 B.C.–A.D. 220)

The primary argument for grouping the Achaemenian and Seleucid periods together and the Parthian period separately stems from numismatic evidence. Coins found at Warka (classical Orchoi) point to a hiatus of about 130 years between the last years of the great Seleucid temple precincts there and the apparent reemergence of the town shortly before the time of Christ.[4] That this lack of continuity was not an isolated development is strongly suggested by similar findings at Nippur and, to a lesser degree, on smaller sites in the Nippur region.[5] Hence the

---

2. A. L. Oppenheim, "Essay on Overland Trade in the First Millennium B.C.," *Journal of Cuneiform Studies* 21 (1967 [1969]): 236–54.

3. Cocquerillat, "Palmeraies," pp. 15–20, plates 3*a*–*b*.

4. H. J. Nissen, "Südbaylonien in parthischer und sasanidischer Zeit," *Baghdader Mitteilungen* 6 (in press); cf. G. Le Rider, "Suse sous les Séleucides et les Parthes: Les trouvailles monétaires et l'histoire de la ville," Mission Archéologique en Iran, *Mémoires* 38 (Paris, 1965): 458.

5. A monograph on the remains of the Parthian period at Nippur is in preparation by E. J. Keall. The region north and east of Nippur was surveyed by the author in 1968, and also will be discussed in a forthcoming monograph.

early Parthian period seems to have witnessed an abrupt decline in settlement and prosperity in the vicinity of some of the major traditional centers of southern Iraq.

The combination of forces that led to this decline is unknown, but some role may be posited for two external factors. Unsettled conditions at the beginning of the Parthian period helped to foster the formation and rapid growth of the kingdom of Characene under Hyspaosines, who refounded and heavily fortified the former Seleucid city of Alexandria-Antiochia near the head of the Persian Gulf under the name of Charax Spasinu. An extension of Hyspaosines's domain into northern Babylonia apparently was short lived, and during his later years and under his successors the kingdom was subjected to Parthian suzerainty. Even as a vassal state, however, Characene retained much of its prosperity and local preponderance.[6] Hence it would not be surprising if there had been some movement away from outlying centers like Warka or Nippur into regions closer to the new regional capital.

In addition, developments at a somewhat greater distance to the northwest may have played a part in the depopulation of the Warka region. The continuing importance of Seleucia, as well as the growth of Ctesiphon into "the crowning ornament of Persia"[7] by the time of Pacorus (d. 38 B.C.) undoubtedly exerted some direct attraction. Moreover, the diversion of a substantial part of the Euphrates flow into canals supplying the hinterlands of those cities may have had a strong indirect effect by creating chronic water shortages farther downstream.

Whatever the factors responsible for this considerable hiatus, the Warka region reemerges in the later Parthian period as one of dense population and apparent prosperity. In fact, the first and second centuries A.D. seem to have constituted the culminating epoch in the entire settlement record. Virtually all parts of the region were occupied, indicating that the extent of cultivated land probably reached a maximum not approached before or since. Individual urban centers apparently attained greater population size at times during the third or early second millennia, but at least at Uruk impressive public building programs and widespread debris indicate a Parthian city not appreciably smaller than any known previously. Reliance on the natural equilibrium of streams in a floodplain was almost wholly abandoned in the interests of extending cultivation to its farthest limits, and unprecedented areas were served by planned, large-scale irrigation systems. And yet, in spite of these achievements, the partial abandonment that followed seems to have been more abrupt and long-lasting than any that had occurred previously.

The context within which this relatively brief apogee was attained is both uncertain and somewhat puzzling. To judge from the ineffectiveness of Parthian control over Characene during most of the latter's history as a commercially oriented vassal state, this region, more remote than Characene and with less to offer, must have been subject to central Parthian control only at rare intervals. If massive resettlement implies extension and improved maintenance of local irrigation systems, this is accordingly difficult to explain as an outcome of hypothetical Parthian capital investments or constructive management. To be sure, the region must have benefited from some backwash of refugees (including a high proportion of skilled urbanites) from northern Mesopotamia and along the Euphrates invasion route who had been dislocated by long periods of sanguinary Parthian-Roman warfare. But in calculating the net effect of vague Parthian suzerainty, account also must be taken of the periodically destructive impact of campaigning that accompanied repeated dynastic upheavals and rivalries.

Charax, on the other hand, was located on the lower Tigris, a long distance to the east across intervening terrain that was almost certainly swampy. To judge from the presence of Characene coins,[8] the Orchoi or Warka region may have been included within the Characene realm for at least a part of the later Parthian period, but it was hardly central enough to have benefited substantially from the latter's prosperity. Nor is it likely that the region gained significantly from the overland transit trade through Charax, largely in Palmyrene hands. Uruk has yielded a single Greek inscription dated early in the second century A.D.,[9] but this is at best a very doubtful indication of the possible survival of a Greek *politeuma* there during the prolonged interval of apparent decline or even abandonment after the Seleucid period.[10] Rather than requiring resident colonies of foreign merchants in towns like Warka, the trade routes commonly either skirted the western desert or else crossed to the Euphrates farther north after proceeding upstream along the Tigris. In short, the impressively widespread settlement within the Warka region during this period must have been largely the consequence of local initiatives that have left no textual or numismatic trace.

With the exception of Uruk and possibly Jidr, Parthian centers for the most part were not comparable in size to earlier centers like Umma, Zabalam, Bad-Tibira, and Larsa. Perhaps they are best characterized as substantial

6. S. A. Nodelman, "A Preliminary History of Characene," *Berytus* 13 (1960): 83–121.

7. Ammianus Marcellinus 23. 6. 23 (Loeb Classical Library ed.).

8. Nissen, "Südbabylonien."

9. C. Meier, "Ein griechisches Ehrendekret vom Gareustempel in Uruk," *Baghdader Mitteilungen* 1 (1960): 104–14.

10. Cf. Le Rider, "Suse sous les Séleucides," p. 41.

towns rather than cities. As is well illustrated along the old levee of what is now called the Shatt al-Nil approaching Uruk from the north, these towns occur at fairly regular intervals along the main trunk, as well as at significant junction points along important branches, of an extensive dendritic canal system (see fig. 20). Whether they were administratively subordinate to local rulers residing in larger centers like Uruk and Jidr is unclear, for traces of imposing buildings—some of them suggesting substantial estates set in largely rural areas, and all of them surely associated with some form of an elite—are not unknown also on smaller sites (e.g., 078 and 313). But at any rate, the pattern as a whole is that of a single realm, even if only a loosely integrated one.

Thus we are not dealing here with a network of largely autonomous, frequently hostile city-states, each jealously guarding its territory and compelling or attracting most of the inhabitants of that territory to take up residence within its walls both for their protection and for its political advantage. Typically, the Parthian town was not compact and nucleated but low and sprawling, its boundaries irregular, ill-defined, and undefended by outer walls. Also typically, unoccupied, interstitial border areas like the "high edin" of earlier times (see p. 32) were no longer made necessary by political fragmentation. Small settlements were numerous, and were widely scattered along the canal branches. Proximity to their fields, rather than subordination to a particular urban center and its strategy for defense, seems to have been the dominant consideration in their placement.

Superficially at least, conditions in the Warka region as just described were both flourishing and stable. Why then was the entire southern half of the region, including its largest concentration of population in and around Uruk, abandoned almost totally in late Parthian times? The same arguments for a substantial degree of local autonomy that were advanced earlier make it unlikely that an abandonment here can be adequately explained by reference to external events. The gradual attenuation of international trade with the Roman Empire, the growing weakness of Parthian authority and the Roman military incursions it prompted (in the main directed at Ctesiphon, and never extending into this area), and the eclipse of Charax by Vologesia all may have exercised some influence. But although the relative importance of each of these factors would be difficult to define—particularly in view of present uncertainties about the timing of the abandonment—even taken together they cannot have been decisive. That occupation continued, and even intensified, in the northern part of the region during the subsequent period suggests instead that the primary explanation is geographical. Even before the end of the Parthian period, the swamps that later were to become the dominant topographic feature in much of southern

Mesopotamia apparently had already begun to engulf large tracts that were formerly fertile and densely settled.

SASSANIAN PERIOD (ca. A.D. 220–640)

The causes of the northward spread of the swamps before and during the Sassanian period are still largely obscure. At least in the Warka region, however, it is clear that the process may be divided into two broad phrases, with the bulk of the Sassanian period falling between them. At Uruk, the latest coins to be found stem from the reign of Ardashīr, the first Sassanian ruler, and seemingly reflect an already much reduced area of occupation.[11] Together with the virtual absence of ceramic indicators of a Sassanian occupation throughout the southern part of the region (see fig. 21), this suggests that the first stage must have been under way even before the end of the Parthian period. The second, leading to a further but less extensive abandonment, seems to have occurred at the very end of the Sassanian period.

The second advance of the swamps may be linked plausibly with effects attributed to unprecedented flooding of both the Tigris and the Euphrates river in A.D. 629. Khusraw Parwīz, one of the last of the Sassanian kings, is said by the historian Balādhurī to have spared neither treasure nor men's lives in unsuccessful attempts to repair the innumerable breaches in the dikes that resulted. In subsequent years, as the Sassanian monarchy crumbled before the Moslem onslaught, massive, state-directed efforts at reclamation could no longer be continued. Balādhurī relates that, as a result, "breaches came in all the enbankments, for none gave heed, and the Dihkāns (namely the Persian nobles, who were the landlords) were powerless to repair the dykes, so that the swamps every way lengthened and widened."[12]

At about the same time as these floods, and possibly as a direct consequence of them, Ibn Rustah informs us that the Tigris shifted from an eastern bed (approximately its present lower course) to a more westerly alignment along which the Islamic city of Wāsit subsequently was constructed.[13] This would have fed immense quantities of water into already swampy districts along the lower Euphrates, certainly explaining their inexorable expansion at the outset of the Islamic period. But we are left then without an adequate explanation of the earlier stage or stages in their formation, which accordingly would have to be attributable to changes in the regime of the Euphrates alone. Balādhurī, to be sure, traces the origin of the swamps to a still earlier Tigris flood, at the time of

11. Nissen, "Südbabylonien."
12. G. Le Strange, *The Lands of the Eastern Caliphate* (London, 1905), p. 27.
13. Ibid., pp. 27–28.

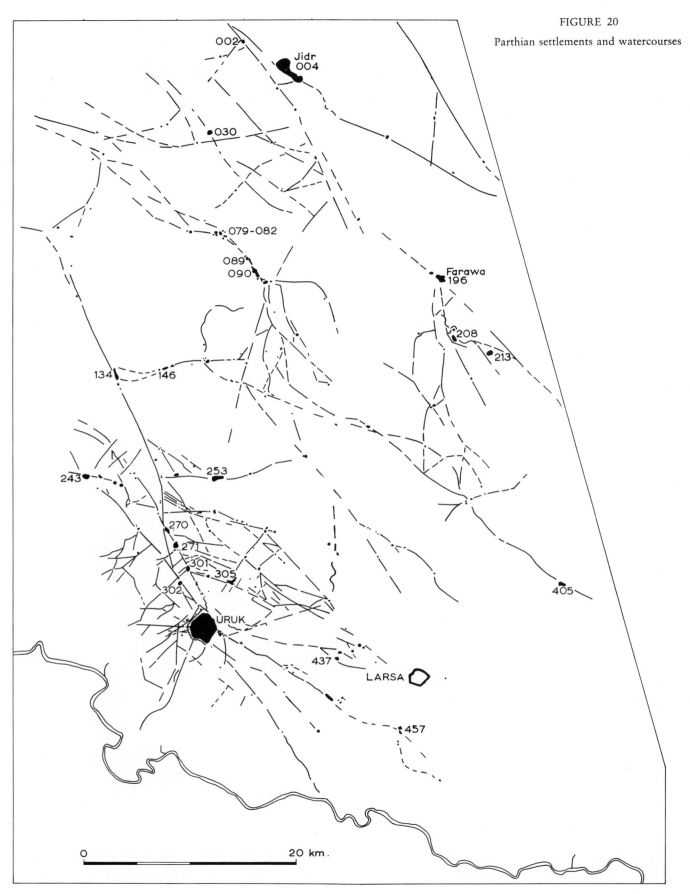

FIGURE 20
Parthian settlements and watercourses

002

Jidr
004

030

079-082

089
090

Farawa
196

208

213

134   146

243

253

270

271

301
305

302

405

URUK

437

LARSA

457

0   20 km.

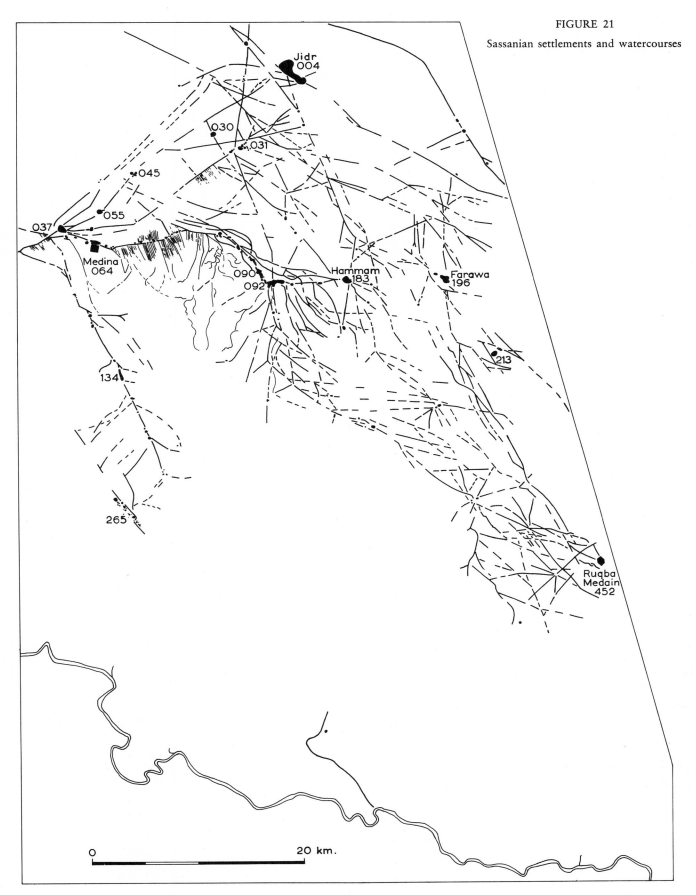

FIGURE 21
Sassanian settlements and watercourses

Jidr
004

030

031

045

037

055

Medina
064

090
092

Hammam
183

Farawa
196

213

134

265

Ruqba
Medain
452

0   20 km.

61

the Sassanian king Kubādh I in the late fifth century. This is, however, entirely too late to explain the onset of extensive swamps in the Warka region by the beginning of the Sassanian period. Moreover, it is difficult to believe that one Tigris flood, or even a series of them, could produce so substantial and long-lasting a change as long as the bulk of the Tigris flow reached the sea along a course far to the east of the Warka region. One is driven, then, at least to entertain the possibility that substantial tectonic changes may have played a part, leading to the general depression of lands along the lower Euphrates. Such a possibility is entirely consistent with the underlying structure of the entire Mesopotamian plain taking the form of a complex, unstable geosyncline,[14] and would help to account for the subsequent westward shift of the lower Tigris.

Within the Warka region, evidence of swampy conditions is provided not only by its partial abandonment but by a number of local features along the margins of the still-inhabited area. One large Sassanian site (265) along the southwestern limit of settlement forms an obvious archipelago. Its occupied portions consist of raised, small islands that are separated by lagoons and channels of varying width, and the whole ensemble closely resembles Maᶜdān communities today along the western margins of the swamps (cf. p. 23). Not far to the east of this site, a great lobe of the swamps seems to have extended northward. Here the insequent, meandering drainage channels along which excess irrigation water spilled out into the swamps still may be traced on the aerial photographs (see fig. 21). Immediately to the north is a distinctive arrangement of closely spaced, parallel canals that must have been more deeply incised than ordinary, shallow field canals, since their traces are still so well preserved. A similar feature, although of middle Islamic rather than Sassanian date, has been noted previously along the margins of a swamp in the Diyala region east of Baghdad.[15] In both cases, some form of specialized cultivation appears to be involved in which large, assured supplies of water were crucial. Rice is perhaps the foremost possibility, and it is noteworthy that even today rice cultivation is concentrated along the margins of swamps.

The Sassanian agricultural system north of the swamps cannot be regarded as only a declining remnant of more extensive Parthian precursors. As the map shows, its major feature was a new large-scale, clearly planned network of irrigation canals that opened east and northeast in a spreading fan more than thirty kilometers in length.

Just as in Parthian and earlier times, the primary concentration of settlements is found along the main trunk of the system, with smaller, more scattered concentrations at connecting points along a few principal branches. But this system involves a more ambitious reshaping of natural patterns of drainage than any previous one, for the orientation of the canals that water this large area is perpindicular to the slope of the region as a whole in a south-southeasterly direction.

The prosperity and impressive organization characteristic of the Sassanian period are attested not only by innovations in the canal system but also by the extent of settlements. Jidr probably attained its maximum size for any period. The major part of the city, in the north, was dominated by a monumental citadel constructed entirely of baked brick; the southeastern end also centered on a smaller fortified enclosure. Other sites were smaller but still very impressive in size. Considering the reduced total area open to occupation because of the swamps, the number that may be classed as of urban proportions is remarkably large (037, 064, 092, 183, 196, 452). Most lie along the main trunk canal referred to earlier, and evidences of planned, monumental construction still survive in at least three of them (Medina, Tell Hammam, and Ruqba Medain). On the other hand, it is also noteworthy that the sprawling, vaguely defined aspect that appeared for the first time in Parthian towns was still further accentuated. Concentrations of sherds and fragmentary fired bricks trace out an irregular but almost continuous ribbon of built-up settlement along the levee of the main east-west trunk canal.

Two important towns illustrate a new application of planning. Medina is laid out in the form of a square 700 meters on a side, and Ruqba Medain is a hexagon enclosing an only slightly smaller area. Both were surrounded by thick mud-brick walls that still form recognizable landmarks after a millennium and a half of wind and rain erosion, and that must have constituted fairly formidable defensive works in their day. The former, located not far downstream of the apex of the main canal system as it fans eastward, may have been intended in part to house a protective garrison for a crucial, and vulnerable, point in the irrigation system. On a much larger scale, it thus recalls the functions of Arab qalᶜas whose much more recently abandoned ruins lie almost within sight, along the now-dry bed of the Shatt al-Kar farther to the east (cf. below, pp. 75–77).

Given the evidence of dense and flourishing settlements under a considerable degree of centralized control, the absence of historical and textual references to the region is curious. In particular, the Talmudic sources, voluminous in anecdotal detail on the northern part of the plain, entirely ignore this area. Clearly this silence can no longer be explained, as Obermeyer sought to, on the

---

14. G. M. Lees and N. L. Falcon, "The Geographical History of the Mesopotamian Plain," *Geographical Journal* 118 (1952): 24–39.

15. R. McC. Adams, *Land behind Baghdad* (Chicago, 1965), fig. 10.

grounds that the Euphrates "lost itself in the swamps a short distance below modern Hilla."[16] There indeed may have been extensive swamps below Hilla during Sassanian times, but if so, settled districts resumed again farther south. Perhaps the most likely explanation is that the districts farther south were generally under the control of the Arab vassal dynasty of the Lakhmids, with its capital in al-Hīra. Jews apparently did not constitute a significant proportion of the population of that realm, suggesting that an ethnic or religious basis for the absence of Talmudic references may be more correct than a topographic one.

At least for a time in the late sixth century, effective Lakhmid control over administration extended as far southeast as Ubulla, below the confluence of the Tigris and Euphrates and near the head of the Persian Gulf. There are references to a series of fortified castles and watchtowers along the desert line of communications to the southeast. Medina and Ruqba Medain probably are parts of the same defensive pattern, having been placed—in their cases within the cultivation zone—along a major artery of waterborne communication to the southeast. Whatever the fluctuating realities of administrative control and ethnic composition, the garrisons in key fortifications like these generally were Persian troops under Persian commanders.[17] Together with the planning evident in the irrigation system, this suggests that the intensive development of the region during the Sassanian period was no longer an essentially autonomous process. To a degree unmatched previously, the region seems to have been incorporated within the structure of an immensely larger imperial unit, as a result of the centralized power and organization that had become characteristic of the Persian realm as a whole.

EARLY–MIDDLE ISLAMIC PERIODS
(ca. A.D. 640–1000)

Two consequences for the Warka region stemmed from the successful Moslem onslaught against the Sassanians. One, already referred to, involved a further northward encroachment of the swamps upon formerly settled areas. Responsibility for this certainly cannot be attributed directly to the invading armies, but the unsettled conditions that accompanied them and remained for a time in their wake precluded organized reclamation efforts on more than a local scale. A second effect, perhaps even more decisive, was only a local manifestation of the

vast redistribution of population that the Arabs initiated through the founding of major new urban complexes at Kūfa, Basra, and Wāsit. Abandonment was accelerated here, in other words, even beyond that which was imposed by the loss of additional cultivated lands to the swamps.

Comparison of figures 21 and 22 provides evidence for each of these interrelated developments. Villages and towns along the southern peripheries of Sassanian settlement disappeared, their ruins probably not often actually covered by the advancing waters but their inhabitants no longer able to subsist agriculturally as more and more of the surrounding lands were engulfed. As figure 22 indicates, the advancing front of the waters was irregular and perhaps discontinuous. Long ganglia of settlement continued to extend southward into the marshes, following the elevated levees of older canal and river systems. In part, the surviving towns continued to depend upon the old irrigation canals along the crests of these levees. But frequently only segments of the former canal systems remained in use, the water for their operation now supplied by meandering, insequent drainage channels that had largely reverted to the natural condition of streams in a floodplain.

In particular, it appears that even the main east-west trunk canal of the Sassanian system remained open no longer. But its substantial levee still would have acted as a barrier to the southward drainage of the overflow from swamps and cultivated districts farther north. Hence, not long after it fell into disuse, a new channel was formed that drained the accumulated waters eastward before breaking through with them to the south at some point where the gradually diminishing height of the now unprotected levee made it less of an obstacle. Along this new channel, of course, there were favorable locations for a few new settlements, probably established by some of those who had been displaced farther south. With slight modifications it also could supply remnants of the old canal system, permitting other communities to remain for a time. This new channel was the upper portion of what became known (at any rate in more recent times) as the Shatt al-Kar. Its lower portion only would have been formed as the swamps began to drain long afterward.

Figure 22 also illustrates an overwhelming reduction in population at the outset of the Early Islamic period, even in those areas not engulfed by the swamps. Most of the major Sassanian towns disappeared utterly, and almost all remaining sites shrank to a small proportion of their former size. Only at Jidr are the remains perhaps extensive enough to justify still claiming the existence of a town. For the rest, the surviving settlement pattern was composed exclusively of dispersed villages and hamlets.

All these trends intensified as the Islamic period continued. By the time marked by the floruit of Sāmarrān

16. J. Obermeyer, "Die Landschaft Babyloniens im Zeitalter des Talmuds und des Gaonats," Gesellschaft zur Forderung der Wissenschaft des Judentums, *Schriften* 30 (Frankfurt, 1929): 97.

17. G. Rothstein, *Die Dynastie der Lahmiden in al-Hīra* (Berlin, 1899), p. 134.

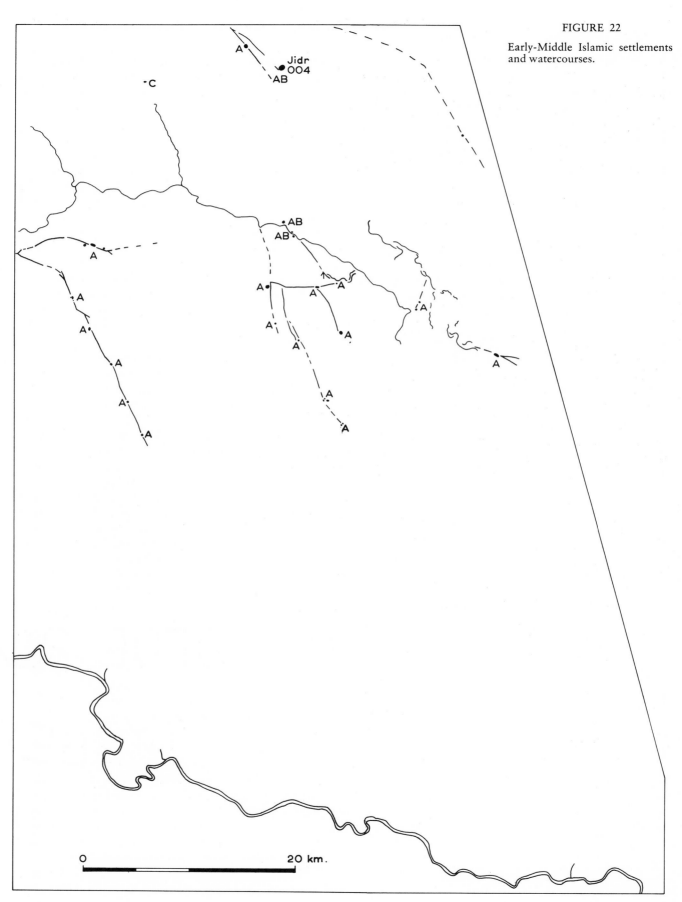

FIGURE 22

Early-Middle Islamic settlements and watercourses.

Jidr
OO4

20 km.

sgraffiato pottery, roughly the later ninth, tenth and perhaps eleventh centuries, seventeen of the twenty Early Islamic sites had been abandoned. The ganglia of settlement along older canal levees all had disappeared, so that only Jidr and a few minor villages directly on the banks of the Shatt al-Kar remained occupied. Then, probably before the twelfth century, even these last settlements were abandoned by their inhabitants. When sedentary folk later began to return, it was as clearers of new fields and founders of new villages in an almost pristine landscape.

5 | Recent Life and Settlement

The long decline of the Warka region that began in late Parthian times seems to have continued unchecked for almost a millennium and a half. Only a single site (006) was noted in the survey, very close to its northern boundary, whose occupation is attributable to the late ᶜAbbāsid period. The brilliant glazed wares of Ilkhanid and later times, not uncommon in more northerly districts of Iraq, are entirely absent here. For a span of at least several centuries shortly antedating and following the collapse of the ᶜAbbāsid caliphate, the available evidence suggests a complete cessation of sedentary settlement and irrigation agriculture.

This hiatus is surely related to the persistence or spread of the so-called Great Swamp, to whose earlier development reference was made in the preceding chapter. To be sure, the presence of widespread seasonal, or even permament, swampy conditions does not entirely preclude settlement. Ibn Rustah refers to the export of salted fish from that region[1] and the virtual absence of named communities there in other classical Islamic geographical accounts and maps[2] may mean only that they were prevailingly small. Indeed, the swamps very likely served as a refuge against the governmentally sanctioned extortions and sanguinary political vendettas that increasingly became the rule after the ninth century, so that the absence of literary references may be more a reflection of the limits of administrative control and important economic interchange than of conditions actually prevailing within the swamps. Nevertheless, the available direct evidence from the survey hardly contradicts the accounts of the ᶜAbbāsid geographers. Either the existing settlements were so small and scattered or they were so lacking in recognizable ceramics of other than strictly local circulation that we failed entirely to notice them. Probably there is some truth in both explanations.

Since political fragmentation only accelerated with the Mongol sack of Baghdad, organized efforts to reverse these conditions through large-scale drainage projects were out of the question. Yet the rise of great tribal polities by no later than the seventeenth century indirectly attests a gradual retraction of the swamps. The change is to be understood, therefore, as primarily a consequence of natural alterations in the hydrological regimes of the Tigris and Euphrates. Principal among these was undoubtedly the reversion of the bulk of the Tigris flow to its present, more easterly course through ᶜAmārah from the Shatt al-Gharraf route it had followed since the Sassanian period. Longrigg reasonably ascribes the shift to the span of time between 1500 and 1650,[3] so that the emergence of at least the broad outlines of modern topographic conditions may be assumed to have occurred by the latter date.

Subsequent archaeological sites are uniformly, and almost exclusively, identified by the presence of handmade bowl sherds of a pinkish, grit-tempered fabric that are decorated with abstract, geometrical designs applied in a fugitive, generally violet paint. This ware has aptly been called "psuedo-prehistoric" because of its resemblance to the Halaf ware of a much earlier period, and at least at Wāsit it has been assigned to the eighth century Hegira "and later."[4] Unfortunately, this fairly diffuse dating is of little assistance for the problems of the Warka region. It

---

1. Ibn Rustah, *Les atours précieux,* trans. G. Wiet (Cairo, 1955), p. 104.

2. Cf. K. Miller, *Mappae Arabicae* (Stuttgart, 1926–31), vol. 3, chap. 3.

3. S. H. Longrigg, *Four Centuries of Modern Iraq* (Oxford, 1925), p. 2, footnote.

4. F. Safar, *Wāsit: The Sixth Season's Excavations* (Cairo, 1945), p. 38.

indicates that the widespread settlement patterns associated with psuedo-prehistoric pottery are unlikely to antedate the fifteenth century A.D., lending some support to the general interpretation just advanced, but it fails to provide a basis for distinguishing between this and later periods. A few sherds of pseudo-prehistoric ware were noted in surface collections even at Qalᶜa Falhīya (399), for example, a site that only was constructed after 1900 and that still had not been completely deserted as late as 1926 (see below, p. 77). These ruins lie along the banks of the Shatt al-Kar, and, since the latter had served for many centuries as an important artery, the observed sherds do not necessarily indicate that the ware continued in use. On the other hand, all of the villages associated with Qalᶜa Sussa (see below, p. 76) were also associated with psuedo-prehistoric ware, and this stronghold appears to have been occupied only after 1850 and until 1890 or later. Hence it is not unlikely that the ware continued well into the second half of the nineteenth century, although in any case the only direct archaeological means for dating that are currently available are admittedly very ambiguous.

Beyond the initial, broad identification of sites occupied during the last 300–500 years, it follows that at present archaeological means are of little avail in reconstructing or interpreting patterns of sequent occupance (fig. 23). The Ottoman archives are potentially of much greater importance, but research based on that immense resource lies entirely outside our competence. What remains are the reports of European travelers, which are rare and sketchy before the nineteenth century but thereafter provide glimpses, sometimes of very high quality, at relatively short intervals. Of course, the temptation to equate the abundance of such evidence with the fullest development of the patterns it illustrates must be eschewed. For the late eighteenth century, for example, no traveler's testimony informs us directly of conditions within the Warka Survey region. Yet we learn indirectly, from the *Baghdad Chronicle,* that conditions along the Shatt al-Kar were already prosperous enough not only to attract raids from tribes in the ᶜAfak confederation but also for the raids to lead to Turkish reprisals.[5] How much more such evidence has been lost, or at any rate has not yet been found and published, can only be surmised.

Before turning to conditions within the region, the orientation and effectiveness of Ottoman policies toward southern Iraq as a whole must be briefly sketched. At least before the mid-nineteenth century, the prevailing opinion of historians with access to the Ottoman source materials is that:

The government did not play more than a limited part in the life of the region. When the Ottomans first conquered Iraq, it was important for them mainly as a buffer province on the frontier of the Empire with Shiᶜi Persia; the first role of the governors who were sent there was to defend the frontier. For this purpose and for purposes of administration they were expected to raise money from the province; but they were also expected to contribute a certain sum to the central treasury in Istanbul. Since Baghdad was considered a place of exile, the governors were usually men who were out of favour, and whose tenure of office was deliberately kept short, so that they would not consolidate their power and seek independence. Their influence hardly extended beyond the walls of the towns, and the authority of the government was scarcely felt in the tribal areas. In these circumstances, the influence of the Arab tribes was supreme; rather than look to the government for protection, they built their own fortifications to defend themselves against each other as well as against the government. When weak they had to pay taxes and other revenues, and in order to avoid this they tended to form themselves into larger groups or confederations.[6]

With the disbanding of the Janissaries, the destruction of the Mamluks, and improvements in communications, conditions began to change shortly before mid-century. But except for the three-year tenure of Midhat Pasha (1869–72), the objective of supplanting tribal authority with that of the government failed to be supported at the local level with consistent policies or execution. As Jwaideh observes,

All the Turks did was to divide and rule, setting various tribes within a confederation against one another and creating dissension within the tribes themselves. Their policy met with only a limited success, and created a wall of hostile and defiant tribesmen to the south of Baghdad.[7]

Part of the Warka region lay within the traditional area of suzerainty of the Muntafiq confederation, and this is another major contender whose local impact must be considered. Traceable in their remote orgins to pre-Islamic times,[8] the Muntafiq emerge into the light of recent history only in the seventeenth century. By that time they had secured control over the region with which they have always since been identified—the tails of the Shatt al-Gharraf and the swamps between the lower Euphrates and the lower Tigris. From this undisputed central heartland more temporary or contingent Muntafiq claims to authority thrust outward in all directions—northward to Kūt, westward to Samāwa, and at times even becoming

5. M. von Oppenheim, *Die Beduinen,* vol. 3, *Die Beduinenstämme in Nord-Mittelarabien und im ᶜIrāk* (Wiesbaden, 1952), p. 305.

6. A. Jwaideh, "Midhat Pasha and the Land System of Lower Iraq," *St. Anthony's Papers* 16, *Middle Eastern Affairs* 3 (1965): 111–12.

7. Ibid., pp. 112–13.

8. Von Oppenheim, *Die Beduinen,* p. 415.

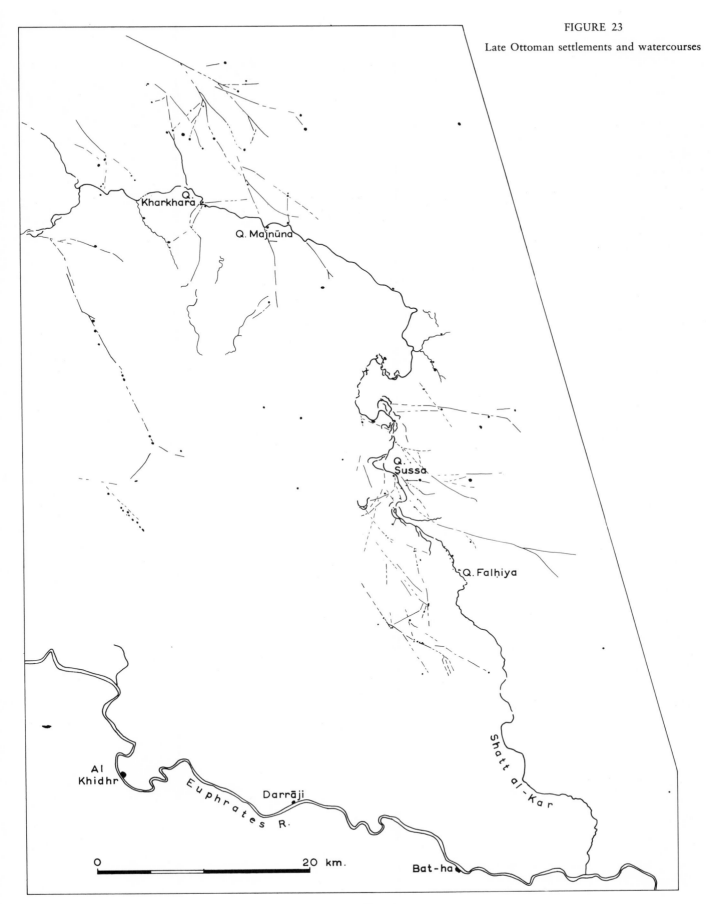

FIGURE 23
Late Ottoman settlements and watercourses

Q.
Kharkhara

Q. Majnūna

Q.
Sussa

Q. Falhiya

Shatt al-Kar

Al
Khidhr

Euphrates R.

Darrāji

0   20 km.

Bat-ha

arbiter to the fate of Basra to the southeast. The Muntafiq are, in fact, the very archetype of a great tribal confederation; "no tribe of ʿIraq became so formidable to its rulers, so long patient of a single government of its own, so famous in the outer world."[9]

Successive phases in Muntafiq control over the Warka region cannot be adequately documented at present. To begin with, conditions were never static. The changing relationships are further obscured by policies of indirect rule, as a result of which the succession of authorities over neighboring groups lends itself to retrospective rationalization according to the interests of the particular chronicler or informant. Von Oppenheim[10] concludes that the first half of the nineteenth century saw the consolidation of Muntafiq authority over at least those components of the Bani Huchaym whose tribal *diras* or territories lay east of the Euphrates in the vicinity of Samāwa. This is supported by the eye-witness testimony of Ainsworth[11] and Loftus;[12] the latter in 1850 not only noted Muntafiq power of appointment of Maʿdān shaykhs along the Euphrates westward to Samāwa, but also described Suq al-Fawwar, northwest of the Warka region, as in Muntafiq hands some years earlier. On the other hand, travelers later in the century report the area to the east of Suq al-Fawwar as in considerable dispute, with actual Muntafiq encampments only being encountered each of the Shatt al-Kar. In 1902 the formal frontier of Muntafiq control crossed the Kar west of Qalʿa Majnūna (see below, p. 76) and thence extended southward to Senkere (ancient Larsa), not far from the stream's western bank.[13] According to Bani Huchaym informants today, the only lands still held by the Muntafiq west of the Shatt al-Kar are those in the vicinity of Senkere. In other areas the Kar serves for the most part as the dividing line, while one Bani Huchaym group (the Toba) now ranges eastward across it all the way to the Shatt al-Gharraf (see fig. 24).

In short, there are some indications of a progressive decline in Muntafiq influence west of the Shatt al-Gharraf that began after a major phase of their expansion culminated in the mid-nineteenth century. Two possible explanations suggest themselves. One is that the gradual drying up of the Shatt al-Kar, about which more will be said presently, converted the patches of cultivation that previously had existed there into uniformly arid steppe suitable only for nomadic or seminomadic herdsmen. The Muntafiq, in other words, may have tended to lose interest in an increasingly inhospitable area with a steeply declining population. Another explanation, not necessarily in contradiction with the first, assigns at least part of the responsibility to changes in Muntafiq relations with the Turks.

After an earlier period of de facto recognition of Muntafiq authority, Ottoman policy shifted in the nineteenth century toward one of systematically dividing and undermining the Saʿdūn family in which tribal leadership was vested. Efforts were made to force members of the latter to register tribal lands in their own names, as well as to accept tax collecting responsibilities and administrative appointments, tending to weaken the link with their followers. Rival claimants to leadership were assiduously

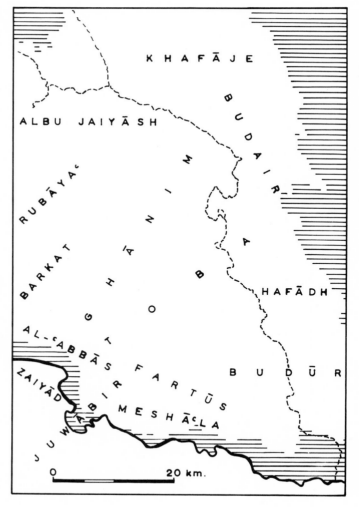

FIGURE 24

Contemporary tribal groupings in the Warka region

9. Longrigg, *Four Centuries*, pp. 78–79.

10. Von Oppenheim, *Die Beduinen*, 336.

11. W. F. Ainsworth, *A Personal Narrative of the Euphrates Expedition* (London, 1888), 2:69.

12. W. K. Loftus, "Notes of a Journey from Baghdad to Busrah, with Descriptions of Several Chaldean Remains," Royal Geographical Society of London, *Journal* 26 (1856): 148; this passage is quoted below, p. 80.

13. W. Andrae, "Aus einem Berichte W. Andrae's über seine Exkursion von Fara nach den südbabylonischen Ruinenstätten," Deutsche Orient-Gesellschaft, *Mitteilungen* 16 (1903): 17.

supported. The outstanding tribal leader of the time, Nasir Pasha, was deprived of authority through being coopted into a position of powerless prestige in the distant Ottoman capital. Finally, when these and similar steps precipitated an open rebellion in 1881, the tribesmen were militarily crushed and the Saʿdūns temporarily banished. In the sequel, however, the Turks were unable to replace the structure they had destroyed with a more subservient one. Opposition may have remained acephalous in the years before World War I, but the reduction of tribal leadership had been achieved only at the expense of a continuing high level of rural anarchy.[14]

A similar break-up of tribal confederations occurred on the Middle Euphrates, west and northwest of the Muntafiq *dira*, during the last quarter of the nineteenth century. Exacerbated by increasingly chronic shortages of water in the Hilla branch, there were confused, internecine, and almost continuous struggles for control of irrigable lands. Again, Turkish tergiversation in land allotment policies played a considerable role, and here too the officals were quite powerless to control, or even benefit from, the unrest that was unleashed. At least in this area, however, it deserves to be noted that loss of strength at the confederational level apparently was not matched by atrophy of the individual tribal units:

in these conditions it was only by means of their collective strength as members of a tribe that the cultivators were able to protect themselves against government officials and *tapu* holders alike. In consequence, both cultivator and government came more and more to be dependent on the good offices of the tribal shaykhs as the wielders of the only effective authority that remained: the tribesmen grew more than ever conscious of the tribe as a unity, and of their lands as a tribal home or *dira,* held collectively by the whole tribe.[15]

The foregoing review of Ottoman policies toward tribes on the Middle and Lower Euphrates, brief and superficial as it necessarily has been, prompts a qualification of the prevailing opinion that the government's influence over the latter was generally minimal. Seen from an urban perspective, this was undoubtedly so. The whole arsenal of policies that were available—military forays, varying means and schedules of tax collections, manipulation of the irrigation system, legitimation of land claims, and intrigue on many levels—failed decisively to produce the pacification that was the primary Turkish goal. Much of the fault, to be sure, lay not so much in the countervailing military potential of the tribes as in ill-considered, inconsistent measures of execution that were a consequence of corruption and short-term tenure

among administrative personnel. But whatever the combination of causes, the effect was to place the tribal system as a whole, not to speak of the day-to-day exercise of the ordinary functions of government in tribal territories, largely beyond the reach of Ottoman officials. Midhat Pasha was indisputably the most able and far-seeing of the latter, and the swift demise, or even unanticipatedly negative effect, of the key elements in his program only underlines the resistiveness of a deeply entrenched, indigenous social system to direct government action.

But the other side of the coin is also worth considering. In different ways, both the Muntafiq and the tribes on the Middle Euphrates were profoundly altered in structure by their relations with the Ottomans. In general, it would appear from the available data that the confederational level of organization was most fragile in the face of the new Ottoman pressures generated from the mid-nineteenth century onward, even though there is some evidence that the emergence of confederacies was itself partly an outgrowth of the weaker, less ambitious forms of Turkish rule current in the seventeenth and eighteenth centuries.

Nor does this exhaust the indirect effects of the imperial Ottoman presence. How much of the strengthening of tribal ties at lower levels of organization, and of the emergence of permanent, institutionalized hostilities between tribal units, was not a feature inherent in the land and local groups but a consequence of Ottoman policies? For this purpose, it does not matter that such policies may have been largely ineffective in reaching their purported ends, or that the pursuit of them was spasmodic at best; the effect in any case was to interpose an unstabilizing element in intergroup relations to which individual tribes would have had to adapt.

Again, to take a feature which has not yet received the scrutiny it deserves from historians of the period, the gun trade may have exerted an important influence on tribal structure and intertribal relationships, an influence linked either directly or indirectly with the Ottoman presence. Surely the enormous military advantages that firearms conferred, against neighboring groups as well as in resistance to Ottoman incursions, made control over the sources of rifles an important adjunct to the powers of tribal leaders. As late as the 1890s, we have the eyewitness testimony of a Muntafiq administrative agent that rifles were still very rare in the Shatt al-Kar region.[16] Not long afterward, it was reported that the Bani Huchaym were beginning to acquire many Martini repeating rifles from the Muntafiq through theft.[17] The latter were in an ad-

---

14. Jwaideh, "Midhat Pasha," pp. 113, 131–32.
15. Ibid., pp. 129–30.

16. Y. N. Serkis, *Mabahith Iraqiyah, Recueils d'articles* (Baghdad, 1955), 2:311.
17. E. J. Banks, *Bismaya; or, The Lost City of Adab* (New York, 1912), p. 418.

vantageous position to secure firearms as a result of their numerical strength, direct access to the port of Basra, and at least periodically favored relationship with the Turks. Hence there was apparently a movement of guns along a gradient from better-armed to less well-armed groups through raids and theft, recalling a strikingly similar process operating among mounted American Indian tribes during the early and middle nineteenth century.[18]

There is even some evidence that the introduction of the gun may have contributed to a shift in settlement patterns and military tactics, in this fashion again reinforcing the position of military leaders in the tribal structure. An early visitor to the Warka region, J. B. Fraser, failed to observe (or at least comment upon) the mud-brick *muftuls* or watchtowers whose ubiquitous presence is unfailingly reported by visitors in the late nineteenth and early twentieth centuries. The slightly later account of Loftus[19] implies that their introduction was associated with the expansion into this area of the better-armed Muntafiq. Farther to the northwest, a visitor just after the the turn of the century was told that "these mud towers with loopholes for fighting had been brought into use on this part of the river only during the last few years."[20] Such indications are suggestive, even if they do not conclusively establish a link with the availability of firearms. They argue for the deployment of permanent armed guards in fixed positions, presumably supported by and responsive to the tribal leadership, as a late development modifying the earlier pattern of reliance on sporadic raids and counterraids.

To summarize, the validity of the assertion that Ottoman influence was very limited outside the cities depends upon what is being studied. It can hardly be questioned with regard to direct administrative controls, and it is nearly as accurate for economic policies. On the other hand, it leaves out of account a whole series of indirect but important modifications in the sociopolitical organization of the countryside.

The significance of this qualification may not be limited to recent history, whether of the Warka region or even of southern Iraq as a whole. To some extent, the nineteenth century provides an obvious model of "pristine" conditions. This is particularly true with regard to low demographic pressure, emphasis on traditional, small-scale agriculture in enclaves of limited area, weakness or virtual absence of extended, superordinate political structures, and the very modest role played by commercial or credit relationships at the command of urban specialists. But as was suggested above, the temptation to uncritically equate all the remaining features of this model with conditions in late prehistoric periods, for which such full and descriptive documentation will never be available, must be avoided. Specifically, the tribal and confederational levels of nineteenth century social organization cannot be fully understood as primitive isolates but must be regarded, at least in part, as complex adaptive responses of indigenous groups to the demands of coexistence with an Ottoman administrative apparatus.

Figure 24 records the approximate distribution today of tribal units in the region of the Warka Survey.[21] No attempt has been made to define precise boundaries, although in most cases these are readily identified by the commonly recognized landmarks (often ancient mounds) through which they run. But the distribution provides a further illustration in microcosm of the fragmentation and displacement that have occurred through time as a result of both natural changes in the river regimes and Ottoman pressure.

The only bedouin who move through the area today, ranging from the Shatt al-Gharraf to the Shatt al-Shamīya, are the Refāᶜi. The euphemistically named *khuwwa* or "brotherhood tax," formerly paid by settled peoples to great bedouin groups like the Shammar on the occasion of their visits in acknowledgement of some vague form of nomadic overlordship,[22] reportedly has disappeared. There are two major groupings of ᶜ*arab* whose followers occupy the area, the Muntafiq and the Bani Huchaym. In both the latter the balance has shifted toward a greater degree of sedentism in recent decades, and both also have tended to be defined more in static, territorial terms than as active focuses of loyalty. This is illustrated by the Badūr, who are generally assigned to the Muntafiq (by Bani Huchaym informants) along with the Budair and the Hafādh, although in fact they broke their bonds with the Muntafiq after a bitter struggle in 1910.[23] Counted among the Bani Huchaym are virtually all of the other tribal components shown on the map: the Albu Jaiyāsh, Rubāyaᶜ, Barkat, Ghānim, Toba, Al-ᶜAbbās, Juwābir, Fartūs, Meshāᶜla, and Zaiyād. Many of these sections

18. Frank R. Secoy, "Changing Military Patterns on the the Great Plains," American Ethnological Society, *Monographs* 21 (1953).

19. J. B. Fraser, *Travels in Koordistan, Mesopotamia . . .* (London, 1840), vol. 2. The passage in Loftus is quoted below, p. 80.

20. H. W. Cadoux, "Recent Changes in the Course of the Lower Euphrates," *Geographical Journal* 38 (1906):272–73.

21. I am indebted to Mr. John Bellingham, a member of the Warka Expedition staff in 1967, who undertook to assemble most of the information recorded in this map through interviews with Toba and Juwābir antiquities guards and workmen in the Warka excavations.

22. E. Sachau, *Am Euphrat und Tigris* (Leipzig, 1900), p. 69.

23. Great Britain, Naval Intelligence Division, "Iraq and Persian Gulf," *Geographical Handbook Series,* B. R. 524 (1944): 365.

furnished the backbone of the great tribal revolt against the British in 1920, and have periodically been involved in small uprisings since.[24] It is keenly to be regretted that no ethnographic accounts are available for any of them.

Whereas the Bani Huchaym had already appeared on the scene as a not unimportant grouping by the time of Niebuhr's journey in 1765,[25] it is interesting to note that at least a few of their components are of much more recent affiliation. The Zaiyād, for example, are a splinter of the Ghazāʿel, for several centuries the dominant confederation on the Middle Euphrates and the most redoubtable opponents of the Ottomans. This confederation was forced to dissolve around 1900 by the westward shift of the main flow of the Euphrates into the Hindīya channel.[26] The same phenomenon may be noted among the Muntafiq. The Budair were particularly hard hit by the drying up of their earlier *dira* well to the northwest, along the tails of the Shatt al-Dhaghara, and by the early years of the twentieth century the Dhaghara group of tribes of which they were a part had been forced to abandon its homelands in a series of migrating fragments and was no longer feared by the Turks.[27] The majority, in fact, moved eastward onto Muntafiq lands along the tails of the Shatt al-Gharraf, there finding means of subsistence only as sharecroppers at the hands of a group with whom previously they had been on terms of bitter hostility.[28] By the time of our survey, as was indicated earlier, Bani Huchaym informants reckoned them a permanent, full-fledged component of the grouping to which they had become attached under duress sixty-five years earlier.

Deeply rooted ecological patterns are evident in these tribal distributions. Major groupings tend to coincide with the ramified "tails" of a particular canal or river branch. Rivalries may exist within this framework, but tribal leadership is ordinarily able to adjudicate disputes and impose a degree of unity at least in the face of external threats. Irreconcilable differences or gross shortages in natural resources that may develop, whether from natural or human factors, are met by out-migration of one or more tribal components. The sharpest conflicts and most deeply felt enmities, on the other hand, run along boundaries traced through arid steppe-lands or zones of marginal cultivation between these larger irrigation enclaves. The latter thus appear to be the "natural" units of loyalty and collective action.

But the patterning does not stop here. Leaving aside the ethnically distinct bedouin with whom interaction is minimal, most tribes are characterized by the simultaneous pursuit of a considerable variety of subsistence alternatives, ranging from fully sedentary to seminomadic. The individual tribal territory tends, in other words, not to follow the zone of irrigation longitudinally along a canal but to extend laterally into the adjoining seasonal depressions or open steppes that are suitable only for grazing. Of course the fortified residences of the shaykhs or sirkals, as well as smaller, more numerous watchtowers, adjoin the banks of the major watercourses whose canal offtakes they are often designed to protect. But the line between cultivator and herdsman usually is not sharply drawn even on the basis of family units. One brother often resides in a black tent and moves with the herds for the greater portion of the year while the other occupies a reed or mud-brick house and engages in cultivation. Moreover, as Heinrich has pointed out in a penetrating discussion of the problem, the specialized products of different subsistence pursuits constitute a unity at a deeper level.[29] The diet of the herdsman and the cultivator is virtually the same. The former provides meat, dairy products, and a crucial contribution of agricultural labor, particularly during the harvest season. The latter provides grain, dates, nowadays rice, and stubble or fodder for the animals during seasons when the steppes and depressions are barren.

The Maʿdān, or Marsh Arabs, constitute an apparent exception to this pattern of lateral variability, for they are usually described as "true" marsh dwellers whose subsistence is intensively focused on the water buffalo.[30] Such a description is indeed fairly accurate today, when the Maʿdān are all said to be concentrated in and around the swamps near the confluence of the Tigris and the Euphrates—hence all at some distance from the Warka region. But it is interesting to note that earlier use of the term was apparently much more flexible. Niebuhr, ascending the Euphrates in 1765, identifies the Maʿdān as "Arabs who herd horses, cattle and buffalo, also cultivate, and move their crude huts from place to place as the

---

24. Von Oppenheim, *Die Beduinen*, p. 338.

25. C. Niebuhr, *Reisebeschreibung nach Arabien und andern umliegenden Ländern* (Copenhagen, 1774–78), 2: 246.

26. Von Oppenheim, *Die Beduinen*, p. 326.

27. Ibid., p. 302.

28. Ibid., p. 310. On the earlier hostility between the Budair and Muntafiq, cf. W. Andrae, ("Ausgrabungen in Fara und Abu Hatab," Deutsche Orient-Gesellschaft, *Mitteilungen* 17 [1903]: 23, passim), who speaks of the relationship as one of "grimmer Feindschaft" and documents this with numerous instances drawn from the daily life of the Fara Expedition. Working at nearby Bismaya, Banks (*Bismaya*) also reports numerous hostile encounters between the Budair and the Muntafiq.

29. E. Heinrich, "Moderne arabische Gehöfte am unteren Euphrat und ihre Beziehungen zum 'Babylonischen Hofhaus'," Deutsche Orient-Gesellschaft, *Mitteilungen* 82 (1950): 40, passim.

30. E.g., Naval Intelligence Division, "Iraq and the Persian Gulf," p. 367.

Bedouin do their tents."[31] Equally significant, he counts the Bani Huchaym and the Ghazā'el among the Ma'dān, suggesting that the term then applied to many times the number of tribal groupings it would include today. Ninety years later, Loftus also speaks of encountering Ma'dān living in tents on open steppes and herding cattle and sheep.[32] Moritz explicitly notes that in his time the name applied not only to specialized buffalo herders but also to semisedentary cultivators given to wandering with their herds after the completion of the harvest.[33] And even today, this usage appears on closer inspection.[34] Thus the exception is more apparent than real. At least in traditional terms, the Ma'dān seem to have exhibited virtually the same variability as other groups.

The adaptive advantage of this pattern is that it provides the tribal unit with subsistence alternatives with which to meet the prevailing conditions of extreme environmental flux and uncertainty. Reductions in cultivated land, whether induced by reduction in stream flow, salinization, or outside conquest, can be met for at least a period by shifting the balance in the direction of seminomadism. Then too, herds are a form of capital, at least as secure as any other that is traditionally available to the local tribesman and under ordinary circumstances readily convertible into a more liquid form to meet emergencies. Beyond a certain point, of course, the only recourse for the greater part of the group will be to seek new irrigable lands along some other canal system, either by conquest or, more frequently, through assuming a client or agricultural laborer status. Since desirable lands were not inexhaustible even with the relatively low population levels of the nineteenth century, this sometimes involved resettlement in marginal areas where only a limited resumption of agriculture was possible. Herein may lie at least one explanation of differences in subsistence emphasis that undoubtedly occur within a major tribal grouping like the Bani Huchaym, and that are not accounted for in the idealized pattern outlined above. The Toba, for example, are less tied to permanent residences and an agricultural way of life than the neighboring Juwābir,[35] although this difference in their home territories now is somewhat offset by annual Toba migrations to provide harvest labor in Muntafiq fields on the tails of the Shatt al-Gharraf.

Our earlier discussion of tribal displacements dealt with natural and social changes whose major effects were initiated and felt elsewhere, and that only involved the Warka region insofar as they precipitated immigration into it. But a well-documented case, the drying up of the Shatt al-Kar in the late nineteenth century, also occurred locally. Moreover, it is particularly interesting in that it affords glimpses of the traditional regime of irrigation and settlement that are significantly at variance with the usual identification of lower Mesopotamia as a region dependent upon large-scale irrigation agriculture.

References to the condition of the Shatt al-Kar in European itineraries have been summarized by Dougherty,[36] and the three stages into which he divides the process of its desiccation can be retained with some modifications. Perhaps the most significant change affects his first stage, which he defines as a swollen seasonal river and dates from the accounts of visitors in 1835 and 1854. Dougherty notes that both of these accounts describe deep crossings in the lower part of the course of the Kar, not far from Senkere (ancient Larsa). Hence, he argues, "farther north it may have been larger, as is often the case with rivers flowing through dry regions which furnish no tributaries." In fact, however, the opposite is true here. The level of the lower Kar was fixed by the level of the Euphrates into which it flowed, and even today, seventy years after water last moved down its channel, high water on the Euphrates backs up the dry bed of the Kar to a point several kilometers northeast of Senkere. In short, although the Kar must have carried a considerable flow at the time (since both accounts imply the presence of water in its upper course as well), there is some reason to doubt that its true flow, even on a seasonal basis, reached the scale suggested by a reported thirty to forty yard channel width occupied by water at shoulder depth.

Dougherty's second stage unfortunately follows the first only after a thirty-year interval. Itineraries in 1885 and 1889 indicate "its survival as a much diminished stream." Fortunately the earlier of these travelers followed the Kar's entire middle course, and includes a locally elicited explanation not only of what had caused the reduction but of some of its indirect consequences:

All day long from Dhahr to Hammam [site 183], and thence to Sheikh Hashm [Kharkhara, site 075], we had seen nothing living on the ground larger than ants, except two toads. All was barren, and yet there were old canals and castle granaries. We were told that there had been some population there, but that six or eight years before a governor had doubled the taxes, which people could not pay, whereupon he had shut off the water which came

31. Niebuhr, *Reisebeschreibung,* p. 246.

32. Loftus, "Notes," p. 146.

33. B. Moritz, "Zur Geographie und Ethnographie von Süd-Mesopotamien," *Gesellschaft für Erdkunde zu Berlin, Verhandlungen* 15 (1888): 195, 199.

34. S. Westphal-Hellbusch and H. Westphal, "Die Ma'dān: Kultur und Geschichte der Marschenbewohner im Süd-Iraq," *Forschungen zur Ethnologie und Sozialpsychologie* 4 (Berlin, 1962): 11.

35. Heinrich, "Moderne arabische Gehöfte," p. 19.

36. R. P. Dougherty, "Searching for Ancient Remains in lower 'Irāq," American Schools of Oriental Research, *Annual* 7 (1927): 26–27.

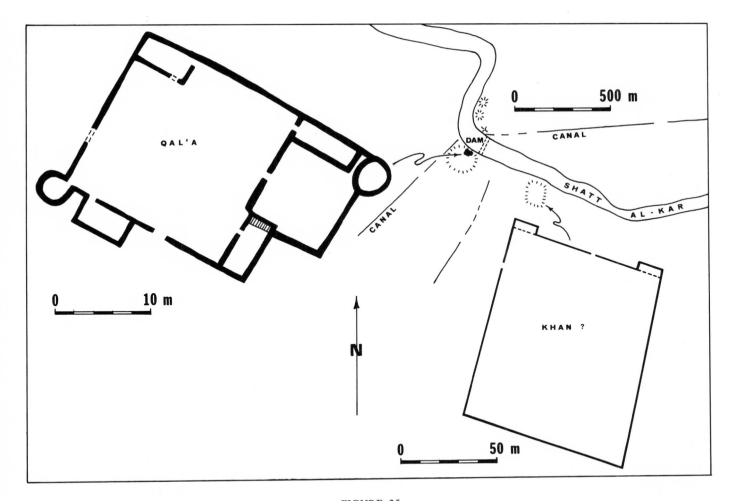

FIGURE 25

Qalᶜa Kharkhara, a late nineteenth century settlement and stronghold.

through the Daghara and the Affech Khor, and now it had gone, they said, to the Hindieh and was lost to the Daghara Canal. This lowered the Shatt-el-Kehr [Kar] also, and famine, followed by plague, resulted, and the country was wholly deserted.[37]

The final stage posited by Dougherty, the Kar's "complete disappearance as a dependable water supply," is covered by excellent accounts dating from 1898 and 1902. In the latter, the report of the excavator of Fara (ancient Shuruppak, near the source of the Kar) on a reconnaissance along its course, we are explicitly told that it was at that time "dry year-in year-out."[38] Yet even under those circumstances, it is interesting to note that Qalᶜa Kharkhara (fig. 25, site 075) still was occupied by one of the shaykhs of the Budair. Its original function undoubtedly had been to protect a dam across the Shatt al-Kar and an associated canal offtake, for remains of both still are to

be seen. That function it had served in the time of Loftus, who found the canal water there "excellent" a half-century earlier.[39] Apparently there was still an agricultural settlement at the time of Ward's journey in 1885, for he and his party were impressed with the size and beauty of the *mudhif* or guest house of the village there in which they were lodged.[40] But by Andrae's time, with the irrigation water gone permanently, it seems to have become only an important outpost along the disputed frontier with the Muntafiq.

Qalᶜa Majnūna is a contemporary fortress six kilometers below Kharkhara on the Shatt al-Kar (site 084). It figures in Andrae's map but is not otherwise identified in his account in spite of its size and proximity to Fara. Surely the reason is that it was in the hands of the Muntafiq with whom Andrae's informants were on hostile terms. Illustrations and a full description have been published[41]

37. W. H. Ward, in *Nippur; or, Explorations and Adventures on the Euphrates,* ed. J. P. Peters (New York, 1897), 1: 329.

38. Andrae, "Berichte," p. 22.

39. Loftus, "Notes," p. 144. Loftus calls the qalᶜa "Khurukha," but there is no question of its identity from the bearings and map location that are given.

40. Ward, in Peters, *Nippur,* p. 330.

41. Heinrich, "Moderne arabische Gehöfte," pp. 29–31.

and need not be recapitulated here, but the accompanying account of circumstances leading to its construction is directly relevant to this discussion and must be included in spite of the numerous problems it raises. Obtained in the 1930s from the oldest Toba shaykh then living, it richly illustrates the character of intertribal relations along an undependable watercourse like the Shatt al-Kar:

In the time of the informant's grandfather, therefore about thirty years previously, the entire district belonged to the bedouin tribe of the Muntafiq. They had installed Sayyid Yāsir as administrator of their territories between the Shatt al-Kar and the contemporary Euphrates course, the Shatt al-Sebil, and he lived in Qalᶜa Sussa [site 375 in the Warka Survey], about twenty kilometers downstream from Majnūna and now also in ruins. At that time the water in the Shatt al-Kar began to be scarce, since the main flow of the Euphrates had shifted to the Shatt al-Sebil. The Albu Budair, living above Majnūna, for this reason built a *sedde,* or earth dam, across the stream in order to keep the existing water supply for themselves. The fields below then could no longer be irrigated. Sayyid Yāsir first sought to open negotiations with the Budair, and when these proved fruitless he overcame them in battle and forcibly destroyed the dam. In this he was helped by tribes of the Bani Huchaym sharing the same interest, namely the Toba, Juwābir, Ghānim, and Fartūs. To assure the security of the disputed place Yāsir built Qalᶜa Majnūna and installed his nephew Sayyid Ridha as its commandant. The latter lived alone in the qalᶜa with his family, only summoning reinforcements from his uncle in time of danger.[42]

One problem that arises at once is the timing of the events that are described. Obviously they had taken place before Andrae's reference to Majnūna in 1902, and probably some time before, since the Kar by then was entirely dry. In fact, a Muntafiq informant indicates that the scarcity of water already had led to a general abandonment of the district before 1896,[43] so that a later date is hardly likely for the construction of what Heinrich regarded as the largest fortress in the area. On the other hand, Ward's 1885 account is graphically explicit in stating that there was no settlement of any kind below Kharkhara. It follows that Qalᶜa Majnūna only could have served its stated purpose for at most a decade or so after 1885. Of course, its function could have been modified later into that of a fortified outpost dependent on wells in the old, dry bed, comparable to Kharkhara but in the hands of the opposing tribal coalition. Its survival for somewhat longer than merely a decade or less perhaps is implied by its present name, drawn not from the Muntafiq overlords who built it, but from a Bani Huchaym shaykh who died in 1920.

Still more troubling is the question of whether Majnūna's stated purpose is consistent with what we know of its location and relationship to Kharkhara. It is situated some distance below the latter, and since Kharkhara continued to be occupied even after the cessation of the Shatt al-Kar's flow the single resident family in Majnūna would hardly have been in a position to halt, or even properly supervise, the diversion of water into the Kharkhara canal. Moreover, a glance at the map (fig. 23) shows that all three contemporary qalᶜas (Kharkhara, Majnūna, and Sussa) are sited at points of stream curvature where canal offtakes can divert part of the flow with minimal problems of silting, following a common irrigation practice in the area at the time,[44] and that one or more such diversionary canals can be traced in each case from the air photographs.

The implication seems clear. Majnūna's purpose, like that of the other qalᶜas, was to supervise and defend its own small irrigation enclave. In times of water shortage undoubtedly there were hostilities between neighboring groups, and there is no reason to doubt that the earthen weirs adjoining these qalᶜas often were a principal focus of attack. But the incident recorded by Heinrich probably was merely an episode in a continuing pattern of hostile coexistence between competitors for the same limited resource. Majnūna is not so situated as to constitute an affirmation of final Muntafiq victory over the Budair; that came only later, with the complete desiccation of the Budair lands so that they had to move in with their former enemies. If anything, Majnūna more effectively proclaims Muntafiq leadership in a cause which also embraced a fragile coalition of Bani Huchaym adherents. Perhaps it indicates that championing the cause of lesser tribes was one of the alternative means by which the Muntafiq sought to extend their control westward, up until the time when the end of cultivation along the Kar made further attempts pointless.

Qalᶜa Sussa (site 375) furnishes a particularly complete and well-preserved example with which to consider the character of these little irrigation enclaves. As is shown in figure 26, the qalᶜa is situated alongside a portion of the Kar's bed that is confined to a single relatively narrow channel. No surface trace survives of the presence of an earth or brushwork weir at this point, although the condition of the bed and confluence of canal offtakes here make it extremely likely that one existed originally. It will be observed that at least half a dozen small villages seemingly were dependent on the canals served by this weir, and still others lie nearby, either directly on the Kar or on smaller canal systems taken from it. The whole ensemble invites comparison with the prehistoric enclave

42. Ibid.
43. Serkis, *Mabahith Iraqiyah,* p. 377.

44. Moritz, "Zur Geographie und Ethnographie," p. 197.

shown in figure 14, and the two figures are drawn to enclose the same area at the same scale in order to facilitate this.

The details of the Kar's course and the associated canals are taken from the air photographs, and they illustrate clearly that this was in no sense a static hydrological system. A large meander above Sussa seems to have been cut off by the formation of a new, shorter channel at a relatively recent time, and traces of other abandoned meanders suggest still earlier variations in the course. Southwest of the qal‘a, in fact, is an isolated reach of the channel which cannot be connected with the present bed at all because of extensive dune movements in the area immediately around it. Surely it is considerably older than most or all other portions of the course that are shown, although, as for the other successive phases of the system, we can only say at present that the pseudo-prehistoric

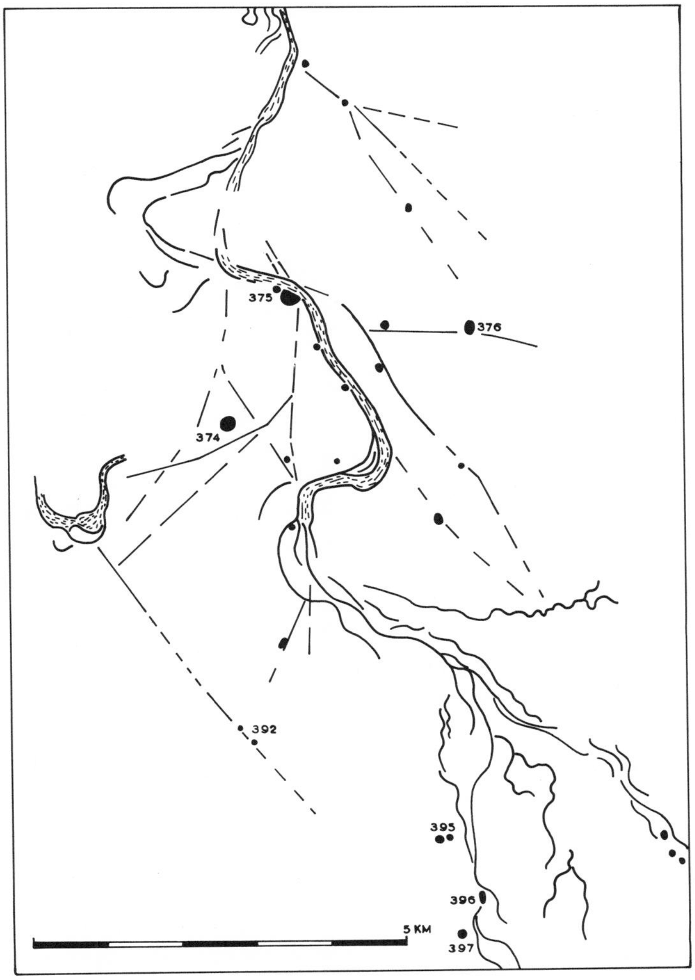

FIGURE 26

Late nineteenth century enclave of irrigation and settlement around Qal‘a Sussa.

pottery scattered along its banks indicates it is probably not to be assigned to a date earlier than the fifteenth century.

The clearest succession of canal patterns occurs in the immediate environs of Sussa. Presumably after the construction of the qal‘a there, a canal offtake a kilometer or so to the west of the qal‘a was replaced by a new one immediately adjoining the site. An effort seems to have been made to provide irrigation water for one or two of the same villages from the new source, perhaps indicating that they were occupied for a considerable period. On the other hand, even the earlier canal postdated the cutoff of the upstream meander, so that the total time period may not be very great. At any rate, Loftus, who assiduously noted the bearings of other qal‘as, and who in 1850 took bearings from nearby Tell Jīd (site 164) and passed the night only about six kilometers away, failed to mention any permanent settlement in these environs at the time.

Qal‘a Sussa itself, in its present ruined condition, is illustrated in figure 27. It will be observed that corner bastions are confined to one narrow end, at a considerable distance from what are apparently the main residential and reception quarters. The plan as a whole also is much more spacious and open than that of either Majnūna or Kharkhara. Possibly because this lay well within the frontier of Muntafiq control, defense was not an important consideration in its layout; emphasis is given instead to the plastered audience chambers in the central enclosure. In this respect it differs completely not only from Kharkhara and Majnūna but also from all of the other "fighting" qal‘as and smaller *muftuls* or watchtowers encountered in the survey (fig. 28). Perhaps the central position in an assured territory of control also explains the numerous smaller villages lying around it. In regions more subject to dispute, the population dependent on each qal‘a generally must have been smaller and may have tended to reside in its immediate vicinity for protection.

In terms of permanent settlement, the history of the Shatt al-Kar does not quite come to an end with Sussa, Kharkhara, and Majnūna. The concluding chapter involves the construction of Qal‘a Falhīya (fig. 29, site 399) in 1902 by Faleh Pasha, a leading member of the Sa‘dūn family and former walī of Nasirīya. Although this was a relatively large and substantial establishment, as Andrae noted after having been a guest there,[45] Faleh Pasha seems to have constructed it in an entirely private capacity. Andrae's own observations make clear that cultivation had entirely ceased by this time in the surrounding area. The numerous scattered outbuildings apparently include

—————

45. Andrae, "Berichte," pp. 17–18.

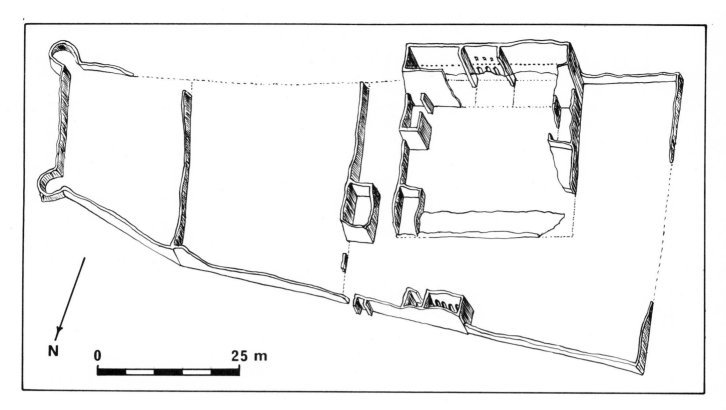

FIGURE 27

Ruins of Qal'a Sussa

a stable for thirty horses, and the defensive towers at the corners are almost vestigial for an enclosure as large as this one. The whole group of buildings thus suggests something more akin to a country estate or hunting lodge than to a functional qal'a like Kharkhara or Majnūna, and hence is only marginally connected with earlier, essentially agricultural, settlement patterns. As was noted earlier, Dougherty found Falhīya "almost deserted" in 1926, but he fails to indicate the nature of the small occupation apparently remaining at the time. With its final abandonment, presumably not more than a few years later, permanent settlement entirely ceased in the region covered by the Warka Survey. Today, as Dougherty already thought likely more than forty years ago,[46] even the bed of the Shatt al-Kar itself has entirely disappeared in many places beneath a blanket of wind-laid silts.

As the accounts given earlier indicate, the drying up of the Shatt al-Kar may have been a fairly localized calamity, but its underlying causes lay in much more generalized administrative decision and hydrological processes. To some degree, the shift of the bulk of the Euphrates flow from the Hilla to the Hindīya channel reflects natural agencies independent of human control, but there is no doubt that human factors were decisive at least in the timing.[47] On the one hand, the irrigation practices of the Arab cultivators involved uncontrolled diversion of a large proportion of the river's flow into swamps east of the Hilla branch, from whence only a small part of it ultimately found its way back into the Euphrates through the Shatt al-Kar. This reduction of flow led to a more rapid siltation of the easterly course, as did the artificial slowing of the current there through the construction of dams.[48] But on the other hand, Arab toleration, or even encouragement, of the formation of swamps was at least partly a defensive response to help them resist Turkish punitive forays. Moreover, as the report by W. H. Ward (quoted above) indicates, the Turks contributed no small amount themselves to the restricting of the Hilla branch's flow as a means of increasing military pressure and extorting tax payments. Midhat Pasha's famous damming of the Daghara canal in 1870, to which that account probably refers, is merely a case in point. Already a generation earlier Loftus relates an otherwise insignificant local incident reflecting the same practice:

Mústapha Beg, the Kiaya of Baghdad, was despatched by Abdi Pasha with a strong force against the rebels, and his first care was to shut off the water completely from the Turunjíeh, by building an enormous dam of earth and brushwood in the usual manner. He then proceeded, to

46. Dougherty, "Searching for Ancient Remains," p. 33.
47. Cf. now the full and critical review of this shift in McG.

Gibson, "The City and Area of Kish," in *Field Research Projects* (Coconut Grove, Florida; in press).
48. Cadoux, "Recent Changes," pp. 270–71.

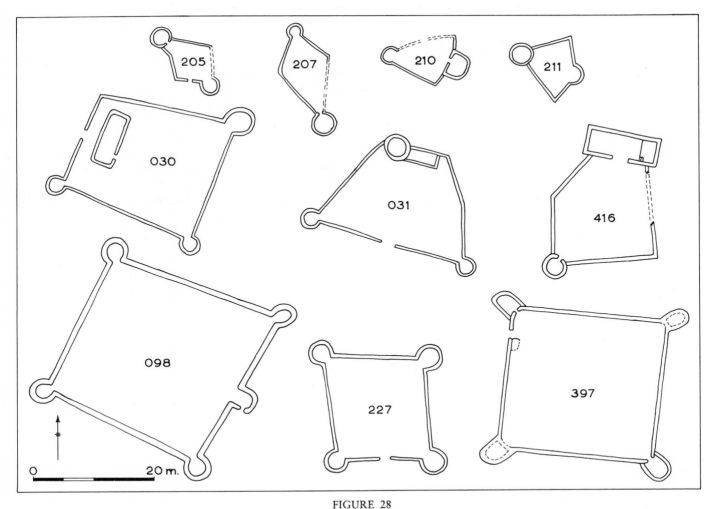

FIGURE 28

Plans of representative Late Ottoman strongholds

besiege a kala‘at, to which the Arabs had retired, and sought to defend. We heard that he had taken possession of it that morning, the besieged having evacuated it during the night with all their movables, leaving behind only mud walls and abundance of filth. No one was killed, no one wounded during the whole affair.[49]

The accidental breaching of weirs on the important watercourses was, of course, quite as disruptive to irrigation and settlement as the damming off of canals as a military tactic. Since the entire system of watercourses in an alluvium is necessarily unstable, its parts are always in mutual adjustment. More or less rapid oscillation in the proportions reaching various channels is the rule, at least in the absence of weirs or dams as regulatory mechanisms, and the agricultural population then can only adjust to the changing conditions through their own movements. Abandonment of land from this cause is already reported as early as 1688, leading to Turkish concern over the ensuing cessation of tax payments. Then as later, the Turks resorted to the familiar expedient of raising taxes

in the surrounding districts in order to obtain the finances to restore the balance of flow—with the predictable consequence that a major uprising followed.[50]

The key instance of this destructive process in the nineteenth century involves the failure of a series of weirs to control the intake of the Hindīya branch of the Euphrates. This branch, originally a canal dug to supply the holy city of Najaf, had already begun to gain ground on the Hilla branch by 1800, and repeated, only briefly successful attempts to stabilize the distribution were made after 1830. By 1880 the Hindīya branch had become the main course of the Euphrates. A masonry dam was completed by foreign engineers in 1891, but this too was breached in 1903 with the consequent diversion of the entire flow into the Hindīya channel. Only the completion of the Willcock Barrage in 1913 finally rectified what had been a recurrently disastrous situation for a major agricultural region.[51]

---

49. Loftus, "Notes," p. 142.

---

50. Von Oppenheim, *Die Beduinen*, pp. 314–15.

51. Longrigg, *Four Centuries*, p. 311; cf. Cadoux, "Recent Changes"; Gibson, "City and Area of Kish."

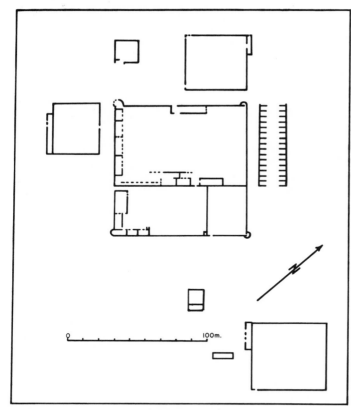

FIGURE 29

Qalᶜa Falhīya, an early twentieth century stronghold

Following the construction of the Willcock Barrage, there was, in fact, a temporary return of water even to fairly remote downstream effluents of the Hilla branch like the Shatt al-Kar. As late as 1916 it was reported that during the flood season only a single bund blocked continuous flow in the Kar from its source near Dīwanīya to the backslope depressions adjoining the Euphrates levee, although much of the Kar was navigable at most for shallow-draft native boats and was dry in other seasons.[52] How long this renewed but periodic flow continued before finally terminating is uncertain, although we have seen that it surely had ceased some years before Dougherty's journey in 1926.

Loftus again has left us a graphic account of the local effects of this irregularity of flow, in a region more than 150 kilometers southeast of the dam in question and immediately northwest of the area included within the Warka Survey:

Nowhere is the effect of the Hindíeh, in abstracting too much water from the Euphrates, better understood than at Súk-el-Fawᶜwar. It was formerly a large and thriving town, like Affej or Súk-es-Sheioukh, the centre of a district belonging to the Montefik Arabs, and surrounded by a series of small towers and watercourses for defence against their more unsettled neighbors. About twenty-five years ago, according to the best information we could obtain, the town was abandoned in consequence of the water having deserted the canal, owing to the breaking of one of the dams at the mouth of the Hindíeh. The country E. of the Euphrates became a waterless desert beyond the borders of the great marshes. At the time of our visit, decayed date-trees and the ruins of the mud houses of Súk-el-Fawᶜwar extended full half a mile along both sides of the stream, and afforded good shelter for jackals and serpents. Abdi Pasha's late work at the Hindíeh had, however, restored a copious stream to the channel of the Fawᶜwar.[53]

The above passage also illustrates a strikingly common, strongly expressed theme in all of the itineraries: the observation of sparse population and very limited cultivation, coupled with many impressions of recent abandonment. This is perhaps easiest to illustrate along the banks of the Shatt al-Kar itself, both because this should have been the area in which irrigation water was most accessible and because it furnished a natural route for travelers. J. B. Fraser, describing a journey fifteen years earlier than Loftus's, approached the Kar from Senkere, to the south. He tells us that "this part of the country had formerly, and at no very distant period, been well cultivated and populous. The remains of many date-gardens were scattered over an extent of more than three miles and a half, and the whole surface of the land still showed the ridges of the rice-grounds which had not long ago existed here."[54] Then moving upstream along the Kar, he reports only thick belts of tamarisk jungle, with scattered tent encampments of nomads or seminomads on higher ground. W. H. Ward followed approximately the same route in 1885, recording precisely similar impressions that have already been quoted. Subsequently, of course, the desiccation of the Kar provides sufficient explanation for the abandonment of its immediate vicinity, but it is worth noting that later visitors like Sachau and Andrae report no compensatory development elsewhere.

The uniformity of these comments obviously attests to a very high degree of flux in settlement. Since there are numerous references to the recency of what must be many successive phases of abandonment, there is no basis for assuming that the observed ruins reflect much earlier, pre-European-contact conditions that were substantially more stable and prosperous. We are left instead with a kaleidoscopic scene of continual formation and desertion of both temporary camps and fully sedentary systems of villages. Under such conditions one would expect, as indeed the survey has recorded, numerous sites with traces

52. Great Britain, Admiralty War Staff Intelligence Division, *A Handbook of Mesopotamia* (London, 1917), 2: 149–50.

53. Loftus, "Notes," pp. 142–43.
54. Fraser, *Travels,* pp. 138–39.

of an occupation during the Ottoman period but few or none with any real depth of refuse. It follows also that a map of "recent" settlements (fig. 23), particularly as identified on the chronologically somewhat insecure basis of pseudo-prehistoric pottery alone, gives a grossly exaggerated picture of the extent of occupation at any one time. And it would be only candid to concede that this in turn raises questions with reference to the interpretation of rural settlement pattern data for other periods, at least in areas remote from the main urban centers and watercourses.

It has been stressed heretofore that there are central themes of ecological continuity connecting the contemporary Warka region with the past. But of course this does not imply an absence of concurrent change in important particulars. Many recent changes are, in fact, dramatic in their immediate impact and even more profound in their probable long-term effects. Among these are surely to be included the substitution of motor transport for many of the old camel caravans; the introduction of pumps and agricultural machinery; the increasing integration of the local economy with that of Iraq as a whole; the extension of education and other social services beyond urban centers into many rural districts; and the at least incipient undermining of purely parochial loyalties through media like the national radio, widespread conscription, and the development of seasonal wage labor patterns.

However, the available evidence does not allow us to document the onset of these new patterns in the Warka region other than at a purely impressionistic level. In any case, they constitute an entirely different subject of inquiry that bears no necessary relationship to the current study. All that we can deal with here are certain broad shifts in settlement and subsistence patterns that provide a contrast between late Ottoman times and the present—and that perhaps help to elucidate underlying features of the former.

Agricultural zones and methods furnish a natural point of departure. The Warka region, as defined for purposes of the survey, is today entirely devoid of cultivation. Yet it is bounded to the west, east, and south by agricultural frontiers that are all expanding more or less rapidly. Clearly this involves a major shift at least in zones of settlement over a period of seventy or eighty years, but the changes in basic pattern of land use are of considerably greater importance than the merely locational changes.

Probably the most important motive force behind the expansion of agricultural frontiers has been unchecked population growth, initiated by externally imposed pacification after World War I and more recently assisted further by the increasing availability of public health services in the cities and towns. On the margins of the Warka region, the construction of new, large-scale canals does not appear to have been the principal means to this end. Instead, the existing canal system has been steadily extended outward in innumerable small increments, principally at the initiative of local shaykhs, in whom effective ownership of the land is still largely vested. Increasing reliance on diesel pumps has been a distinguishing technical characteristic of this process. Not only do they permit new lands to be irrigated without the construction of long gravity-flow canals, but also their initial cost and maintenance requirements strengthen the positions of the landowners and shaykhs, who alone have the means for capital investments.

The corollary to this agricultural expansion is that water has become an increasingly scarce resource. Moreover, its application to the land, particularly along the outer fringes of cultivation, increasingly is associated with the costs of running pumps rather than flowing freely through a gravity-flow canal network. As a result, the spillover of unneeded water surpluses into uncultivated interior depressions has declined substantially. This in turn has reduced the importance of the latter as a potential source of fodder for the nomadic and seminomadic proportion of the population, probably doing more to hasten their conversion into agriculturalists than any conscious government measures. Of course, the intensification of this contrast between the desert and the sown must not be exaggerated. The distance still left to be traveled is perhaps suggested by a recent estimate that less than 15 percent of the available land along the lower Euphrates has yet been brought under cultivation in modern times.[55]

The character of irrigation in the Warka region during Ottoman times contrasted considerably with these modern practices. Most obviously, the extreme flux and uncertainty to which we have referred would have encouraged minimal reliance on relatively permanent capital facilities like extensive canal systems. Some fairly long canals are shown, to be sure, in the map of settlements in the region during the Ottoman period (fig. 23), but they were all of very modest width and, presumably, carrying capacity. As a substitute, greater reliance was placed on the margins of seasonal depressions, and on temporary, small-scale, ad hoc canal construction that took advantage of limited portions of the insequent drainage patterns where the topography was locally favorable. Walter Andrae has left a revealing account of the slight impact of such a system on the natural landscape in the northern part of the Warka Survey region just after the turn of the century:

One can represent the territory in question . . . as an ex-

_____
55. E. Wirth, "Agrargeographie des Irak," *Hamburger Geographische Studien* 13 (1962): 146.

tremely shallow depression that in the main takes the character of a marsh. The deepest places, the *haurs*, generally are filled during flood time and become reedy swamps. Suitable for cultivation is the somewhat higher lying land covered with thickets, through which there are channels that allow the water to pass from one *haur* to another. This situation on a large scale may be observed often enough in alluvial Mesopotamia. The watercourses change from deeply incised channels into wide, shallow ones, then come together again into one or more deep cuts that often may be assigned other names. Thus one can receive very different impressions of different beds of one and the same watercourse, particularly in the dry season. . . . The activity of the modern inhabitants is confined to the building of small earth dams that direct the water from the channels to their fields, and in the latter they dig the scantiest possible field canals for irrigation. That is all. Enormous canal constructions like those that are still undertaken, for example, near Babylon and Hilla are entirely unknown here and surely have been unknown for centuries.[56]

Before the advent of large-scale private landownership as a result of land registration policies put into effect after World War I, the organization and execution of irrigation tasks was the responsibility of the communities themselves. It may be thought that the absence of durable, centralized, coercive direction was one of the factors contributing to the limited extent and effectiveness of the irrigation system. In the late nineteenth century, however, there is excellent eyewitness testimony to the successful operation on this basis even of fairly large-scale projects, drawing water from the lower Shatt al-Gharraf not far east of the Warka region:

All of the male inhabitants of one or more villages belonging to the same tribe unite themselves for the construction of large canals and dams. Then the entire body of workers is divided into several parties, each raising a flag and inciting one another on through improvised war songs and mutual challenges. Thus the excitement often climbs to the point where the men throw off their clothes and run about as if possessed. One certainly hears nothing of such noise when the work concerned is undertaken at the requisition of the government.[57]

Even under modern conditions in which the internal cohesiveness of the tribes has been fundamentally shaken by policies of land registration that have favored the ruling lineages and by the penetration into the countryside of agencies of a strong, centralized government, a similar attachment of tribal rituals to work on irrigation projects still continues. Robert A. Fernea's recent account of the El Shabana in the Daghara region provides a strikingly

similar description of the ceremonies attending the annual cleaning of the shaykh's canal:

Tribal sections arrive on horseback in full regalia—guns held aloft, knives roped on. Flags of different colors bearing religious inscriptions are carried by men in each section. Enthusiastic hosas are often performed before the men, somewhat anticlimactically it seems, tie up their long garments and jump into the silt-clogged canals to begin work. The arrival, the dress, the hosa performance, are much the same sort of behavior as occurs on the occasion of ashira feasting. Informants agree that in "the old days" similar activity took place when the ashira gathered for attack or defense in warfare.[58]

Although he does not reject the "simplest explanation" of the continuing willingness of tribesmen to be mobilized for arduous, unpaid corvee service, self-interest in retaining the shaykh's favor, Fernea feels that this cannot account for the heavy overlay of ritual. More than the charismatic but ephemeral force of the shaykh's leadership provides for relations of cooperation as well as those of competition within the tribal structure. This hints at adaptive potentialities inherent in Arab tribes that are too little understood: "inclusive segmentary groupings may be capable of a more constructive social action than mere 'opposition' to groupings of similar size and composition."[59]

The underlying issue here is broader than the effectiveness of kin-based social systems in managing fairly extensive irrigation networks. The central emphasis in Fernea's study is on a closely argued defense of the continuing viability of Iraqi tribal units, in the face of all the ecological constraints associated with the practice of irrigation agriculture on the Mesopotamian plain:

I have tried to emphasize that there was a congruence or fit between traditional tribal methods of cultivation and land tenure, and the nature of the land, water, and climate in southern Iraq. The tendency of this land to become saline under conditions of intensive use was avoided under tribal control when fluctuating supplies of water limited cultivation to a single harvest each year and tribesmen were encouraged to shift about the areas under cultivation, leaving sections fallow for a year or more at a time. Even under contemporary conditions, . . . there are two situations which result both in the highest income levels for individual cultivators and sustained yields from the land: large units of land under cultivation, permitting strict fallowing, and family economics based on a combination of cultivation and animal husbandry.[60]

56. W. Andrae, "Die Umgebung von Fara und Abu Hatab," Deutsche Orient-Gesellschaft, *Mitteilungen* 16: 24–26.

57. Moritz, "Zur Geographie und Ethnographie," p. 198.

58. R. A. Fernea, "Shaykh and Effendi: Changing Patterns of Authority among the El Shabana of Southern Iraq," *Harvard Middle Eastern Studies* 14 (1970): 131.

59. Ibid., p. 132.

60. Ibid., p. 152.

Fernea's conclusions parallel and supplement those arrived at in this study, the manuscript for which was essentially finished before his volume appeared in print. A similar perspective also leads him to reject the prevailing confutation of tribal resistance to Turkish and British authorities with tribal incapacity to enlarge agricultural production. After all, there is evidence of a sustained rise in agricultural exports during the late nineteenth and early twentieth centuries. External stimuli like improvements in transport undoubtedly played a crucial part in this, but by themselves cannot provide a sufficient explantation. The basis for expansion "was not a rural population reorganized under new political auspices but a tribal society still dependent on local leadership and techniques." Had the effects of Ottoman control been less disruptive, the possibility is at least open that indigenous economic development would have begun sooner and carried further.[61]

Taken as a whole, the landscape of settlement in the Warka region during late Ottoman times as it has been sketched out in this chapter differed considerably from patterns sometimes assumed to have been inseparably associated with Mesopotamia. Population was sparse and, prevailingly, only semisedentary. Even the seemingly settled villagers maintained a hedge against a variety of natural or man-made disasters in the form of extensive herds of livestock in the hands of noncultivating kinsmen. Irrigation was conducted essentially at local initiative. Its success and continuity were subject not only to local rivalries over water but to major shifts between channels that were, from the local viewpoint, entirely unpredictable and uncontrollable. Cities were distant, in the hands of an alien government regarded in the countryside as simply predatory, and frequently beleaguered. The viable, basic social units were groups of kinsmen or putative kinsmen, organized in tribes that claimed the territory around one or more villages and encampments. Warfare, or at least petty raiding and skirmishing, was virtually continuous. For all of the renowned productivity of Mesopotamian agriculture, the attainment of even the bare margin of subsistence was always precarious.

The challenging question, to be resolved only by future fieldwork, is how far this set of conditions parallels those that existed in late prehistoric times. The overall settlement patterns of the two periods, barring only the presence of the extraordinary urban center of Uruk, were not dissimilar. Many, perhaps most, of the early watercourses on which irrigation depended must have been as small and unreliable as the Shatt al-Kar.

If the parallels were close and all-inclusive, the precocious growth of centers like Uruk would be all the more enigmatic. Obviously the explanation for the initial phase of rapid urbanization will not be found in the countryside alone, particularly if one is wholly dependent, as at present, not on excavations but on the results of only surface reconnaissance. But equally obviously, no adequate explanation can be formulated which ignores the rural sources of the agricultural and labor surpluses upon which the city's growth ultimately depended.

To consider only the accounts of nineteenth century travelers and Ottoman administrators is to discount heavily the possibility of major evolutionary advances ever having been initiated in southern Iraq. Yet once this was so. Hence the nineteenth century model must not fully apply to the late fourth millennium. Since the available evidence makes it only reasonable to assume basic continuity in subsistence practices, settlement patterns, and the natural environment, the major divergences must concern the radically different sociopolitical setting to which the Bani Huchaym and their Muntafiq neighbors had to adapt. For all of the weakness of Ottoman authority, so obvious to those who furnished the only existing historic records, we must not underestimate its unstabilizing and cumulatively destructive impact upon tribal societies within its sphere of control or even influence. And at the same time, seeing those societies through the foreign and never very sympathetic eyes of literate chroniclers and itinerants writing for European audiences, we may have failed to notice potentials for change and development that were always inherent and that still await only a more propitious moment for expression.

The baffling and important problems, in other words, are not limited to the prehistoric and early historic fields. Even from a generalizing, evolutionary standpoint, there are equally relevant questions to be answered from nineteenth and early twentieth century archaeology and ethnohistory as well.

---

61. Ibid., p. 30.

6 | The Uruk/Warka Region in Historic and Comparative Perspective

In common usage, the idea of a region implies a bounded area whose limits are more or less fixed by natural features or enduring bonds of human association. In such terms, the changing configurations of settlement traced in the foregoing chapters for the most part fail to qualify as a regional unit. As was explained in chapter 1, the limits of the Warka Survey were largely imposed by the arbitrary (and rapidly changing) frontiers of modern cultivation, as well as by the relatively brief period of time available for the reconnaissance. Hence there is nothing to suggest that conditions immediately outside this zone differed significantly from those within it, or that the territorial boundaries of centers like Uruk ever coincided with those of the reconnaissance. It is clear, in fact, that intervals of disunity, during which even the limited terrain covered by the survey was transected by sharply contested political frontiers, must have been comparable in duration to those other, more easily identified periods when it was subject to unified control.

Probably the Mesopotamian plain as a whole constitutes the only fully acceptable "natural" unit within which to trace changing configurations of settlement as a largely self-contained historic phenomenon. By itself, the information on the Warka region presented here constitutes an extremely modest contribution toward that still remote end. On the other hand, data are also now available on a number of other segments of the plain, representing a considerable diversity (if not necessarily the full range) of ecological and historic conditions. These other segments include central Akkad, with special reference to the hinterlands of ancient Kish, the alluvial fan laid down by the Diyala River above its confluence with the Tigris, the upper Khuzestan plains around ancient Susa, the enclave of settlement around ancient Ur, immediately southeast of the Warka region, and the hinterlands of ancient Nippur in northern Sumer. It would be premature

to offer full-scale, systematic comparisons with all these other regions, particularly since the results of surveys in several of them are not yet available in published form. On the other hand, some preliminary, gross comparisons can help to place the results of our work around Warka in clearer perspective.

For this purpose, it is useful first to summarize the findings outlined in the foregoing chapters in a more abbreviated, less contingent form. To be sure, brief descriptive characterizations are not a complete substitute for the fuller account of quantitative variation offered earlier. Moreover, brevity requires the omission of many of the uncertainties with which the interpretation heretofore has been qualified. Hence, individual statements in the synoptic account that follows differ widely in their degree of reliability. The reader is also warned that the account as a whole is not intended as a condensation of all the survey's findings but rather as a paradigm of certain key features of the natural and cultural landscape that may be effectively compared with other regions.

To begin with, we may reconstruct some of the characteristic features of the landscape upon which the impressive but more transitory traces of former settlements have been imposed. In partial contrast with present conditions, it appears that numerous Euphrates branches formerly watered the area. More closely resembling the nineteenth century Shatt al-Kar than the now unified Euphrates course below Samāwa, they were typically rather small and at least in some cases ephemeral. Given a favorable relationship of stream levels to land surfaces, irrigation never required the gigantic canal systems that were brought into use in more northerly regions of the plain during later historic periods.

Only during rare intervals of prosperity and political stability, as in the Third Dynasty of Ur and more particularly during the Parthian and Sassanian periods, were major artificial programs of canal construction undertaken that significantly altered natural drainage patterns. More commonly, inhabitants of the region settled in discontinuous enclaves, indicating that population levels were low in relation to the potentially arable area. Water rather than land was the critical determinant, and so the network of permanent settlements closely adjoined a largely natural system of meandering, bifurcating, and rejoining distributaries. To be sure, these natural watercourses were periodically diked, straightened, and artificially maintained, and they certainly supplied numerous artificial canal offtakes leading into nearby fields.

It must be stressed that this traditional system offered little security about the availability of water during the winter growing season. Large variations in flow, capriciously supplemented with variations in the small but often crucial local rainfall, still produce alternating periods of abundance and suffering today. In earlier times, before the widespread introduction of pumps and the construction of permanently effective weirs and regulators, these variations were much more devastating. Particularly during periods of political fragmentation and instability, shifts in the balance of flow between various channels—whether naturally or artificially induced is immaterial—would have precipitated abrupt declines in the sustaining capacity of the land that were entirely beyond the possibilities of control by local cultivators. The history of the region accordingly has been punctuated by a rapid ebb and flow of population into better watered districts. Even the major towns were correspondingly subject to sudden shifts in their economic strength, as well as in the size of the population that could be mobilized for military purposes.

Chronic uncertainties about the availability of irrigation water had another, quite opposed effect that had more serious consequences in earlier times than in the Warka region today. Coming in the late spring, the Euphrates floods are badly timed to be of any assistance in the agricultural growing cycle; in fact, they represent only a source of danger to the mature field crops as they are about to be harvested. In the absence of modern regulatory mechanisms such as the Lake Habbānīya flood control scheme, and of the more extensive canal distribution system that has been developed in response to currently much higher population levels in lower Iraq as a whole, the local impact of floods formerly was much more serious. As a result, seasonal and permanent swamps formed a much more conspicuous part of the ancient landscape. Their presence in now-desiccated regions east and north of Uruk may be indirectly inferred from our pre- and protohistoric settlement pattern data, and they were well attested in textual sources from the Third Dynasty of Ur and the Neo-Babylonian, Sassanian, and Islamic periods. Water impounded in the swamps was, of

course, largely beyond use with the available agricultural technology. On the other hand, the swamps supplied a variety of important subsistence and other resources, including fish, marsh fowl, reeds for basketry, mats, and building, and fodder for livestock. Rather than the circumscribed Maᶜdān area of the lower Tigris and Euphrates marshes of today, increasingly focused on the commercial production of water buffalo dairy products and reed mats for urban markets, we must think of the ancient pattern as one in which swamps, arid steppes, gardens, and fields were continuously interspersed. The traditional habitat, in short, was a complex mosaic of relatively small, shifting, interdependent areas in which the principal variable was the availability of water.

It follows that the growth of the great uninterrupted expanse of arid steppe that is now to be seen in the Warka region is an atypical phenomenon. The present pattern results in part from improved control of flooding and from more effective employment of the available flow during the remainder of the year through the use of pumps for irrigation. Extensive areas of dunes, which inhibit drainage and the reclamation of lands for cultivation, probably are an even more important contributing factor. At least in the enlarged areas they now occupy, dune formations appear to be a progressively accumulating product of wind erosion of elevated local land surfaces such as ancient, disused levees and settlements. On a considerably smaller scale, and for quite different reasons, arid steppes also occurred at times in earlier antiquity. Most notably, much of the region north and east of Uruk lay abandoned during the third and second millennia B.C. In that earlier instance, the rivalry of city-states situated along different Euphrates branches seems to have been the major factor that diverted both the settled rural population and its water supplies elsewhere. The interests of all the emergent cities converged on the formation along the disputed frontiers between them of broad, empty zones suitable only for small groups of pastoralists.

Having traced the relatively enduring natural features of the Warka landscape, we can now briefly recapitulate the developments accompanying its earliest extensive settlement, as well as the crucial phase of urbanization which followed. As currently known, the record of human occupation extends well back into the fifth millennium B.C. Until perhaps the middle of the fourth millennium, however, it seems to have consisted of only a small handful of widely dispersed villages and small towns. Of Uruk itself, little more can be said than that the site surely was occupied for most of this interval; probably the site had already become a center of some prominence by the end of it.

The great transformation began with the Uruk period, around the middle of the fourth millennium. Small rural settlements began to increase in frequency in Early Uruk times, and it is likely that the ceremonial precincts of Uruk (or of Eanna and Kullab, if later literary references imply that those were once separate corporate entities within what subsequently became a single urban area) more or less contemporaneously attained monumental size. Only with the Late Uruk period, however, came a swift increase in the number of settlements by a full order of magnitude. The rapidity of this increase, the substitution of a markedly clustered pattern of small sites for the earlier, dispersed pattern of somewhat larger ones, and perhaps the technological and stylistic reorientation evident in Uruk pottery, all seem to point to a massive shift from seminomadism to a more settled way of life or possibly to an infusion of new population elements into the region. Although Uruk surely became a center of major importance during this period, its architectural emphasis and forms of extramural influence were still predominantly theocratic rather than political. Moreover, it was isolated, perhaps even unique. The baseline for the subsequent Urban Revolution in southern Mesopotamia, as a linked growth of the political institutions associated with the dynastic city-state and of the administrative and economic institutions of a class society,[1] accordingly is to be found in the Uruk period.

The data of the Warka Survey concern primarily the nonurban components of settlement patterns in the region. We are further handicapped in accounting for basic demographic trends by the limited extent of excavations outside Uruk, and by the focus of the archaeological program at that site almost exclusively on its central ceremonial precincts. On the other hand, there is no reason to doubt that trends toward urban growth both profoundly influenced and were intimately dependent upon changes in the organization and density of settlements in the neighboring countryside. In addition, fairly detailed (although admittedly unsystematic) surface inspection of the ruins of Uruk supplements what is known from excavations. To judge from what is known, Uruk seems to have attained its maximum urban size in a process of rapid growth during the Early Dynastic I period, approximately at the time of the initial construction of its great outer wall and when Enmerkar is said to have "built" the city. Linking this with the results of reconnaissance, a reasonably consistent picture of some previously unrecognized aspects of the urban transformation can be formulated.

The central fact which emerges is that Uruk and its sister cities grew through the depopulation of the countryside around them. From a predominantly rural pattern of settlement in the Late Uruk period, with the great bulk of the population residing in hamlets, villages, and small towns, the Warka region had been transformed by late Early Dynastic times into an overwhelmingly urban one. This change was of course accompanied by a steep decline in the number of occupied places, with whole districts seemingly abandoned as their inhabitants were persuaded or compelled to migrate to the cities.

For reasons set forth more fully in chapter 2, population estimates must remain extremely tentative. As is suggested there, however, the population of Uruk may have grown from 10,000 or so in Jemdet Nasr times to perhaps four times that number in the Early Dynastic I period. Other urban centers in the region, headed by Umma in rank order of size and political importance, seem to have been somewhat later in development as well as considerably smaller.

Even aside from the formation of cities, we can discern a progressive increase in the average size of other settlements. Equally important, the normal unimodal distribution of small sites in the Late Uruk period gives way during the Jemdet Nasr and Early Dynastic I periods to a well-developed hierarchy of differentiated site sizes. Since Uruk retained or even strengthened its preponderant importance during this interval, these newly developing local centers are not to be understood as independent rivals to it. Instead, they apparently reflect the extension into the countryside around Uruk of a new series of economic or administrative networks. Undoubtedly subordinate to the city, these increasingly complex networks fostered a growing differentiation between small, subservient peasant communities and larger settlements that also housed social, economic, or administrative elites identified with each district. It is not improbable, of course, that such districts also were differentiated from one another by ethnic features or by presumed bonds of common descent or local affinity. An attempt is made in figure 8 to delineate these districts provisionally on the assumption that small hamlets are more likely to have been subordinated to the town nearest them than to any other.

Not unnaturally, the presence of Uruk tended to inhibit the growth of a tiered hierarchy of subordinate towns and villages in its immediate vicinity. Out to a distance of about ten kilometers from the city there was little differentiation and the average size remained very small. Perhaps we may assume that within this range local elites would have elected to reside within the center of religious prestige and emerging political power. It is also possible that at least a few of the small sites close to the city were not primarily residential communities of local cultivators. Instead they may have served, for example, as specialized collecting depots, or as places of seasonal occupation by groups whose primary place of residence lay at Uruk itself from the Late Uruk period onward. Such

---

1. The author's views on this process are set forth in detail in *The Evolution of Urban Society: Early Mesopotamia and Prehispanic Mexico* (Chicago, 1966).

patterns of differentiation can only remain speculative, of course, until they can be tested with excavations and intensive, controlled surface collections.

The primary impulse toward urbanization seems to have culminated with the consolidation of Uruk as a new kind of centrally administered domain in the Early Dynastic I period. By that time, trends also must have been underway leading toward the formation of similar, ultimately competitive domains in districts too far away to be subject to its continuing, immediate influence. Shuruppak may have been one of these, if the tradition of an antediluvian dynasty there reflects an earlier political reality. Much larger and more significant was Umma, although less is known of trends in settlement in its vicinity because of dense formations of dunes.

To judge from a district south of Umma that lies outside the dune zone, the process of urban growth in this "secondary" case may have been considerably different. Here we find an area rapidly and intensively occupied only in Jemdet Nasr and Early Dynastic I times, and not beginning with a widespread array of small villages but instead with a densely clustered, linear arrangement of substantial towns. There is a more consciously planned aspect to this pattern of settlement than was true earlier in districts around Uruk, including its apparent placement along a canal fifteen kilometers or more in length for which there is no evidence of a natural antecedent watercourse. Distributional evidence makes clear that at least part of the population influx into this area must have come at the expense of areas formerly within the ambit of Uruk's authority. It is also clear that the entire pattern was only transitional. These towns all were abandoned after the Early Dynastic I period, their inhabitants presumably moving into Umma as the latter grew to become a major urban center.

With the abandonment of large tracts of rural settlement went a reduction in the number of small, natural watercourses that earlier had formed a bifurcating and rejoining network across the region. The new urban centers would have sought to concentrate the available supplies of water within districts subject to their immediate control. Within those districts, it is likely that a variety of control works were implemented along the major streams, shifting them along the continuum from natural rivers in the direction of artificial canals. To assure better protection, as well as to provide for economical transport of food supplies to the concentrated urban populace, there also must have been an intensive development of subsidiary canal systems as closely adjacent as possible to the centers themselves. Thus by late Early Dynastic times we may visualize an increasing emphasis on intensive cultivation around the urban centers, while other, formerly settled areas were allowed to retrograde to disused swamp and steppe.

Such is the pattern of initial urbanization that emerges from the data of the Warka Survey. How does it compare, we then must ask, with roughly coeval patterns in other regions? One would like to know more of comparably important areas like the kingdom of Lagash, for which, unfortunately, survey data are not yet available. But for those other areas currently known (in varying degrees of completeness), the main lines of similarity and contrast appear to be as follows.

Nearest at hand is the region centering on ancient Ur and Eridu; it lies to the south and southeast of the Warka region, adjoining the opposite backslope of the modern Euphrates meander-belt levee. In spite of proximity, the developmental sequences differ considerably. Fourteen sites of the Ubaid period have been identified in the vicinity of Ur, for the most part following the Warka pattern of a fairly regular, or at any rate nonclustered, distribution. Also as in the Warka region, small towns were present by this time at Ur and Eridu. The remainder of the sites, occupying a slightly larger aggregate area, are said to have been only rural villages and hamlets.[2]

Divergent developments seem to have followed quickly in spite of this roughly similar base line. The massive infusion of clustered rural sites around Uruk in the Uruk period had no parallel farther south and southeast, where small settlements of this period are described as "rare." Like Uruk, to be sure, Eridu went on at this time to become a large temple-centered town, although afterward it was abandoned as population became concentrated around Ur. By Early Dynastic I times settlements seemingly were confined to a small (ninety square kilometers) enclave, including the town of Ur, covering about twenty hectares, one smaller town, three villages, and a small rural center.[3] This constriction of the settled area, coupled with the relatively slight growth of the largest population center, contrasts with trends concurrently under way at Uruk. It may argue that Uruk was drawing in some rural population even from as far away as the hinterlands of Ur, at a distance of forty or fifty kilometers.

A truly urban phase seems to have come to Ur only in the later Early Dynastic period, at a time when Uruk had shrunk considerably in size. Wright estimates the area and population of Ur at this time as about fifty hectares and 10,000 inhabitants, much smaller than Uruk at its maximum. Whereas the decline of rural settlement around Uruk continued progressively throughout the Early Dynastic period, Wright has found a somewhat more complex picture around Ur that included the abandonment

2. H. T. Wright, "The Administration of Rural Production in an Early Mesopotamian Town," University of Michigan, *Anthropological Papers* 38 (1969): 25, and fig. 2.
3. Ibid., p. 27.

of certain zones while elsewhere rural centers and estates possibly were being newly founded.[4]

In general then, the region around Ur and Eridu seems to have been less strongly affected by an early phase of intensive rural settlement than the region around Uruk. Moreover, the Ur-Eridu region was substantially later in becoming urbanized, and never carried the process of city growth (and consequent abandonment of the countryside) to the extremes seen at Uruk. In this sense, the Ur region resembles the northern limits of the Mesopotamian alluvium somewhat more closely than it does the districts around Warka that are directly adjacent to it .

The principal body of data available for the northern part of the plain concerns the lower Diyala region. Some correction must be noted at once in the published account of settlement patterns there during the Ubaid and Uruk periods, as a result of an earlier misapprehension of the dating of clay sickles. These very common artifacts are now known not only to have occurred in the Ubaid period (as assumed in the Diyala study) but to have remained immensely popular through at least the Uruk period. Hence only sites with Ubaid painted pottery as well as clay sickles can be reasonably ascribed to the Ubaid period, whereas sites where only sickles were found are more likely to be of Uruk or even later date. On this basis, the twenty-two Ubaid sites originally described as having been found in the Diyala region should be reduced to nine. The observation that all of them were small is of course not changed by the reduction in number, but it can no longer be maintained that they "tended to cluster loosely in linear enclaves in the southern part of the lower Diyala basin."[5] Instead, the configuration of the reduced number is very similar to what has been described for the Ubaid period around Uruk and Ur. Throughout the Mesopotamian plain, it appears, Ubaid sites tend to be isolated at considerable distances from one another rather than clustered.

The clustered pattern previously ascribed to the Ubaid period appeared in the Diyala region only in Uruk and Jemdet Nasr times. From a total of nine widely dispersed sites, the number increased to forty-three, now unquestionably grouped into enclaves. Although not permitting a precise comparison, the available data strongly suggest that the bulk of this increase came only in the Jemdet Nasr period rather than earlier. Excavations in the Diyala region make it apparent that by late Jemdet Nasr times at least a few of the larger sites were no longer villages but

towns, with temples and other public buildings. This extension in the size and number of settlements seems to continue uninterrupted through most of the following Early Dynastic period, by the end of which the occupation pattern included ten large towns (over ten hectares), nineteen small towns, and sixty-seven villages.[6]

Contrasting these conditions along the branches of the ancient lower Diyala with those around Uruk, Ur, and Eridu, the foundation of large numbers of clustered or "contagiously distributed" settlements occurred in the Uruk area in Late Uruk times, in the Diyala region probably only in the subsequent Jemdet Nasr period, and in the neighborhood of Ur and Eridu not at all. Then, during the Early Dynastic period, the pattern in the Diyala region diverges from that around Uruk. There is little to suggest any further increase in the population of the Uruk region after Late Uruk or Jemdet Nasr times; instead, the predominant trend was toward concentration of the formerly dispersed population around a few major urban centers. On the other hand, in the Diyala region a very substantial increase continued through at least part of the Early Dynastic period, and no comparable trend toward urbanization occurred.

It appears that the Diyala counterpart of the highly nucleated city-states farther south followed a pattern that was more dispersed but no less durable. Small walled towns maintained local hegemony as district capitals, but the bulk of the population continued to reside in smaller towns and other rural settlements. Generalization about the Ur region may be somewhat premature, since relatively few sites have yet been reported there, but this reconstruction of the lower Diyala pattern is certainly at least as close to what has been described for Ur as the account of trends toward urbanization around Uruk. Granting that Ur may have shared with Uruk the corporate character of a Sumerian city-state rather than an Akkadian township, it was less than twice as large as northern provincial towns like Eshnunna and Tutub and only an eighth of the area of Uruk. And around it and associated with it, as we have seen, were at least a limited number of villages and rural centers. Centers of this kind were even more common in the north, whereas they were virtually absent around Uruk.

In the northern part of the alluvial plain between the Tigris and the Euphrates, ancient Akkad, conditions appear to have been roughly intermediate between those around Uruk and those in the Diyala region. As in both the latter areas, there was a rapid increase in the number of occupied sites during the Uruk and Jemdet Nasr periods. Subsequently there was at least a localized trend toward urbanization, culminating in the growth of a

4. Ibid.

5. R. McC. Adams, *Land behind Baghdad* (Chicago, 1965). A reexamination of the field records indicates that only the following sites in the Diyala numbered series still may be assigned unequivocally to the Ubaid period: 12, 244, 267, 397, 421, 515, 634, 818.

6. Ibid., p. 42.

single major city-state at Kish, while elsewhere systems of towns and villages continued as the characteristic units of settlement. Hence, unlike the Diyala region, there was some reduction in the total number of sites during the Early Dynastic period, although not as large a reduction as around Uruk.[7]

Slightly farther south, in the vicinity of ancient Nippur, conditions were different again. The surveyed area is particularly small in this case, and so there may be danger of overgeneralizing from what were only fairly local clusterings or abandonments related to minor shifts in the watercourse system. However, the available evidence at least suggests that clustered rural settlements made their appearance as early as the Early Uruk period, whereas by Jemdet Nasr times occupation of such sites had essentially come to an end. Thus there may have been a rapid concentration of population in towns or cities like Nippur and Abū Salabikh by the Jemdet Nasr period, somewhat earlier than the same process occurred at the great cities of southern Sumer like Uruk.

Finally, we may consider briefly the upper Khuzestan plains in southwestern Iran, the area around the ancient Elamite capital of Susa. Rural population in this geographical extension of the Mesopotamian alluvium reportedly reached its apogee by the Susa A period or even earlier, by which time also there is some evidence that Susa itself had become a regional center of substantial size. Intensive recent work may modify the published findings of an earlier survey,[8] but during the subsequent Susa B and C periods an abrupt decline in the number of sites suggests a decline in settled population in spite of a marked increase in average settlement size. Susa A must continue into or even through the Early Uruk period in southern Mesopotamia, and B and C are roughly contemporaneous with Late Uruk and Jemdet Nasr. Hence a densely clustered pattern of small rural settlements appeared at least as early in Khuzestan as in any other portion of the plain yet identified. Processes of urbanization and concurrent abandonment of rural areas also began early in Khuzestan, perhaps at about the same time as in the Nippur region and ahead of southern Sumer. However, the significance of Khuzestan's slight priority with regard to certain trends affecting community patterning should not be overemphasized. The evidence thus far available from early texts and excavations does not suggest that this putative priority extended into other realms

such as technological or administrative complexity. Moreover, neither the size of Susa nor the scale of monumental construction there ever approached that at Uruk. And Uruk was only one of a number of contending Sumerian city-states, whereas all the resources of Elam seem to have been concentrated at Susa.

Drawing together these necessarily brief and perhaps superficial comparisons, it is clear that the aspects of the Urban Revolution in Mesopotamia involving demographic changes and shifts in community patterning did not follow a single, simple paradigm. Even where similar trends seem to have occurred in the same order in different parts of the alluvium, their onsets and terminations seldom were closely in phase. From this it seems certain that future accounts of the growth of Mesopotamian civilization will need to reckon with far greater local differences and variability than have customarily been considered. The history of the growth of a particular town or city for which textual and archaeological data happen to be available cannot even serve adequately as a loose metaphor for the development of civilization within the entire region.

It may be reasonable to simplify the picture slightly by excluding ancient Elam. One justification for doing so is the presence of an entirely different adaptation there, less dependent on irrigation than on rainfall agriculture and with a distinctively mixed society that balanced sedentary cultivators with transhumant herdsmen.[9] So also, at a different level, are the pervasive stylistic differences between the proto-Elamite artifact inventory and its southern Mesopotamian counterparts. To an even greater degree than stylistic differences, the development of an independent Elamite language and script argues for a minimum of direct contact and intermixing between the population of that area and the Sumero-Akkadian population occupying the greater part of the alluvium to the west. Even within the Iraqi portion of the lower Mesopotamian plain, however, it must be conceded that the processes of development summarized above are as noteworthy for their regional differences as for their common features.

Perhaps the most widely recurring similarity is an initial rapid, pronounced rise in rural settlement. The earlier pattern, continuing through at least the Ubaid period, is one of widely dispersed sites. This was replaced by a much denser, more or less highly clustered pattern in which large numbers of small villages or hamlets are found grouped closely together. In the Warka area, such a transformation occurred at the beginning of Late Uruk times. Around Nippur it may have been slightly earlier,

7. McG. Gibson, "The City and Area of Kish," including appendix by R. McC. Adams, "Settlement and Irrigation Patterns in Ancient Akkad," in *Field Research Projects* (Coconut Grove, Florida; in press).

8. H. T. Wright, personal communication; cf. R. McC. Adams, "Agriculture and Urban Life in Early Southwestern Iran," *Science* 136 (1962): 109–22.

9. R. McC. Adams, "The Study of Ancient Mesopotamian Settlement Patterns and the Problem of Urban Origins," *Sumer* 25(1970):111–24.

while still farther north, in the Diyala region, it appears to have been delayed until the subsequent Jemdet Nasr period. But whatever these disparities in date, the suddenness in the increase in the number of sites and the accompanying reduction in average size suggest something more than the hiving off of new villages from old ones as a result of any natural rise in population. Either the adoption of a more settled way of life by formerly migratory folk or some form of fairly large-scale immigration into the alluvium appears to be indicated.

Although the arrival of at least some new population elements seems likely, this provides little help with identifying them or their source. They might already have been advanced sedentary cultivators elsewhere, merely migrating with their skills into a new, lightly populated, and very promising region. On the other hand, it is no less likely that their earlier subsistence patterns tended more in the direction of hunting, herding, or collecting in a near-desert setting to the west or south. Such areas and pursuits would have become increasingly untenable as the post-Pleistocene climate slowly became more arid. In the latter case, the newcomers would have had to acquire the greater part of their agricultural knowledge from the residents of the scattered Ubaid townships on the alluvium who preceded them. It is of course a possibility—on the slight available evidence one cannot claim it is more than that—that the new arrivals were speakers of the language later to be identified as Sumerian.

To the degree that this initial intensification of settlement in much of the alluvium (but apparently excluding at least some districts, like that around Ur and Eridu) must be traced to massive population movements, several possible lines of explanation appear for subsequent trends toward urbanization. One arises from what must have been at least a transient scarcity of land that confronted the new settlers in spite of seemingly low overall population densities. The indigenous inhabitants surely first appropriated the areas that were most favorable for irrigation agriculture at existing, fairly primitive levels of technique. Later arrivals, forced to deal with the remainder, would have found large areas locked in swamps or inaccessible to available sources of water. Of course, many of these conditions could be rectified when time and the slow development of new technology permitted more ambitious drainage, flood control, and irrigation projects. But the initial effect would have been to greatly accentuate differences among the inhabitants of the area in the relative degrees of control over land and water, the crucial resources of agricultural production.

To state the matter differently, reconnaissance findings in the Warka region and elsewhere prompt a reconsideration of the role of "population pressure" as an important historical variable. In an earlier appraisal, the then available evidence seemed to show that:

appreciable population increases generally followed, rather than preceded, the core processes of the Urban Revolution. Particularly in Mesopotamia, where the sedentary village pattern seems to have been stabilized for several millennia between the establishment of effective food production and the "take-off" into urbanism, it may be noted that there is simply no evidence for gradual population increases that might have helped to precipitate the Urban Revolution after reaching some undefined threshhold.[10]

Now the evidence of widespread substantial, rapid increases makes that formulation no longer acceptable. Moreover, the idea of population pressure clearly need not imply the gross imbalance of a whole society's food intake requirements over its available food supplies. Even if only a portion of the immigrant population found itself unable to secure the resources to meet its own subsistence needs, the dislocation arising from their depressed socio-economic position would have engendered or profoundly reinforced trends toward the establishment of class-stratified dynastic states. Such groups also would have tended at times to resort to brigandage, or even to more formally organized attacks on neighboring communities that were favorably situated but nonetheless vulnerable. The result would be a decrease in the security of the countryside, further encouraging a process of urban concentration that played directly into the hands of the new elites who were dominant in the cities.

Urban concentration was, at any rate, the next major trend that comes to light, not only in the data of the Warka Survey but also in other areas of Sumer. The formidable fact is that, within the space of no more than a few centuries, dwellers in small towns and rural settlements all over southern Mesopotamia overwhelmingly either chose to abandon conditions of rural insecurity with which they could no longer cope or were compelled to do so by the emerging military and administrative elites who were the chief protagonists (and beneficiaries) of the formation of walled city-states. And for this trend at least, Uruk was one of the very largest and earliest examples and hence may serve as a paradigm or prototype. We have traced in detail how it grew by devouring its hinterlands. However indissolubly wedded to city life the Sumerians and their Akkadian successors later may have become, this evidence suggests that the initial appearance of the urban settlement form was forced rather than natural.

With the full attainment of an urban way of life in the Warka region by the Early Dynastic period, it is less useful to continue systematic comparisons with other parts of the Mesopotamian plain. The greater continuity of occupation at later sites, as well as technical problems

---

10. Adams, *The Evolution of Urban Society*, pp. 44–45.

of dating the ceramics, for the most part have meant that the remains of later periods can be studied with survey techniques only more impressionistically and less completely. Perhaps even more important, a reconstruction of settlement patterns from reconnaissance is intrinsically of less importance after the proliferation of textual sources makes genuine historiography possible.

In any case, there is a later radical reduction in the divergences between developmental paths followed in different regions. Differences in the density and configuration of settlements continue to occur in later periods, but increasingly they become differences of degree rather than of kind. Surely contributing to this convergence were the more inclusive, better coordinated forms of political and economic administration that were imposed upon broad areas of the alluvium by a succession of later states and empires. Cumulative changes in the technology of agricultural subsistence probably also affected settlement patterns throughout the area in similar ways. No attempt can be made to survey themes of this kind here, however, since they are virtually as comprehensive as the later history of the area. A brief overview of the later sequences of change within the Warka region can only illustrate the application in microcosm of trends that probably prevailed much more widely.

The primacy of southern Mesopotamia with respect to the development of cities contained throughout the third millennium B.C. and even into the second. Upon closer inspection, to be sure, this seemingly impressive continuity dissolves at virtually every site into a number of local phases of urban extension and retrenchment. The Akkadian and Gutian periods, in particular, are not well represented in surface collections made throughout the region. Interrupted by brief intervals of local prosperity or political ascendancy like the so-called Fourth Dynasty of Uruk, the cities are likely to have shrunk back to vestigial urban populations dwelling within the crumbling shell of their unmaintained outer walls. Then at other periods, above all during the Third Dynasty of Ur and the later hegemony of Larsa, powerful kings and secure conditions quickened the pulse of urban reconstruction and resettlement.

It is interesting to note that urban and rural settlement tended to be stimulated under the same auspices. The increased number of outlying small towns and villages noted in the Warka region during periods of strong political consolidation probably reflects the application of conscious state policies to force nomads and semi-nomadic groups into sedentary pursuits. With this went a concomitant extension of the system of lateral canals leading inland from the main trunk waterways, both to provide for an enlarged agricultural population and to take advantage of cultivable areas where the former hazards of raiding and brigandage had been largely

eliminated. Under the same circumstances, urban dwellers who formerly would have journeyed considerable distances to seek the protection of their walls now might elect to take up residence closer to their fields. Yet the important point is that, in spite of these centrifugal tendencies, the cities also flourished during times of political centralization and stability.

It has been argued that these periods of florescence held the seeds of their own subsequent decay. Under conditions of high summer heat and aridity, and of minimal surface slope and subsurface drainage, irrigation agriculture inevitably is accompanied by progressive salinization. A number of converging lines of evidence, including declining crop yields, shifts to the cultivation of more salt-tolerant crops, and explicit records of growing areas excluded from cultivation because of salt, all point to a cumulative, extremely destructive process of salinization in the late third and early second millennia B.C.[11] Such a process would have been accelerated by the improvement and enlargement of the irrigation network, and by lengthening periods of stability during which it could be operated without disruption.

In the sequel, although surely only in part for this reason, political hegemony shifted northward to Babylon under Hammurabi and his successors. Around Warka as elsewhere, a predominantly urban pattern of settlement disappeared forever from southern Iraq. Individual cities continued in occupation for varying periods, maintaining where and to the degree they could the traditional urban institutions and occupations that had been associated with them. But throughout the alluvial plain, in the south no less than in the north, Cassite and Middle Babylonian times saw a massive retraction in the frontiers of cultivation and an equally decisive decline in the proportion of settlement that may be considered in any sense urban. Even in the Neo-Babylonian period, in spite of a return of political stability and of the intensive development of large-scale date plantations as a mode of agriculture well suited to the environmental conditions, we have seen that the population of centers like Uruk apparently attained only a fraction of its former levels.

Developments in the Warka region following the Neo-Babylonian period also are consistent with patterns obtaining throughout the Mesopotamian alluvium. The Parthian, and to still greater extent the Sassanian, period everywhere saw an intensification and extension of irrigation to its furthest limits. Probably more significant than any increase in the gross area under cultivation was the transformation of the system into a planned, essentially artificial one. Earlier practices for the most part had in-

11. T. Jacobsen and R. McC. Adams, "Salt and Silt in Ancient Mesopotamian Agriculture," *Science* 128 (1958): 1251–58.

volved the construction of no more than lateral offtakes, from streams maintaining a natural equilibrium with their floodplains. For such systems to continue without quickly choking up with silt, only a limited portion of the flow of the primary waterways normally would be diverted into the fields for agricultural purposes. Now whole districts were brought under cultivation through straight (non-meandering), entirely artificial, branching canal systems that included an increasingly differentiated hierarchy of major trunk canals and secondary and tertiary distributors. Annual desilting hence became an indispensable requirement for the maintenance of the entire system, rather than merely for its minor effluents. The need to follow the natural northwest-southeast drainage patterns declined as this became institutionalized, so that some of the major components of later systems were designed to flow at right angles to virtually all earlier patterns.

These trends have been noted and described previously in regions as diverse as the alluvial fan of the lower Diyala and the upper Khuzestan plains.[12] Their application to the Warka region is somewhat obscured by the advance of swamps in late Parthian and Sassanian times, apparently as a result of natural hydrological or tectonic changes with which not even large-scale, state-financed economic enterprises could cope. But the new configuration of settlements and canal systems in the parts of the Warka region that remained habitable makes clear that there too the system was undergoing essentially the same transformation as elsewhere.

Surveys on the Diyala and upper Khuzestan plains suggest that the apogee of settlement generally was attained during the late Sassanian period, followed by an abrupt, extensive decline during the disorders accompanying the collapse of Persian rule before the Arab onslaught. Subsequently there was a partial recovery, followed by a protracted but irregular decline to still lower population levels and areas cultivated during the last few centuries of the ʿAbbāsid Caliphate. The Mongol invasion seems to have dealt no more than the coup de grace to an urban civilization whose roots in rural agriculture had already withered.[13]

However, gross generalizations like these fail to take into account the reemergence for a time of substantial regional differences. On the lower Diyala plains, for example, the selection of Baghdad for the ʿAbbāsid capital only a little more than a century after the fall of Ctesiphon suggests that continuity of settlement may have been the dominant theme. Elsewhere, the founding of new Arab cities like Basra, Kūfa, and Wāsit may imply that major emphasis in the Early Islamic period was placed on urban

and agricultural development in formerly marginal regions, perhaps because the rights and claims of the indigenous inhabitants there could be more easily ignored or overridden. Within the area of the reconnaissance around Warka, the process of abandonment before the advancing waters of the Great Swamp merely accelerated. In fact, there is so little evidence of an occupation in this region during classical Islamic times that comparison with other regions probably is meaningless. Quite possibly most of its remaining population at the end of the Sassanian period later was drawn off to swell the growth of these new urban centers and their agricultural hinterlands.

The final chapter in the history of the Warka region is the slow process of resettlement that began in late Ottoman times. Again the pattern is a common one, varying only in detail according to the strengths of individual tribal units and their degree of exposure to Ottoman power emanating from Baghdad. After World War I, and especially in more recent years, the pace of agricultural expansion has quickened. However, these recent developments take place in the context of modern statehood. They also reflect the impact of entirely unprecedented, externally derived economic and technological forces. Hence they are not a part of the long series of evolving configurations of local settlement that have been the central subject of this discussion.

Our sequence thus may be said to end not very differently than it began, with petty tribes squabbling over rights to land and water along ephemeral swamps and streams in an otherwise harshly arid landscape. The difference is, of course, that in the earlier case the groups in question found and used the keys to one of humanity's small handful of truly decisive advances. Five millennia later, groups that may have included their remote descendants could claim none but the most circumscribed, local leadership. In any wider perspective, they were bitterly engaged in holding off a world whose accelerating changes they regarded as almost wholly inimical to their interests—in defending a position of deeply entrenched historical backwardness.

As we have seen, the explanation for the ironic parallels between these conditions is not the absence here of massive change and even upheaval, in which many intervening generations played a part. We have to deal not with five millennia of stagnation but with the tragic return of a wheel to the point of its beginning, under the pressure of larger external forces than the inhabitants of this region could cope with. The tribesmen at the end of our story were held in check by the remote and largely ineffective regime of a crumbling empire, but still a regime that commanded more decisive forces than they could ordinarily bring to bear even in concert. Perhaps in the earlier case it was precisely the absence of any counter-

12. Adams, "Agriculture and Urban life in Early Southwestern Iran," pp. 116–17; *Land behind Baghdad*, pp. 74–79.
    13. Ibid., pp. 105–7.

93

vailing force of this kind that encouraged local villagers and townsmen to exercise their ingenuity in devising larger and more complex settlements and social combinations.

Several ruined cities that arose from their efforts may be seen in the distance from almost any high dune on the plains around Warka. Generally they can be distinguished by the high, swelling irregularity of their summits, and often also by the faint shadow of fallen brickwork. Around them the land and sky usually merge as clouds of dust obscure the horizon. To generate the proportions of distance, there is little more than a rare cluster of black tents or a slowly moving file of camels. The potentialities of this monochromatic, limitless, unresisting landscape are difficult for the traveler to discern; yet he knows that they are still held dear, fought over, and patiently labored for. Then the dust subsides momentarily and another subtle shadow hints at the riverine sinews of past and future: a line of tamarisks hovers on the edge of focus, their roots groping for moisture in the bed of an ancient canal while their last lacy branches disappear beneath encroaching dunes.

Here once, in a brief but heroic age, the need, the means, and the will converged to shape the first urban society. One can share with Gilgamesh the pride he felt in Uruk's ramparts, of which the epic sings. Even as ruins in an empty desolation, it is his city—and the endless line of its successors—that brings him the immortality man could not obtain otherwise.

2| Analysis of Archaeological Surface Collections
Hans J. Nissen

7 | Typological Dating Criteria

The main purpose of this chapter is to present and discuss the dating indicators for the different periods. No general discussion of the periods is intended—in a sense even the opposite is true, as the stress has to be laid here on the features which separate the periods, rather than on those which show continuity.

Since only pottery is abundant enough on the surface of any site and shows enough change through time to aid in identifying characteristic features, only pottery was used for dating. Consequently only pottery will be discussed here, and of this find category we will consider only those types which we actually used for establishing the date of the sites.

The discussion is somewhat uneven, in that the pottery of the earlier periods is discussed more intensively than the pottery of the periods after Early Dynastic I. This is a result of both a larger body of material for the earlier periods and the greater uniformity of the later pottery. Within these earlier periods emphasis is given to the discussion of the "mass-produced types" of the periods from Early Uruk through Early Dynastic I. The importance of this group for dating was discovered only shortly before our survey, and reliance on these wares during our survey helped to demonstrate the validity of the ideas about mass-produced pottery.

A short introductory note is necessary in regard to the designations of the periods used in the following discussion. Mainly, the most commonly accepted terms are used, following Edith Porada's outline,[1] though the separating lines drawn there did not always fit our finds.

Agreeing with her that the proposal of a new terminology only confuses the issues even more, we abstained from proposing a new system.[2] The only change we felt was necessary is the subdivision of the Uruk period. Owing to the lack of scientifically controlled excavations covering this entire time span outside of Uruk, any subdivision has to be based on what little is known from Uruk. There, the pottery sequence from the deep-sounding unfortunately offers too many possibilities for subdivisions, so that any system is based on equally well-founded distinctions.[3] In the absence of any quantitative approach to the pottery or other evidence favoring one line of distinction over the other, we found ourselves unable to follow the scheme proposed by Porada, which divides the Uruk period into Early, Middle, and Late Uruk. In particular, we were unable to accept her dividing line between Middle and Late Uruk between the Archaic levels VI and V in the deep-sounding,[4] as there is no evidence from Uruk that this point marks anything which could be taken as the basis for introducing a new subdivision. Instead we relied entirely on the distribution of the earliest mass-produced pottery, the beveled-rim bowls, since in our surface pottery there was a clear distinction within the Uruk pottery between one assemblage of features which always is associated with the frequent appearance of the beveled-rim bowls and another assemblage which is not

---

1. Edith Porada, "The Relative Chronology of Mesopotamia I," in *Chronologies in Old World Archaeology*, ed. R. W. Ehrich (Chicago: University of Chicago Press, 1965), p. 133 and charts on p. 175.

2. Porada, "Relative Chronology," p. 134.

3. The pottery from the deep-sounding is published in A. Nöldeke, "Vierter Vorläufiger Bericht über die . . . ," in *Uruk unternommenen Ausgrabungen* (Berlin, 1932) (henceforth *UVB* IV), plates 16–20.

4. There is no clear distinction between the pottery of VI and V (*UVB* IV, pl. 19–20), and that we know major architectural remains only from as far down as level V is due entirely to the excavation process, as large-area excavations did not penetrate beyond level V.

connected with this mass-produced type.[5] That this is a temporal distinction is shown by the fact that the one assemblage without the mass-produced type finds its closest parallels in Eanna XII to VII. Thus our material allows only for two subdivisions of the Uruk period, Early and Late Uruk, with the dividing line somewhere in or around Archaic level VII.

UBAID I-II (Eridu–Hajji Mohammed)

These two periods, or rather subphases, of the Ubaid period are known in stratigraphical context only from the lowest layers in Eridu,[6] the material of which still remains largely unpublished. It is therefore almost impossible to separate the pottery of these phases from each other, and to find out shapes or patterns which are used exclusively in one of them. Although the pottery from one or the other of our sites left the impression of belonging more to the older or more to the later stage, this cannot be confirmed. Another serious obstacle was that we found very few sites of these periods. Thus it was impossible to work out a differentiation from internal criteria of the surface pottery.

It cannot be more than an assumption that the sunburst pattern painted on the interior of large dishes and the double rims are indicators of the later part of the early Ubaid stages.[7]

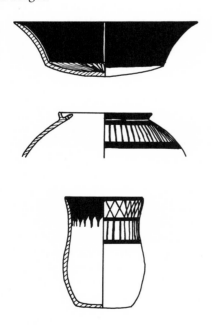

We observed two different kinds of ware in the pottery, but found no way of separating them either in time or in the patterns used. The one kind is very highly fired and often gives the impression of china. The colors are often burned in deeply, the edges of the patterns being unsharp. Tempering consists of very fine sand.

All vessels are hand formed. Main types are a high tall beaker with sinous sides, and a large open dish.

The colors range all the way from buff to yellowish to greenish. Although painting is monochrome, contrasts are achieved deliberately by different thickness of the applied paint. Colors of the painted designs are black, dark brown, brown, yellow, purple, sepia, and dark green.

Special attention is called to site 298, where besides a few sherds of the above-mentioned kinds, sherds of a different kind of pottery have been found, which was not previously known from southern Iraq. In particular, there are two fragments of dishes on high hollow bases, with the interior of the dishes painted in a way distinctly different from what we know about Ubaid. In addition to

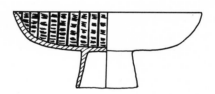

these fragments there were many sherds of open bowls decorated inside and outside with pendant triangles made of parallel lines. Shapes and patterns point to the pottery found in the Mandali area, and ultimately to Sāmarrā.[8] The ware is much cruder than the Ubaid wares, the tempering sand being fine to medium fine, and the ware seems to be fired at a lower temperature than the Ubaid pottery. The color of the sherd is buff, with a buff to creamy slip occasionally applied before the painting.

UBAID III (Standard Ubaid)

It is not easy to separate this phase from either the earlier or the later ones, for the same reasons mentioned before. Yet a bit more is known and thus the identification of sites of this phase is possible to a certain extent. The finer ware of Ubaid I–II comes to an end, as do details like the sunburst pattern and the double rims. Patterns used in Ubaid III are much more elaborate than those in Ubaid IV.

The ware resembles most closely that of the previous phases which was fired at a lower temperature. Sometimes a black core can be observed. All vessels are hand formed

---

5. See the discussion below in this chapter.

6. The latest summary of the pottery of these layers can be found in J. Oates, "Ur, Eridu, and Prehistory," *Iraq,* vol. 22.

7. Cf. Ch. Ziegler, "Die Keramik der Qalᶜa des Haǧǧi Mohammed," *Ausgr. in Uruk* vol. 5, pl. 31; D. Stronach, "Ras el-ᶜAmiya," *Iraq,* vol. 23, pl. 48–49, 53–54.

---

8. See the detailed discussion of site 298 in chapter 8.

and tempered with fine sand. In most cases the color of the ware is greenish, but there are also, very rarely, buff sherds. There are no distinctive shapes. The main types are open shapes like beakers, dishes, or bowls. In most cases the patterns consist of horizontal bands with geometrical designs in the space between. Painting is concentrated on the upper part of the vessels.

There are few cases of painting in colors other than black or very dark green, primarily in a kind of sepia color.[9]

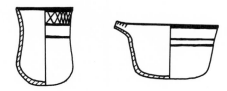

UBAID IV (Late Ubaid–Eanna Archaic Levels XVIII–XV)

In many instances a separation of Ubaid III and IV is difficult, if not impossible, but there seem to be some innovations both in shape and in design. The tendency toward simplification in design has already been mentioned. Often one or two bands of black paint are the only decoration, or at most a garland pendant from the rim.

A wide open dish with flattened inverted rim seems to be new. The interior of these dishes is often entirely or mostly covered with black paint. Another specialty are dishes or open bowls, the lower part of the interior of which is scratched by a blunt comblike instrument, using a circular movement.

In addition to the above-mentioned items there probably were in the Ubaid IV pottery early examples of the Uruk ware, as in the lower levels of Eanna.[10] But since most of our Ubaid IV sites continued to be inhabited at least into the Early Uruk period, there is no way of telling from our material.

THE EARLY MASS-PRODUCED POTTERY TYPES

Sherds of these wares[11] were the primary basis for our distinction of the periods from Late Uruk through Early Dynastic I, and hence deserve a special discussion. They belong to three main types of open bowls, which can be well separated from each other chronologically. On a number of sites they make up 50 percent or more of the total sherd collection, providing an opportunity to date these sites from the sherds of the mass-produced types only. From what we know, the "beveled-rim bowls" are confined to the Uruk period and give way abruptly to the "conical cups" at the beginning of Jemdet Nasr; the latter remain in mass use through Early Dynastic II. The tallest variant form of these conical cups, the "solid-footed goblet," makes its appearance at the beginning of Early Dynastic I and becomes the hallmark of that period, disappearing at its end.

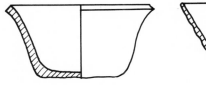

The beveled-rim bowl is easily recognized from its obliquely cut rim. It is a bowl made in a form, of heavily chaff-tempered clay, and is rather brittle. Most vessels are of a dirty yellowish color. The conical cup is made on the wheel of rather fine, sand-tempered clay, has a thinning out, rounded rim, and is well fired. The vessels are reddish brown. Although quite different, the types have features in common which let us lump them together under one heading: they were all manufactured in vast numbers, rather carelessly, with no attempt to apply any finishing technique to their surface. The conical cups especially are made with a minimum of care, the bowls often having become badly warped during firing, although only in severe cases did this preclude their use.

Pottery of these types is found in many places in Babylonia and beyond, but probably owing to its ubiquity and extreme ugliness it has almost never received the attention it deserves. Almost nowhere is its stratigraphic position clearly established. There is essentially only one spot in Uruk where it has been possible to trace the relation of these types to each other and the other archaeological remains, in a trench connecting the Eanna district with the large platform under the latter Bit Resh.[12] Elsewhere

---

9. Whenever in the following discussions the term "sepia" is used, this refers only to the impression of the color. By no means is it intended to point to the organic origin of the paint, as the paint used was most probably of the same kind, which under slightly different firing temperatures also produced dark purple or dark brown.

10. *UVB* IV, p. 37.

11. A fuller discussion of this topic was contained in a paper read before the XVIIth Rencontre Assyriologique Internationale 1969 in Brussels. Good evidence for these questions is now available from the sounding in "K/L XII," in Uruk (*Bagh. Mitt.*, vol. 5, 1970).

12. Cf. E. Heinrich, *UVB* X, p. 29. In both earlier and later

the evidence is insufficient for a clear corroboration of the temporal sequence given above; however, nowhere does the evidence contradict it.[13]

The chronological sequence of these mass-produced types thus provides us with a reasonably firm chronological framework for the Late Uruk through Early Dynastic I periods, into which most of the sites inhabited during these periods can be fitted on the basis of the distribution of the mass-produced types alone. This applies particularly to the Late Uruk and Early Dynastic I periods, which are unmistakably defined by the presence of either beveled-rim bowls or solid-footed goblets. The weak point, however, is the Jemdet Nasr period, for the conical cups that first appear at this time also are found in the same shapes in Early Dynastic I and even later. To be sure, there are other kinds of pottery, a polychrome and a monochrome painted ware (cf. fig. 30 s and t) which are confined to the Jemdet Nasr period, but these are so rare that they cannot be expected to be found on every site inhabited during the Jemdet Nasr period. Thus the dating of a site in the Jemdet Nasr period cannot be confirmed from the evidence of the mass-produced pottery alone.

From the observation that a number of sites produced sherds of only a single mass-produced pottery type, the possibility emerged that they were occupied only during all or a part of a single period. Furthermore, starting from the known sequence of mass-produced types, wider pottery assemblages could be worked out. Ultimately, it was these more complex pottery assemblages that provided the basis for assigning sites to one or more periods. This approach was first worked out for Late Uruk through Early Dynastic I. Subsequently it was extended by the observation of sites which lacked not only painted Ubaid pottery but also Late Uruk beveled-rim bowls or other contemporary index fossils. Pottery from these sites was found to form a coherent assemblage of its own, with clear parallels in the pottery of Eanna Archaic levels XII–VII–Early Uruk. Thus we are able to speak also of sites occupied only during the Early Uruk period.

Figures 30 and 31 list the main components of the various pottery assemblages of the periods from Early Uruk through Early Dynastic I.

EARLY URUK (Eanna XIV–VIII/VII)—Figure 30 a-f

On a number of sites we found sherds apparently forming an assemblage which was clearly separated from the Ubaid pottery, but also from the pottery of Eanna VI–IV. Especially in terms of the mass-produced types, the difference from the later time is that beveled-rim bowls either are absent or occur only in very limited quantities.

The dating indicators are found in fig. 30 a-f. Particularly, there is the pointed-base bottle, vessels with long straight spouts or a very characteristic split spout. Many vessels are made on the fast wheel. Painting occurs, but is different from the Ubaid painting. The space between horizontal bands is covered by netlike ornaments, with triangles or lozenges left free by these designs often filled in by stippling. The color of the ware normally resembles that of the Ubaid wares, but is normally finer. Often a green slip is applied to the surface before painting. The color of the paint varies between black and dark green. About 90 percent of the pottery, however, is unpainted, being reddish to yellowish in color.

The closest parallels to this assemblage are found in Eanna XII–VII, but since certainly XIII and XIV cannot be separated from XII, we are taking this group to be contemporary with XIV–VIII or VII. The ambiguity of the end is a result of the insufficient evidence as to when the beveled-rim bowls made their mass appearance in Eanna.

LATE URUK (Eanna VII/IV)—Figure 30 g-q

There are close ties to the preceding phase, especially in the ware but also in shapes. However, there are also a number of innovations, predominantly in surface finishes such as rocker bands, reserved slip, ridges with finger impressions, and incising. Also, lumps of clay are sometimes applied to the surface, forming irregular patterns.

The most popular features, the beveled-rim bowls and the rope handles, are found in the Eanna sequence somewhat earlier than VII/VI, but are most abundant in levels VI–IV. The same applies to the drooping spouts.

Other typical shapes are small or big strap- or rope-handled cups, the handles being drawn out of the rim. The handle may also consist of two or three parallel ropes. Characteristic also are horizontal rope handles which usually are placed near the rim of big vessels opposite a vertical handle or another horizontal one. There may be continuity between these horizontal rope handles and ledge handholds, the upper part of which show parallel grooving imitating a rope.

Spouts attached to the rim and false spouts are peculiar to this period, as are long drooping spouts. Restricted to this period are thick, almost flat sherds with deep interior scoring which must have been the bottoms of large husking trays.

reports the conical cups were mixed with a much larger kind of cup, which typologically belongs in a different context. This confusion proved to be particularly detrimental, as this second kind ranges over different periods from the conical cups. (For a full discussion see "K/L XII" in *Bagh. Mitt.*, 5: 132–42.)

13. "Pottery from the Diyala Region," *OIP* 63, p. 39.

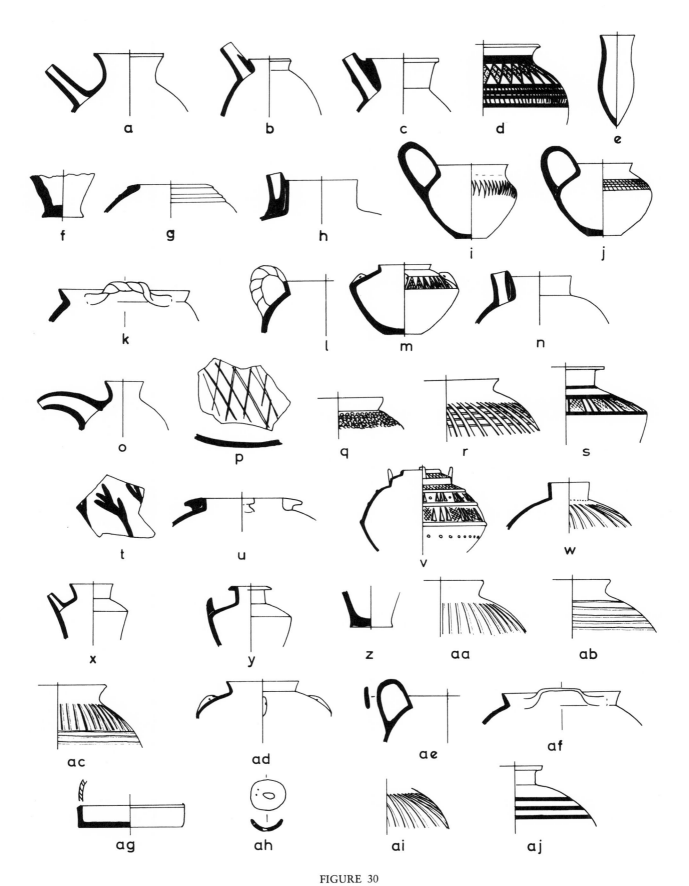

FIGURE 30

Pottery type chart: Early Uruk–Early Dynastic I

101

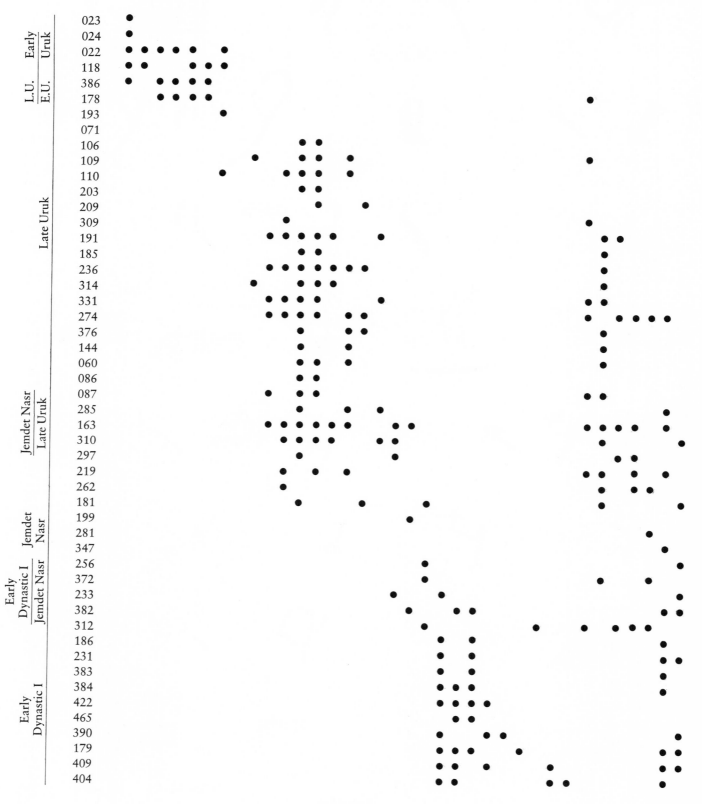

FIGURE 31

Distribution of the types in figure 30

102

Mostly the ware is yellowish to buff to reddish, in different granulations of the tempering sand. Many vessels have a yellowish slip, in particular the reddish vessels. Three kinds of manufacture are employed: manufacture in molds (only the beveled-rim bowls), forming by hand, and, most commonly, manufacture on the fast wheel.

No sherds with painted designs were found, coloring, in rare cases only, being done by applying a colored slip to the entire surface of the vessel. In this category a number of sherds of the combed gray ware have been found, besides very few of the "red Uruk" ware.

JEMDET NASR (Eanna III)—Figure 30 *r-t*

As was pointed out in the discussion of the mass-produced types, the trouble with the normal pottery of the Jemdet Nasr period is that it cannot be separated from the Early Dynastic I pottery, except in very infrequently occurring luxury types such as painted pottery. However, as will be seen from the discussion of the pecularities of the Early Dynastic I period, there are very distinctive Early Dynastic I features, so that whenever a site produced the common Jemdet Nasr–Early Dynastic I but none of the Early Dynastic I characteristics we assumed that the site was inhabited in Jemdet Nasr but not in Early Dynastic I. In strict terms only the well-known polychrome kind of painting is taken for Jemdet Nasr, and a less well-attested kind in which concentric circles in red, purple, or black paint applied around the shoulder. These are sometimes accompanied by stars or branches (or trees).

EARLY DYNASTIC I—Figure 30 *u-ac*

As was already mentioned, there is continuity coming down from Jemdet Nasr in almost all shapes. Even the features which are characteristic of the Early Dynastic I period almost all can be traced back in their origins to earlier times. Thus, in spite of the rather distinctive look of Early Dynastic I pottery, there is no "break" between this and the preceding period.

As the main indicator for Early Dynastic I the solid-footed goblet was taken, on the basis of its restricted occurrence at all places where remains of this time range have been found. Also new is "cut ware" consisting of rather sophisticated shapes, the upper parts of which bear bands of cut-in or cut-through triangles alternating with holes, as well as the singular triangular handle on the shoulders of tall carinated, narrow-necked vessels.

Reserved slip was already known and used extensively, mostly on the shoulder of big, almost globular vessels. This kind of decoration starts right below the neck and obliquely covers the entire shoulder. Typical for Early Dynastic I, however, are fixed combinations of this kind with other kinds of decoration, as, for instance, the men-

tioned oblique reserved slip with a line of punctations right at the junction of neck and shoulder. Also peculiar to this time are reserved slip patterns with either vertical or horizontal stripes, or even a combination thereof.

Restricted to Early Dynastic I are four rim tabs (fig. 30 *u*) arranged around the rim and sometimes decorated on the upper side with parallel groovings, thus suggesting a connection with the Late Uruk ledge handholds and the horizontal handles. Real handles seem to be entirely absent. They seem to have been replaced by the already mentioned triangular lugs on the shoulder of carinated vessels. The advantage of this aid would have been that it allows one to lift the pot with one hand. These lugs apparently are the forerunners of the "goddess handles" of the later Early Dynastic phases.

EARLY DYNASTIC II–III

Both phases are badly attested in our area, owing to a complete shift in the settlement pattern. Compared with other periods, we know the pottery of this time range relatively well from the excavations in the Diyala area and in Ur, Kish, and Nippur. However, only a few features are characteristic enough to serve as dating criteria. Among those are the "fruit stands," a heavy, almost cylindrical beaker, and a small cup with inverted rim.

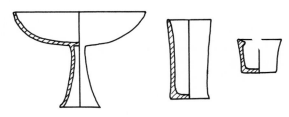

AKKAD–UR III

Although one would like to have these two stages separated, the excavated materials from Ur, Nippur, and the Diyala area do not provide us with pertinent evidence. The distinction seems to lie in a gradual change; this could be made useful for dating purposes only through the application of quantitative methods, which our material does not permit.

Characteristic for the time range are certain types of ribbed ware, very articulated rims, and a prevalence of ring bases. The ware is reddish to yellowish and in most cases a yellowish slip is applied. There is no painting and no incising.

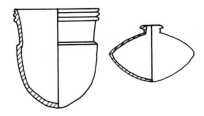

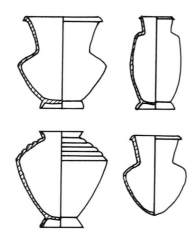

ISIN/LARSA–OLD BABYLONIAN

These two periods also could not be separated on the grounds of their pottery. To be sure, there exist some pottery types whose occurrence is restricted to one of these periods, as we know from the evidence from areas TA and TB in Nippur, but we were not able to trace them in our surface material. We did not find, for instance, a single sherd of the Isin-Larsa painted ware. Main types are a peculiar kind of carinated dish and the column decoration around the neck of large vessels.

CASSITE

To a large extent the Cassite pottery is not very characteristic. There are, however, two widespread index fossils, in the solid foot of a tall jar and the knob base. Unlike other regions the latter never was found smaller than depicted.

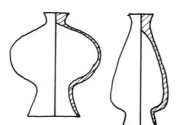

NEO-BABYLONIAN–ACHAEMENID

Dating criteria for this and later periods require a treatment largely outside the scope of the present discussion. Many common types were extremely long lasting, perhaps even having originated in the Old Babylonian or Cassite periods. Thus only a single characteristic shape of bowl can be taken as an indicator, along with the rare sherds of stamp-decorated vessels.

SELEUCID–PARTHIAN

This pottery also remains not well understood, having only in a few cases been excavated and published stratigraphically. There are a number of diagnostic indicators of these periods, but it is not possible to make subdivisions within a 500 year span.

Diagnostic indicators are one-handled jars, often glazed, oil lamps, and two- or three-handled storage jars with elongated bases. Stippling in the interior of dishes and a crude kind of rocker pattern on the shoulder of large vessels date to these periods.

SASSANIAN

The pottery of this period is even less known for lower Mesopotamia than that of the Parthian period. The large storage jars with elongated bases of the Parthian period become thicker, and the glaze tends to be a darker blue than previously. Frequently the still-wet surface of large vessels is crudely decorated by finger impressions (honeycomb).

8 | Surface Collections

In this chapter an attempt is made to publish the groups of surface finds as fully as possible, within the obvious limitations of the usefulness of unstratified surface material. Collections that are richly varied and can make a useful contribution to the understanding of an entire contemporary corpus of pottery, or that can help to reduce chronological difficulties, are fully illustrated. Others, falling within a more limited series of types, are shown more schematically. Some categories of finds, such as terra-cotta figurines, are not illustrated at all owing to the unsatisfactory state of preservation in which all specimens were found. A few unique objects, including a temple model which may be the single most important object recovered by the survey, are both discussed and illustrated.

POTTERY

As has been mentioned earlier, our surface collections of pottery are among the most complete currently available from lower Mesopotamia for the time range between the Ubaid and the Early Dynastic II periods. Adding to their importance is the fact that many of the surveyed sites apparently were occupied only during one or two short phases of this span of time. It is particularly these sites that we have chosen to emphasize in description and illustration, although collections from some multiperiod sites also are shown in full.

Our dating procedures began with the identification of a succession of types of mass-produced pottery. Other less common types were related chronologically to these through a study of multiple occurrences in what seemed to be single-period collections. In this way it was possible to place most of the unstratified surface pottery in rather sharply separated groups, which then may be regarded as well-defined, largely sequential, pottery assemblages. Although such assemblages naturally are not full replacements for large, well-stratified bodies of material obtained from excavations, they are, owing to the paucity of published accounts of excavated pottery from the region, the best substitutes that are currently available.

A much smaller number of sites was found dating from the various subphases of the Ubaid period, so that much less material of that more remote age is illustrated. In addition, because a sequence of mass-produced types is lacking for these earlier periods, the chronological placement of the remaining material is less satisfactory. With the Eridu sequence still remaining largely unpublished, even a rough separation between the subphases of the Ubaid period remains problematical. Hence it has seemed justifiable to publish the surface collections from the better-documented Ubaid sites in full, providing the available evidence not only for our own chronological placements but also for alternative reconstructions that others may offer subsequently as accounts of excavations become more plentiful. Also illustrated in full is the collection from a site at which was found a hitherto unknown kind of pottery that apparently is older than or contemporary with the oldest known subphase of the Ubaid period, the Ubaid I or Eridu phase.

Descriptions of a particular ceramic collection will be found on the page facing the appropriate pottery drawing. The presentation is arranged according to the sequence of Warka Survey (WS) numbers of the sites, rather than according to a chronological order, in order to facilitate reference to the appendix giving the catalog of site descriptions and to the text as a whole.

LIST OF SITES FROM WHICH THE POTTERY IS PUBLISHED

A. Sites according to WS Numbers

Site	Ub.	E.U.	L.U.	J.N.	E.D. I	Fig.
022		●				33
042	●	●	●			34–36
087		●	●	●		37
109			●			38–39
137	●	●	●			40–43
163			●	●		44–47
177				●	●	48
178	●	●	●	●		49
191			●			50–51
201		●	●	●		52
218	●	●	●			53
219			●	●		54
256				●	●	55
264			●	●		56–59
267	●	●	●	●		60
274			●			61–62
275	●					63
276			●	●	●	64–65
298	●					66–67
310			●	●		68
312				●	●	69
382				●	●	70
386		●	●			71–72
387			●	●	●	73
390					●	74
411	●					75–76
422					●	77
460	●	●				78–80

B. According to Periods

Site	Ub.	E.U.	L.U.	J.N.	E.D. I
275	●				
298	●				
411	●				
460	●	●			
042	●	●	●		
137	●	●	●		
218	●	●	●		
178	●	●	●	●	
267	●	●	●	●	
022		●			
386		●	●		
201		●	●	●	
109			●		
191			●		
274			●		
087			●	●	
163			●	●	
219			●	●	
264			●	●	
310			●	●	
276			●	●	●
387			●	●	●
177				●	●
256				●	●
312				●	●
382				●	●
390					●
422					●

FIGURE 32

EXPLANATION OF THE NUMBER-CODES
ACCOMPANYING EACH SHERD

The code consists of three digits:

        1st digit: color of the sherd

        2d digit: consistency of the clay

        3d digit: slip or other kind of surface treatment.

In particular the numbers of the code mean:

Number	1st digit	2d digit	3d digit
0	yellowish	very fine	yellowish
1	reddish	fine	reddish
2	buff	medium fine	cream
3	orange (brick red)	medium coarse	cream burnished
4	gray	coarse	greenish
5	greenish	very coarse	red
6	black		plum red
7	green (overfired)		plum red burnished
8			gray

WS 022

Early Uruk single-period site. Most of the characteristics of Early Uruk pottery can be found here, such as the split spouts (022/4,7), high, narrow bottles (022/3), long, straight spouts (022/5), and Early Uruk painting (022/12).

Figure 33

022/1   Thumb impressions on a plastic right; below a wavy plastic ridge.
022/12 Black green paint.

Scale 2/5. 1:53–; 2:03–; 3:040; 4:034; 5:514; 6:03–; 7:020; 8:02–; 9:04–; 10:524; 11:03–; 12:524.

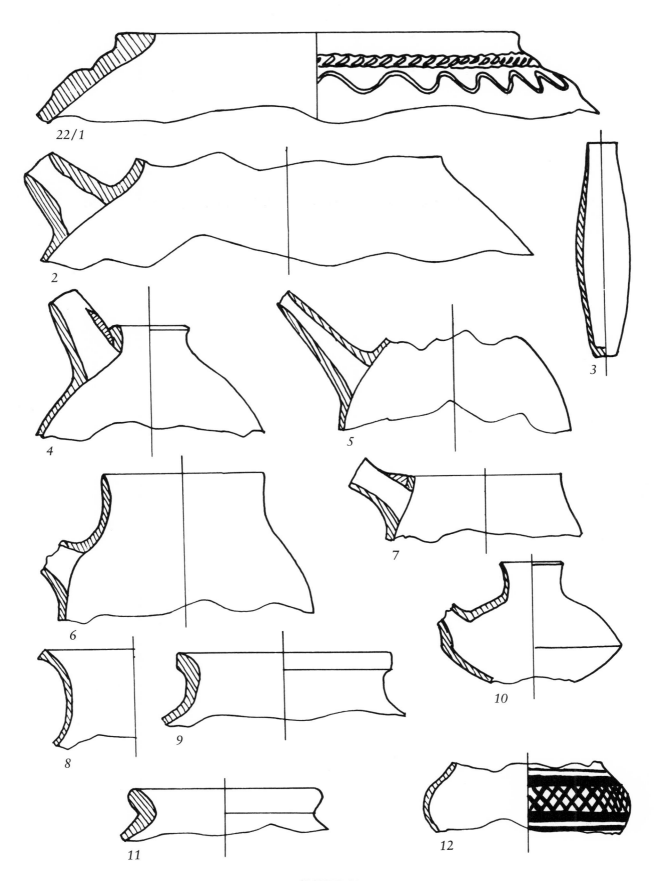

22/1

2

3

4

5

6

7

8

9

10

11

12

FIGURE 33
WS 022

109

WS 042

Ubaid II–Early Uruk (–Late Uruk). The best examples for the very frequent double rims are found in the pottery from the Qal°a of Hajji Mohammed and Ras al-°Amiya.[1] A ladle with a broad band handle is unique in Babylonia, but is certainly of Ubaid date.[2] Examples of the very highly fired "china" ware were found here. No clear Ubaid I pieces. The spouted vessels and the pointed-base bottle are characteristic of Early Uruk. Very few beveled-rim bowls may indicate an occupation into the Late Uruk period.

Figure 34

042/1 Black green paint.
042/2 Dark brown paint.
042/3 Dark sepia.
042/4 Dark brown.
042/5 Dark sepia.
042/6 Dark green.
042/7 Dark purple.
042/8 Dark green paint.
042/9 Dark brown bands, light brown/yellow filling.
042/10 Dark brown.
042/11 Dark brown.
042/12 Light olive.
042/13 Black green.

Scale 2/5. 1:51–; 2:51–; 3:52–; 4:01–; 5:01–; 6:52–; 7:01–; 8:51–; 9:51–; 10:51–; 11:51; 12:52–; 13:51–.

---

1. Ziegler, *AU* 4, pl. 29, 31. Stronach, *Iraq,* vol. 23, pl. 53, 54. Hole et al. *Deh Luran,* fig. 58 *a-e.*
2. Hole et al. *Deh Luran,* fig. 53 f. ("Mehmeh" phase = Ubaid III)

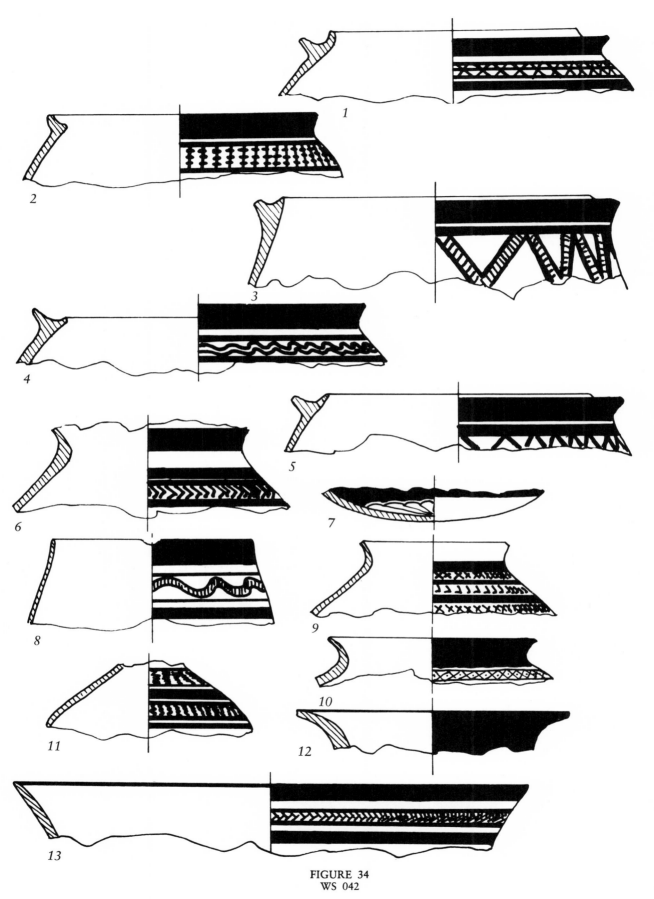

FIGURE 34
WS 042

111

Figure 35

042/14 Ext: dark brown; int: dark green.
042/15 Green.
042/16 Sepia. Good example of "china."
042/17 Dark green.
042/18 Dark green.
042/19 Black.
042/20 Dark green.
042/21 Dark sepia.
042/22 Dark green.
042/23 Dark green.
042/24 Dark green.
042/25 Sepia, changing to dark purple.
042/26 Dark green.

Scale 2/5. 14:52–; 15:02–; 16:01–; 17:52–; 18:51–; 19:01–; 20:51–; 21:014; 22:54–; 23:52–; 24:51–; 25:514; 26:51–.

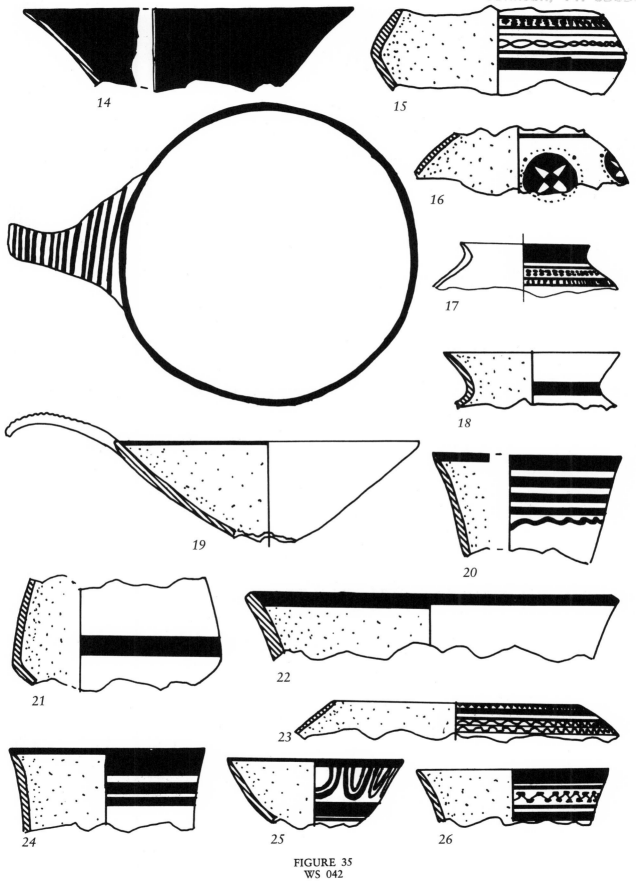

FIGURE 35
WS 042

113

Figure 36

042/27 Black brown.
042/28 Brown.
042/29 Dark purple.
042/30 Open pouring spout.
042/31 Dark green.
042/39 Upper part of pointed-base bottle.

Scale 2/5. 27:51–; 28:51–; 29:01–; 30:020; 31:020; 32:02–; 33:020; 34:13–; 35:12–; 36:13–; 37:52–; 38:020; 39:13–.

FIGURE 36
WS 042

115

WS 087

The site was mainly inhabited during Late Uruk, but also in Jemdet Nasr (conical cups). Characteristic features in pottery all date to Late Uruk, like combed gray ware (087/7) and rope-handled cups (087/9). No distinctive Early Dynastic I features, hence the conical cups are taken to represent only a Jemdet Nasr occupation.

Figure 37

087/1 Oblique reserved slip.
087/4 Three bands of incised hatchings are bordered by incised lines.
087/5 In a thick gray slip, impressions are made with a comblike instrument.
087/6 A ring of stitches around the base of the spout.
087/9 The handle consists of three parallel ropes; over a band of concentric incisions, there are oblique incisions.
087/10 Square in section with rounded edges. Stand?
087/11 Strap handle cup with a hole pierced through the handle. Band of stitches.

Scale 2/5. 1:044; 2:52–; 3:240; 4:04–; 5:439; 6:130; 7:030; 8:22–; 9:54–; 10:130; 11:52–; 12:02–; 13:51–.

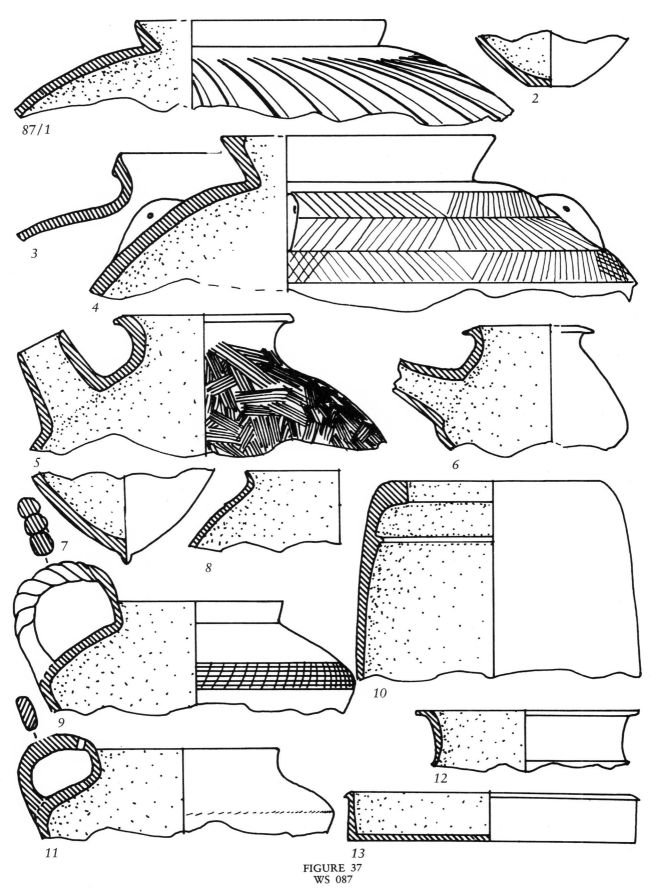

87/1

2

3

4

5

6

7

8

9

10

11

12

13

FIGURE 37
WS 087

117

WS 109

Late Uruk single-period site established from the mass pottery, though not many characteristic Late Uruk features are present.

Figure 38

109/4   Red Uruk ware.

109/7   According to the traces, a strap handle must be restored.

109/8   False spout. Not enough preserved even to reconstruct diameter.

Scale 2/5. 1:54–; 2:53–; 3:04–; 4:316; 5:12–; 6:110; 7:110; 8:030; 9:040; 10:52–.

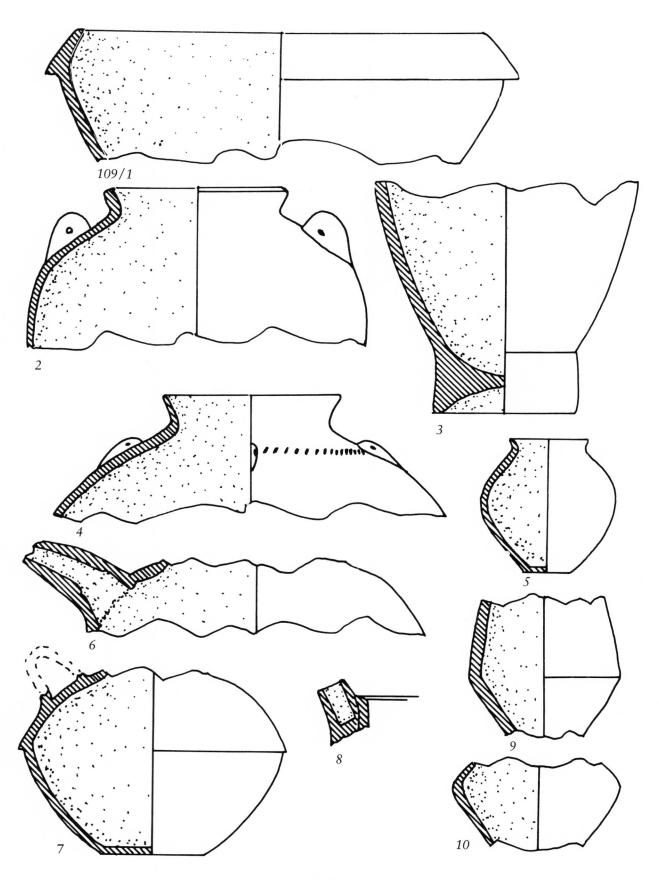

109/1

2

3

4

5

6

7

8

9

10

FIGURE 38
WS 109

119

Figure 39

109/13 Band of stitches on the shoulder.

Scale 2/5. 11:53–; 12:11–; 13:130; 14:53–; 15:53–; 16:03–; 17:020; 18:010; 19:030.

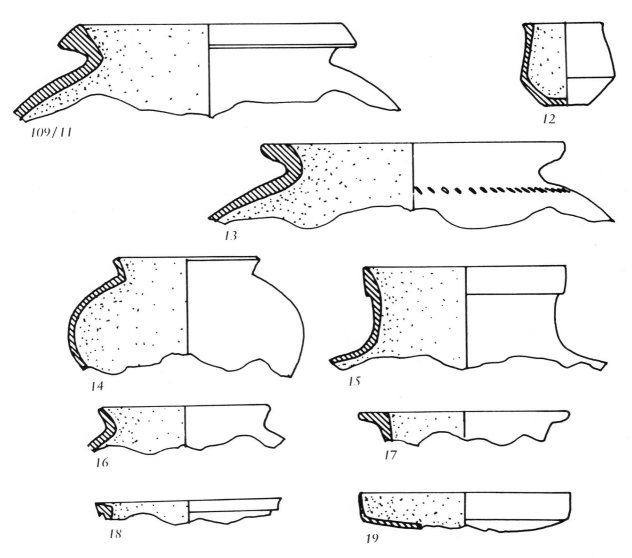

109/11

12

13

14

15

16

17

18

19

FIGURE 39
WS 109

121

WS 137   *Figure 40*

Late Ubaid through Late Uruk, with the stress on Late   137/1 Green black paint.
Uruk. Only a few distinctive Early Uruk features were   137/2 Green black paint.
found: 137/3 Green black paint.
137/4 (?); 137/13.   137/4 Dark brown paint.
                                                              137/6 Deep combing on inside.
                                                              137/7 Dark green paint.
                                                              137/8 Dark green paint.
                                                              137/9 Black stripes on rim.
                                                              137/11 Dark brown paint.

Scale 2/5. 1:53–; 2:52–; 3:53–; 4:52–; 5:52–; 6:52–; 7:52–; 8:52–;
9:53–; 10:52–; 11:220.

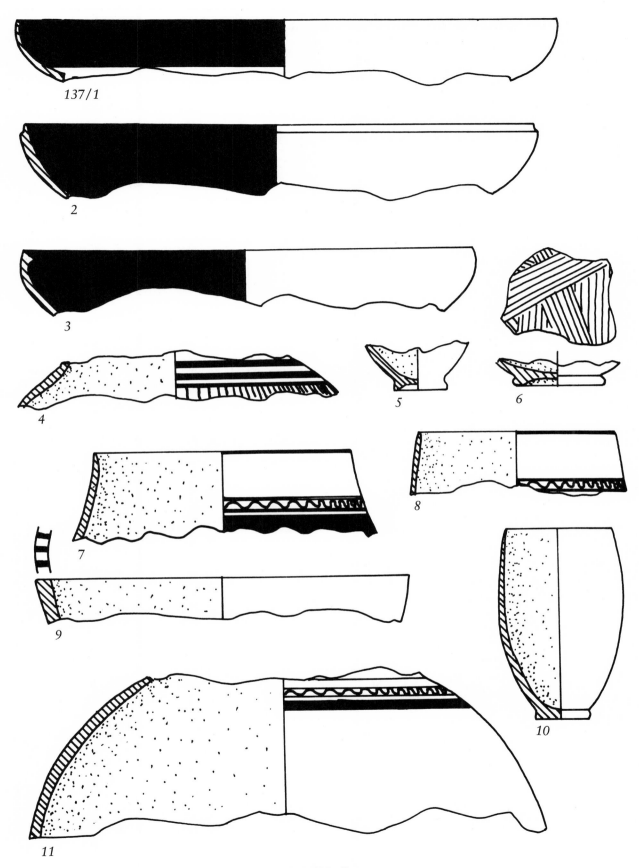

137/1

2

3

4

5

6

7

8

9

10

11

FIGURE 40
WS 137

123

Figure 41

137/12 Spout attached to rim.

137/13 Spout attached to rim.

137/16 Strap handle subdivided by grooves; rocker incision on upper part of cup.

137/17 Attached spout.

137/19 Strap handle must be reconstructed.

137/22 Horizontal rope handle.

Scale 2/5. 12:120; 13:020; 14:010; 15:030; 16:54–; 17:020; 18:220; 19:72–; 20:22–; 21:22–; 22:73–.

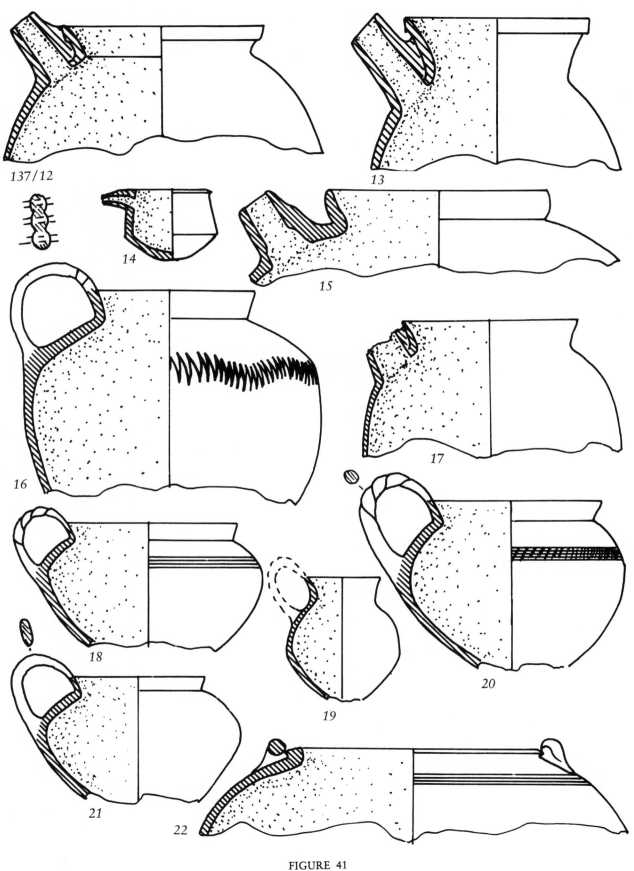

137/12

13

14

15

16

17

18

19

20

21

22

FIGURE 41
WS 137

Figure 42

137/23 Two ledge handholds.
137/24 Band of incised cross-hatchings below incised triangles.
137/26 Incised lines on rim.
137/27 Band of stitches.
137/29 Band of stitches near rim; one knob handhold.
137/30 Four rows of finger impressions.
137/31 Finger impressions on three plastic ridges.
137/32 Finger impressions on a plastic ridge.

Scale 2/5. 23:03–; 24:120; 25:05–; 26:74–; 27:03–; 28:010; 29:220; 30:73–; 31:73–; 32:73–.

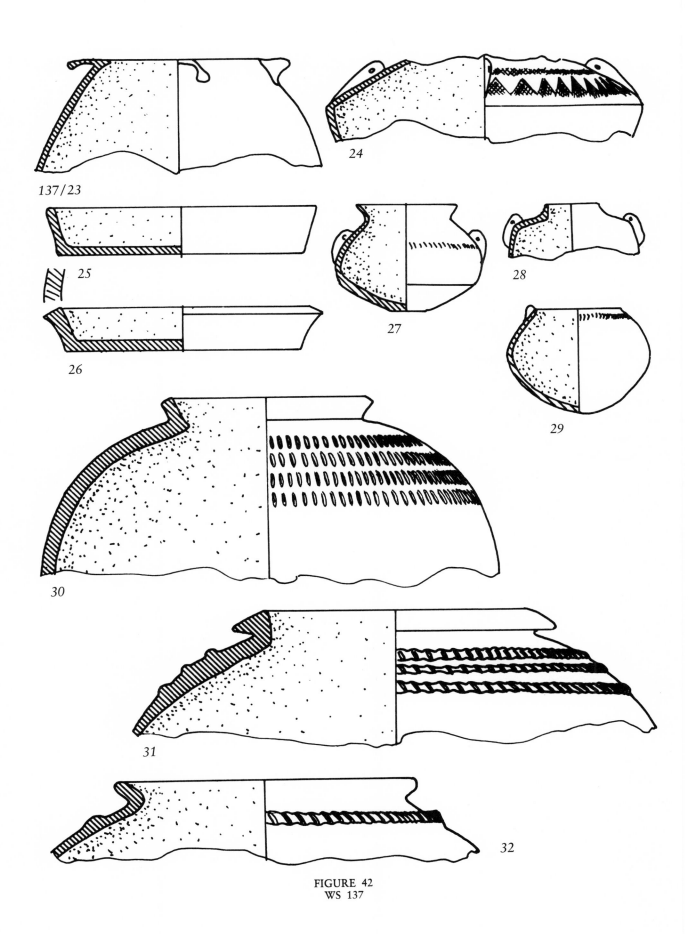

137/23

24

25

26

27

28

29

30

31

32

FIGURE 42
WS 137

127

Figure 43

137/33 Gray, soft ware.
137/35 Gray, soft ware.
137/37 Two rows of stitches.

Scale 2/5. 33:44–; 34:73–; 35:44–; 36:73–; 37:73–; 38:120; 39:020; 40:010; 41:120.

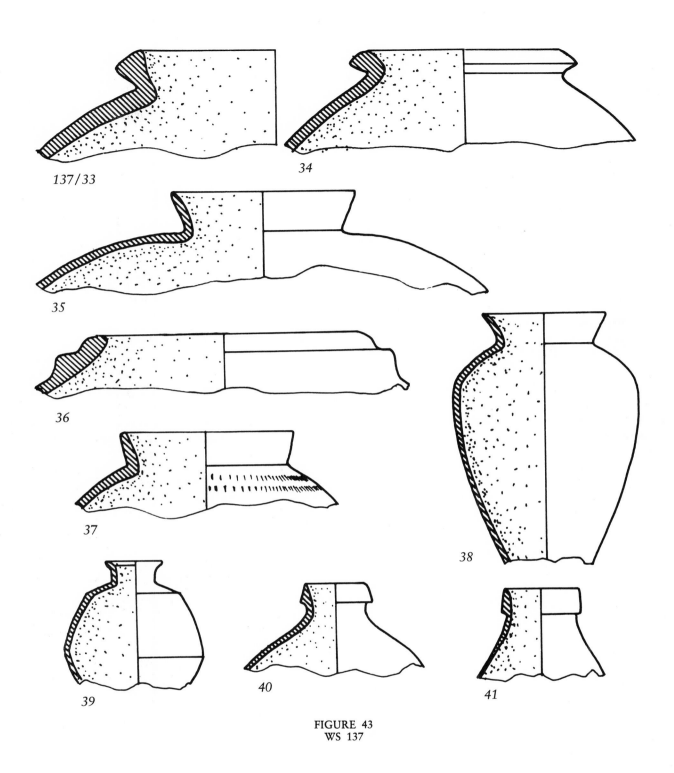

137/33

34

35

36

37

38

39

40

41

FIGURE 43
WS 137

129

WS 163

Multiple site consisting of five adjacent settlements (a-e) (cf. plan on fig. 11). All places were inhabited in the Late Uruk, but only a, d, e continued into the Jemdet Nasr period.

Figure 44

163a/1 Finger impressions on plastic ridges.

163a/2 Band of herringbone incising.

163a/3 Pattern which is produced by drawing broad bands over a bundle of parallel incisings (cf. chap. 7, fig. 30r).

163a/4 Base of heavy bottle; to be compared with the bottles used to reinforce the edges of the Anu-Ziggurat Terrace? (cf. UVB XXIII, pl. 1a; 2b; 3a).

163b/1 Groovings on the strap handle seem to imitate rope handle.

163b/4 Horizontal rope handle.

163b/5 Crosshatched incising on rim of oval plate (12 × 20 cm).

163b/6 Crosshatched incising in metopelike fields.

Scale 2/5. 163a, 1:030; 2:740; 3:02–; 4:15–; 5:030; 6:02–; 7:020; 163b, 1:73–; 2:020; 3:72–; 4:02–; 5:02–; 6:02–.

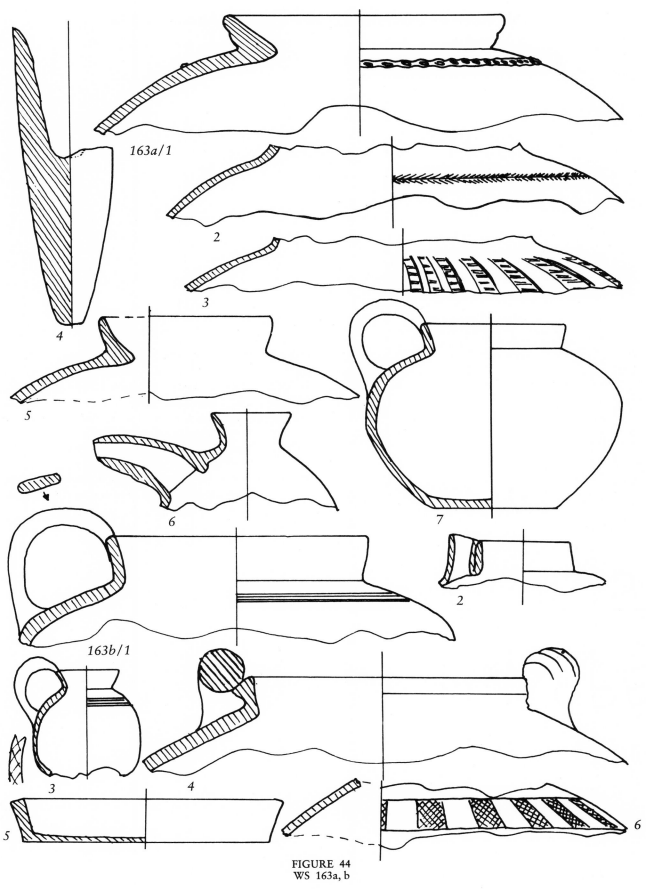

163a/1

2

3

4

5

6

7

163b/1

2

3

4

5

6

FIGURE 44
WS 163a, b

131

Figure 45

163*c*/1 Horizontal rope handle over spout. Ridge with finger impressions.
163*c*/2 Attached spout. Oblique reserve slip.
163*c*/5 Two ledge handholds.
163*c*/7 Fused together with a beveled-rim bowl, hence unusual shape.
163*c*/8 Incised double lines on rim of an oval plate 18 × 13 cm).
163*c*/9 One row of triangles of a row of semicircles. Both are filled with crosshatched incisions.

Scale 2/5. 1:23–; 2:01–; 3:020; 4:72–; 5:01–; 6:02–; 7:73–; 8:73–; 9:03–.

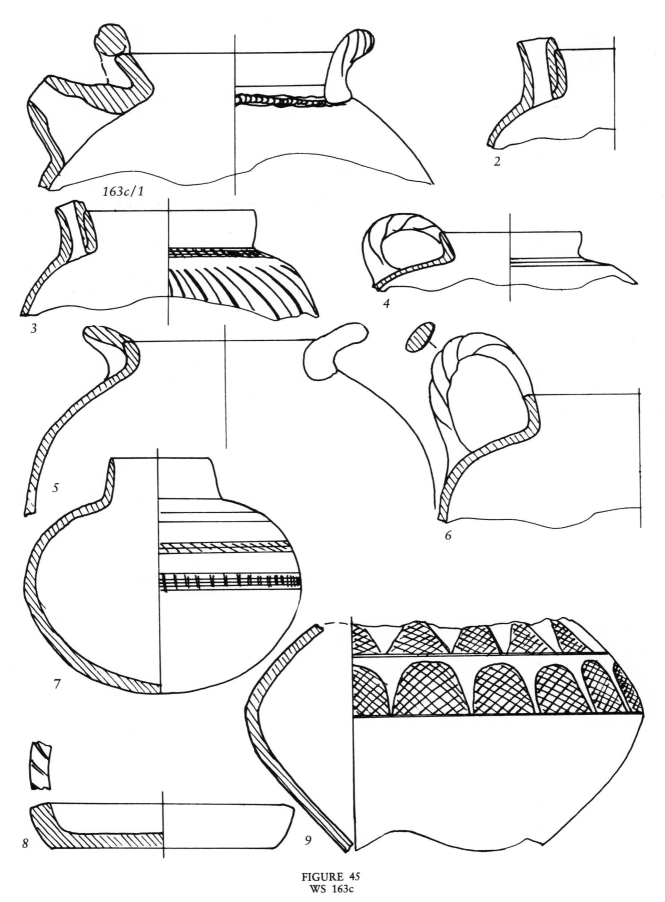

163c/1

2

3

4

5

6

7

8

9

FIGURE 45
WS 163c

133

Figure 46

163*d*/1   (Water)pipe, handformed.

Scale 2/5, except 1, which is 1/5. 1:02–; 2:120; 3:120; 4:12–; 5:010; 6:010.

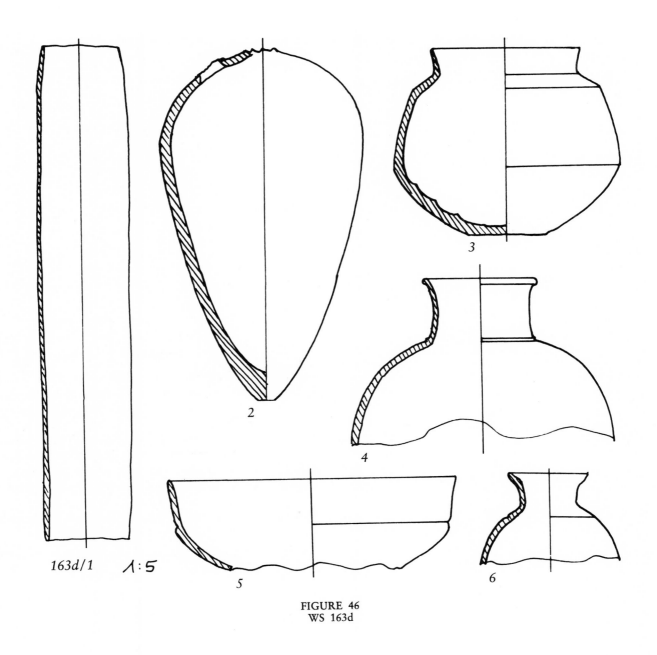

163d/1   1:5

2

3

4

5   6

FIGURE 46
WS 163d

135

Figure 47

163*e*/1 Small variety of beveled-rim bowl.
163*e*/3 Two shallow containers fixed to both ends of an oval plate (18 × 26 cm). Double line incisions on rim.
163*e*/4 Strap-handled cup with vertical ridges around the neck and incised decoration on shoulder.
163*e*/5 Traces of plum red paint on the shoulder.
163*e*/7 Band of triangles filled with crosshatched incisings.
163*e*/8 Two bands of triangles filled with crosshatched incising.

Scale 2/5. 1:75–; 2:02–; 3:74–; 4:73–; 5:120; 6:020; 7:020; 8:020.

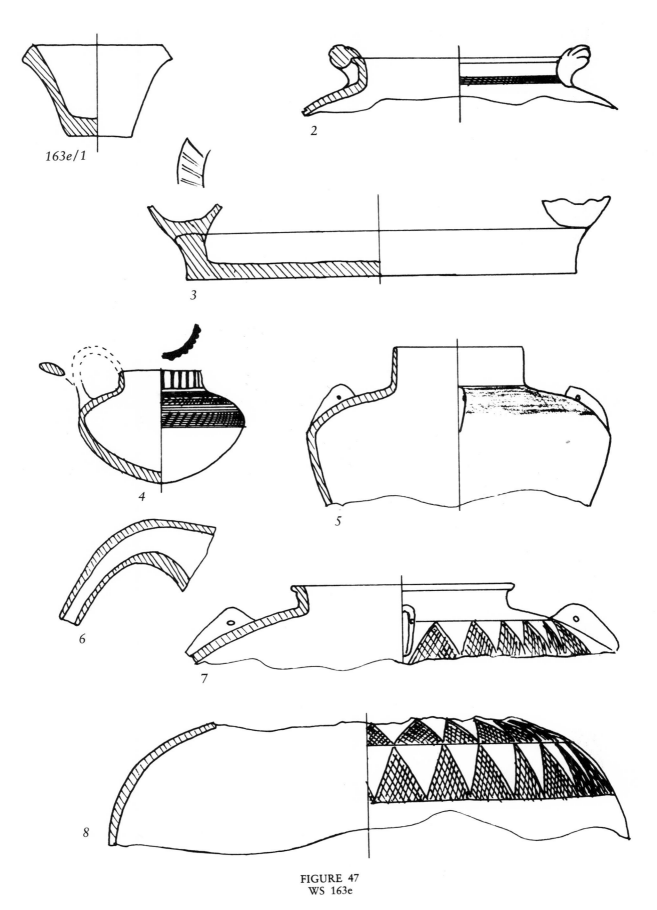

163e/1

2

3

4

5

6

7

8

FIGURE 47
WS 163e

137

WS 177

Inhabited during Jemdet Nasr (painted ware: 177/2, 4, 6, 11) and Early Dynastic I (solid-footed goblets and stone vessel type 8). Characteristic of the latter period is also 177/8 (cf. *K/L* XII).

Figure 48

177/2 Few traces of red and dark brown paint. No pattern recognizable.

177/4 Faint traces of plum red paint.

177/6 Traces of plum red paint on neck and shoulder.

177/11 Traces of dark brown paint on sherd of very large vessel (presumably over 60 cm diameter).

Scale 2/5. 1:13–; 2:13–; 3:14–; 4:147; 5:13–; 6:147; 7:13–; 8:03–; 9:130; 10:130; 11:22–; 12:230.

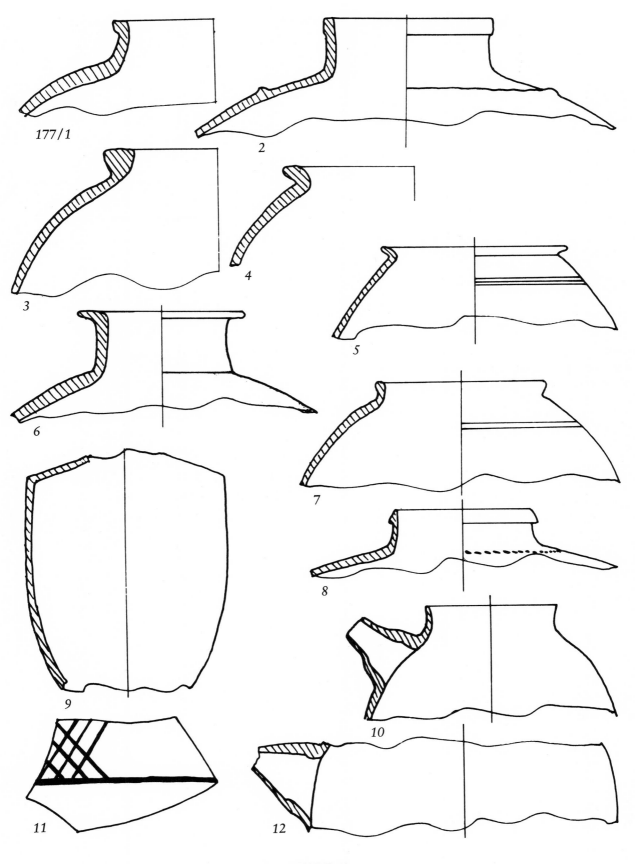

FIGURE 48
WS 177

139

WS 178

Rather small mound with sherds from Ubaid III through Jemdet Nasr. The collection is shown here mainly because of the good Early Uruk samples (178/3, 5, 7).

Figure 49

178/1   Dark sepia paint, inside and out.
178/2   Dark green paint.
178/3   Dark brown paint.
178/4   Dark green paint.
178/7   Faint traces of almost vertical reserved slip.
178/8   Two knobs near each other.
178/11   Row of applied clay dots.
178/12   Band of crosshatched incising.
178/15   Thumb-impressed plastic ridge.
178/18   Two wavy plastic ridges.

Scale 2/5. 1:52–; 2:51–; 3:020; 4:52–; 5:220; 6:15–; 7:524; 8:524; 9:02–; 10:524; 11:02–; 12:53–; 13:72–; 14:02–; 15:03–; 16:01–; 17:53–; 18:030.

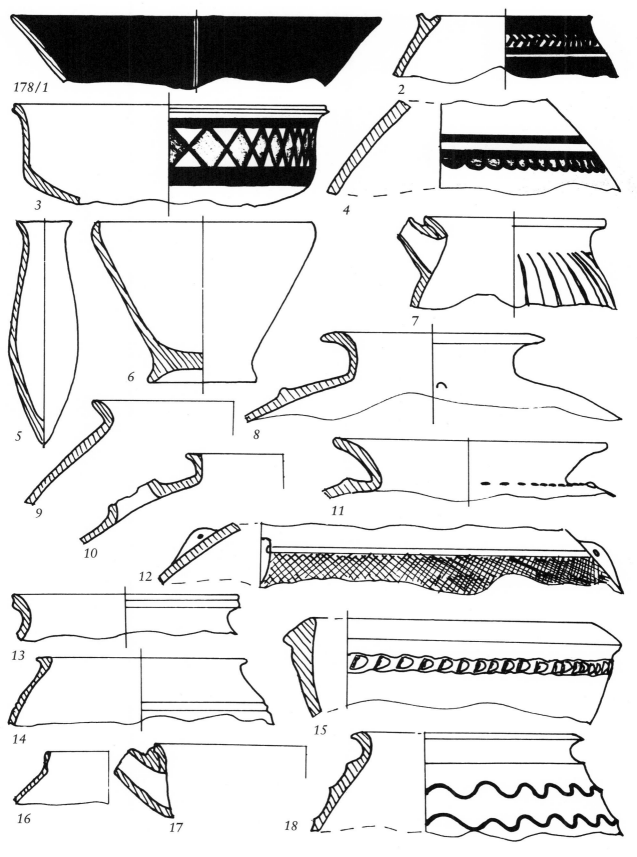

178/1

2

3

4

5

6

7

8

9

10

11

12

13

14

15

16

17

18

FIGURE 49
WS 178

141

WS 191

A Late Uruk single-period site, the pottery of which was distinctive especially by the many variations of incised, stitched, impressed decorations, as well as by the application of lumps of clay. Some sherds remind one of Early Islamic Barbotine ware.

Figure 50

191/1   Soft gray combed ware; combing is restricted to upper part of vessel.

191/4   Soft gray ware; traces of burnishing.

191/9   Finger impressions on plastic ridge.

191/10 Combination of bundle of incised lines and crude kind of reserved slip (cf. chap. 7, fig. 30*r*).

Scale 2/5. 1:439; 2:030; 3:03–; 4:44–; 5:03–; 6:020; 7:02–; 8:03–; 9:02–; 10:05–.

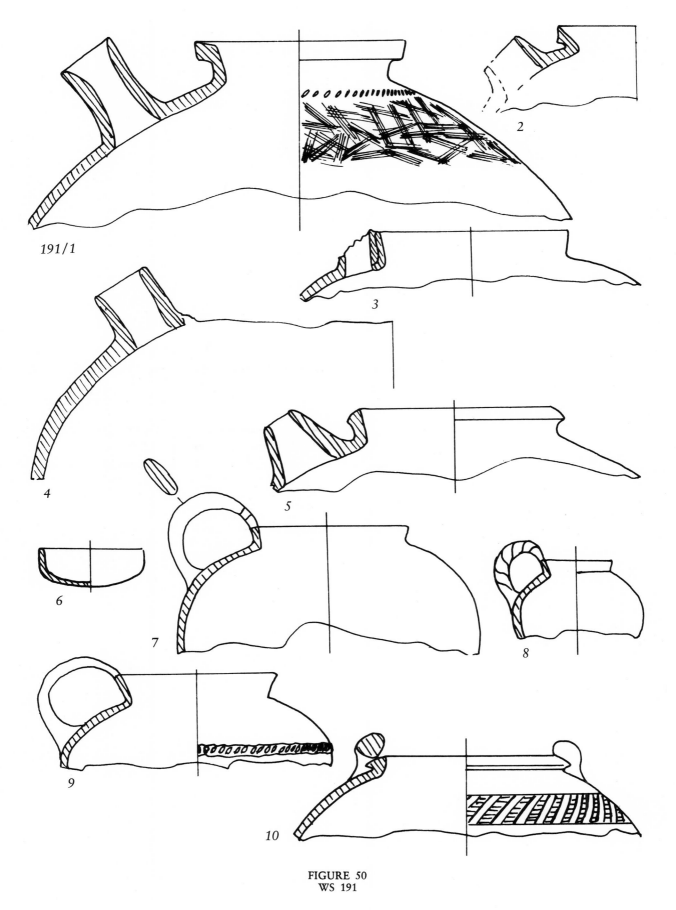

191/1

2

3

4

5

6

7

8

9

10

FIGURE 50
WS 191

Figure 51

191/11 Bands of crosshatched incisions below filled, incised triangles.

191/12 Soft gray ware with finger-impressed plastic ridge.

191/14 Finger-impressed plastic ridge.

191/16 Soft gray ware, burnished.

191/17–26 Various kinds of incising with all kinds of instruments (reeds), sometimes combined with plastic application.

191/20, 22 Soft gray ware.

Scale 2/5, except 1, which is 1/5. 11:05–; 12:44–; 13:05–; 14:120; 15:03–; 16:439; 17:03–; 18:02–; 19:02–; 20:42–; 21:03–; 22:42–; 23:02–; 24:03–; 25:03–; 26:03–.

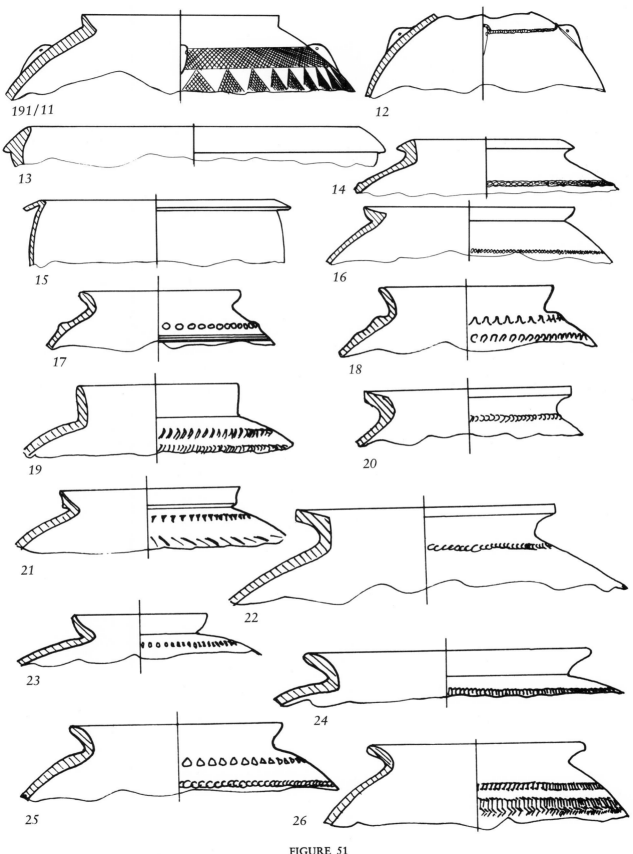

191/11

12

13

14

15

16

17

18

19

20

21

22

23

24

25

26

FIGURE 51
WS 191

WS 201

The collection is shown mainly because of Early Uruk samples (201/1, 2, 3, 4, 7). Rope and strap-handled cups, incising, etc., point to a larger Late Uruk occupation, but these shapes are omitted here.

Figure 52

201/1 Split spout; green black paint.
201/2 Black paint.
201/3 Dark brown paint.
201/6 Band of black paint; traces of vertical painting below.
201/7 Split spout; decorated plastic ridge not parallel to rim, but pattern not recognizable.
201/12 Oblique reserved slip.
201/13 Crisscross incising over the vessel.

Scale 2/5. 1:524; 2:52–; 3:020; 4:52–; 5:130; 6:02–; 7:03–; 8:034; 9:24–; 10:04–; 11:03–; 12:024; 13:04–; 14:72–.

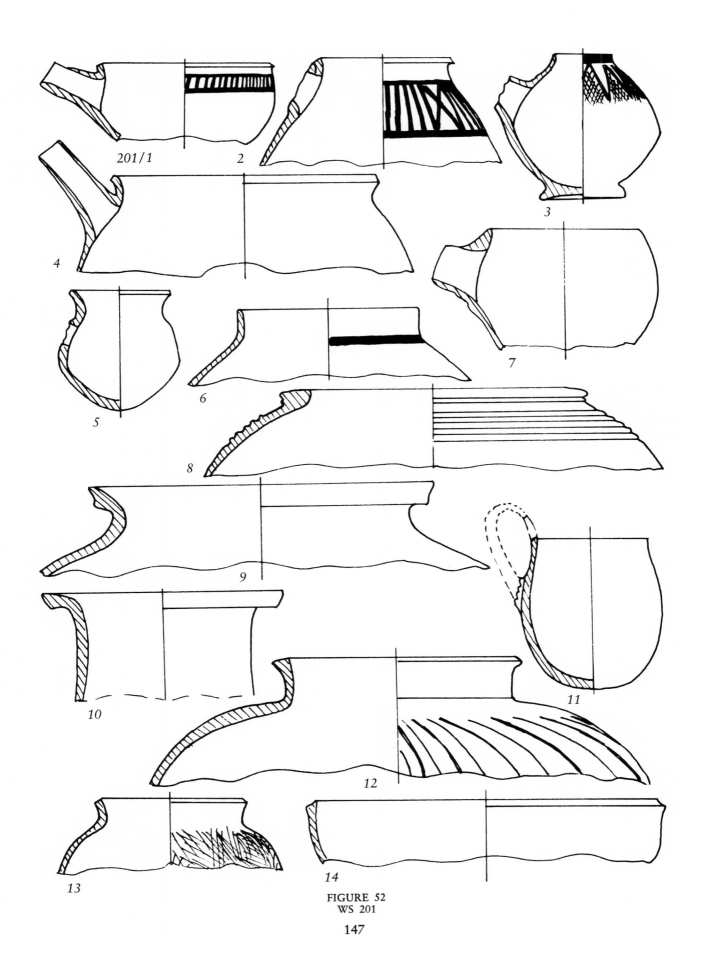

201/1
2
3
4
5
6
7
8
9
10
11
12
13
14

FIGURE 52
WS 201

147

WS 218

Late Ubaid (218/1, 2, 3, 4, 5, 15), Early Uruk (218/6, 7, 10), and Late Uruk (218/8, 9, 12) are about equally represented. Late Uruk rope-handled cups were only recorded; they are not given here.

Figure 53

218/1 Green black paint.
218/2 Green black paint.
218/3 Green black paint.
218/4 Below a band of green black paint, a broad zone covered with crosshatched incising.
218/5 Black paint.
218/7 Light, vertical reserved slip.
218/8 Finger-impressed plastic ridge.
218/9 Crosshatched incising on two plastic ridges.
218/12 Band of crosshatched incising.
218/15 Green black paint.
218/16 Thumb-impressed plastic ridges.

Scale 2/5. 1:52–; 2:52–; 3:52–; 4:53–; 5:52–; 6:514; 7:514; 8:54–; 9:53–; 10:230; 11:14–; 12:02–; 13:130; 14:52–; 15:53–; 16:53–.

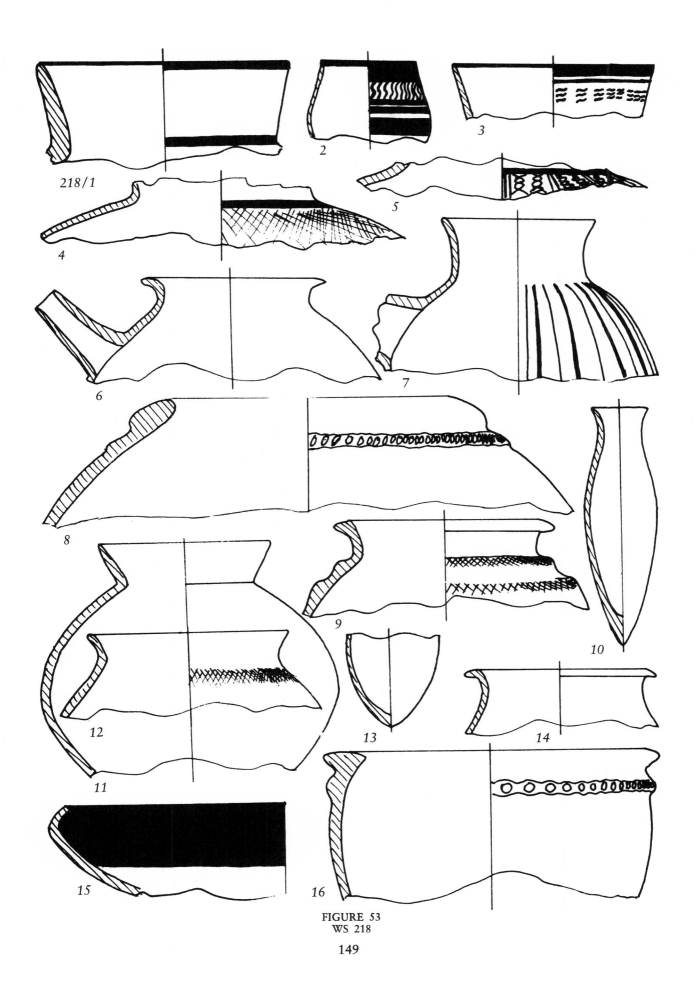

218/1

2

3

4

5

6

7

8

9

10

11

12

13

14

15

16

FIGURE 53
WS 218

149

WS 219

Rather rare conical cups and the painted sherd (219/8) point to a limited Jemdet Nasr occupation; otherwise everything is Late Uruk.

Figure 54

219/1 Oblique reserved slip.

219/2 Horizontal rope handles; crude kind of reserved slip.

219/3 One vertical ridge on neck.

219/6 Shallow cup fixed to one (two?) end of oval plate (18 × 11 cm); incised crosshatching on rim.

219/8 Dark brown paint.

219/9 Band of herringbone pattern incisions.

219/11 Bands of incised semicircles and standing triangles filled with incised crosshatching.

Scale 2/5, except 9–11, which are 1/5. 1:130; 2:53–; 3:72–; 4:12–; 5:73–; 6:73–; 8:230; 9:020; 10:232; 11:530.

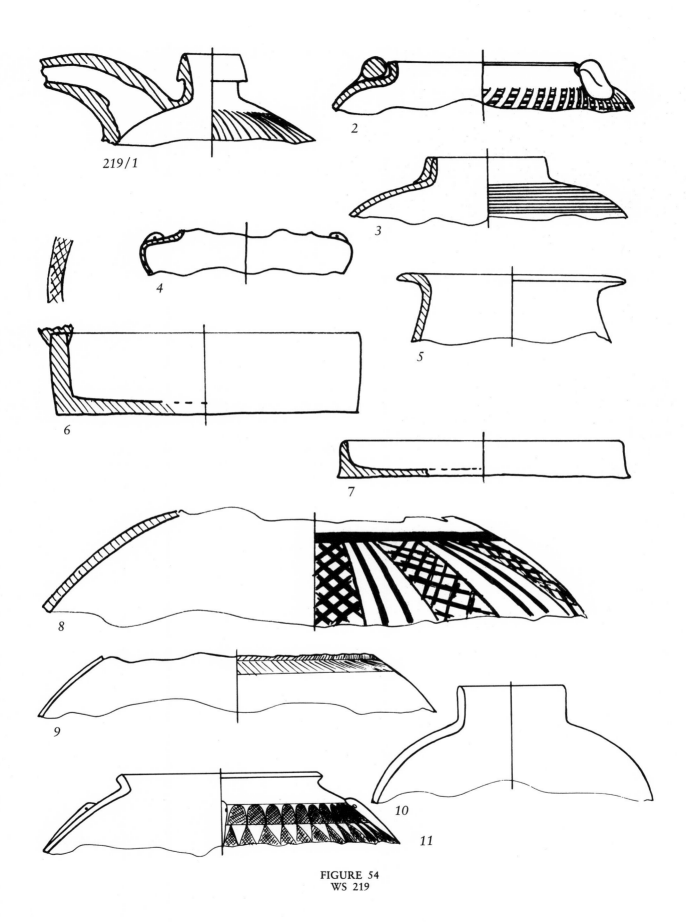

219/1

2

3

4

5

6

7

8

9

10

11

FIGURE 54
WS 219

151

WS 256

Figure 55

The examples of simple painting (256/2, 3, 8) point to a Jemdet Nasr occupation, while features like 256/6 and solid-footed goblets confirm the continuation into Early Dynastic I.

256/2   Dark brown paint.

256/3   Purple brown paint.

256/5   Pierced combination of two lugs with a bridge, used as a handhold.

256/8   Traces of brown paint, better preserved where the leaves(?) had been painted thicker.

Scale 2/5. 1:03–; 2:23–; 3:23–; 4:13–; 5:03–; 6:12–; 7:12–; 8:120.

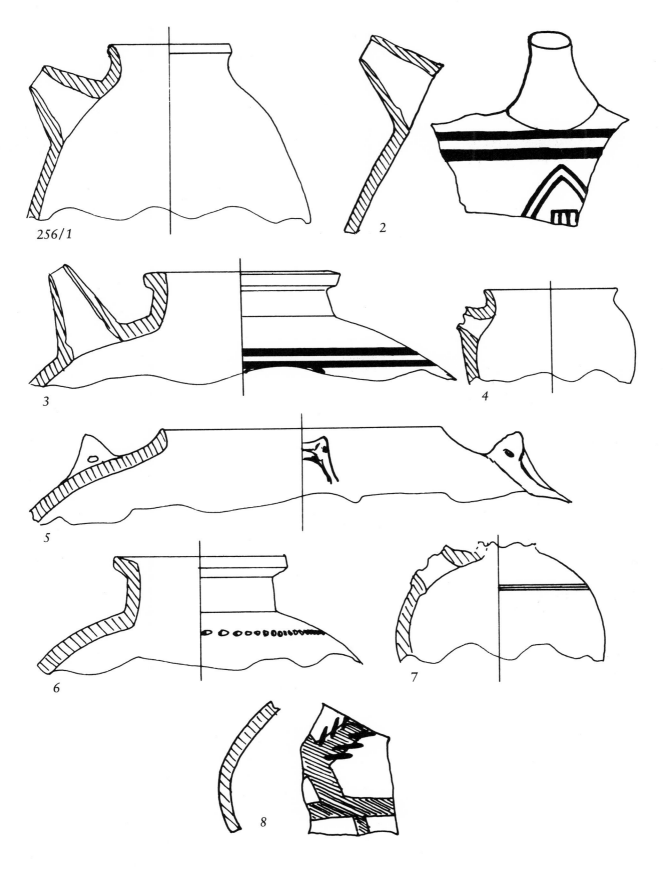

256/1

2

3

4

5

6

7

8

FIGURE 55
WS 256

WS 264

A long settlement with three centers (fig. 11), all settled primarily during Late Uruk, but also Jemdet Nasr sherds are present. Early Dynastic I occupation is attested only by a few solid-footed goblets at the extreme ends of the site.

Figure 56

264/7   Oval plate with broken-off shallow cup at one end.

Scale 2/5. 1:120; 2:02–; 3:05–; 4:230; 5:02–; 6:02–; 7:54–; 8:120; 9:02–; 10:040; 11:020.

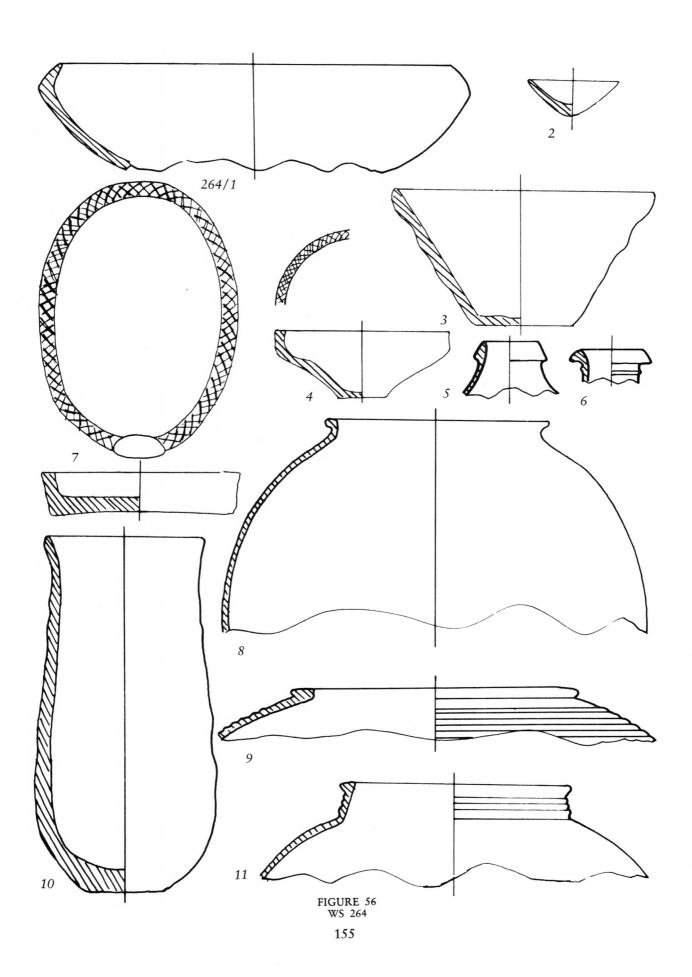

264/1

2

3

4

5

6

7

8

9

10

11

FIGURE 56
WS 264

155

Figure 57

264/16 Thumb-impressed plastic ridge. The rim is at two opposite places flattened and broadened to form handholds. These spots are decorated with incising.

264/19 Oblique stitches on an incised line.

264/20 Sherd with horizontal reserved slip; of a large vessel (diameter more than 60 cm).

Scale 2/5. 12:12–; 13:520; 14:030; 15:53–; 16:02–; 17:720; 18:72–; 19:01–; 20:010; 21:03–.

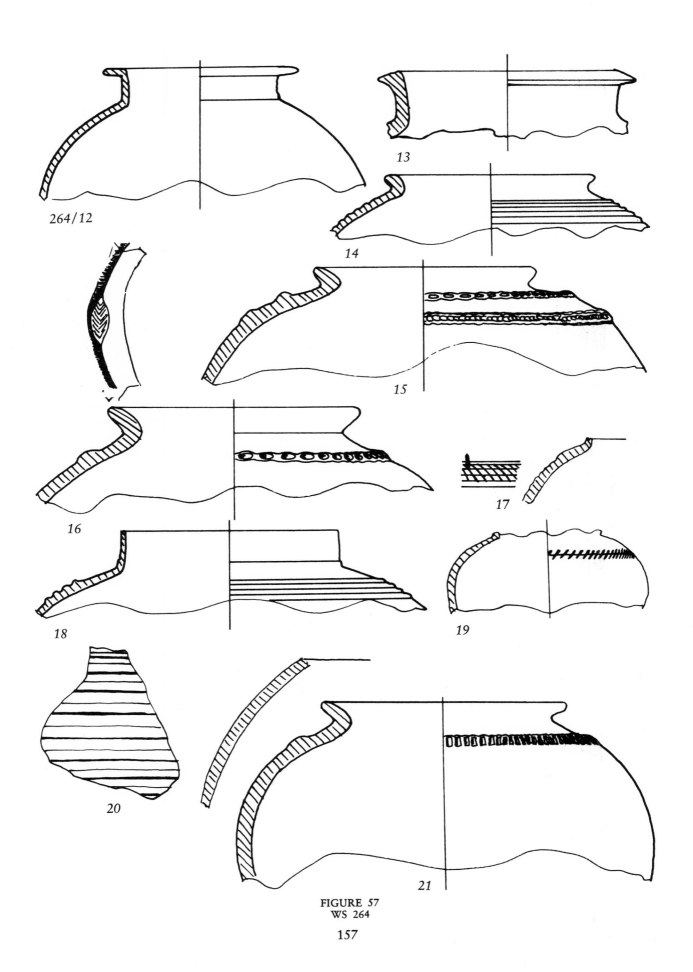

264/12

13

14

15

16

17

18

19

20

21

FIGURE 57
WS 264

157

Figure 58

264/22 Dark green paint.

264/24 Fragment with three bands of fingernail impressions. Probably the point of fracture of a rope handle.

264/26 Upper side of a ledge handle decorated with impressions of fingernail.

Scale 2/5. 22:520; 23:132; 24:03–; 25:02–; 26:130; 27:72–; 28:02–; 29:72–; 30:23–.

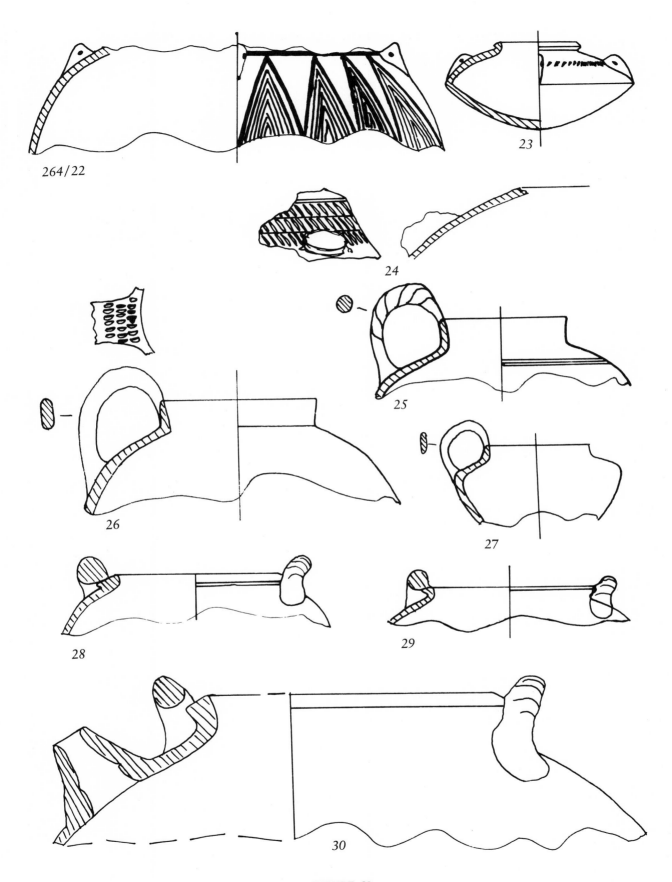

264/22

23

24

25

26

27

28

29

30

FIGURE 58
WS 264

159

Figure 59

264/36 Oblique reserved slip.

Scale 2/5. 31:030; 32:030; 33:030; 34:130; 35:010; 36:020; 37:02–; 38:02–; 39:02–.

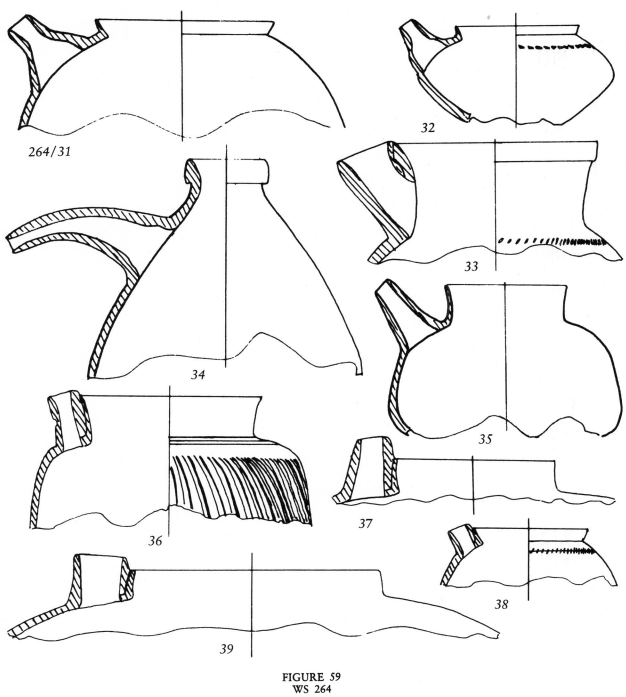

264/31

32

33

34

35

36

37

38

39

FIGURE 59
WS 264

WS 267

The site was inhabited in Hajji Mohammed (Ubaid II) and Late Uruk–Jemdet Nasr; later reoccupied during the Akkadian period through the Larsa period. Here only the Ubaid specimens are given. Especially notable is 267/9, as it may even belong to the Ubaid I phase.

Figure 60

267/1 Double rim pierced into the interior. Black green paint.
267/2 Black brown paint.
267/3 Black green paint.
267/4 Black green paint.
267/5 Black paint.
267/6 Reconstruction of a dish. Inside the pattern is black green paint; outside it is dark purple.
267/7 Inside black green paint; outside, same, slightly lighter.
267/8 Black green paint.
267/9 Fragment of a base of a dish with a central pattern, black green paint.

Scale 2/5, except 6, which is 1/5. 1:03–; 2:02–; 3:52–; 4:52–; 5:52–; 6:02–; 7:53–; 8:51–; 9:02–.

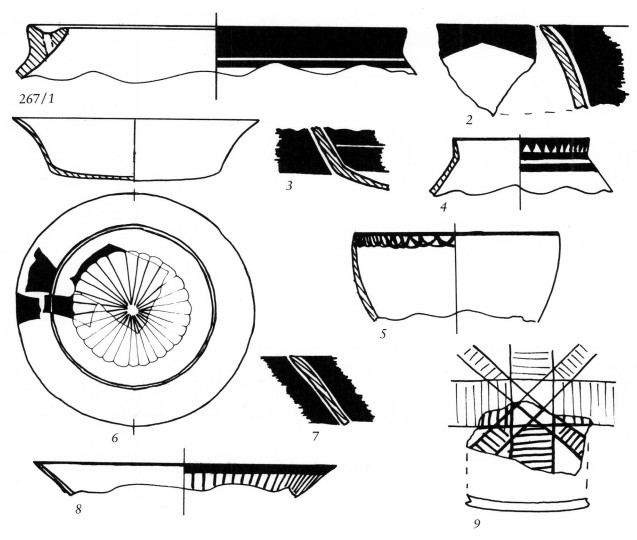

267/1

2

3

4

5

6

7

8

9

FIGURE 60
WS 267

163

WS 274

Late Uruk single-period site. In addition to the illustrated material, large sherds with deep rectilinear scoring have been found of the type on fig. 30 *p*.

Figure 61

274/1 Fingernail impressions around rim.
274/15 Below a band of incised crosshatching, another band of filled incised triangles.

Scale 2/5. 1:240; 2:514; 3:524; 4:112; 5:010; 6:020; 7:220; 8:53–; 9:524; 10:22–; 11:120; 12:030; 13:514; 14:030; 15:224; 16:12–.

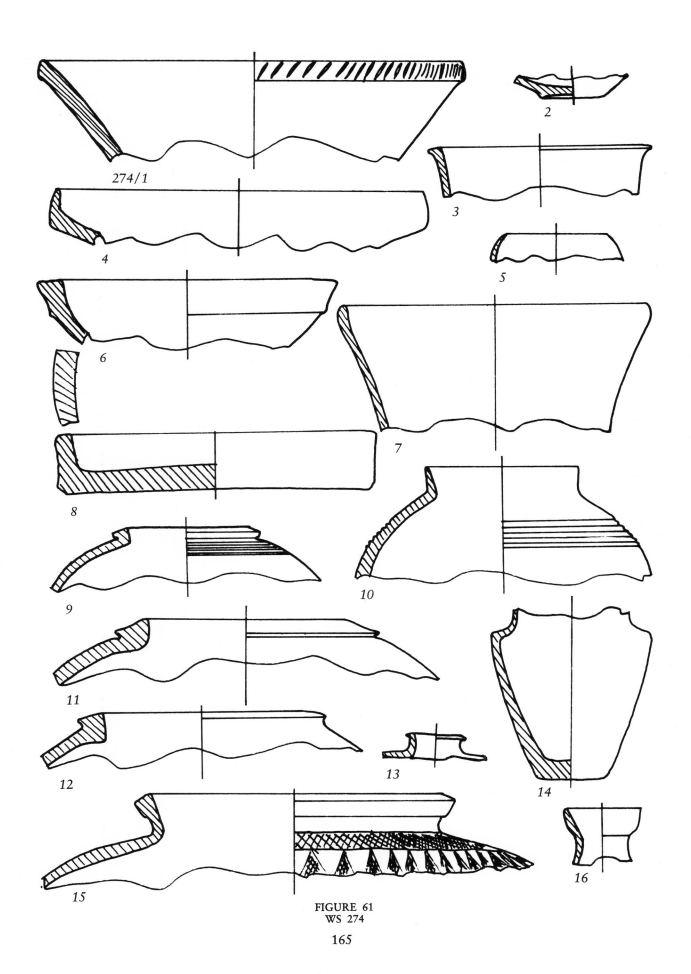

274/1
2
3
4
5
6
7
8
9
10
11
12
13
14
15
16

FIGURE 61
WS 274

165

Figure 62

274/17 Cup with a handle consisting of three parallel ropes.

274/22 Two ledge handholds.

274/23 Oblique reserved slip.

274/25 Pottery part of a ladle, originally with a wooden haft (?).

274/26 Red burnished slip, "red Uruk ware."

Scale 2/5. 17:020; 18:524; 19:220; 20:514; 21:120; 22:024; 23:024; 24:52–; 25:120; 26:125; 27:120; 28:120; 29:020; 30:020.

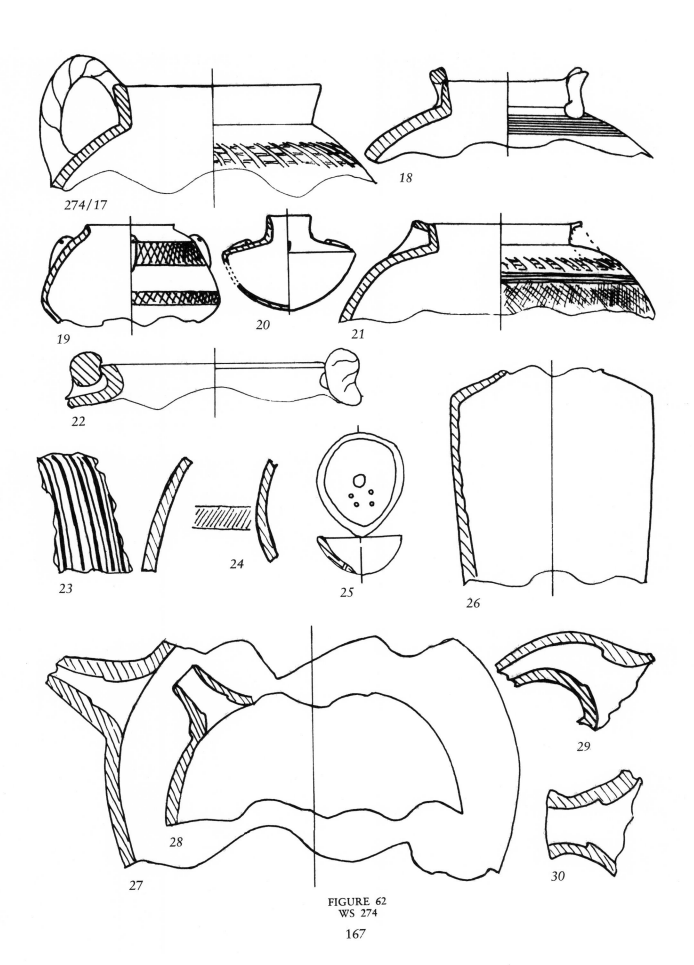

274/17

18

19

20

21

22

23

24

25

26

27

28

29

30

FIGURE 62
WS 274

167

WS 275

Occupied during Ubaid III and IV, perhaps even only during the latter stage.

Figure 63

All painted sherds display a black green color.

275/12 Deep interior scoring.

275/17 Band of black green paint around the base of the spout.

Scale 2/5. 1:52–; 2:51–; 3:52–; 4:024; 5:52–; 6:51–; 7:52–; 8:53–; 9:52–; 10:52–; 11:52–; 12:02–; 13:52–; 14:52–; 15:022; 16:03–; 17:52–.

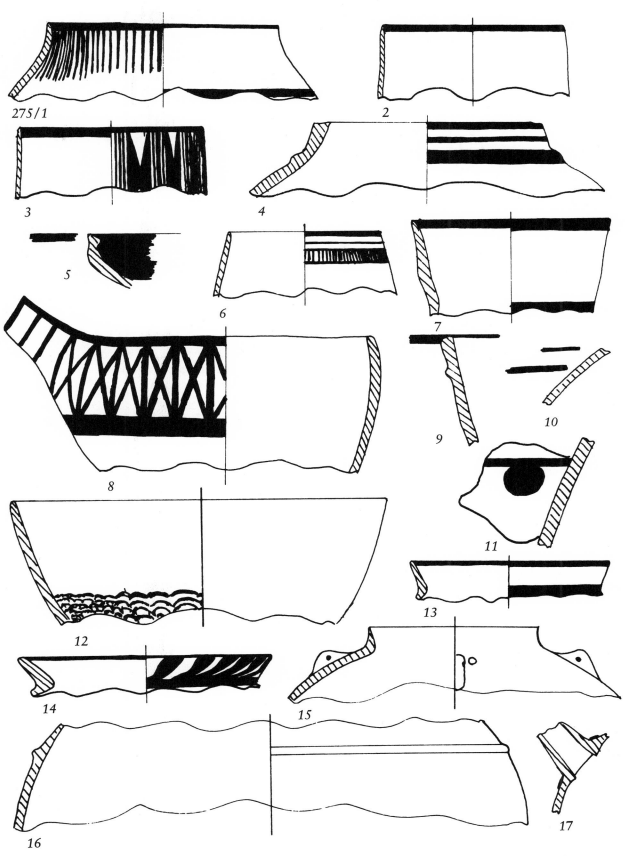

275/1

2

3

4

5

6

7

8

9

10

11

12

13

14

15

16

17

FIGURE 63
WS 275

169

WS 276

Beginning in Late Uruk (beveled-rim bowls; 276/11, 13, 14), the site was inhabited in Jemdet Nasr (276/5, 10, 12, 20, 21, 23) and through Early Dynastic I (solid-footed goblets; 276/24, 28).

Figure 64

276/5 Traces of plum red coating.
276/10 Bands of light green paint.
276/12 Black green paint.

Scale 2/5. 1:130; 2:030; 3:020; 4:02–; 5:137; 6:030; 7:020; 8:020; 9:73–; 10:030; 11:03–; 12:03–; 13:72–; 14:020; 15:120; 16:12–; 17:03–; 18:130.

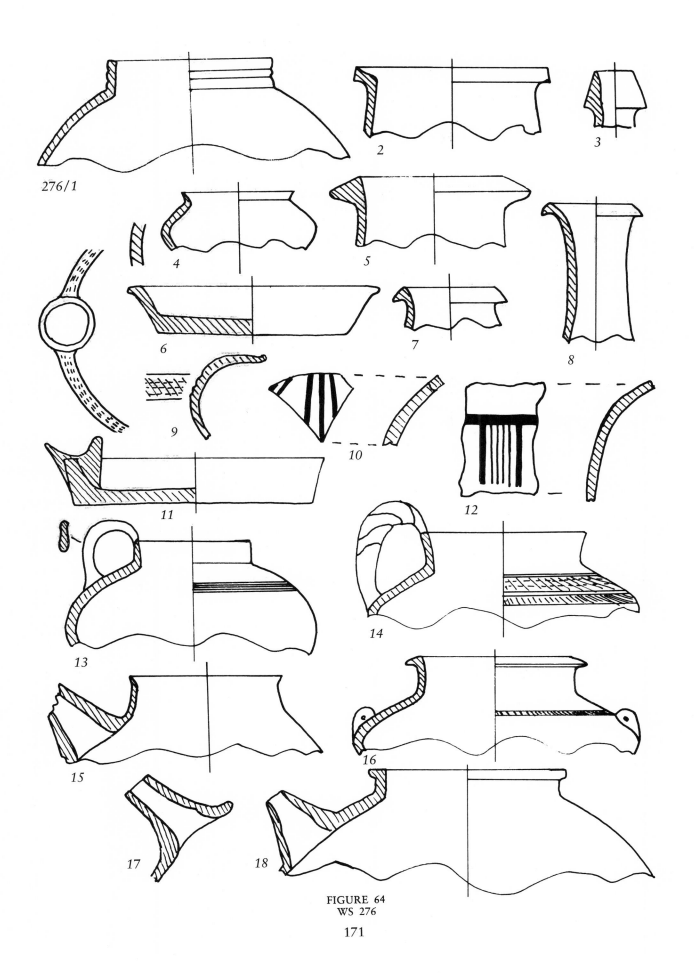

276/1

2

3

4

5

6

7

8

9

10

11

12

13

14

15

16

17

18

FIGURE 64
WS 276

171

Figure 65

276/19 Thin horizontal bands of reserved slip.

276/20 Dark purple paint.

276/21 Dark green paint.

276/22 Black green paint.

276/23 Black green paint.

276/24 Lower fragment of a large vessel of Early Dynastic I cut ware (cf. 422/7).

276/25 Lines impressed with a blunt instrument, not incised.

276/27 Stand which in its uppermost part has a rest for something to be inserted.

Scale 1/5. 19:520; 20:52–; 21:020; 22:020; 23:22–; 24:24–; 25:132; 26:120; 27:130; 28:13–; 29:72–.

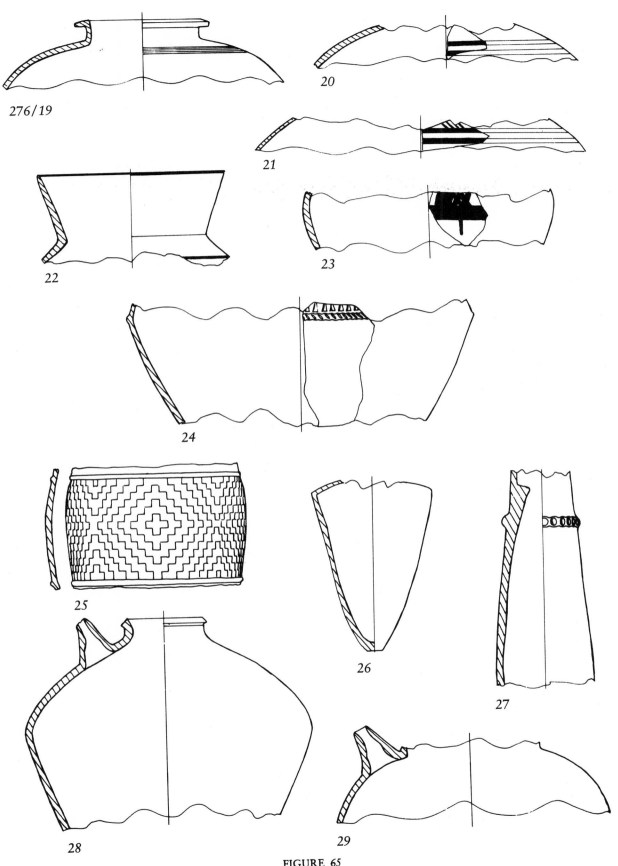

276/19

20

21

22

23

24

25

26

27

28

29

FIGURE 65
WS 276

WS 298

This small site yielded sherds of a kind which had not been found before in Southern Iraq; at least nothing is reported about them in the summaries on the early pottery from Eridu (cf. J. Oates, "Eridu and Prehistory," *Iraq* 22: 32 ff.). In designs the pottery compares with the material found in the Mandali area, especially in the excavations of Chogha Mami (Oates, *Iraq* 30: 1 ff.; 31, 115 ff.); but the comparisons with that area are even more conspicuous because we find similar wares in Chogha Sefid phase 5 (prior and contemporary with Ubaid I) (Prelim. Report Rice Univ. Proj. in Iran 1968/69 figs. 11–15).

Uncentered patterns inside of oval dishes are known from Eridu (*Iraq* 22, pl. 5, no. 21) but not on a pedestal base, for which parallels can be found in Sāmarrān Baghouz (Baghouz, pl. XXII 1–3), and in the abovementioned level 5 of Chogha Sefid, for which strong Sāmarrān connections are claimed. Thus there can be no doubt that the bulk of the pottery from this site is contemporary with Eridu (Ubaid I) or even earlier. The ware of this distinctive kind of sherd however, is different from that of both the Sāmarrān and the Chogha Mami examples, as they are much coarser and the thickness of the walls averages around 0.6–0.7 cm.

Figure 66

298/1 Faint light brown paint.
298/2 Light brown paint.
298/3 Light brown paint.
298/4 Light brown paint.
298/5 Olive green paint.
298/6 Light brown paint.
298/7 Inside purple paint; outside light brown paint.
298/8 Light brown paint.
298/9 Black paint.
298/10 Light brown lines, dots in dark brown.
298/11 Brown paint.
298/12 Bands of dark green paint.
298/13 Olive green paint.
298/14–16 Dark green paint.
298/17 Green paint.

Scale 1/5. 1:23–; 2:23–; 3:02–; 4:03–; 5:52–; 6:020; 7:52–; 8:22–; 9:52–; 10:22–; 11:22–; 12:52–; 13:524; 14:52–; 15:52–; 16:53–; 17:23–.

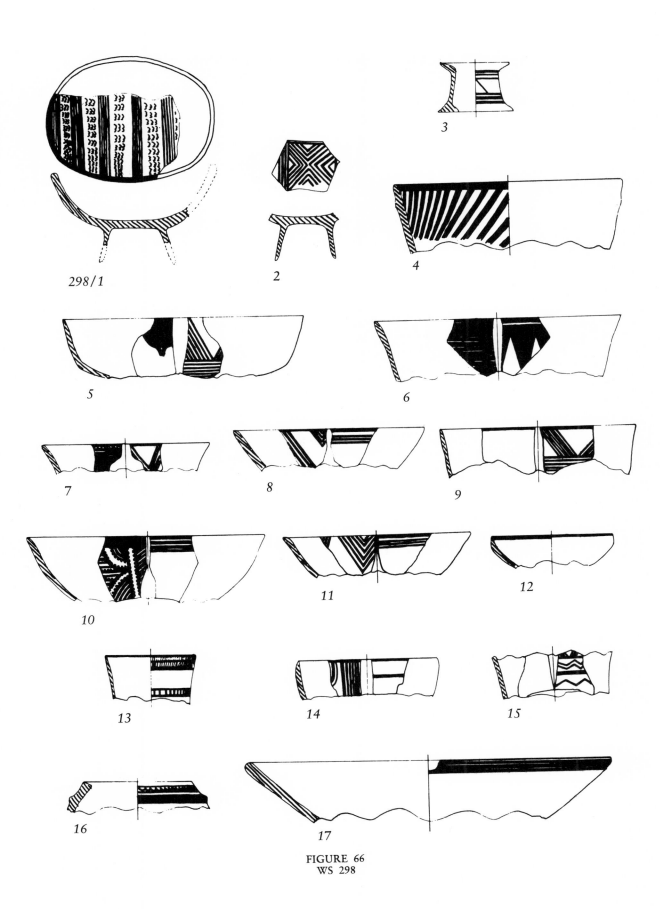

298/1

2

3

4

5

6

7

8

9

10

11

12

13

14

15

16

17

FIGURE 66
WS 298

175

Figure 67

298/18 Light brown paint.
298/19 Dark green paint.
298/20 Inside dark green paint.
298/21–22 Dark green paint.
298/23 Olive green paint.

Scale 1/5. 18:020; 19:524; 20:01–; 21:52–; 22:22–; 23:02–; 24:52–; 25:22–; 26:22–; 27:02–; 28:02–; 29:22–.

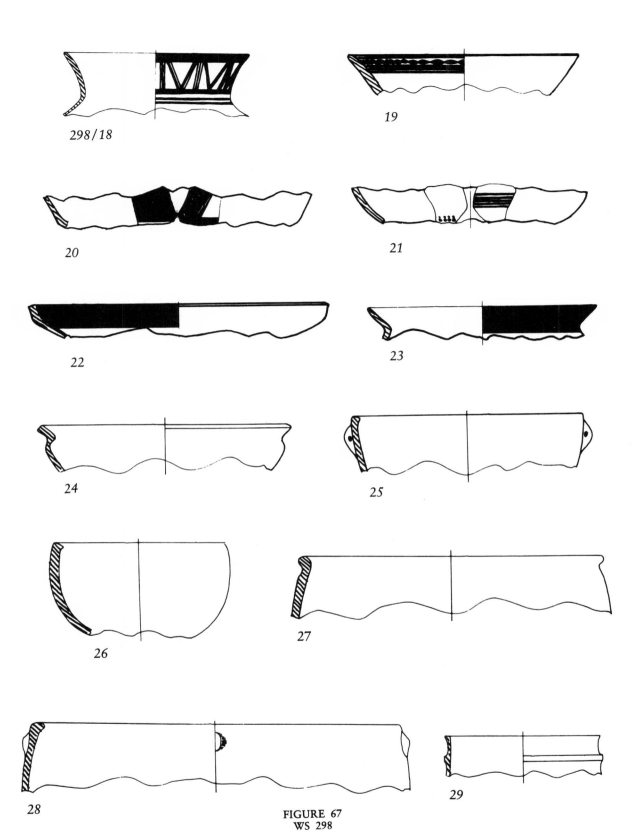

298/18

19

20

21

22

23

24

25

26

27

28

29

FIGURE 67
WS 298

177

WS 310

According to the mass-produced types, this site was occupied mainly during Late Uruk and Jemdet Nasr (no Early Dynastic I solid-footed goblets or other features). In general the other sherds comply with that dating, except 310/2, 4; these would better fit an Early Dynastic II context. Thus there may be an occupation at that time, though very small, as we found no other evidence.

Figure 68

310/1 Oblique reserved slip below two bands of incising.
310/2 Pedestal of a low "fruit stand"? (perhaps together with 310/4).
310/3 Bands in black green paint.
310/4 Upper part of a fruit stand?
310/6 Band in black paint.
310/7 The entire surface is decorated in rows of applied lumps of clay; double rope handle.

Scale 2/5, except 1, which is 1/5. 1:220; 2:02–; 3:52–; 4:02–; 5:53–; 6:52–; 7:72–; 8:120; 9:72–; 10:02–; 11:020.

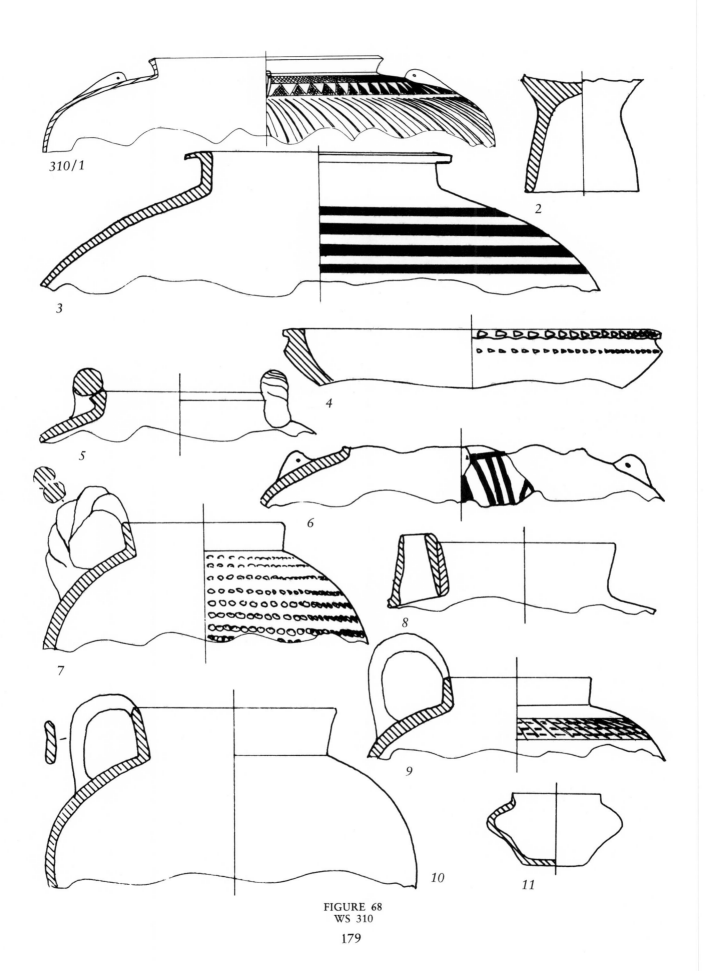

310/1

3

2

5

4

6

7

8

9

10

11

FIGURE 68
WS 310

179

WS 312

No single sherd of Late Uruk date, but many conical cups and solid-footed goblets confirming an occupation in Jemdet Nasr to Early Dynastic I. The illustrated sherds correspond to this date.

Figure 69

312/6 Two ledge handholds.
312/7 Nonconcentric plastic ridges; geometric designs in dark brown–sepia paint.
312/8 Vertical reserved slip.

Scale 2/5. 1:02–; 2:53–; 3:020; 4:122; 5:120; 6:520; 7:020; 8:020; 9:02–; 10:120; 11:020; 12:130; 13:03–; 14:120; 15:12–.

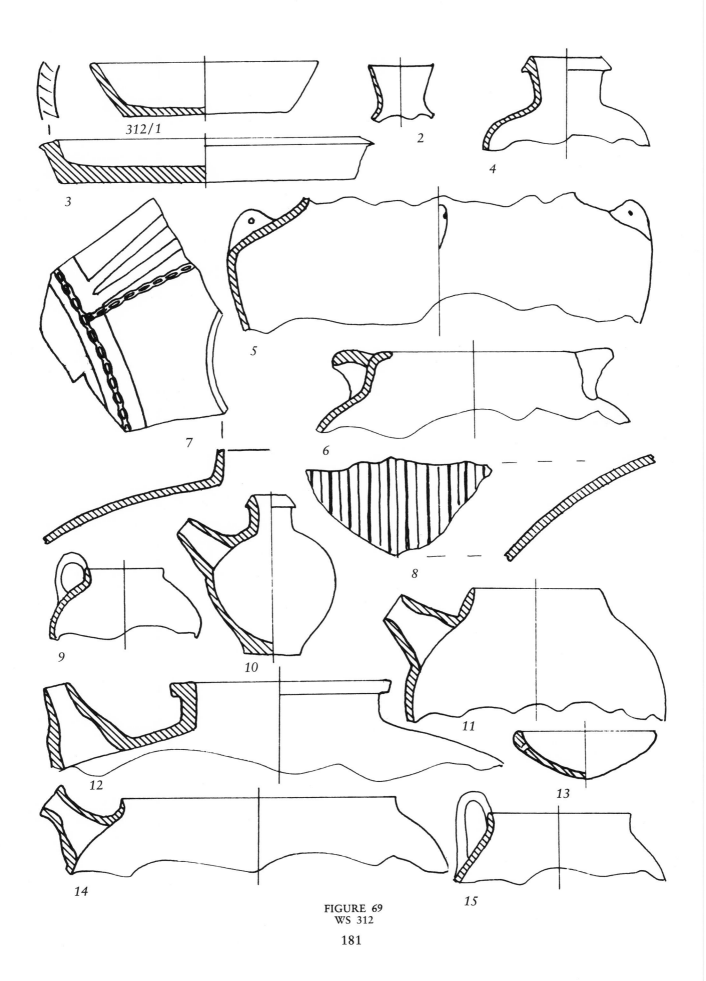

312/1

3

2

4

5

7

6

8

9

10

11

12

13

14

15

FIGURE 69
WS 312

WS 382

According to the mass-produced types, occupied during the Jemdet Nasr–Early Dynastic I, a date suggested also by Jemdet Nasr painting (382/8, 11); a good example of Early Dynastic I cut ware (382/14).

Figure 70

382/1 Brown bands on rim.
382/2 Four (?) crescent-shaped handholds with two buckles underneath; oblique reserved slip below a row of stitches.
382/8 Plum red and black paint.
382/11 Plum red and black paint.
382/14 Early Dynastic I cut ware with holes pierced through, triangles cut halfway through wall.

Scale 1/5. 1:020; 2:230; 3:120; 4:020; 5:120; 6:120; 7:030; 8:020; 9:120; 10:130; 11:12–; 12:130; 13:030; 14:120; 15:120.

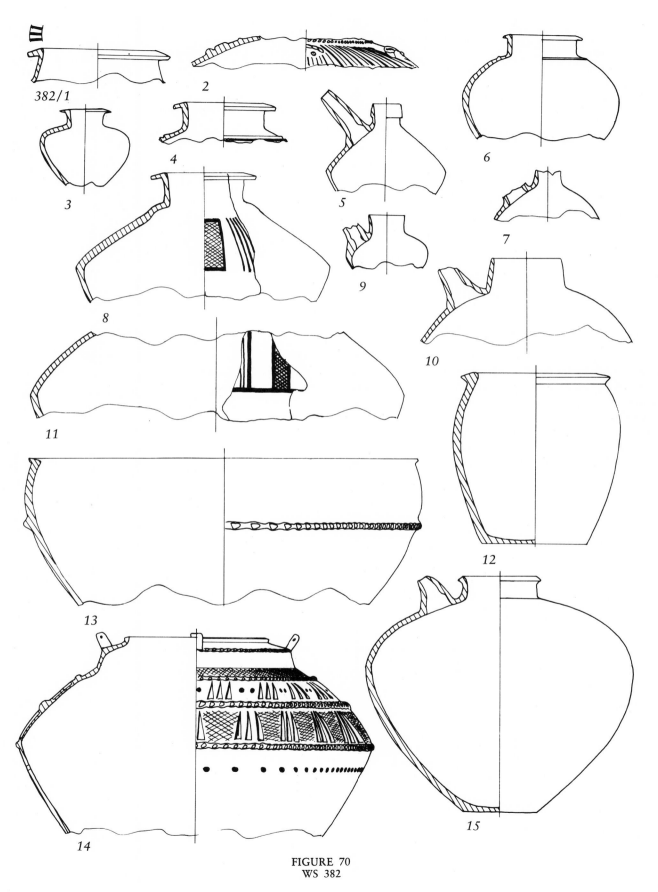

382/1

2

3

4

5

6

7

8

9

10

11

12

13

14

15

FIGURE 70
WS 382

183

WS 386

No sherds of conical cups were found, as opposed to many beveled-rim bowls; hence occupation was probably restricted to Late Uruk and Early Uruk (as 386/3, 16, 20 show). Of special interest are 386/18, with a combination of horizontal and vertical bands of crosshatched incising, and 386/17, a sherd with the remains of a plastic snake (?), resembling similar plastic decoration on sherds from the Late Uruk levels in *Uruk K/L* XII (layer 41).

Figure 71

386/3 Traces of vertical burnishing.
386/11 Black paint.

Scale 2/5. 1:03–; 2:22–; 3:020; 4:52–; 5:15–; 6:02–; 7:52–; 8:010; 9:020; 10:53–; 11:04–; 12:426.

2

386/1

3

4

5

6

7

8

9

10

11

12

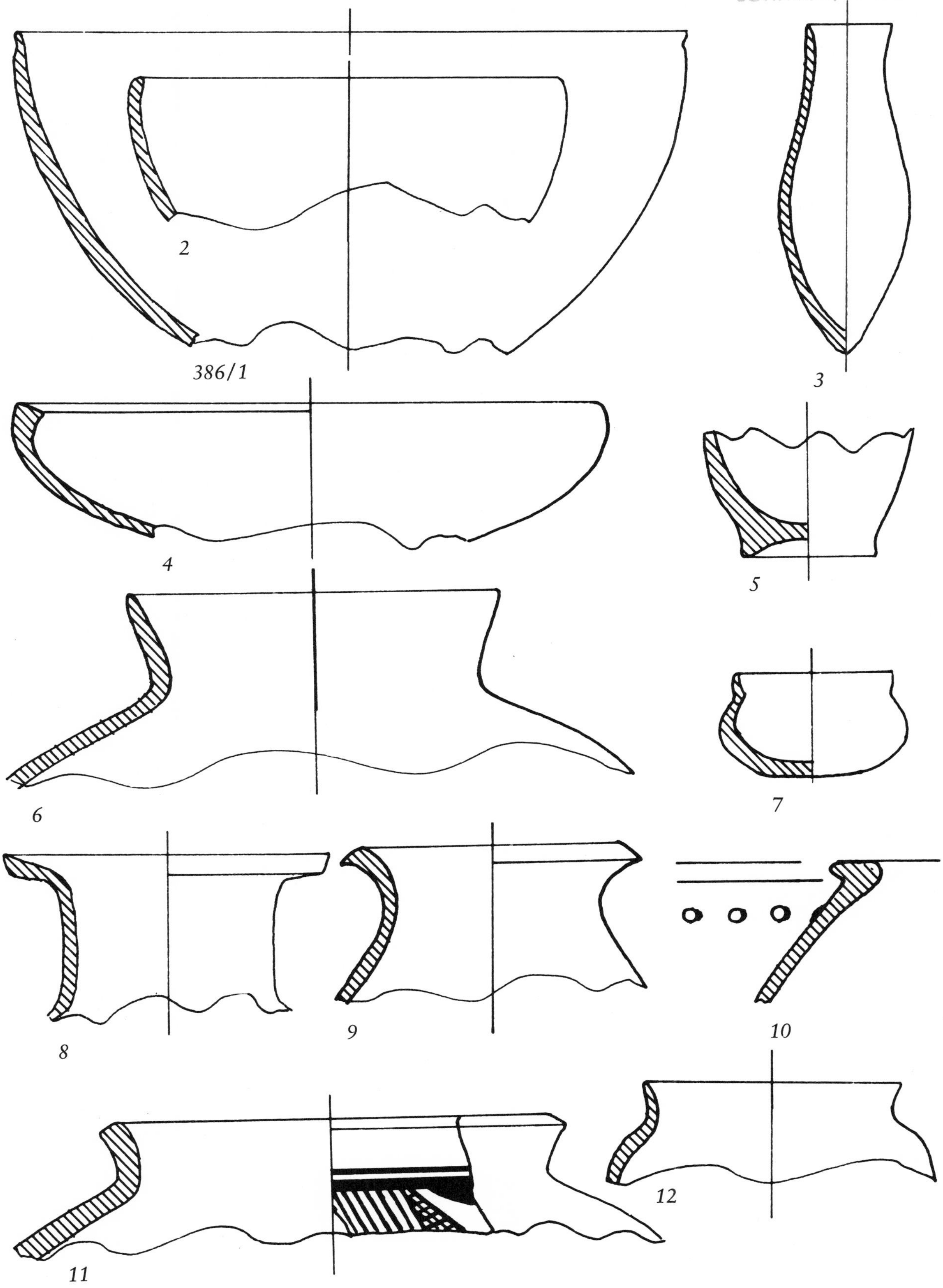

FIGURE 71
WS 386

Figure 72

386/14 Crosshatched incising below a finger-impressed plastic ridge.
386/16 Fine example of Early Uruk painting in dark brown paint.
386/17 Sherd with plastic decoration.
386/18 Sherd with horizontal and vertical bands of incising.

Scale 2/5. 13:53–; 14:03–; 15:220; 16:014; 17:52–; 18:020; 19:020; 20:72–.

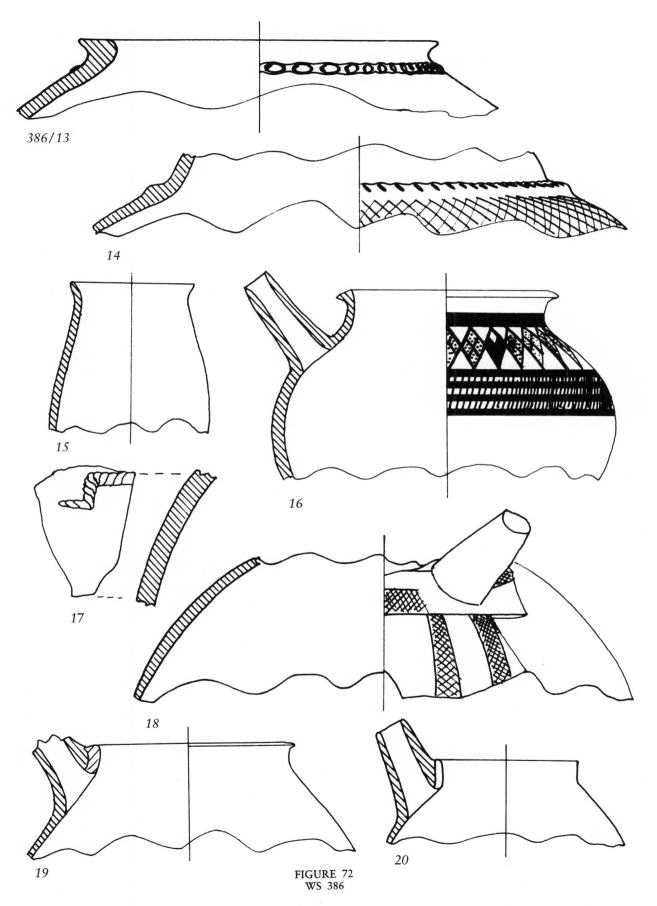

386/13

14

15

16

17

18

19

20

FIGURE 72
WS 386

187

WS 387

Although not very informative, this sherd collection is illustrated because of the importance of establishing the date of the abandonment of this site as an indication of the date of the temple model found on its surface. The mass-produced wares (few beveled-rim bowls, very frequent sherds of conical cups and solid-footed goblets) point to an occupation during the Late Uruk through Early Dynastic I periods. As far as the few sherds are characteristic they confirm this time range: Late Uruk, 387/6, 11; Jemdet Nasr, 387/1, 3/10. Early Dynastic I; 387/2, 8. There is nothing which can be dated to a period later than Early Dynastic I.

Figure 73

387/1 Black paint.
387/2 Dark brown paint.
387/3 Dark brown paint.
387/4 Dark green paint.
387/5 Stand with cut-through triangles.
387/8 Four rim tabs.
387/10 Concentric bands in black as well as a black band around the base of the spout.
387/11 Vessel with twin spouts, elsewhere attributed to Late Uruk (*UE* IV p. 23, pl. 25).

Scale 2/5. 1:224; 2:22–; 3:020; 4:52–; 5:13–; 6:020; 7:02–; 8:73–; 9:130; 10:030.

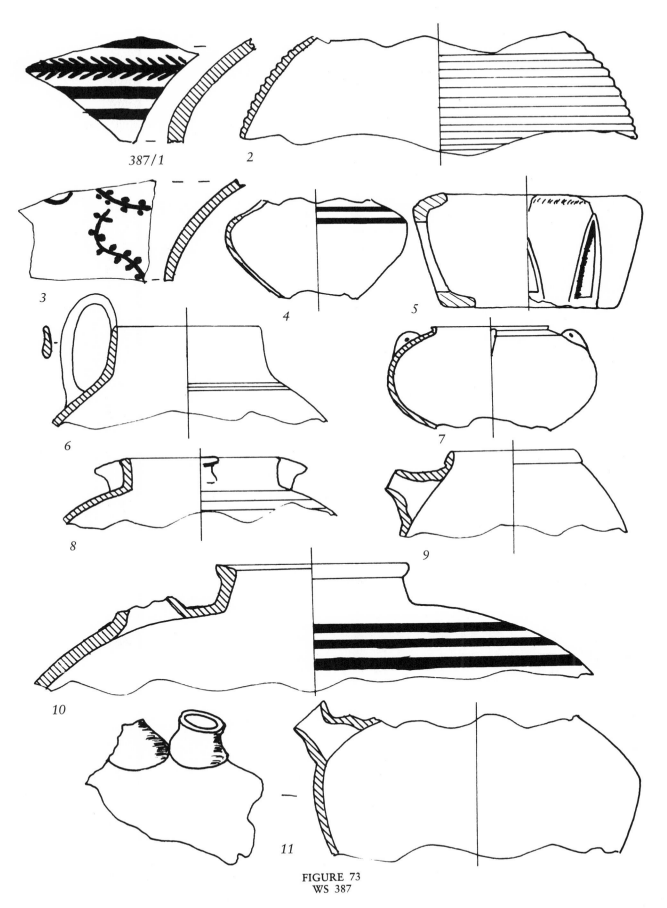

387/1

2

3

4

5

6

7

8

9

10

11

FIGURE 73
WS 387

WS 390

Primarily occupied during Early Dynastic I, with some sherds dating to the Jemdet Nasr period (390/1, 6?).

Figure 74

390/1   Very faint traces of plum red (?) paint.
390/3   Band of black green paint.
390/6   Band of black paint.
390/7   Ribbed ware with four rim tabs.
390/10   Example of carinated jars with one triangular lug on the shoulder.

Scale 2/5. 1:120; 2:230; 3:034; 4:02–; 5:02–; 6:024; 7:120; 8:130; 9:130; 10:030.

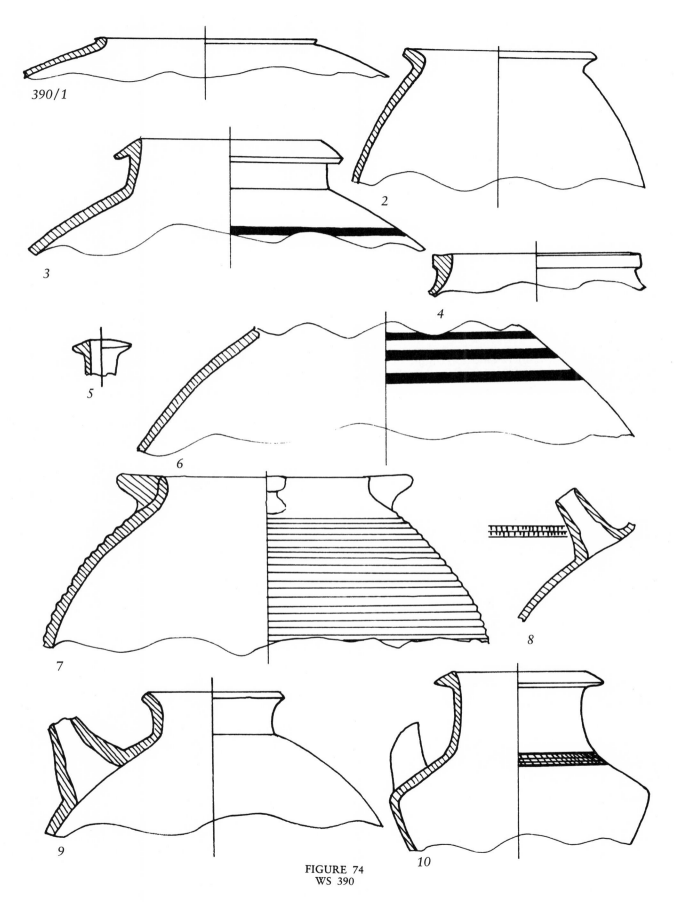

390/1

2

3

4

5

6

7

8

9

10

FIGURE 74
WS 390

191

WS 411

Probably a Late Ubaid (Ubaid IV) single-period site, although no definite proof can be given that the site was not inhabited in Ubaid III. Definitely no Early or Late Uruk features.

Figure 75

All painted sherds display a black green color.
411/10 Semicircular inside scoring.
411/12 Base of bowl like 411/10 with interior scoring.

Scale 2/5. 1:52–; 2:534; 3:02–; 4:51–; 5:52–; 6:51–; 7:52–; 8:52–; 9:52–; 10:52–; 11:01–; 12:22–; 13:02–; 14:02–.

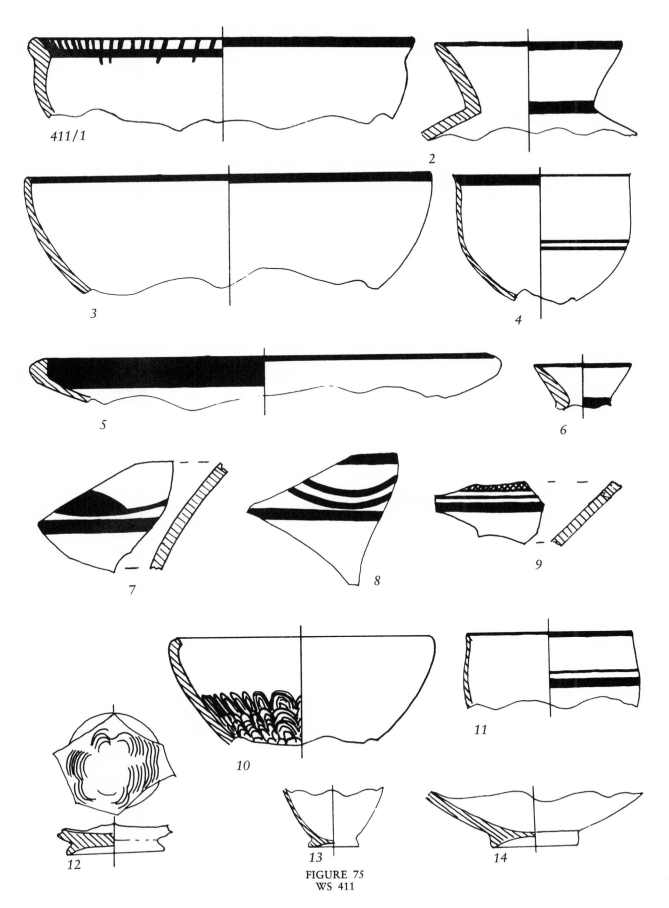

411/1

2

3

4

5

6

7

8

9

10

11

12

13

FIGURE 75
WS 411

14

193

Figure 76

411/16 Remains of a handle (?).

411/22 Only two of these buckles are preserved; thus it is only conjectural whether more can be reconstructed or whether there never were more than two.

Scale 2/5. 15:04–; 16:030; 17:03–; 18:02–; 19:73–; 20:020; 21:020; 22:02–.

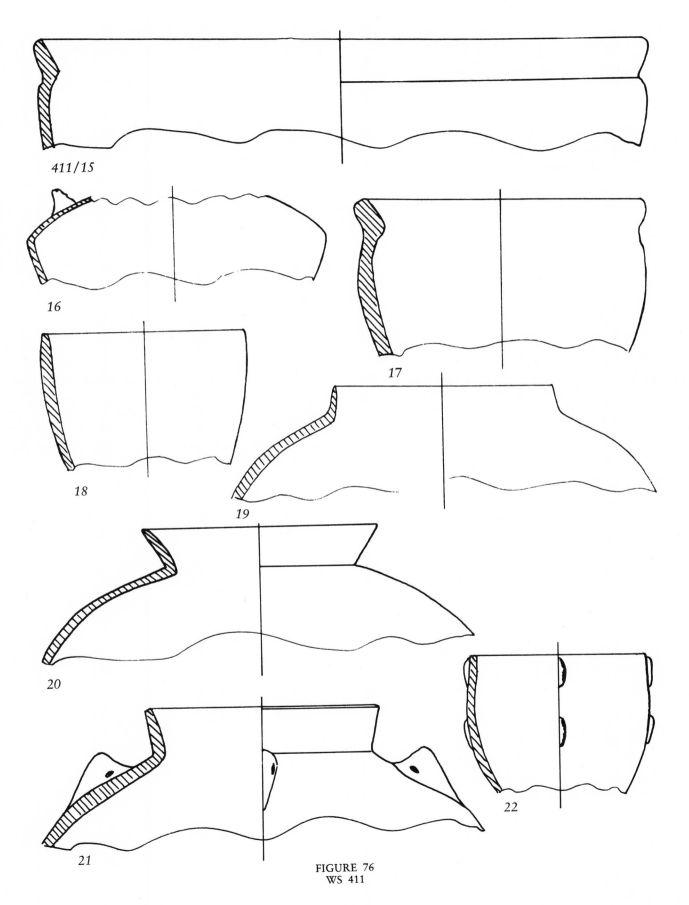

411/15

16

17

18

19

20

21

22

FIGURE 76
WS 411

WS 422

All characteristic sherds date to the Early Dynastic I period (422/3, 7, 8, 10, 11). Together with the frequent sherds of the solid-footed goblets, this speaks for an Early Dynastic I single-period site.

Figure 77

422/3   Four rim tabs.

422/7   Imitation of cut ware, as the holes and triangles are only incised.

422/8   Fragment of true cut ware.

422/10–11 Below a row of stitches oblique reserved slip.

Scale 2/5. 1:120; 2:120; 3:020; 4:020; 5:020; 6:41–; 7:030; 8:130; 9:12–; 10:020; 11:220.

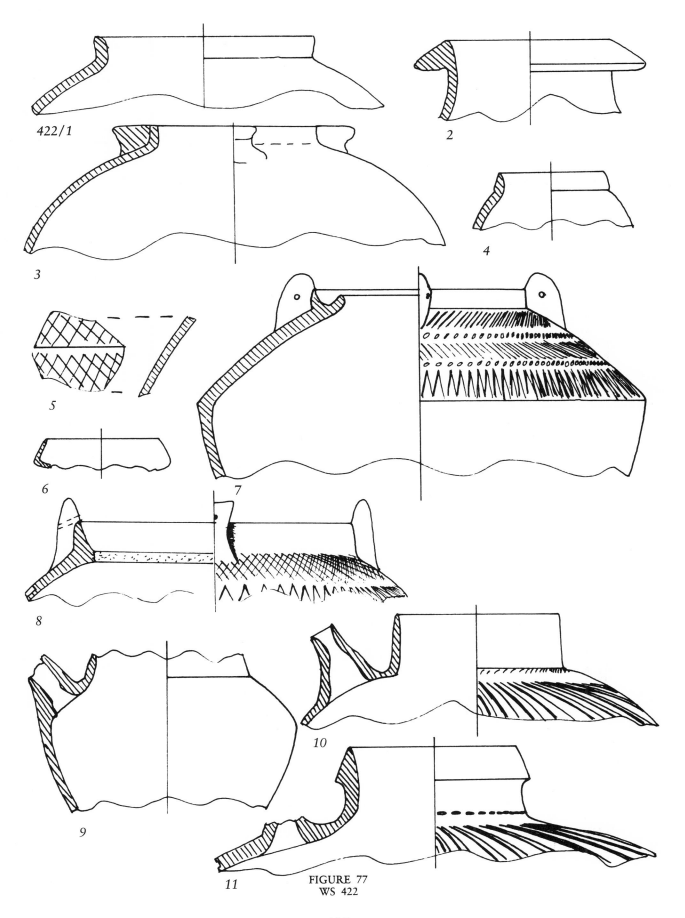

422/1

2

3

4

5

6

7

8

9

10

11

FIGURE 77
WS 422

197

WS 460

This site was visited by members of the French expedition to nearby Senkere in 1967 independently of our visit (a short account appeared in *Syria* 45:234 ff. with fig. 26–29). In addition to the overwhelming majority of Ubaid III and IV remains (ibid. fig. 28–29 and our following plates) we were able to secure few sherds of Early Uruk (460/43, 44, 45, 53) date and even of Late Uruk (infrequent sherds of beveled-rim bowls and 460/48, 52).

Figure 78

460/1 Black green paint, open pouring spout.
460/2 Black green paint.
460/3 Black green paint.
460/4 Brown paint.
460/5 Dark brown paint.
460/6 Brown paint.
460/7 Black paint.
460/8 Sepia paint.
460/9 Dark brown paint.
460/10 Black green paint.
460/11 Dark brown paint.
460/12 Black paint.
460/13 Dark brown paint.
460/14–16 Black green paint.
460/17 Brown paint.

Scale 2/5. 1:53–; 2:53–; 3:02–; 4:224; 5:02–; 6:01–; 7:020; 8:02–; 9:52–; 10:52–; 11:020; 12:53–; 13:52–; 14:53–; 15:53–; 16:01–; 17:020.

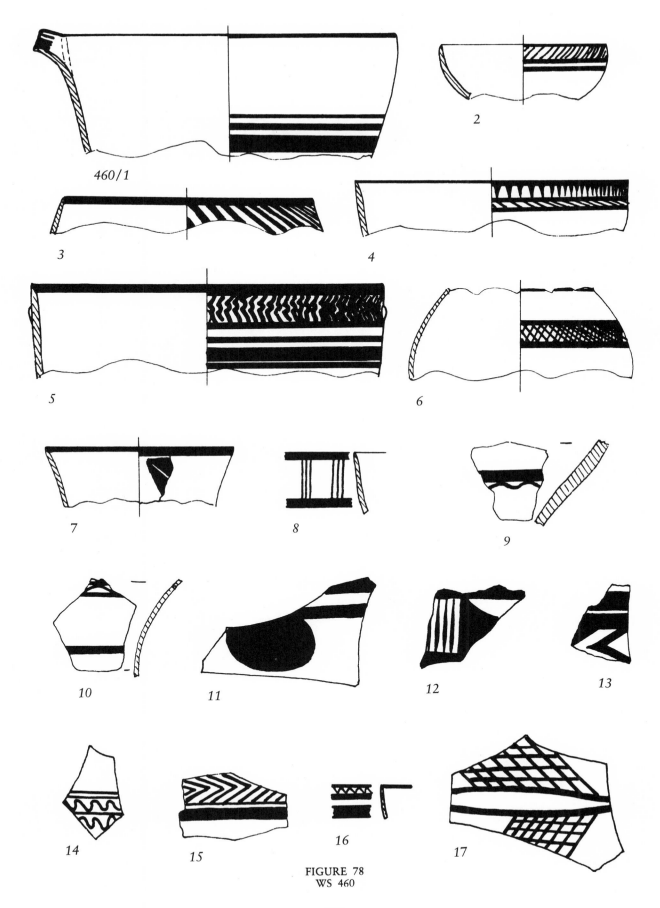

460/1

2

3

4

5

6

7

8

9

10

11

12

13

14

15

16

17

FIGURE 78
WS 460

199

Figure 79

460/18–20 Black green paint.
460/21 Black green, the same on rim.
460/22 Dark brown, the same on rim.
460/23 Sepia, the same on rim.
460/24 Black green paint.
460/25 Black green, the same on rim.
460/26 Brown paint.
460/27–28 Black green paint.
460/30 Base with semicircular inside scoring.
460/31 Inside stippling to reach an effect similar to that in 460/30, 34.
460/32 Like 460/30, band of black green paint.
460/33 Black green.
460/34 Like 460/30.
460/35 Black green, the same on rim.
460/36–37 Black green paint.
460/38 Light brown paint.
460/39 Black green paint.

Scale, 18–34, 1/5; 35–39, 2/5. 18:53–; 19:53–; 20:53–; 21:53–; 22:53–; 23:52–; 24:53–; 25:234; 26:13–; 27:53–; 28:52–; 29:54–; 30:52–; 31:52–; 32:52–; 33:53–; 34:53–; 35:53–; 36:534; 37:020; 38:02–; 39:52–.

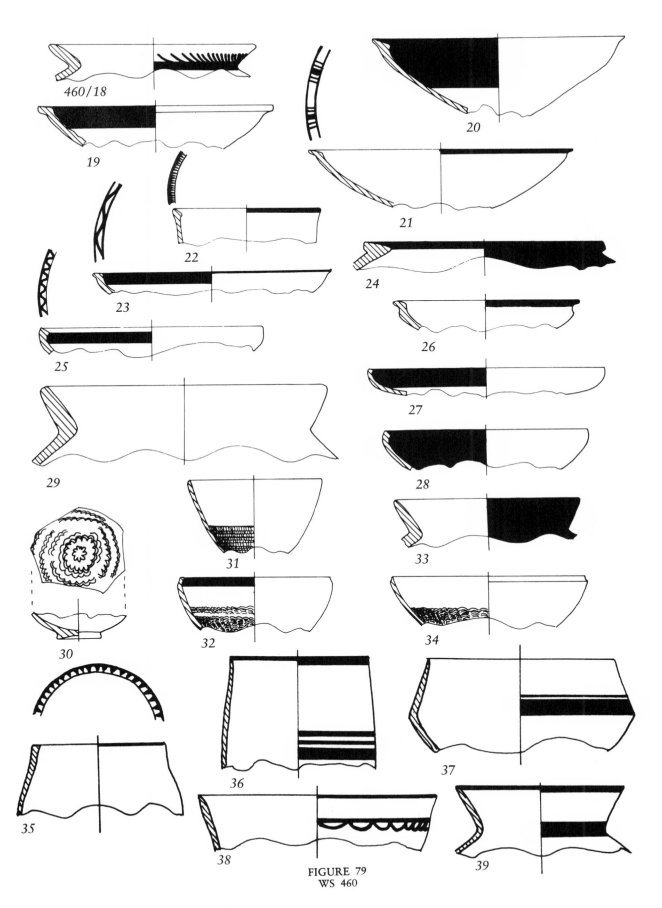

460/18

19

20

21

22

23

24

25

26

27

28

29

30

31

32

33

34

35

36

37

38

39

FIGURE 79
WS 460

201

Figure 80

460/40 Basket handle.
460/42 High hollow base.
460/43 Black green paint.
460/44 Brown paint.
460/45 Base of pointed-base bottle.
460/53, 57 Black green paint.

Scale, 40–52, 2/5; 53–57, 1/5. 40:52–; 41:52–; 42:04–; 43:73–; 44:02–; 45:04–; 46:02–; 47:112; 48:72–; 49:73–; 50:220; 51:13–; 52:73–; 53:534; 54:04–; 55:53–; 56:53–; 57:54–.

460/40

41

43

42

44

45

46

47

48

49

50

51

52

53

54

55

56

57 FIGURE 80
WS 460

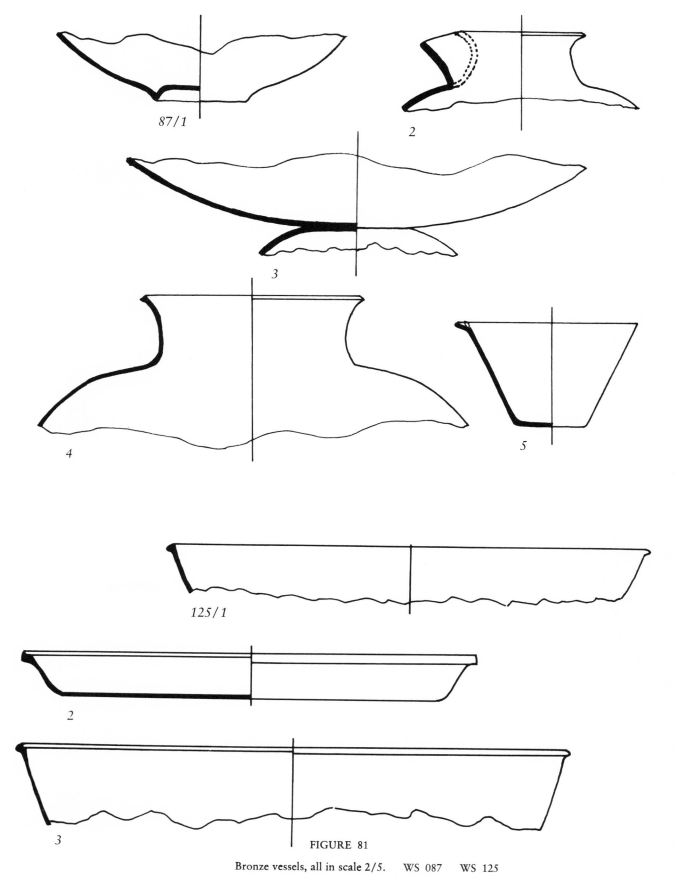

87/1

2

3

4

5

125/1

2

3

FIGURE 81

Bronze vessels, all in scale 2/5.   WS 087   WS 125

204

METAL VESSELS

Broken pieces of bronze or copper that can be identified as fragments of vessels were found at eight sites. On the basis of the associated ceramics, all can be dated to the span between the late Uruk and the Early Dynastic I periods. The thin sheeting naturally had suffered more from weathering than any other category of surface materials, so that in four cases nothing could be determined of the sizes and profiles of the original vessels. In four other instances, however, individual fragments providing some information about form could be separated from clumps of many pieces that had corroded together. Two concentrations, each containing numerous fragments, were observed on the surface of one site (WS 177). Most

of these fragments were either completely shapeless or hopelessly corroded together, leaving us with the impression that already in ancient times they had been broken and collected for reuse.

Among the fragments from WS 177 occurred one from the side of a large vessel that was decorated with an embossed rosette. Another consisted of part of a foot with a riveted attachment. A third was a piece of a plate, in the corroded surface on whose underside could be detected the impressions of a reed mat. Also from this site was a small, entirely amorphous piece with the low stump of a connection between two metal sheets and traces pointing to the use of solder in the joint.

Among the eight find-spots of these metal fragments were two sites that appeared to have been occupied only

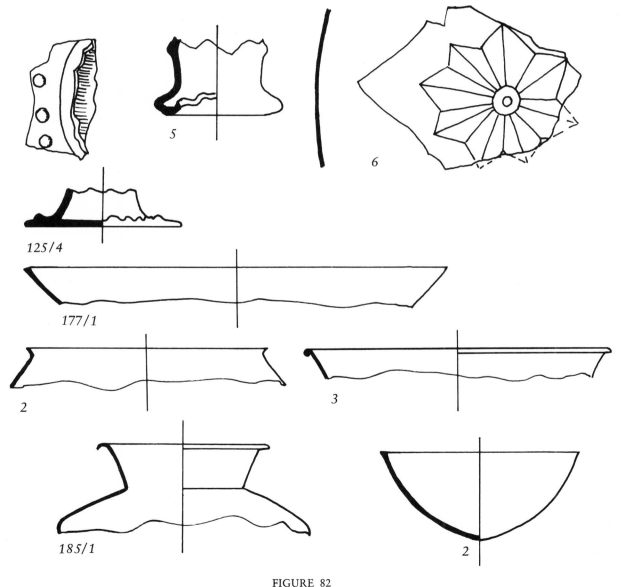

FIGURE 82

Bronze vessels: 125, 4–6, scale 1/5; all others 2/5.   WS 125   WS 177   WS 185

205

during the late Uruk period, and in five additional cases the occupation began at that time but continued later. Although certainly not unexpected, this is somewhat surprising in that no metal vessels have yet been recovered from excavations of late Uruk levels. On the other hand, two installations connected with metalworking have been excavated in late Uruk levels at Uruk itself.

With regard to date and site of origin, the fragments of metal vessels recovered during the survey may be conveniently summarized as follows:

Site Number	Late Uruk	Jemdet Nasr	Early Dynastic I
WS 185	————————		
WS 274	————————		
WS 087	————————————————		
WS 285	————————————————		
WS 406	————————————————		
WS 125	————————————————————		
WS 162	————————————————————		
WS 177		————————————————	

In addition to vessel fragments there were sporadic finds of metal tools and weapons. These included, among the sites tabulated above, a chisel at WS 274 and projectile points (spears?) at WS 087 and 125. Heavy, chisel-shaped implements also were found at WS 314, a single-period Late Uruk site, and at WS 272, occupied from Late Uruk into Early Dynastic I times. An apparent arrowhead was found at WS 321, which was occupied only during the Jemdet Nasr period.

STONE VESSELS

Fragments of stone vessels were very common, especially on sites falling within the span of time between the late Uruk and Early Dynastic I periods. The range of variation is very limited, however, so that almost all examples can be classified into one of nine types.

By far the most common are bowls with simple rounded rims, or with rims folded down perpendicular to the outside so as to leave the impression of a horizontal band. These two variations occur so commonly that one

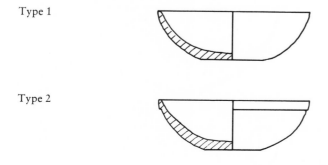

Type 1

Type 2

Site	Ub.	E.U.	L.U.	J.N.	E.D. I
137	- - - - - - - - - - -				
160	- - - - - - - - - - - - - - -				
023		- - - - -			
386		—————			
020		————————————————————————			
107			- - - - -		
109			—————		
191			• • • • • • • •		
193			————————		
314			- - - - -		
331			• • • • • • • •		
087			- - - - - - - - - - -		
144			• • • • • • • • • • • • • • • •		
163			- - - - - - - - - - -		
181			————————————————		
219			————————————————		
262			- - - - - - - - - - -		
267			————————————————		
292			- - - - - - - - - - -		
297			————————————————		
310			————————————————		
317			————————————————		
334			————————————————		
028			————————————————————		
082			————————————————————		
125			————————————————————		
162			- - - - - - - - - - - - - - -		
230			————————————————————		
242			————————————————————		
264			• • • • • • • • • • • • • • • • • • •		
272			————————————————————		
276			————————————————————		
282			• • • • • • • • • • • • • • • • • • •		
387			• • • • • • • • • • • • • • • • • • •		
321				—————	
177				————————	
233				————————	
288				————————	
312				- - - - - - - -	
372				————————	
382				————————	
179				- - - - - ———	
306				- - - - - ———	
383				- - - - - ———	
409				- - - - - ———	

Type 1	————	Types 1 and 2	- - - - -
Type 2	• • • • •		

Summary of available data on the provenance and dating of the principal types of stone vessels.

might expect to find some evidence of chronological differences in their periods of major popularity. Although there appears to have been some tendency for type 2 to be favored in earlier periods (it occurs at four single-period sites of late Uruk date), however, it also occurs at a site of Jemdet Nasr–Early Dynastic I age like WS 312. Type 1, on the other hand, is found in seemingly equal numbers in all periods from early Uruk to Early Dynastic I.

It is hardly possible to say more about the dating of the remaining types, since they occurred in such small numbers that assignments of exact date on the basis of surface findings can be attempted only with caution. As a whole, however, it appears that their time of greatest popularity lay in the late Uruk and Jemdet Nasr periods. Only in the case of type 8 were all three sites at which it was found still occupied as late as the Early Dynastic I period. And one can in fact assign this type to the Early

Dynastic period on the basis of its obvious similarity to a ceramic vessel form known to be of that date with four evenly spaced lugs attached directly to the rim.

Most vessels were carved out of whitish, grayish white, or yellowish limestone or gypsum. Only rarely were other types of limestone employed exhibiting other colors or bands of color. Also very little used were harder types of stone. Basalt was used only for relatively crude, very thick-sided vessels and for mortars, pestles, and querns.

The frequency of stone vessel fragments declines in the Early Dynastic I period. Since we know from the findings of excavations, however, that stone vessels remained common throughout the Early Dynastic period and rapidly began to decline in importance only after the Ur III period, this finding is open to another interpretation. Probably it reflects no more than the decline during and after the Early Dynastic I period in the occupation of rural settlements of the kind recorded by the survey.

Type 3, Deep bowl with spout

Site	Ub.	E.U.	L.U.	J.N.	E.D. I
357				———	
312					———

Type 4 — Height 8–10 cm; Diameter 8–11 cm

Site	Ub.	E.U.	L.U.	J.N.	E.D. I
137	———————————				
185			———		
262			————————		
162			———————————————		
306				- - - - ———	

Type 5 — Height 12–22 cm; Diameter 10–25 cm

Site	Ub.	E.U.	L.U.	J.N.	E.D. I
060			———————————		
087			———————————		
292			———		

Type 6 — Height 12–14 cm; Diameter 22–24 cm

Site	Ub.	E.U.	L.U.	J.N.	E.D. I
087			———————————		
130					———

Type 7 — Height 3.5–4 cm; Diameter 13–15 cm

Site	Ub.	E.U.	L.U.	J.N.	E.D. I
185			———		
264			———————————————		

Type 8 — Height 25–32 cm, Diameter 15–18 cm

Site	Ub.	E.U.	L.U.	J.N.	E.D. I
125			————	————	————
230			————	————	————
272			————	————	————
177				————	————

Type 9 — Height a 7–9 cm, 15–19 cm; b 27–35 cm

Site	Ub.	E.U.	L.U.	J.N.	E.D. I
042	————	————	————		
386		————	————		
107			————		
110			————		
163			————	————	
297			————	————	
272			————	————	————
282			————	————	————
293			————	————	————
177				————	————
256				————	————
231				- - - -	————

CLAY SICKLES

All sickles we found were made for use with the left hand. They are made of medium fine clay, highly fired and of greenish color. On two sites (WS 042, 411) we found sickles with the cutting edge painted with the usual Ubaid black paint. The purpose of these is unknown, but it seems unlikely that they served the same purpose as the unpainted ones.

That the sickles look like the normal Ubaid ware in texture and color and often were found in Ubaid context led to the assumption that clay sickles were confined to the Ubaid period. However, we found them to be an essential part of the Early and Late Uruk assemblages, extending into the Jemdet Nasr period as indicated by their presence in Jemdet Nasr single-period sites. That sickles were actually made also after the Ubaid period is shown by a lump of fourteen sickles fused together, found on WS 119, a Late Uruk single-period site.

We found sickles of exactly the same size on 104 sites, of which 88 are within the time range from Ubaid to Early Dynastic I. On four sites we found, in addition to the normal-sized sickles, smaller specimens, the "blade" of which measured only up to 15 cm. From the distribution of these one gets the feeling that the smaller size is peculiar to the earlier periods. The limited number, however, does not permit us to be more accurate.

In addition to these early sites we found single sickles on the surface of sixteen sites dating from Larsa to Sassanian times. In these cases we assumed that this sickle was a stray find, and did not draw any chronological conclusions.

Site	Ub.	E.U.	L.U.	J.N.	E.D. I
275	————				
460	————	————			
218	————	————			
009			————		

Distribution of small clay sickles

Site	Ub.	E.U.	L.U.	J.N.	E.D. I	Site	Ub.	E.U.	L.U.	J.N.	E.D. I
247	▬					095			▬▬▬▬		
275	▬					105			▬▬▬▬		
460	▬▬▬					114			▬▬▬▬		
042	▬▬▬▬▬					127			▬▬▬▬		
051	▬▬▬▬▬▬▬▬▬▬					129			▬▬▬▬		
137	▬▬▬▬▬					144			▬▬▬▬		
218	▬▬▬▬▬					153			▬▬▬▬		
160	▬▬▬▬▬▬					219			▬▬▬▬		
260	▬▬▬▬▬▬					292			▬▬▬▬		
022		▬▬				310			▬▬▬▬		
023		▬▬				334			▬▬▬▬		
024		▬▬				406			▬▬▬▬		
118		▬▬				453			▬▬▬▬		
215		▬▬				373			- - - -	▬	
020		▬▬▬				317			- - - - -		
386		▬▬▬				330			- - - - -		
107		▬▬▬▬▬				028			▬▬▬▬▬▬		
201		▬▬▬				082			▬▬▬▬▬▬		
009			▬▬			125			▬▬▬▬▬▬		
071			▬▬			162			▬▬▬▬▬▬		
083			▬▬			166			▬▬▬▬▬▬		
106			▬▬			168			▬▬▬▬▬		
108			▬▬			169			▬▬▬▬▬		
109			▬▬			190			▬▬ - - - - -		
110			▬▬			197			- - - - - - -		
112			▬▬			198			- - - - - - -		
115			▬▬			230			▬▬▬▬▬▬		
119			▬▬			242			▬▬ - - - - -		
133			▬▬			276			▬▬▬▬▬▬		
152			▬▬			282			▬▬▬▬▬▬		
185			▬▬			293			▬▬▬▬▬▬		
191			▬▬			387			▬▬▬▬▬▬		
193			▬▬			407			▬▬▬▬▬▬		
209			▬▬			164			- - - - - -	▬	
236			▬▬			155				▬▬	
274			▬▬			358				▬▬	
314			▬▬			370				▬▬	
318			▬▬			380				▬▬	
331			▬▬			401				▬▬	
350			▬▬			047				▬▬▬▬	
367			▬▬			174				▬▬▬▬	
376			▬▬			186				- - - ▬▬	
044			▬▬▬▬			256				▬▬▬▬	
060			▬▬▬▬			384				- - - ▬▬	
086			▬▬▬▬			130				▬▬▬▬	
087			▬▬▬▬								

Distribution of normal-sized clay sickles.

BENT CLAY "NAILS"

Site	Ub.	E.U.	L.U.	J.N.	E.D. I
275	▬▬▬				
411	▬▬▬				
460	▬▬▬▬▬				
218	▬▬▬▬▬▬▬				
160	▬▬▬▬▬▬▬▬▬▬▬				
156			▬▬▬▬▬		
262			▬▬▬▬▬		
125			▬▬▬▬▬▬▬		
245			▬▬▬▬▬▬▬		
289				▬▬▬	

The general find situation is similar to that of the clay sickles. These objects also have been taken as indicators for the Ubaid period on grounds of their association with Ubaid pottery in excavations and of their greenish color. We found them on nine sites, of which five start in the Ubaid period. Three other settlements started, however, only in the Late Uruk period and only one in the Jemdet Nasr period. These objects, whose purpose is enigmatic, thus range in time from the Ubaid through the Jemdet Nasr periods.

HOES

Site	Ub.	E.U.	L.U.	J.N.	E.D. I
051	▬▬▬▬▬▬▬▬▬▬▬				
267	▬▬▬▬		▬▬▬▬▬		
460	▬▬▬▬		- - - - -		
297			▬▬▬▬▬		
109			▬▬▬		
245			▬▬▬▬▬▬▬		
079				- - - - ▬	
148	Achaem.-Parth.				

Hoes made of flint or, less frequently, of clay have also mostly been found in Ubaid context and thus were taken to be peculiar to this period. We found stone hoes on eight sites, of which three fit an Ubaid date. There are, however, three sites which start only in Late Uruk and one starts only in Jemdet Nasr.

The same is to be said about hoes made of clay. Three sites out of seven were already settled in Ubaid times but two sites started only in Early Uruk, two more in Late Uruk.

In spite of the limited number of sites, we are safe in taking the hoes also as part of the normal Early and Late Uruk assemblages and thus defining their time range as Ubaid through Late Uruk.

Site	Ub.	E.U.	L.U.	J.N.	E.D. I
247	▬▬▬▬				
275	▬▬▬▬				
218	▬▬▬▬▬▬▬				
215		▬▬▬▬			
386		▬▬▬▬▬			
193			▬▬▬		
292			▬▬▬▬▬		

MACE-HEADS

This designation was adopted with some hesitation, as we did not reach a conclusion about the use. Made of stone—mostly basalt—they weigh from one-half to almost two kilograms. One side, taken as the base, is flattened. On the upper side one finds on most of the specimens cross-groovings which continue down the sides. These groovings point to the stone's being attached to something by thongs or cord. Because of the flat base and the general macelike appearance they are normally taken as mace-heads fixed to handles, but manifold problems arise from such a combination. They might also be part of a sling, but then the flattened base would remain unexplained.

These implements were found on fourteen sites which include Early Uruk, Late Uruk, and Jemdet Nasr sites. The time range thus includes these three periods, with a possible peak in the Late Uruk period.

Site	Ub.	E.U.	L.U.	J.N.	E.D. I
260	▬▬		▬▬▬		
215		▬▬			
109			▬▬		
152			▬▬		
274			▬▬		
129			▬▬▬▬		
219			▬▬▬▬		
262			▬▬▬▬		
162			▬▬▬▬▬▬		
230			▬▬▬▬▬▬		
276			▬▬▬▬▬▬		
242			▬▬▬- - - - - -		
091				▬▬	
189				- - - - -▬▬	

CLAY CONES

All possible variations in length and appearance were found, from cones 15 cm long with a hole in the head to cones only 5 cm long. They were found on the surface of eighteen sites, of which two must be mentioned in particular: WS 181, the marsh settlement of the Jemdet Nasr period, where the smallest variety of cones lay on the area which we assumed to be the site of the public buildings of this settlement. The cones were found in heaps along the outer face of what we thought was a kind of enclosure wall. On WS 245 a part of a wall with clay cones in situ still stood above the surface.

Almost all settlements were inhabited during the Late Uruk or the Jemdet Nasr period or both, and thus the dating fits nicely with the date established for cone mosaics in Uruk. Other large sites with cones include Tell Shmīd (168) and Umm al-Aqarib (198), but it is interesting to note that cones also occur on much smaller sites. Apparently this kind of decoration was not confined to large sacred or public buildings.

Site	Ub.	E.U.	L.U.	J.N.	E.D. I
260	▬▬		▬▬▬		
218	▬▬▬▬▬▬				
215		▬▬			
133			▬▬		
181			▬▬▬▬		
219			▬▬▬▬		
406			▬▬▬▬		
082			▬▬▬▬▬▬		
245			▬▬▬▬▬▬		
293			▬▬▬▬▬▬		
407			▬▬▬▬		
273				▬▬	
281				▬▬	
174				▬▬▬	
212				▬▬▬	
288				▬▬	

POT STANDS

Massive round pot stands up to 10 cm high were found on seven sites. The fact that all these sites were inhabited during the Jemdet Nasr period points to this period as the minimum time range, the maximum ranging from Late Uruk through Early Dynastic I.

Site	Ub.	E.U.	L.U.	J.N.	E.D. I
044					
219					
230					
272					
177					
256					
288					
Type 1					
Type 2					

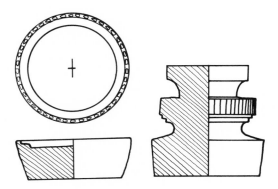

CLAY WHEELS

Mostly heavily damaged, clay wheels were found on eight sites. When they were reconstructible, the outer diameter varied from 15 to 25 cm. Nothing on the find-spot gave a hint as to their use. One may think of the cult wagon from Khafajah, or of the chariot models of the Old Babylonian period. However, for the normal-sized chariot models our wheels certainly were too big. As is shown in the diagram, the dates of the sites are too inconsistent to allow any comments.

Site	L.U.	J.N.	E.D. I	E.D. II	Akk	Ur III—Larsa	O.B.
242							
177							
256							
130							
131							
204							
100							
444							

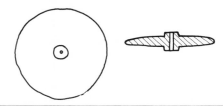

SPINDLE WHORLS

Spindle whorls were found on sixteen sites, covering the periods from Late Uruk to Early Dynastic I. All were similar in shape and were undecorated.

Site	Ub.	E.U.	L.U.	J.N.	E.D. I
137					
260					
185					
274					
181					
219					
082					
407					
189					
404					

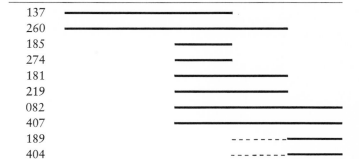

NET WEIGHTS

Two kinds of finds may perhaps be combined under this heading, though they are very different from each other. Easy to recognize as such are round or trapezoid clay plates with two holes near each other near the edge. They were found on eight sites, dating from Early Uruk through Early Dynastic II/III.

Site	Ub.	E.U.	L.U.	J.N.	E.D. I
042	————————————————				
022		———————			
118		———————			
110			———————		
219			———————————————		
256				———————————————	
179					———————
259					E.D. II/III

The second kind remained enigmatic to us until similar examples were found in Warka itself, with a slightly different shape that may suggest how they were used. Instead of being cylindrical objects which were thickened at both ends, the Warka pieces had only one sharply defined deep groove around their center. From this it seems obvious that they have been used as weights for something which could be tied to them. For the Warka examples an explanation as fish net weights seems possible, since they were made of limestone. However, this explanation does not fit all of our specimens, as some were made of unburned clay or of bitumen, which floats on the water. An explanation as weights used in fowl nets fits better. It must remain open, of course, whether the two kinds of net weights were clearly functionally divided; that is, the one kind for fish nets, the other for fowl nets. Alternatively they could serve different purposes on the same net, for instance, the heavier ones for the corners and the others for the sides.

Site	Ub.	E.U.	L.U.	J.N.	E.D. I
411	———————				
042	————————————————————————				
218	————————————————————————				
024		———————			
201		——————————————————————			
020		———————————————————————————			
191			———————		
219			———————————————		
297			———————————————		
028			———————————————————————		
048			———————————————————————		
282			———————————————————————		

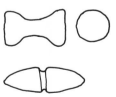

Whether there is any connection to the similarly shaped but larger "clay hammers," found at other places, for instance during the Nippur Survey, remains unproved but not unlikely.

213

U-SHAPED TROUGHS

We found fragments on five sites which range in time from the Late Uruk period to Early Dynastic I. Interesting is the one end of such a trough found on WS 262 which shows how the different parts are connected with each other. The walls are funnellike, bent outward so that the following piece could be inserted. Two holes in the bottom part probably corresponded to holes in the next piece to allow a secure connection. These troughs probably were used for open water drains.

Site	Ub.	E.U.	L.U.	J.N.	E.D. I
262			———————		
230			—————————————		
288				———————————	
372				———————————	
384				———————————	

FLINT IMPLEMENTS

Significant numbers of blades and some cores were met only on four sites, the dates of which are very inconsistent. Their occurrence on one site which starts only in Late Uruk is quite interesting, but any kind of conclusion is excluded by the small number of sites.

Site	Ub.	E.U.	L.U.	J.N.	E.D. I
275	—————				
051	————————————————————————				
264			—————————————————		
103	Neobab.-Achaem.				

BOATS

On two sites we found two fragments of clay objects which can be explained only as parts of large models of boats, although they do not resemble the normal shape of boat models. Both times too little is preserved to tell us much about the original form. However, the one preserved compartment of one fragment alone measures 20 cm in length, so that the complete model, consisting of at least three compartments, was at least 60 cm long. This large size may account for the fact that the ends are not bent upward as in smaller boat models. But one may also think of these models as representing another type of boat, possibly cargo boats. The dating of both sites involved: WS 242 Late Uruk–Old Babylonian and WS 97 Akkadian?/Ur III–Old Babylonian points to a date of these objects in the Ur III–Old Babylonian range.

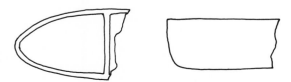

CRESCENT BASE

Among the noteworthy individual finds is a crescent-shaped clay disk, coated on the sides and upper surface with a fine, yellow green slip, while the underside was left unfinished. There are three broken places on the surface where legs of some sort were attached. Apparently it served as a base for some sort of object, although the nature of the latter is unknown. From the form of the plaque it is clear that the object erected on it was aligned to one side. Possibly it was meant to fit the curve of a large vessel. The find-spot, WS 109, is a Late Uruk single-period site.

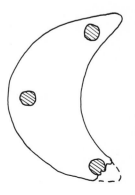

TEMPLE MODEL

On the surface of WS 387, in an area of about 5 m diameter and partly hidden under drifting sand, we found fragments of a baked clay architectural model. Only unimportant sherds from the floor and the roof were missing. The object has three adjacent rooms, one open and thus to be identified as the courtyard, and the other two roofed. The arrangement of the rooms with the door along one axis resembles the plan of a temple more than that of a private house or any other recognized type of structure; therefore we feel justified in speaking of it as a temple model and in calling the rooms courtyard, antecella, and cella.

FIGURE 83
A baked clay temple model

The courtyard is entirely enclosed by a wall; probably, however, this results from the construction requirements of a model and does not necessarily represent reality. From the court one enters a wide antecella through a door with projecting lintel and sides. This room receives light only through its door; there is neither a window nor a skylight. From this room a further door along the same axis leads into the equally wide cella which received its light through a trapezoidal opening in the roof, possibly meant to be square. Perhaps the size of this roof opening, like the height of the doors relative to the total height of the building, also is distorted by the nature of the model. The opening is located over the rear of the cella in alignment with the doors, thus over the spot at which one would expect a niche, which, however, is missing. Both the roof and the opening in the roof are surrounded by a ledge.

The dating of the find cannot be definitely fixed. The pottery on the surface of WS 387 all derives from the Late Uruk–Early Dynastic I periods, Early Dynastic I being without question the final period. (Cf. the publication of the pottery in extenso above.) Within this potential time range, the fact that the fabric of the model agrees in appearance and composition with that used in the conical cups, the solid-footed goblets, and other pottery of Jemdet Nasr–Early Dynastic I date appears to argue for a Jemdet Nasr–Dynastic I dating for the model.

An assignment to this time range admittedly creates a problem, since a ground plan consisting of two wide rooms lying behind each other with axially aligned doors is first known in a much later period. The earliest excavated example is the cult layout in the west corner of the Egipar from the time of the Third Dynasty of Ur.

The question of the purpose of the find is difficult to answer. We have spoken of a "model," but by no means in the contemporary sense of an architectural model, a small prototype of a building to be constructed. Here certainly the opposite must be true, that for some reason the representation of an existing building or building type was attempted. Because the plan corresponds best to that of a temple, the reason for the reproduction probably should be sought in the religious sphere. Therefore it seems reasonable to think of a votive offering or a kind of house altar. Naturally nothing definite can be concluded from surface observations, but it is worth noting that the entire find-spot was densely covered with sherds. This might suggest a habitation area, supporting an explanation of the object as a house altar.

TERRA-COTTA FIGURES

Fragments similar to the one given were found on three sites:

WS 168 Early Dynastic II/III–Akkadian

WS 204 Early Dynastic II/III–Larsa
WS 360 Early Dynastic II/III–Akkadian–Ur III?
thus we are rather safe about dating the fragments in the Early Dynastic II/III–Akkadian range.

The objects are totally asymmetrical. About oval in section, one of the larger sides is obviously meant to be in open view, since it is much better executed and bears three vertical, though not parallel, ridges. Toward the top the object widens and then is broken off, as is also the lower end.

We see in these fragments the uppermost parts of the legs of life-size animal figures, in particular the part immediately below the shoulder of the forelegs of sitting or standing animals. The ridges are then representations of tendons. Nothing can be said about the kind of animal, as no traces are to be found of hair or fleece. As our pieces all are only the uppermost part of the legs and all are about 15 cm high, the height of the complete figures at the shoulder must have been between 1.00 and 1.20 m.

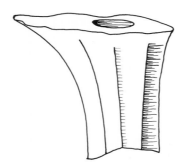

Only a few small terra-cotta figurines were found, often completely mutilated and defaced. None were sufficiently well preserved to be illustrated here.

PIPES

Specimens were found on two sites, WS 163d (163d/1) and 262, both dated to the Jemdet Nasr period. They are hand formed of yellowish clay, measuring about 10 cm in diameter and about 70 cm in length. Here also the ends are made in such a way that the narrower end of one pipe can be inserted into the wider end of the next pipe.

FRAGMENT OF A STELA

A fragment of a stela of gray white limestone with a very weathered surface was found on the surface of WS 097. Although no traces of working were recognizable on one side, traces of low relief were preserved on the upper part of the other side. The feet and the lower part of the legs of a figure walking to the right are discernable approximately 60 cm above the lower end of the stone plaque. The bottom of the tapering base is completely unworked, and probably is the part of the stela which was inserted into a socket or into the earth. The entire surface, including the worked part, is so weathered that nothing can be said about the details—sandals or clothing, for instance.

Although traces of earlier settlements were also found, the main settlement period of WS 097 is established from its surface pottery as having been in the Ur III–Old Babylonian period. A date for this fragment of a stela in this time span seems probable.

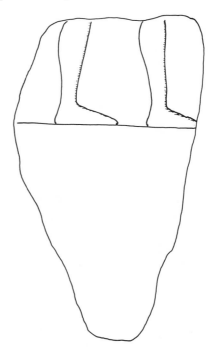

QUERNS

Those made of stone have been discussed already as type 9 of the stone vessels. Only one specimen remains to be discussed, as it differs by being made of clay and having a peculiar outlet near one corner. The actual use remains questionable, but because of the soft material and the outlet one might think of a quern used for grinding seeds. WS 272 dates from Late Uruk to Early Dynastic I.

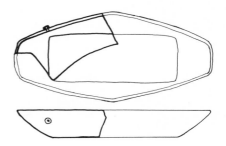

BRICK INSCRIPTIONS

Stamped inscriptions on bricks were found at various sites scattered over much of the area, but all referred to buildings in the capital of the ruler in question, or in religious centers of his area, rather than to local buildings at the sites where the bricks were found.

The oldest are two bricks with inscriptions of Gudea of Lagash found on the surface of Tell Jidr (= WS 004). They were located—apparently in situ—with many other examples of the same inscriptions in a wall which projected above the surface. Both inscriptions were meant for buildings in Gudea's capital, Girsu, specifically for the Ningirsu Temple "Eninnu" (*SAK* 142 t, Brick F), and for the Baba Temple in Uruku, which was probably a part of Girsu at the time of Gudea (*AnOr* 30, 147, 10). This last inscription is practically an exact duplicate of the brick in *VS* I, 20, except that the epithet of Baba, "mistress of Uruku," in line 4 is missing here. The appearance of bricks of this ruler in Tell Jidr is not surprising, since we have long known of inscriptions of Gudea from Adab, lying slightly to the northwest of Tell Jidr (*OIP* 14, no. 33; for the construction of the Eninnu). Unfortunately, among the topographical names of the Gudea period documents there is none which would be applicable to Tell Jidr (*AnOr* 30, 42 ff.).

Fragments of an already known brick inscription of Urnammu (*SAK* 186 Id) were found on the surface of two small sites (WS 078 and 369). It is the inscription intended for the construction of the Inanna Temple in Uruk (*UVB* I 50, 3). Neither of the sites lies on a main watercourse, and so the presence of important buildings of this ruler seems unlikely.

Bricks with inscriptions of Amarsuena were found at eight sites, including all duplicates of the known building inscription of the construction of the Abzu of Enki in Eridu (*SAK* 196 3c) in five, and duplicates of the short inscription which only gives the titles of the ruler (*SAK* 196 3b) in three. It is interesting that these bricks were found not only at major towns like Uruk (surface find made in 1967 in the area of the Sinkashid Palace), Adab (*OIP* 14, 40, and 42), Bad-Tibira (*Iraq* 22:198), and Kisurra (*MDOG* 17, 15), but also at smaller sites, WS–039, 097, 100, 131, 242, and 439. As has been discussed in chapter 3, all the latter sites lie along the western branch of the Euphrates.

In addition to the Amarsuena bricks on the surface of WS 439 (Umm al-Wawīya) ten fragments were found of a stamped brick of Gungunum of Larsa. No fragment includes the entire text, and so it is not possible to present the entire wording of the inscription. The text is a duplicate of *SAK* 206, 1a (find-spot unknown) and Roux, *RA* 52, 233 ff. (picked up in Larsa). Here too the line next to the last is illegible:

line 9 ša Mu.AŠ.KA.x-bi   of y its x
line 10 ù bàd-bi mu-dù   and its city wall he built.

Although in the 1967 campaign in Larsa a complete brick bearing this inscription was found, apparently there too the next to last line cannot be read (Birot, *Syria* 45:242[2]).

Found some years ago on the surface of Tell Ibzaykh (= WS 169 = Zabalam) was a brick with a building inscription of Hammurabi of Babylon, which at that time made possible the identification of Ibzaykh with Zabalam (Goetze, *Sumer*, 11:127 f.). Bricks with this inscription still are to be found in large numbers in situ in the walls of a building which is almost completely visible on the surface. It probably thus is to be identified with the temple named in the inscription. Since only the identification of the site based on the inscription has been published heretofore, the full wording of the inscription is given below (a small fragment from Adab, *OIP* 14, 12 can now be identified as part of the same inscription).

Size of the brick   30 × 33 × 8 cm
Size of the stamp   16.5 × 6 cm

1	ha-am-mu-ra-pí	Hammurabi,
2	lugal kal-ga	the mighty king,
3	lugal	the king
4	babilim[ki]	of Babylon
5	lugal an-ub-da-limmu-ba ke₄	the king of the four quarters
6	ba-dím	built
7	é-zi-kalam-ma	the Ezikalama
8	é-ᵈinanna	the temple of Inanna
9	zabalam[ki]-ta	of Zabalam

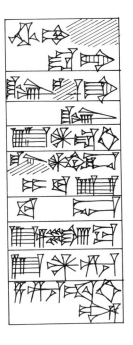

Appendix
Catalog of Surveyed Sites
Robert McC. Adams

001 250 meters in diameter × 6 meters high; entirely surrounded and partly covered by high dunes. Ur III–Cassite.

002 300 NW × 260 × 4. Immediately southeast is a mound at least 400 diam. × 2.4; limits of latter obscured by dunes. High mound is Early Dynastic II/III–Old Babylonian, with dominant component of surface debris suggesting Ur III as period of maximum occupation. Lower mound Achaemenian–Early Islamic, mainly Sassanian–Early Islamic. Small quantities of Achaemenian–Parthian debris on the high mound may reflect only its use as a cemetery.

003 170 diam. × 2.2. Achaemenian–Parthian, some Recent.

004 Tell Jidr. A very large and long-lived ancient town, whose full importance has yet to be recognized. Outline and contours of site suggest that it may have been two settlements initially, coalescing into one during the Parthian and Sassanian periods. Older and larger is in northwest. An area 1,300 NE × 1,000 is considerably elevated, its central part rising 10–12 m in a series of well-defined mounds suggestive of very large buildings. Nearest the center is a steeply elevated citadel (?) 200 m in diam. Numerous yellowish baked bricks (34 × 34 × 7 centimeters) here bear a stamped impression of trifurcating wavy lines, for both of which a Sassanian date seems probable. Immediately southwest of citadel is a square mound, 200 m along each side and with corners oriented to cardinal directions, that rises almost to same height. Here there are bricks of same dimensions (but without stamp), and much mortar.

Imām Dhāhir, built of 22 × 22 brick and partly fallen into ruin, stands surrounded by dunes on extreme northwest edge of this older, larger and higher part of the site. Early Islamic–Samarran pottery predominates in the immediately surrounding area, but elsewhere occurs only very sparsely. Ubaid III painted ware occurs in low places, and clay sickles are widespread and numerous. Southwest and south of the citadel there are areas where conical cups and Early Dynastic I goblets are perhaps the dominant surface component, and on the outer flanks of the site in this area Old Babylonian baked bricks (25 × 17 × 7) are widespread. Northeast of the shrine and citadel most surface material is of Ur III–Cassite date, but plano-convex bricks (28 × 18 × 4) in situ in walls and Akkadian bricks (42 × 42 and 46 × 46) suggest that an earlier settlement underlies this part of the site also. The east and south outskirts of this part of the site are Old Babylonian–Cassite and Parthian. (Cf. W. Andrae, "Die Umgebung von Fara und Abu Hatab," Deutsche Orient-Gesellschaft, *Mitteilungen* 16 [1903]: 28–29, fig. 9).

To the southeast the elevation is lower, although still several meters above plain level. Debris in an area 1,400 SE × 700 is mainly Parthian–Sassanian, although one small hummock is covered with Old Babylonian–Cassite sherds. Several reused bricks in this area bore stamps of Gudea (cf. p. 217).

The southeast end of the site forms another elevated area 850 NE × 600. Again this centers on what may be a citadel, a thick-walled 200 m square, lower in the center, with corners oriented to cardinal directions. Sparse Cassite sherds and clay sickles occur here, and Parthian pottery is found along the outer flanks, but the bulk of the surface material on and near the citadel is Sassanian.

In short, Ubaid III, Early Dynastic I through Cassite, and Parthian through Sāmarrān are well represented. The Uruk and Jemdet Nasr periods are suggested but not fully confirmed by conical cups and clay sickles. The Neo-Babylonian and Achaemenian periods are not attested by the observed surface material, although the size, height, and long-term continuity of the site suggest that it must have been occupied for at least a limited time during these periods also.

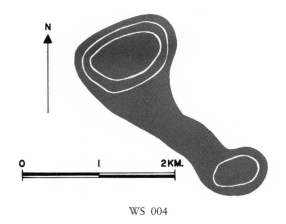

WS 004

005 220 diam. × 0.9. Larsa–Cassite.

006 130 E × 20 × 0.2. Late Uruk. 200 m west is a second mound, 170 E × 80 × 0.7. Turban handles, circular "bull's-eye" stamp impressions on buff sherds, and blue and olive lead glazes define a unique occupation within the survey area. Recent "pseudo-prehistoric" ware is present but rare. Post-Sāmarrān ʿAbbāsid. 80 m southwest of second mound is a small, low third mound with a recent watchtower, in ruins.

007 60 diam. × 1. Recent.

008 120 diam. × 1.8. Sassanian.

009 260 N × 180 × 0.7. Late Uruk.

010 40 NE × 15 × 2.1. 30 m northeast is a small contemporary mound, 60 N × 30 × 0.6. Both are Recent. The high, irregular contours of the former suggest that it may be the fallen remains of a muftul or watchtower. If so, the total absence of observable features suggests that it must have been abandoned considerably before most of the recent watchtowers identified in this survey.

011 140 NW × 30 × 3, widening to 50 at southeast end. The low ruins of a qalʿa stand on the middle of the main ridge of the site, and a meandering watercourse bed passes just northeast. Larsa–Cassite, Recent. An unusual amount of plain, utilitarian blue-glazed pottery and the presence of one "turban" handle may argue that this site is somewhat earlier than most other Recent sites recorded in the survey.

012 Large, irregular clusters of sherds at plain level. Limits diffuse, but perhaps fall within an area 280 m in diam. Late Uruk.

013 200 (330°) × 100, but debris is sparse, there is no noticeable elevation, and limits of the site are cor-

respondingly uncertain. Probable Jemdet Nasr; Early Dynastic I; Recent.

014 Central mound 120 diam. × 0.9. There is a second mound 60 E × 30 × 0.7 that lies 25 m south-southeast, and a third, 130 diam. × 1.6, 160 m south. 200 m north of central mound is a small, ruined tower with a survey triangulation stake, and immediately northwest of it is another small, low mound. Sparse Recent sherds around the latter two mounds; otherwise Sassanian.

015 220 SW × 80 × 0.3. Sassanian.

016 300 diam. × 1.8. Cassite–Achaemenian, limited Parthian. Chalice bases diagnostic of the Cassite period occur only on spoil banks around one pit. This may suggest that full-scale occupation of the site began only in the Neo-Babylonian period.

017 200 diam. × 3. Achaemenian–Sassanian, Recent.

018 240 diam. × 1. Late Uruk, limited Jemdet Nasr.

019 250 NE × 200 × 1. Early Dynastic II/III, Ur III–Larsa, Sassanian, Recent.

020 Abū Bogaʿ. Early Uruk probable. Late Uruk–Old Babylonian. Rare Parthian sherds may reflect only graves. Dominant surface materials are late Early Dynastic.

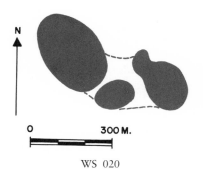

WS 020

021 150 NE × 70 × 1.2. Larsa–Cassite.

022 180 N × 140 × 0.9. Early Uruk. Surface collection described in chapter 8.

023 110 E × 90 × 0.3. Early Uruk.

024 95 diam. × 0.2. Early Uruk.

025 140 diam. × 1.8. Cassite–Achaemenian. Also some evidence of small Parthian, Recent occupations.

026 160 diam. × 2. Parthian, Recent; the latter is the dominant surface component.

027 240 diam. × 1.8. Larsa–Cassite; also a smaller Recent occupation.

028 190 (340°) × 150 × 2.4. Late Uruk; Jemdet Nasr probable but not certain, Early Dynastic I. Also a more limited Recent occupation.

029 140 diam. × 2.4. Parthian, Recent.

030 Qalʿa Huwaysh al-Pasha. 720 NE × 410 × 2. Qalʿa is located near west edge of site (see fig. 28). Recent "pseudo-prehistoric" sherds occur in the mud brick walls of the qal°a, indicating that a settlement here antedated the latter. Parthian–Sassanian, Recent.

031 Qal°a al-Tawwīl. 250 diam. × 0.3 Qal°a on northwest end of site, rises 4.5 m (see fig. 28). Sassanian pottery observed here and on outlying smaller mounds to northeast, east, and southwest. Recent pottery confined to the central mound. The small mound at northeast end of group may consist of a single building built of 31 × 31 cm brick.

032 250 (350°) × 140 × 3, reaching that height only at a cairn near north end. Larsa–Cassite. Lower, smaller mounds to southeast and southwest are Larsa–Cassite (secondarily transported materials?), Parthian.

033 Two adjoining tells separated by bed of old canal running from northwest. Together they form a compact, almost continuous site 340 NE × 260 × 3. A few plano-convex bricks on site are assumed to have been brought secondarily from nearby Tell Shmīd (site 168). Achaemenian–Parthian.

034 300 N × 140. Sparse but continuous sherds at plain level. Numerous clay sickles indicate a probable Uruk or Jemdet Nasr occupation that cannot otherwise be defined. Achaemenian–Parthian.

035 350 NW × 200 × 1.8. Numerous 22 × 22 cm bricks on surface. Sassanian, Recent.

036 Tell Salbukh. 300 diam. × 1.9. Bricks 30 × 30 × 5 and 24 × 24 × 5. Late Sassanian–Early Islamic, the latter apparently a reduced occupation.

037 This ill-defined group constitutes the west end of chain of tells called Jezāziyāt. See map for distribution of main summits. Central mound rises 3.5, north mound 2.6; others are lower. Parthian debris common on high central mound only. Continuous sherd distribution on other mounds and surrounding plain suggests a Sassanian settlement 400 m in diameter.

038 220 SE × 160 × 1.6, with thickly strewn sherds continuing farther southeast at plain level. Sassanian.

039 Part of Jezāziyāt. 650 WNW × 420, rising to 2.6 m along southeast edge, where it adjoins an old bed of the Euphrates visible here in air photographs. Also jocularly referred to as Umm al-Haffriyat, "mother of excavations," reflecting major, large-scale pitting and looting under way at the site. Ur III–Old Babylonian.

040 240 (020°) × 100 × 0.4. Larsa–Old Babylonian, Recent.

041 250 N × 120 × 2. Wind erosion has traced parallel north-south furrows immediately west of site that suggest stratified alluvial deposits reflecting presence of an old, major watercourse. Early Dynastic possible but unconfirmed. Akkadian–Larsa. Old Babylonian, Parthian very limited.

042 280 N × 200 × 2.6. Ubaid II–Late Uruk, mainly the former. Surface collection described in chapter 8. Parthian burials, small Recent occupation.

043 Two mounds about 100 diam. × 1. They are located 200 m apart on a 030° axis. Sassanian, Recent.

044 110 NW × 70 × 0.2. Late Uruk–Jemdet Nasr.

045 Small mound in northwest is conical in shape, 3 m high; others all are 2.0–2.3 m. Primarily late Sassanian. Some Recent pottery and 19 × 19 cm brick on conical mound (which in fact is composed entirely of such brick) and southernmost mound.

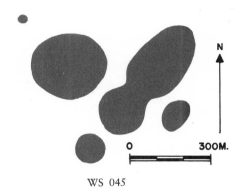

WS 045

046 290 E × 180 × 2. Neo-Babylonian–Achaemenian, limited Parthian.

047 140 diam. × 1.5, with a ruined tower on northwest end rising to 4 m. Jemdet Nasr–Early Dynastic I, Recent.

048 120 diam. × 1.8, with low, small extensions to northwest and southeast. Late Uruk–Early Dynastic I.

049 280 (340°) × 200 × 4.2. Plano-convex bricks. Late Early Dynastic–Cassite, Parthian. Parthian debris also continues south-southeast along old canal bed for almost 1 km.

050 Two mounds 100 m apart along a 012° axis. The northern one is 130 diam. × 0.4. The southern one is 190 NW × 130 × 1.4, and has a small, ruined tower on its summit. Late Early Dynastic, Parthian, Recent.

051 190 diam., rising to 1.8 m high summit near northwest end. Numerous stone hoes and large flint blades. Ubaid II–Jemdet Nasr. Early Dynastic I sparse.

052 350 N × 150 × 2.5. Ur III–Larsa, Sassanian–Sāmarrān, Recent.

053 140 N × 70 × 1.2. Parthian, Recent.

054 200 NE × 110 × 2. Primarily Neo-Babylonian–Achaemenian, Parthian rare.

055 Tell al-Dhiba°i. 500 diam. × 4, with smaller outlying mounds to the east. Sassanian.

056 280 E × 240 × 3.3. 150 m away at 065° is a second mound, 240 E × 120 × 2.5. Directly east of the first mound and 30 m south of the second mound is a third, 300 E × 250 × 2. The entire group is Sassanian.

APPENDIX

057 Muftul Sindāl. 200 NW × 120 × 0.3. Small fallen tower. Recent.

058 140 (070°) × 80 × 0.3. 150 m away along probable old canal course (340°) is a small outlying settlement 40 diam. × 0.2. A third lies 1.5 km northeast, 100 diam. × 0.3. All Sassanian.

059 280 (280°) × 120 × 3. Very sparse Early Dynastic I remains may or may not reflect a significant occupation. Mainly Parthian–Sassanian. Much lime mortar and many 29 × 29 and 30 × 30 cm bricks may reflect terminal use of site for a single building in late Sassanian or even later times.

060 150 N × 120 × 0.4. Late Uruk–Jemdet Nasr.

061 230 diam. × 1. Ur III–Larsa, Parthian graves.

062 Part of Jezāziyāt. 250 diam. × 5. Wasters and slag suggest large pottery kilns here. Mainly Sassanian, limited Early Islamic.

063 Part of Jezāziyāt. See map for outlines of this irregular settlement. Elevations to 3.8 m. Mainly Sassanian. Limited Early Islamic, Recent.

064 Tell al-Dhibaʿi or Medina. A square, walled town, 700 m along each side, oriented slightly east of north. The wall is composed of large mud bricks; traces along west side show that it was originally 7 m thick. Its present summit is marked by a regularly spaced series of hillocks rising to 3 m. These may be indications of close-spaced semicircular buttresses, although no conclusive evidence for this could be detected on the surface. There are low places in the outer wall, suggesting gates, in the middle of the north, west, and south sides. Within the enclosure are scattered building remains, but they may be at least in some cases later that its period of primary construction and use, since they do not appear to line up with each other or anything else. Baked fragments (26–28 cm square and 30–31 cm square) outline these fairly sparse remains, but do not appear elsewhere on the surface within the enclosure. Moreover, roughly a third of the area, in the southeast corner, essentially lacks any surface debris at all. Glazed pottery is rare, and all observed classifiable types were Sassanian.

065 Part of Jezāziyāt. Most prominent mound in group is 120 diam. × 3.4. Presence of much mortar and bricks (30 × 30) in situ suggests that this may be the remains of a single large building. 150 m away at 250° is a smaller mound, 90 diam. × 3.2, and immediately north of the latter is a still smaller settlement. 450 m from the first mound at 282° is a mound 250 diam. × 3. Early Islamic pottery in addition to Sassanian pottery is present on the last; on the others there is only Sassanian.

066 230 NW × 180 × 2.4. Neo-Babylonian–Achaemenian.

067 Two mounds 60 m apart on a north-south axis. South mound 180 diam. × 1.6; north mound 80 diam. × 1. Neo-Babylonian–Achaemenian.

068 200 diam. × 2. Jemdet Nasr.

069 250 (330°) × 200 × 2. Neo-Babylonian–Achaemenian.

070 200 NE × 140 × 0.8. Larsa–Cassite.

071 See figure 11. South tell is 250 m northeast of site 070, 0.5 in ht; north tell, 0.4. Both are dark, soft-surfaced, highly saline; hence sherds are sparse. Late Uruk.

072 Main tell 350 NW × 160 × 2.2. 400 m away at 250° is a mound 140 diam. × 0.9. 1,150 m west of latter is a third, 300 diam. × 1.3. All Sassanian.

073 Main tell 300 E × 200 × 5. Sassanian, Recent. Smaller mounds up to 150 diam., exclusively Sassanian, extend northeast from here for almost 1.5 km. See map for location.

074 A ruined qalʿa, walls still rising 3.5 m. Square in plan, 30 m along each side, walls oriented at 330°. Main tower in south corner, 8 m in diam., projects 1 m beyond line of walls. There was also a much smaller projecting tower in north corner. Recent.

075 Qalʿa Kharkhara. See figure 25 and pp. 75–77. A large and well-preserved fort protecting a weir and strategic canal inlet on the Shatt al-Kar. 400 m east is a contemporary walled enclosure that may represent a khān.

076 140 diam. × 1.9. Late Uruk, probable Jemdet Nasr, Early Dynastic I.

077 90 diam. × 2.1, located 90 m east of site 076. Scattered early debris occurs here also, but may have been secondarily transported from the latter. At any rate, the site is mainly Parthian.

078 Abū Dhubaʿ. 250 diam. × 2.3. Jemdet Nasr uncertain. Early Dynastic I. Two brick fragments bore standard Ur Nammu inscriptions, but presumably were brought to the site secondarily. Mainly Parthian. To this last period may be assigned very extensive traces of a large, well-preserved, formal building with mud brick walls up to 2 m thick. Also Parthian is a smaller site 100 m W, 180 E × 100 × 2.

079 Part of Ishin al-Mʿammar. 300 diam. × 3.5. Jemdet Nasr uncertain, Early Dynastic I, Parthian–Sassanian. Included under the rubric of Parthian are bricks bearing circular, presumably Seleucid, stamps.

080 Part of Ishin al-Mʿammar. 200 NW × 100 × 6. An outlying settlement, 150 diam. × 2.3, lies farther northwest and is also located on south bank of old major canal course.

081 Part of Ishin al-Mʿammar. 340 NE, ranging in width from 350 at northeast end to 220 or less at opposite end, 3 m height. Fairly numerous remains of Jemdet Nasr–Early Dynastic I date are tentatively assumed

to represent the transport of materials from 079 nearby. Otherwise the site is Neo-Babylonian–Parthian.

082 Part of Ishin al-Mᶜammar. Northeast mound rises to 3.2 m, west mound 3 m, south mound 1 m, others 2 m. Northeast mound Late Uruk, probable Jemdet Nasr, Early Dynastic I; Parthian–Sassanian graves. South mound Neo-Babylonian–Sassanian. Others Parthian–Sassanian.

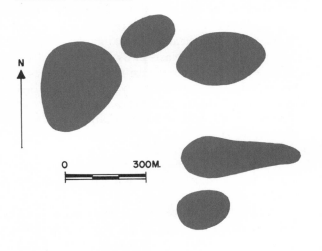

WS 082

083 220 NE × 50 × 0.3. Late Uruk, Neo-Babylonian.

084 Qalᶜa Majnuna. See pp. 75–76.

085 250 E × 200 × 3. Site lies on south bank of the Shatt al-Kar, the dry bed of which is 1.2 m below plain level at this point. 250 m northwest, on opposite bank of Shatt al-Kar, lies a companion site 90 E × 50 × 0.9. Sassanian–Sāmarrān, although sgraffiato ware was not noted on the smaller mound.

086 260 (330°) × 160 × 0.3. Mainly Late Uruk; a smaller occupation continued for a time into the Jemdet Nasr period.

087 280 diam. × 0.8. Surface collection described in chapter 8. Late Uruk–Jemdet Nasr.

088 350 NW × 200 × 2.6. Most of the tell is much lower, but it rises to this height at northwest end, where there are well-preserved traces of a large brick (31 × 31 cm) building with plastered walls. Sassanian.

089 250 NW × 110 × 3, with large, lower areas of debris extending northwest and southeast. See map for outline. Main mound is 100 m north of latest course of major supply canal, and presumably was built at the time an earlier bed was in use. Parthian–Sassanian.

090 See map for outlines of continuous strips of debris extending for more than 1 km along both banks of old canal bed. Most prominent mound on north bank, 180 diam. × 6.5. Immediately southwest, on opposite bank, is another, 240 diam. × 3. Another

major mound forms southeast terminus of settlement 600 m (at 160°) from first mound, 260 NW × 140 × 4. Average width of debris on each bank, 100 m. Parthian–Sassanian.

091 170 diam. × 1.2. Mound forming the southeast end of site 090 is 200 m north. Jemdet Nasr, Parthian–Sassanian.

092 Part of Ishin al-Mᶜammar. See map for irregular limits of this very large site. East part forms a continuous ridge rising to 6 m near east end; here there are large quantities of glass slag. West part of site is generally lower, divided into segments by old canal beds, but rising occasionally in high, conical mounds. The westernmost of these mounds is primarily Neo-Babylonian–Parthian, but the maximum extent of occupation of the site came in the Sassanian period. Some Early Islamic pottery also occurs in west part of site.

093 250 diam. × 0.3, with hummocks near east end rising to 2.5 m. Sassanian.

094 400 E × 180 × 3. Sassanian–Early Islamic. Rare Recent sherds also.

095 80 diam. × 0.3. Late Uruk–Jemdet Nasr. Some sherds suggest a possible small reoccupation in the late Early Dynastic period.

096 280 (340°) × 90 × 1.9. A small, low area of contemporary debris lies immediately west across old canal bed; another lies 150 m away at 160°. Sassanian–Early Islamic.

097 Part of Tūlūl al-Hummar. 400 diam. × 3.4. Three stamped Amarsuena bricks. Late Early Dynastic possible, Akkadian probable, mainly Ur III–Old Babylonian; Parthian graves.

098 Qalᶜa Dulūᶜ or Abū Sūda (latter on British ¼″ map). See figure 28. The ruined fort lies near the east edge of a dune-covered area containing hummocks of Sassanian and Recent pottery. The area of settlement must have been at least 300 m in diam.

099 140 diam. × 1.4. Sassanian. 250 m away at 160° is a second Sassanian mound, 320 N × 180 × 0.9, which also has Early Islamic, Recent pottery.

100 Part of Banaat al-Hassan. 550 NW × 300 × 2. Akkadian–Larsa, rare Old Babylonian, rare Recent.

101 1,440 (153°) × 100–160, varying in height from plain level to 0.4. Possibly this represents a strip of settlement along a watercourse, but possibly also it reflects secondary disturbance of a now-buried site by later canal construction. Jemdet Nasr–Early Dynastic I.

102 Sparse debris at plain level, scattered low hummocks; limits not clear, but perhaps 300 m in diam. Jemdet Nasr, rare Early Dynastic I.

103 360 E × 220 × 0.7. Clay sickles and flint blades in considerable numbers, suggesting a possible Uruk

or Jemdet Nasr occupation nearby. Neo-Babylonian–Achaemenian.

104 180 diam. × 0.1. Sparse debris. Neo-Babylonian–Achaemenian.

105 Extremely sparse, scattered sherds within an area 80 m in diam. at plain level. Vague linear clusterings may suggest that all visible debris was brought to surface in later canal diggings. However, no direct trace survives of such a watercourse. Late Uruk, Jemdet Nasr.

106 130 diam. × 0.1. Dark, spongy, saline; hence surface debris is meager. Late Uruk.

107 160 diam. × 0.8. Early Uruk. Very small Jemdet Nasr occupation.

108 100 diam. × 0.4. Late Uruk.

109 See figure 11. Southwest tell 0.2 ht., NE tell 0.3 ht. Surface collection described in chapter 8. Late Uruk.

110 See figure 11. Maximum elevation at northwest end, 0.8 m. Late Uruk. Southeast end was reoccupied in Neo-Babylonian–Achaemenian times.

111 Two irregular clusters of low hummocks composed of closely packed sherds. One is 200 m diam.; another, 300 m southwest, is 180 m diam. The plain surface around the hummocks is sterile in both clusters, suggesting that wind erosion has reduced sparsely settled sites to scattered heaps of sherds with no remaining cultural debris in situ. A line of vegetation between the two sites follows a 340° course, suggesting the broad bed of a former watercourse. Neo-Babylonian–Achaemenian.

112 220 diam. × 2. Late Uruk, mainly Neo-Babylonian–Achaemenian.

113 250 diam. × 0.4, but debris is sparse and largely confined to scattered hummocks within this area. Neo-Babylonian–Achaemenian.

114 260 N × 110 × 0.3. Late Uruk–Jemdet Nasr.

115 130 diam. × 0.1. Late Uruk.

116 160 N × 90, rising to 1 m near north end, 2.4 near south end, and with low saddle in middle. Site is composed primarily of 20 × 20 × 5 baked bricks and mortar, somewhat obscured by drifting sand. Extremely rare sherds include glazed ware and stamp impressions as well as Recent "pseudoprehistoric" ware. Possibly a Late ʿAbbāsid or Ilkhanid occupation, and certainly a Recent one.

117 170 N × 130 × 0.4, but consisting mostly of scattered hummocks. Neo-Babylonian–Parthian.

118 See figure 11. All mounds 0.2–0.4 m ht. Early Uruk.

119 140 (030°) × 90 × 0.6. Late Uruk, with superimposed later kiln debris that is possibly Neo-Babylonian–Achaemenian in date.

120 Sparse sherds and debris obscured by wind-laid sand; 140 m diam. is little more than a guess. Very slight elevation. Late Uruk.

121 250 diam. × 1.4. Sassanian.

122 120 E × 80 × 2.5. Parthian–Sassanian.

123 160 NW × 100 × 1.7. Late Uruk.

124 Continuous debris at plain level within an area 160 m in diam., slightly covered in places by low wind-laid sand hummocks. Late Uruk.

125 See figure 14. Main tell 0.8 m ht., Late Uruk–Early Dynastic I. Bulk of surface debris probably is of Jemdet Nasr date. Three concentrations of copper noted on surface here in spite of absence of pits; see illustrations in chapter 8. Northwest tell 0.6 m, Late Uruk only. Northeast tell mainly Late Uruk, but with some Jemdet Nasr–Early Dynastic I debris on southwest slope facing main tell. The plain between them is sherd-strewn and may represent the bed of a watercourse (either contemporary or more recent). The small mound immediately adjoining the northeast tell is Sassanian–Early Islamic.

126 200 diam. × 0.5. Late Uruk.

127 200 diam. × 0.3. Late Uruk–Jemdet Nasr.

128 See figure 11. South tell 0.4 m ht., north tell 0.2. Late Uruk.

129 260 diam. × 1.6. Rare chalice bases indicate a probable Cassite occupation. Mainly Achaemenian–Parthian, with a minor Early Islamic reoccupation. A scatter of debris at plain level 150 m northwest indicates a Late Uruk–Jemdet Nasr site.

130 Part of Banaat al-Hassan. 2.1 m ht.; badly looted, leading to a wide array of surface materials. Jemdet Nasr through Akkadian well represented. Ur III and Larsa present but less plentiful; may derive primarily from graves during floruit of nearby site 131.

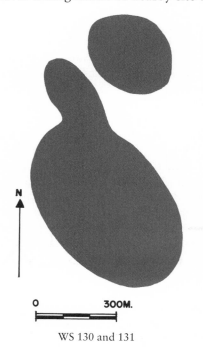

N

0   300M.

WS 130 and 131

131 Part of Banaat al-Hassan. 4.2 m ht. Jemdet Nasr possible but uncertain. Early Dynastic I–Old Babylonian, but primarily Ur III–Larsa. Numerous baked bricks with Amarsuena stamps. Widespread Parthian graves, scattered Sassanian sherds (particularly on east slope). Small mound extending north from north end Sassanian–Early Islamic, with the remains of building with pillars or curving walls constructed of baked brick (27 × 27 × 6) and mortar.

132 160 diam. × 0.2. Jemdet Nasr.

133 80 NW × 30 × 0.3. Late Uruk.

134 Part of Banaat al-Hassan. Scattered mounds extending 1,200 m northwest, rising up to 4.4 m ht. Parthian–Sassanian; Recent.

135 240 diam. × 2.6. Achaemenian–Parthian.

136 440 NW × 240 × 4. Achaemenian–Parthian, the latter possibly reflecting not a full occupation but only graves.

137 190 NW × 80 × 0.6. Ubaid IV–Late Uruk, the former apparently localized in southeast.

138 400 E × 150 × 2. East end Sassanian, Recent; west end Sassanian–Early Islamic, Recent.

139 180 (340°) × 150 × 1. Late Uruk–Jemdet Nasr probable. Akkadian–Larsa. Old Babylonian very limited.

140 120 (340°) × 70 × 1. Ur III–Larsa.

141 250 (060°) × 180 × 0.9, divided into two segments by old canal bed. Sassanian.

142 Low hummocks of sparse debris within an area 120 m diam. Larsa–Cassite.

143 180 (290°) × 150 × 4.2. Neo-Babylonian–Achaemenian.

144 250 NE × 80 × 0.7. Very thick, extensive shell deposits cover the plain southeast of mound. Late Uruk, Jemdet Nasr limited to southwest quadrant of site.

145 150 NE × 110 × 0.8. Cassite–Achaemenian.

146 Main settlement a continuous ridge 550 NE × 150 × 3.8. Large, low, irregular outliers 400 m east and northeast. Other low, irregular areas of debris trail off at 250°. Parthian.

147 Low hummocks, sparse debris within an area 120 m diam. Parthian.

148 Ishan al-Jerin. Large east mound rises to 3.2 at north end, northwest mound to 1.9 m, others lower. Northwest mound Cassite–Achaemenian, east mound Achaemenian–Parthian, others only Parthian.

149 140 E × 80 × 0.7. Cassite–Neo-Babylonian, a limited Sassanian reoccupation.

150 180 diam. × 0.6. Surface debris mainly Cassite–Achaemenian; Parthian rare. Same dating applies to a mound 200 diam. × 0.5 that is 700 m away at 240°.

151 60 diam. × 0.2. Mainly Cassite–Achaemenian; limited Parthian occupation.

152 300 (025°) × 220 × 0.7. Late Uruk, Cassite.

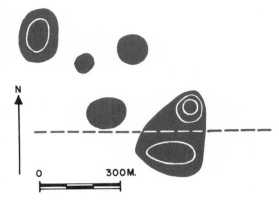

WS 148

153 140 diam. × 0.2. Late Uruk–Jemdet Nasr, limited Achaemenian–Parthian.

154 300 NE × 180 × 0.6. 700 m away at 200° is a contemporary, smaller site, 160 (020°) × 90 × 0.4. Parthian.

155 350 (300°) × 140 × 0.2, with sparse clusters of debris suggesting that settlement may not have been dense or continuous within this area. Jemdet Nasr, mainly Achaemenian–Parthian.

156 A curious outer ring of sherds, nowhere in excess of 0.4 m ht. Plain surface in center contains only very sparse debris. Rare clay sickles may imply an Uruk or Jemdet Nasr occupation. Primarily Larsa–Cassite.

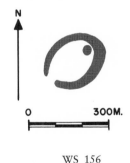

WS 156

157 Present surface debris may have been thrown up secondarily on later canal banks. Larsa–Cassite.

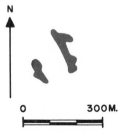

WS 157

158 250 diam. × 0.8. 250 m north is a contemporary

settlement, 150 m diam. Achaemenian, limited Parthian.

159 A thin band of debris at least 250 m long (350°) and 20 m wide, rising in occasional hummocks to 0.7 m ht. A circular area of debris lies just east of its center, 120 m in diam. Sassanian.

160 Irregularly spaced hummocks of sparse debris forming an area roughly 90 m in diameter. Ubaid IV, probable Early Uruk, and Late Uruk are present on west half of site. To east, on opposite bank of possible later canal course (330°) through site, is predominantly Jemdet Nasr. Small quantities of "pseudoprehistoric" ware may date this canal to Recent times.

161 250 diam. × 0.3. Debris sparse. A few sherds suggest an Uruk or Jemdet Nasr occupation nearby. Primarily Cassite–Achaemenian.

162 See figure 11. Only spoil banks around numerous recent pits rise above 0.2 m. Late Uruk; probable Jemdet Nasr; Early Dynastic I. Also a small Larsa–Old Babylonian occupation on north end of main mound. Sparse Parthian and Recent surface remains.

163 See figure 11. Low, except around dense pits on larger mounds. Mainly Late Uruk, with Jemdet Nasr limited to west end, extreme northeast, and rare sherds elsewhere.

164 Tell Jīd. The ancient settlement is 300 diam. × 4. Probable traces of a Late Uruk occupation occur on west slope. An Early Dynastic I and probable Jemdet Nasr occupation is documented by surface collections on south edge of mound. Main occupation Ur III–Old Babylonian. A steep, knife-edge ridge, virtually sterile and with discolorations or cleavage plains that would indicate mud brick, runs in a northwest line along southwest edge of site. Rising to 24 m ht., this ridge is a major landmark. Its date of construction is uncertain, but possibly is much later than the terminal occupation of the site. (Cf. W. K. Loftus, "Notes of a journey from Baghdad to Busrah . . . ," Royal Geographical Society of London, Journal 26 (1856): 118–20; Andrae, "Umgebung," pp. 18–19, fig. 2; note that orientation of latter is 180° in error.)

165 200 diam. × 0.2. Sparse debris, with other, smaller clusters extending north for 500 m. Cassite–Achaemenian.

166 200 diam. × 1.6. Late Uruk. Probable Jemdet Nasr. Early Dynastic I.

167 170 diam. × 2.2. Lies 180 m south of site 166. Late Uruk sherds here may have been transported secondarily from 166. Mainly Neo-Babylonian–Achaemenian.

168 Tell Shmīd. 800 diam. × 6, but reaching that height only in a suggestively square citadel (?) at north end of mound. Late Uruk–Early Dynastic I, with many clay sickles and cones. Surface debris preponderantly late Early Dynastic. Akkadian wares and bricks (39 × 39 × 6 and 41 × 41 × 6) present in smaller quantities, later periods probably are not represented.

169 Ibzaykh (Zabalam). 1,100 (110°) × 520 × 6. Northwest end of mound is only 5 m ht., and it is lower still in middle. Rare clay sickles suggest a beginning of occupation in Uruk or Jemdet Nasr times. A late Early Dynastic occupation indicated by widespread (although not numerous) plano-convex bricks and other diagnostic types. Surface material preponderantly Akkadian–Old Babylonian. See chapter 8 for stamped brick inscription of latter period identifying site as Zabalam.

170 Tell Khayta. 190 NW × 140 × 11. Northwest end rises steeply to maximum height, then falls away in a series of badly eroded ridges giving site the appearance of a giant molar tooth. Debris very sparse, suggesting that it may not represent a natural accumulation through settlement but rather a tower or platform of some sort. This recalls Tell Jīd (site 164), which is just within visual range. Perhaps only Parthian–Sassanian, with late Early Dynastic and Larsa–Old Babylonian sherds secondarily transported from nearby Ibzaykh (site 169).

171 240 NW × 150 × 3. Many clay sickles suggest an Uruk or Jemdet Nasr occupation in the vicinity, but site is Parthian–Sassanian.

172 180 diam. × 3. Akkadian–Ur III.

173 160 diam. × 0.4. Late Uruk–Jemdet Nasr.

174 300 diam., low, vaguely defined. Jemdet Nasr–Early Dynastic I.

175 Northeast mound very slightly elevated. Very limited Early Dynastic I, mainly late Early Dynastic–Akkadian, continuing into Larsa period only at south end. Main mound primarily Ur III–Larsa, but with some late Early Dynastic–Akkadian wares, thin Neo-Babylonian–Parthian debris, and much late kiln slag. Surface debris is also found in intervening area between the two mounds, suggesting that they form parts of what was originally a single large settlement.

176 470 NW × 50 or less × 2.2, a curiously narrow ribbon of settlement. Ur III–Old Babylonian.

177 230 NE × 200, rising to 1.2 m ht. only near northeast end. Surface collection illustrated in chapter 8. Jemdet Nasr–Early Dynastic I.

178 120 N × 60 × 0.6. Surface collection illustrated in chapter 8. Ubaid II, Early Uruk. Late Uruk limited, Jemdet Nasr confined to north end of site.

179 See figure 11. 2.3 m ht. at north end. Jemdet Nasr possible but uncertain, major occupation Early Dynastic I, small Sassanian reoccupation concen-

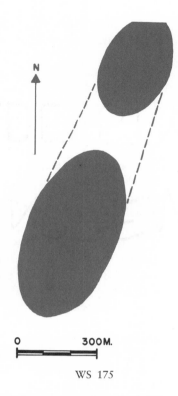

0   300M.

WS 175

trated mainly near north end of site.

180 210 NE × 160 × 1.9. Bed of old canal runs south from here and crosses the later course of the Shatt al-Kar 500 m away. Two small contemporary sites, each about 80 diam. × 1, adjoin each other in between. Sassanian.

181 240 diam. × 1.2, Late Uruk–Jemdet Nasr.

182 80 E × 40 × 0.7. Primarily Sassanian. Possible Early Islamic occupation also.

183 Tell Hammam. Area of continuous debris is about 870 E × 600, bounded on the east by the massive ruined tower by which the site may be identified from a great distance. Most of the area is low, although large mounds occur at intervals; (cf. Andrae, "Umgebung," fig. 4). No attempt was made to survey this extensive site in detail, but all diagnostic debris noted was apparently Sassanian, with two exceptions. 350 m away from the tower at 257° is a mound 280 NE × 130 × 4.6. Sassanian is still the dominant surface component here, but there are also numerous Early Dynastic I sherds and possible Jemdet Nasr remains. In addition, there is widespread, although rare, Recent pottery. (Cf. Loftus, "Notes," p. 113; Ward, in Peters, *Nippur,* 1:329; Peters, *Nippur,* 2:273).

184 200 diam. × 0.6. Sassanian.

185 210 diam. × 0.6. Profiles of copper vessel fragments illustrated in chapter 8. Late Uruk.

186 110 diam. × 0.3. Early Dynastic I, possible Jemdet Nasr.

187 110 NW × 50 × 0.2. Late Uruk.

188 Qalᶜa Rodhan. Extends for 180 m east along north bank of Shatt al-Kar × 80, but is closely surrounded and partly covered by dunes. Wind erosion has virtually destroyed the qalᶜa, leaving only suggestions of a four-cornered lozenge shape with the main tower (5 m diam., now rising 2 m) at one of the acute angles nearest the Shatt. The tower can be distinguished from many wind-eroded natural bluffs in this area only by the layers of reeds used in its construction. Recent "pseudoprehistoric" ware predominates, although blue lead glazes also are fairly frequent. In comparison with Kharkhara (site 075) and Majnūna (site 084), the advanced state of erosion here may suggest considerable age. Alternatively, the presence of active dunes may indicate an increased rate of wind erosion.

189 170 NW × 80 × 1. Possible Jemdet Nasr, definite Early Dynastic I. Mainly Neo-Babylonian–Parthian.

190 Part of Abū Bott. 500 (020°) × 300 × 6.2. Late Uruk, possible Jemdet Nasr, probable Early Dynastic. Akkadian–Larsa, reduced Old Babylonian occupation.

191 250 NW × 160 × 0.2. Surface collection illustrated in chapter 8. Late Uruk.

192 250 NW × 200 × 0.2. Sassanian.

193 200 (330°) × 150 × 0.1. Surface collection illustrated in chapter 8. Late Uruk.

194 210 NE × 180 × 2.5. Sassanian–Early Islamic.

195 110 diam. × 0.6. Sassanian–Early Islamic.

196 Tell Farawa. Main mound irregularly outlined (see map) but about 1,000 NW × 700, rising steeply to 6 m at northwest end and then falling away gradually. Much kiln debris. 300 m northwest is an area of low contemporary ruins, 400 E × 300. Parthian–Sassanian.

197 Jokha (Umma). Site not surveyed in detail. Andrae ("Umgebung," pp. 20–21, fig. 3) describes it as a main west-southwest–east-northeast ridge 15 m high and 1,000 m long, with lower extensions to the northeast and southeast. Topography is obscured by many dunes, as it was also in Andrae's day, but our impression is that this description includes only the more elevated proportions of the site and does not give the outer limits. On the basis of limited surface reconnaissance and plotting of discoloration in aerial photographs, it is tentatively suggested instead that the site covers an area about 1,500 m in diameter. Late Early Dynastic and Old Babylonian are dominant in surface collections, but intervening Akkadian, Ur III, and Larsa periods also are well represented. Uruk, Jemdet Nasr, and Early Dynastic I possible but unconfirmed.

198 Umm al-Aqarib. 1,700 (120°) × 840. Height difficult to measure because of dense surrounding sand dunes,

but at least 10 m. Uruk through Early Dynastic I probable but unconfirmed. Late Early Dynastic, including plano-convex bricks (21 × 14 × 5, 27.5 × 17 × 4, 37 × 20 × 4.5, and 31 × 20 × 4.5).

199 220 diam. × 2. Jemdet Nasr.

200 350 NW × 280 × 3. A few Ur III–Larsa sherds may or may not represent a significant occupation. Bulk of surface is Sassanian–Early Islamic.

201 500 (020°) × 220 × 3. Early–Late Uruk. Jemdet Nasr sherds are widespread but infrequent, and must represent a small or brief terminal occupation.

202 170 (020°) × 140 × 2.1. Sassanian.

203 80 diam. × 1.9. Late Uruk.

204 Part of Abū Bott. 490 NE × 290 × 4.8. Most of tell's surface is obscured by drifting sand, with recent robbers' pits in exposed areas. Late Early Dynastic–Larsa.

205 Qalᶜa Dermān al-Mūminīn. See figure 28. Settlement around qalᶜa 300 NW × 160 × 0.7. Low surrounding dunes partly cover site, bed of Shatt al-Kar immediately west. Recent.

206 250 NW × 180 × 2. Mainly Parthian. Also Early Dynastic I, possible Jemdet Nasr.

207 Small qalᶜa, see figure 28. Surrounding Recent settlement is 150 NW × 80 × 1.3.

208 Abū Ruwaysh. Main tell 700 NW × 300 × 1.2. 400 m north, connected by a sterile ridge that may be an ancient levee or river bank, is a smaller contemporary mound 170 m in diameter. Pottery and debris sparse on both. Parthian.

209 120 diam. × 0.8. Late Uruk, mainly Parthian.

210 Qalᶜa Umm al-Hicham. See figure 28. On east bank of old, dry watercourse bed, low mound 160 diam. on opposite bank at this point. Recent.

211 Also known as Qalᶜa Umm al-Hicham. See figure 28. On west bank of same old watercourse as site 210, accompanies mound 160 N × 120 × 0.4. Recent.

212 260 diam. × 2. Jemdet Nasr–Early Dynastic I.

213 Tell Zicharīya. 900 N × 500 × 4.5, attaining this height only near north end. Late Early Dynastic, probably also Akkadian. Main occupation Ur III–Larsa, with a thick overlying layer of Parthian–Sassanian debris only on north part of site.

214 350 NW × 200 × 1.5. Sassanian–Early Islamic.

215 50 NW × 15 × 0.2. Early Uruk.

216 60 diam. × 0.1. Achaemenian–Parthian.

217 Four adjoining Sassanian–Early Islamic sites northeast of Tell Jīd (site 164): 180 diam. × 0.3, 140 (325°) × 70 × 1.1, 120 diam. × 0.2, and 220 E × 180 × 0.7. See map for location.

218 280 (030°) × 230 × 1. Surface collection illustrated in chapter 8. Ubaid IV–Late Uruk.

219 140 NW × 100 × 0.6. Predominantly Late Uruk, reduced Jemdet Nasr occupation.

220 160 diam. × 1.6, Jemdet Nasr. Immediately adjoining to southeast is another tell, 100 diam. × 0.6, Parthian.

221 60 NE × 40, hummocks rising up to 0.3 m. A still smaller outlying area of debris 30 m northeast, with sparse debris at plain level suggesting that both originally formed a single settlement. Early Islamic.

222 180 N × 140 × 0.5, but only south half of site is perceptible as a mound above plain level. Much glass, some glass slag. Sassanian, Recent.

223 100 diam. × 0.8. Sassanian.

224 350 E × 200 × 0.6. Recent.

225 Two adjoining tells separated by an old canal line from northwest. To the northeast, 260 NW × 150 × 0.8. To the southwest, 360 NW × 180 × 0.6. A third contemporary tell lies 200 m southeast of the latter, 180 diam. × 0.8. Parthian–Sassanian.

226 180 (340°) × 130 × 0.4, with a small, ruined qalᶜa immediately to the southeast. Recent.

227 Qalᶜa Umm al-Hammad. See figure 28. Surrounding Recent settlement 300 E × 130 × 0.6.

228 120 NW × 40 × 0.6. Surrounding dunes also cover much of mound. Neo-Babylonian–Achaemenian.

229 Qalᶜa Maltūs (al-Hafāz). Main mound 350 (070°) × 220 × 2, with well-preserved small watchtower on its west end. 100 m southwest is a contemporary mound, 200 NE × 160 × 2.2. Clay sickles are rare, but might reflect an Uruk or Jemdet Nasr occupation. Primarily Parthian–Sassanian, with a much reduced Recent reoccupation.

230 Part of Umm al-ᶜAjjāj. 1,200 N × 440 × 2.6. Late Uruk rare, Jemdet Nasr, Early Dynastic I.

231 Part of Umm al-ᶜAjjāj. 600 (330°) × 400 × 1.7. Jemdet Nasr uncertain, Early Dynastic I.

232 Part of Umm al-ᶜAjjāj. 320 (330°) × 230 × 1.7. A southward continuation of 231, interrupted by a slight, narrow depression with sparse sherds. Jemdet Nasr–Early Dynastic I.

233 500 (330°) × 240 × 2.1. 150 m southwest is another, 160 (330°) × 100 × 0.6. See figure 11. Jemdet Nasr–Early Dynastic I.

234 220 diam. × 0.6. Jemdet Nasr. Early Dynastic I limited to south end of mound.

235 220 N × 180 × 2. Larsa–Cassite, Parthian.

236 220 diam. × 0.2. Surface collection illustrated in chapter 8. Mainly late Uruk. A limited Recent reoccupation.

237 130 NW × 70 × 2. Late Uruk. A reduced Recent reoccupation.

238 220 diam. × 2.4. Sassanian–Early Islamic, Recent. 250 m away at 340° is a mound 120 (340°) × 80 × 1.2. A third mound is 300 m away at 160°, 150 diam. × 2. Both of the latter are Sassanian only.

239 Imām Mahdi, also known as Abū Jamara. The small,

crude imām stands on a cone of debris 10 m diam. ×
2. It is constructed of secondarily reused brick laid up
without mortar, and roofed with reed matting. Hummocks of debris and fairly dense sherds at plain
level suggest a fairly continuous settlement within
an area 350 m diam. centering on this shrine. Sassanian, Recent (the latter including graves around
the shrine that apparently postdate the settlement).

240 140 NE × 80 × 1.5. 100 m northeast lies a smaller
contemporary tell, about 80 m diam. Parthian.

241 Low hummocks, sparse debris within an area 120 m
diam. Sassanian, Recent.

242 Part of Suheri. Probably this important site has
escaped earlier notice because it is very low, exceeding 1–1.5 m only in rare hummocks of late debris.
Moreover, high dunes cover part of the site and obscure its true size. Late Uruk, and possibly Jemdet
Nasr–Early Dynastic I, well represented particularly
in northeast quadrant. Conical cups of Jemdet Nasr
or Early Dynastic date occur in profusion in the same
area but also are common to the south, suggesting
that these levels are widespread. Late Early Dynastic
debris also common, but the dominant surface components are Akkadian–Larsa. Old Babylonian pottery confined to a very small area at extreme south
end of mound. One baked brick noted with a
stamped inscription of Amarsuena. Numerous Parthian graves, particularly on west half of site, but
nothing to suggest an actual settlement at that
period.

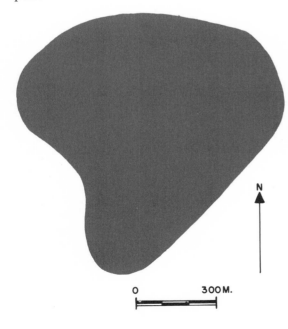

WS 242

243 Part of Medain. 700 E × 450 × 3.8. Parthian.

244 Larger mound rises 2 m, smaller one 2.4 m. Primarily
Achaemenian–Parthian, with a few early sherds
thought to have been introduced from site 245, and
with some Cassite and rare Recent pottery.

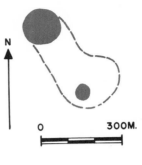

WS 244

245 See figure 11. The outer dashed line encloses a
slightly elevated area with sparse debris. If this defines the limits of early settlement, it was an impressively large one. North mound 2 m ht.; Jemdet Nasr
remains dominant here, but in addition there was
much Late Uruk and probably also Early Uruk.
Large clay cones occur in great numbers in the northeast part of this mound, suggestively outlining the
right-angled intersection of two walls of a temple
enclosure (?). Early Dynastic I pottery is present but
rare. On the other two mounds, both only 0.6 m ht.,
Jemdet Nasr was again the dominant surface component but there was little or no earlier pottery. A
little Parthian and Recent debris occurs on southwest mound.

246 Part of Medain. Irregularly bounded, approx. 400 m
diam. Low, but with many hummocks rising to 0.7
m and one to 1.2 m. Many baked bricks with wedge-
shaped Seleucid impressions. Neo-Babylonian–Parthian, with the latter perhaps representing only
graves now being exposed by wind erosion.

247 Part of Medain. Almost totally engulfed by dunes,
rendering limits and ht. obscure. At least 400 m diam.
One Ubaid II rim sherd, one clay celt and one clay
sickle point to a probable early occupation nearby.
Larsa–Neo-Babylonian, rare Parthian.

248 Single elongated mound at west end of illustrated
group. Ht. 2.9 m. Larsa–Neo-Babylonian, with Recent pottery along canal levees immediately west.

249 Remainder of illustrated group. Two mounds in
north 2.2 m ht., southeast mound 2 m, west mound
0.8. Parthian.

250 Main mound 140 NW × 110 × 1.8. Much glass, including slag fragments. Sassanian. 50 m south is a
second tell, 80 diam. × 1.6, exclusively Parthian. A
third tell, also Parthian, is of approximately the same

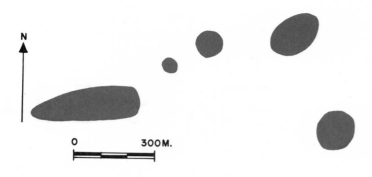

WS 248 and 249

size and lies 100 m farther south. In almost the opposite direction from the main mound (340°), irregular clusters of sherds and small hummocks of debris trail off along old canal levees for almost 1 km. Probably this represents a primarily Sassanian settlement.

251 450 E × 300 × 0.5, but with debris thinning out toward edges so that limits of site are hard to define. Site is bisected by a meandering, fairly narrow canal bed. Parthian.

252 At least 150 m diam., but the scatter of sherds continues without sharp limits. No perceptible elevation. Parthian.

253 About 1,000 × 250 × 4, obscured by dunes. Cassite–Parthian.

254 80 diam. × 0.2. Larsa–Cassite.

255 180 E × 130 × 2.2. Larsa–Old Babylonian probable but unconfirmed. Mainly Cassite–Neo-Babylonian.

256 190 NW × 100 × 0.3. Numerous robbers' pits. Surface collection illustrated in chapter 8. Jemdet Nasr–Early Dynastic I.

257 250 NE × 120 × 0.1. Adjoining soil discoloration indicating a wide, old canal bed. Achaemenian–Parthian.

258 260 NW × 110 × 2.8. Numerous clay sickles and one stone hoe suggest an ill-defined Uruk or Jemdet Nasr occupation nearby. Rare Cassite sherds, mainly Neo-Babylonian–Achaemenian.

259 Main mound 2.8 m ht., east mound 1.7 m, south mound 1.4 m. Nature of the four mounds shown suggests that they form parts of a single settlement whose lower-lying areas have been submerged by alluviation. An apparent old canal course cuts through site from the northwest, with absence of contour breaks in mounds suggesting it is contemporary with or older than main occupation. This course is marked by an intact plano-convex brick wall north of main mound, continuing across plain southeast of mound as a clear band of discoloration. Detailed plan of part of large building on east mound drawn from clean mud brick walls, 0.5 m thick and

very straight, visible on surface. Numerous baked plano-convex bricks are strewn on the eroded lower land surface to the southwest of the surviving portion of this building. Surface collection is predominantly late Early Dynastic, and this may be the only period of significant occupation. There are also rare Akkadian sherds, and perhaps some Ur III–Larsa sherds as well.

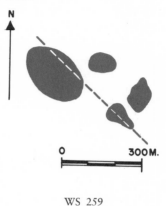

WS 259

260 Abū 'Ilba. Main tell 300 (330°) × 240 × 4, but with a parallel, lower extension to the west 200 m long × 120 m wide. Relatively dense debris also is found at plain level over an area at least half again as large as these dimensions. Dunes occur thickly to the north, and partly cover north half of tell. One sherd Ubaid IV painted ware. Late Uruk–Jemdet Nasr common, Early Dynastic I less numerous. Surface debris mainly Parthian, suggesting that only the high, central part of site is early.

261 Abū Khāwa. 320 N × 240 × 2.4, with an old canal apparently cut subsequently into west edge of site. 30 m east—across another old canal bed?—is a contemporary mound 160 diam. × 4. Possible Jemdet Nasr. Early Dynastic I–Akkadian, mainly late Early Dynastic.

262 220 (285°) × 160 × 0.2. Badly pitted. Late Uruk–Jemdet Nasr, the former predominant.

263 Irregular mounds and hummocks within an area perhaps 250 m in diameter. Highest mound 2 m; another, lower one is a late kiln site. Akkadian–Ur III. A few sherds of "pseudoprehistoric" ware probably date a Recent canal junction whose spoil banks occur in middle of occupied area.

264 See figure 11. Southeast tell 0.3 m high, others lower. Hundreds of flint cores and many more blades and flakes suggest the presence here of a specialized stoneworking site. Many stone bowl fragments also observed. Surface sherd collection illustrated in chapter 8. Late Uruk–Jemdet Nasr, the former predominant. A few Early Dynastic I sherds occur on extreme northwest and southeast ends.

265 Part of Medain. An extremely large, sprawling, irregular settlement, forming a discontinuous ribbon —presumably along a former river or canal—almost 5 km long. See map for principal debris clusters as sketched from air photographs, but no attempt was made to trace outlines in detail or to confirm them on the ground. Quite large, continuously built-up areas occur at intervals; one at extreme northwest end is about 400 m diam. Average size of sherd clusters is much smaller, however, perhaps little more than 25 m diam. The width of strip within which these clusters occur is mostly 1–200 m, widening in places to 400 m. Clusters are low, rising to 1.2 m only near southeast end. Sinuous, depressed, largely sterile areas between them give the entire site the appearance of an archipelago, suggesting that it once lay on the edge of marshes. Most of the site Sassanian, Recent, with a Parthian occupation seemingly limited to southeast end.

266 Abū Halifa. 70 diam. × 2. Tell now stands deep in seasonal swamp or haur, and is accordingly very salty. Parthian.

267 The sizes and relationships of this group of sites are obscured by later canal levee deposits. Most pronounced mound 120 diam. × 2, Parthian. 120 m south of this is a lower mound, 120 diam. × 0.7, Akkadian–Larsa, Parthian. Spoil banks along old Shatt al-Nil 200 m east of latter are littered with Ubaid I–II and Late Uruk–Jemdet Nasr pottery. This may form an early settlement 160 N × 20 width on either side of later bed. However, these sherds are more likely to have been thrown up during canal clearance.

268 Two mounds, both about 50 diam. × 0.2, 400 m apart on a 350° line. Parthian.

269 An important junction on old Shatt al-Nil. One main affluent, flowing from the north, is joined by another from the northwest; combined course continues directly south. Debris particularly thick along northwest branch, extending for 500 m x 250 m width. Most prominent elevation is a small mound, 60 m diam. × 3, on west bank of other affluent. Neo-Babylonian–Achaemenian, little Parthian.

270 Main mound on Shatt al-Nil, 400 (330°) × 250 × 3, bisected by bed of the old canal. 400 m east is an outlying settlement, 80 diam. × 3.5. Achaemenian–Parthian.

271 al-Tine. At least 450 (330°) × 300 × 2.5, but limits of site are obscured by dunes and canal deposits. Neo-Babylonian–Parthian.

272 See figure 11. Ht. 0.4 m. Surface collection illustrated in chapter 8. Late Uruk, Jemdet Nasr, Early Dynastic I.

273 Two adjoining small areas of scattered sherds at plain level, not exceeding 5 m diam. each. Jemdet Nasr.

274 See figure 11. Badly pitted, reaching 0.4 m ht. only in spoil banks. Surface collection illustrated in chapter 8. Late Uruk.

275 30 diam. × 0.2. Ubaid III–IV.

276 See figure 11. Central mound badly pitted, hence spoil banks reach max. ht. of 0.3 m. Nature of apparent ring of settlement or debris to west unclear. Surface collection illustrated in chapter 8. Late Uruk–Jemdet Nasr–Early Dynastic I.

277 80 diam. plain level. Jemdet Nasr. Debris sparse.

278 400 E × 120 × 2. Rare Cassite. Neo-Babylonian–Achaemenian possible but unconfirmed. Mainly Parthian.

279 Main mound 190 NE × 140 × 2. Another mound 200 m west, about half as large. Rare Cassite. Neo-Babylonian–Achaemenian possible but unconfirmed. Mainly Parthian.

280 350 NW × 180 × 2.5. Sand dunes occupy a low saddle crossing the middle of this tell perpendicular to its length, but the underlying debris appears to be continuous. Cassite, Parthian.

281 See figure 12. Clusters of debris suggestively outline a marsh settlement interrupted by sinuous natural watercourses. An apparent temple enclosure is prominently situated along one of the main offtakes from the parent watercourse. Within the slightly raised area shown in dark hachure are broken bits of stone, mortar, and baked brick, but no pottery. Except on the southeast, this area is enclosed by what appears in places as the remains of a thick wall with masses of small, well-made clay cones on its outer surface. It may be noted that, within the limits of accuracy of a prismatic compass bearing (corrected for magnetic declination), this apparent Jemdet Nasr temple is directly north of the Eanna ziggurat and Nafiji.

The remainder of the site consists of sparse clusters of Jemdet Nasr debris at plain level, although a much later canal cuts across it from the west-northwest. The watercourses appear as very slight depressions accompanied by some soil discoloration. There is a curious contrast between the appearance of this settlement and that of adjacent site 282. At least the main mounds of the latter are thickly strewn with sherds, somewhat regular in shape, noticeably (even if slightly) elevated, and badly pitted, like most other contemporary sites found during the survey. This site is clearly irregular in shape, less dense, and lacking a nucleus in spite of the presence of an apparent temple enclosure. Since both were occupied during the same period, and since no local differences are evident in erosional or depositional processes, the contrast is hard to explain.

282 See figure 12 and comments under 281. Max. ht.

0.4 m. Late Uruk, Jemdet Nasr, very limited Early Dynastic I.

283 90 m diam., low hummocks and scattered debris at plain level. Larsa–Cassite.

284 140 NW × 110 × 0.8. Neo-Babylonian–Achaemenian, very limited Parthian.

285 90 diam. × 0.3. Badly pitted, obscured by low, drifted sand. Late Uruk–Jemdet Nasr.

286 Sparse patches of debris, apparently partly covered by drifting sand. Late Uruk.

287 220 diam. × 2.5, with sparse debris trailing off westnorthwest 300 m to low, hummocky remains which may represent a single building. The latter possibly recalls site 336. Larsa–Cassite.

288 290 NE × 200 × 2, with the second dimension possibly much larger but obscured by overlying dunes. Jemdet Nasr, very limited Early Dynastic I.

289 Patches of Jemdet Nasr debris at plain level, partly dune covered. Immediately east is an apparent old levee that has been wind-scoured and is now largely below the level of the site. Site gave impression of having been similarly affected.

290 180 diam. × 2. 400 m east is a contemporary tell, 240 diam. × 2. Parthian.

291 140 diam. × 1.6. Achaemenian–Parthian.

292 See figure 11. Appearance of the site is that of dispersed, low hummocks; in this case the regularity of the outlines shown is somewhat misleading. Surface collection illustrated in chapter 8. Late Uruk, limited Jemdet Nasr.

293 170 E × 100 × 0.7. Late Uruk–Jemdet Nasr, limited Early Dynastic I.

294 Center mound 3 m, southwest mound 1.1 m, other 0.5–1 m ht. Northeast mounds Late Early Dynastic, limited Old Babylonian. Central mound, and plain surface adjoining to the NE, Larsa–Old Babylonian. Southwest mound Late Early Dynastic–Ur III.

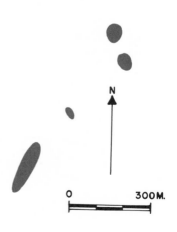

WS 294

295 Tell al-ʿAwaydīya. A prominent triangulation point, reaching 4.5 m ht. Parthian.

296 200 diam. × 0.8. Parthian.

297 250 N × 65 × 0.2. Badly pitted. Late Uruk–Jemdet Nasr.

298 80 diam. × 0.3. Surface collection illustrated in chapter 8. Ubaid I–II, possibly also pre-Ubaid.

299 160 (150°) × 110 × 2. Parthian.

300 50 diam., plain level, just clusters of debris. Cassite-Neo-Babylonian.

301 Sur. 450 (330°) × 250 × 2, but these dimensions include the bed and spoil banks of the old Shatt al-Nil which divide the site. Limited Cassite, mainly Neo-Babylonian–Parthian.

302 Definition of site obscure, a low, hummocky settlement 300 m in diameter. Parthian.

303 Parthian settlement on both banks of the Shatt al-Nil. Beginning on south end, it extends north for 200 m mainly on west bank (width 100 m). At that point bulk of settlement shifts to east bank and continues north for 200 m farther, finally disappearing under very high dunes.

304 150 diam. × 1.5, but with sherds at plain level covering an area 400 m diam. and extending farther to northwest. Parthian.

305 Tell al-Hawīya. Most of site is low, limits are vaguely defined. Broad, eroded traces of a large or repeatedly redug canal parallel the northeast arm of site, and another old canal levee approaches site from the west-northwest. Neo-Babylonian–Parthian.

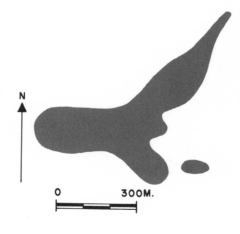

WS 305

306 90 diam., rising only in scattered hummocks to 0.5 m ht. Possible Jemdet Nasr. Early Dynastic I.

307 240 NE × 180 × 1.5, but mostly lower, discontinuous, perhaps badly wind eroded. Parthian.

308 Parthian cemetery, the interment vessels exposed above plain surface through the scouring action of wind. Completely surrounded by dunes, so that the

presence of an accompanying settlement cannot be confirmed.

309 80 E × 70 × 0.2. Late Uruk.

310 95 diam. × 0.7, badly pitted. Surface collection illustrated in chapter 8. Late Uruk. Jemdet Nasr limited to east end of site.

311 140 diam., but at present only scattered hummocks up to 1.5 m ht. emerge through a covering layer of drifted sand. Hence the presence of a continuous settlement cannot be confirmed. Possible Larsa–Cassite, mainly Neo-Babylonian–Parthian. An outlying Parthian cemetery is being exposed by wind erosion several hundred m south-southeast.

312 220 N × 190 × 1.4. Mainly Jemdet Nasr, limited Early Dynastic I. Very limited Parthian debris also is present, and there is a Parthian brick kiln a short distance east of mound and a Parthian cemetery being exposed by wind erosion 300 m northeast. Surface collection illustrated in chapter 8.

313 60 NE × 25, rising to 2.5 m only near southwest end. Apparently a single Parthian building. Baked brick floors and walls are visible, as well as four column bases up to 1.1 m diam. with several coats of stucco.

314 80 E × 70 × 0.4. Surface collection illustrated in chapter 8. Late Uruk.

315 130 NW × 110 × 2. One Cassite sherd may or may not reflect a significant occupation. Mainly Neo-Babylonian–Achaemenian, sparse Parthian. Wind erosion is exposing Neo-Babylonian graves on east and southeast parts of mound.

316 140 diam. × 0.8. Low, level areas within site suggest courtyards. Neo-Babylonian–Achaemenian, sparse Parthian.

317 40 E × 30 × 0.4. Limited surface debris indicated an Uruk or Jemdet Nasr date or both. Considerable obsidian noted.

318 140 N × 80 × 0.2, but with dunes making site limits imprecise. Late Uruk.

319 180 E × 140 × 0.6, but with second dimension obscured by dunes. Neo-Babylonian–Achaemenian.

320 Perhaps 100 diam. × 0.5, but limits imprecise because of enclosing dunes. Larsa–Cassite.

321 See figure 11. Larger mound rises in a few hummocks to 0.2. Jemdet Nasr.

322 Four small clusters of debris, each 40–50 m diam. × 0.5–1 m ht. Parthian.

323 50 diam. × 2.5. Probably the remains of a brick kiln. Parthian.

324 40 diam. × 0.5. Parthian.

325 190 (030°) × 110 × 0.2. Late Uruk. Probable Jemdet Nasr. Early Dynastic I.

326 80 diam. × 1. Parthian.

327 180 NE × 120 × 0.8. Soil highly saline, possibly

explaining why only greenish, overfired sherds are present on surface. Jemdet Nasr.

328 60 diam. × 0.6. Presence of fused pottery and brick slag may indicate later use as kiln site. Jemdet Nasr.

329 Possible Uruk or Jemdet occupation reflected by a few sherds, which might instead have been secondarily transported to site. Surface collection Parthian, except for one complete Sassanian incantation bowl (inscription illegible).

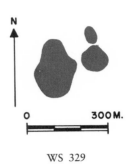

WS 329

330 130 E × 95 × 0.8. Soil highly saline, surface sherds accordingly sparse and poorly preserved. Ill-defined occupation in the Uruk or Jemdet Nasr range.

331 See figure 11. Surface collection illustrated in chapter 8. Late Uruk.

332 60 diam. × 0.2. Neo-Babylonian–Parthian.

333 200 (290°) × 110, mostly low, but with a few hummocks rising to 1 m. Larsa–Neo-Babylonian.

334 90 (120°) × 40 × 0.7. Late Uruk–Jemdet Nasr.

335 50 NW × 15 × 0.1. Neo-Babylonian–Achaemenian.

336 An isolated enclosure or administrative center. Baked brick in place in center platform (36 × 36 × 7) may postdate site. Highest debris 0.5 m. Larsa–Cassite.

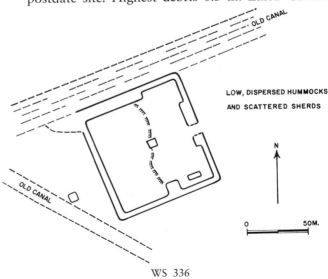

WS 336

337 80 diam. × 0.2, with two smaller but slightly higher mounds just northeast. Parthian.

338 160 diam. × 1.3, but slightly elongated to southeast and tailing off in that direction for perhaps 100 m of largely sterile but slightly elevated (levee?) deposits. Mainly an Uruk site, but also with a Parthian occupation concentrated around highest elevation near southeast end.

339 30 diam. × 0.8. 200 m away at 200° is a low, vaguely defined, saline swelling perhaps 80 m diam. Neo-Babylonian–Achaemenian.

340 Small Parthian kilns (?) along an old road or canal course. The larger, to the north, is 20 diam. × 0.9. The other is 75 m away at 205°.

341 140 E × 90 × 1.3. Badly pitted. Larsa–Old Babylonian.

342 30 diam. × 1. A still smaller mound of same type is 40 m northwest. Probably Parthian kilns.

343 A string of small mounds adjoining an apparent old canal bed 20–30 m in width. 20–80 m diam., mostly low. See map for location. Parthian.

344 Buwayrīya. Max. ht. near northeast end, 2.5 m. Parthian.

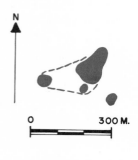

WS 344

345 Hnēfisāne. 220 (070°) × 120 × 3. Two smaller mounds tail off at 30 m intervals from southwest end. Parthian.

346 300 diam., hummocks rising to 0.5 m. Sherd piles left after decay and erosion of mud brick walls outline possible courts. Neo-Babylonian–Achaemenian. Parthian is limited to west end of site.

347 Sparse surface debris, interspersed by canal levees, within an area about 100 diam. Jemdet Nasr.

348 Abū Shuwaych. 60 NW × 50 × 3.5 Parthian.

349 120 NW × 50 × 1.5, with a small outlying mound to the northeast. Achaemenian, probably also Neo-Babylonian.

350 See figure 11. Both mounds 0.4 m ht. Late Uruk.

351 200 (330°) × 90 × 1.8. Ur III–Larsa, Neo-Babylonian–Achaemenian.

352 50 diam. × 1.3. Mainly Ur III–Larsa, probably also Akkadian.

353 240 (330°) × 190 × 2.6. Ur III–Larsa.

354 100 NW × 70 × 2.4. Neo-Babylonian–Achaemenian, limited Parthian.

355 Ishān Nahle. 270 (330°) × 80 × 2.4, tapering to a low north end. Saline. Ur III–Larsa.

356 Umm Muʿilim. 50 NW × 25 × 2.5. Very sparse sherds. Age indeterminate.

357 Only clusters of sherds on plain surface, surrounded by dunes; perhaps 30 m diam. Jemdet Nasr.

358 400 diam. × 1.5. Jemdet Nasr was major occupation. A thin, limited Larsa–Cassite reoccupation occurred on north and east parts of mound.

359 120 diam. × 0.8. Cassite–Neo-Babylonian.

360 Abū Dhīb. Highest part of site is its northeast extension, which seems to consist of a single baked plano-convex brick building. Similar bricks are found all over site in smaller numbers. Dominant ceramic component is late Early Dynastic, with a few possible Akkadian or Ur III sherds also noted. In the area of mound shown in hachure soil discolorations suggest a large building which may be of Neo-Babylonian date, since pottery of this period also is widespread on site. Probably of this date also is the small mound to the southwest, which again may be a single baked brick building.

WS 360

361 Five small (5 m diam.) clusters of Larsa–Old Babylonian debris on plain surface.

362 280 NE × 160 × 0.6. 200 m southwest lies a contemporary mound, 80 diam. × 0.4. Traces of mud-brick architecture survive in southwest part of latter. Parthian.

363 150 NW × 50 × 1.3. Neo-Babylonian–Parthian.

364 120 diam. × 0.8. Cassite–Neo-Babylonian.

365 170 E × 160 × 1.6. Saline, dark-surfaced, pottery sparse except around robbers' pits. One of these exposes a well 1.8 m diam. lined with plano-convex brick. Possible Jemdet Nasr. Rare Early Dynastic I. Late Early Dynastic.

366 40 (330°) × 30 × 1. Mainly Achaemenian, limited Parthian.

367 Tell Abū Zumal. 200 NW × 150 × 2.3. Late Uruk, Achaemenian–Parthian.

368 240 diam. × 2.3, although on one side wind-laid sand has elevated the plain an additional meter. Old

enclosure of mud brick on southwest edge. Neo-Babylonian–Achaemenian.

369 Tell Umqtaif^c. 160 diam. × 1.9. Jemdet Nasr.

370 160 diam. × 1.8. Jemdet Nasr, Neo-Babylonian–Achaemenian.

371 Imām Nur. 30 diam. × 7, a small, conical mound very difficult to approach through completely sursounding dunes. The crude, small shrine is of baked, reused bricks laid up loosely without mortar and covered with a reed mat. The extent of the surrounding Recent settlement, if any, is hidden by sand.

372 Dimensions obscured by dunes but perhaps 250 (330°) × 80–100, rising above plain level only in spoil banks around old pits. Surface collection illustrated in chapter 8. Jemdet Nasr–Early Dynastic I.

373 250 N × 150; sherds and debris at plain level. Jemdet Nasr, probably also Late Uruk. Surface collection mainly Neo-Babylonian–Achaemenian.

374 200 diam., low hummocks of debris with sparse sherds. Recent.

375 Qal^ca Sussa. See figure 26 and pp. 76–78. Accompanying settlement is immediately downstream from standing ruins, 220 (120°) × 160, low. Recent.

376 220 diam. × 0.8, with main elevation to east of center. Late Uruk. Low west part of site is mainly Recent.

377 225 N × 190 × 2. Possible Jemdet Nasr. Early Dynastic I, Recent.

378 See figure 11. Southwest mound 0.8 m, but other part of site is really little more than a scatter of sherds at plain level. Possible Jemdet Nasr. Early Dynastic I.

379 110 NW × 70 × 1. Achaemenian–Parthian.

380 150 E × 110 × 2.1. Jemdet Nasr, Neo-Babylonian–Parthian.

381 Tūlūl Gayyarat. Central mound 165 E × 130 × 2.2. A second lies 500 m away at 068°, 200 E × 100 × 2.1. A third lies 100 m away from former at 160°, 180 N × 160 × 2.2. Parthian–Sassanian.

382 Tell Baydha. 420 NE × 300 × 4, reaching max. ht. between center and southwest end. Surface collection illustrated in chapter 8. Primarily Jemdet Nasr–Early Dynastic I, but with a sparse Neo-Babylonian–Achaemenian reoccupation of southwest slope.

383 Tell Mansurīya. 630 NW × 350 × 2.8. Possible Jemdet Nasr. Early Dynastic I.

384 Tell Twaimi. See figure 11. Both mounds 1.9 m ht. There is a small mud-brick watchtower on the west one. Probable Jemdet Nasr. Early Dynastic I.

385 160 E × 125 × 2.5. Perhaps one-third of larger dimension is without elevation or debris but contained within a ridge of sherds that may be the remains of an eroded mud-brick wall. The elevated area, 125 m

diam., is sharply contoured at edges, perhaps also suggesting an enclosing wall. Late Early Dynastic–Larsa.

386 245 (100°) × 70 × 0.3. Some pits. Surface collection illustrated in chapter 8. Early–Late Uruk.

387 Central part of mound is compact and elevated, 150 diam. × 3, suggesting a possible citadel. But debris continues, forming a recognizable mound 420 NW × 260 with outlying hummocks and clusters for an additional 40 m to northeast and 60 m southeast. Surface collection illustrated in chapter 8. Late Uruk–Jemdet Nasr–Early Dynastic I.

388 260 diam., reaching 0.8 ht. only in discontinuous hummocks. Parthian.

389 300 (330°) × 80 × 1.5. Neo-Babylonian–Parthian.

390 170 E × 100 × 1. Surface collection illustrated in chapter 8. Possible Jemdet Nasr. Early Dynastic I.

391 140 diam., rising to 0.4 ht. only in hummocks. A still smaller outlying settlement lies to the southeast. Parthian.

392 90 diam. × 0.8. Cassite–Parthian, Recent. 100 m southeast is a second mound, 80 diam. × 1.6. In spite of the greater elevation here, only a single Cassite sherd was noted and Neo-Babylonian–Achaemenian types apparently were absent. As on the other mound, there was sparse Recent, in addition to Parthian, pottery.

393 40 diam. × 0.2. Parthian.

394 Sikne, also known as Imām Hussayn. 160 diam. × 6, with a west extension of sherds at plain level for an additional 200 m. The shrine is of crude baked brick, laid up without mortar, and there are several modern graves around it. Parthian.

395 120 diam. × 1.5, with debris trailing off to west along a broad old levee. Parthian, also some Recent pottery.

396 180 (330°) × 1.5. Recent.

397 Qal^ca al-Arayfāt. See figure 28. Surrounding Recent settlement is 120 diam., with sherds continuing to north along old canal bed.

398 160 (300°) × 110 × 1. Neo-Babylonian–Achaemenian, limited Parthian.

399 Qal^ca Falhīya, also known as Qal^ca Fali. See figure 29 and pp. 77–78. A large, well-preserved country estate, including enclosed courts surrounded by galleries of small rooms, and outlying stables. Surface collection included a few sherds of "pseudo-prehistoric" ware as well as china teacups and other trade items.

400 Ht. 1.9 m. Larsa–Cassite. See illustration on next page.

401 220 NW × 170; ht. not recorded but about 1 m. Mound tails off to southeast, and debris in this area is mainly Jemdet Nasr. The higher part of the mound

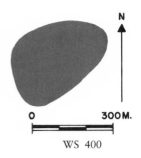

WS 400

is Neo-Babylonian–Achaemenian, with a limited Recent occupation.

402 170 N × 140 × 2.1, with the remains of a small mud-brick tower on the crest of the mound. A few clay sickles suggest a possible Uruk or Jemdet Nasr occupation. Mainly Neo-Babylonian–Achaemenian.

403 130 diam. × 1.3. Site map shows drainage channels or canals radiating in all directions from this mound, and these are strikingly apparent both on the ground and in air photographs. Cassite–Achaemenian.

404 Tell Awayli. 200 diam. × 2.6. Possible Jemdet Nasr. Early Dynastic I.

405 700 E × 250 × 3.2. Cassite–Parthian.

406 110 NE × 70 × 0.7. Late Uruk, limited Jemdet Nasr.

407 250 E × 220 × 2. Very gradual contours and outcrops of debris at some distance east and west of mound suggest its original size may have been somewhat larger. Late Uruk, Jemdet Nasr, limited Early Dynastic I.

408 180 E × 140 × 1. Neo-Babylonian–Parthian.

409 See figure 10. Elevation of main mound 2.2 m. Surface collection illustrated in chapter 8. Possible Jemdet Nasr. Early Dynastic I.

410 A scatter of sherds 40 m diam. at plain level. There is an uncertain and ill-defined Uruk or Jemdet Nasr occupation. Most debris is Neo-Babylonian.

411 190 E × 125 × 2. Surface collection illustrated in chapter 8. Ubaid IV.

412 220 NE × 200 × 3.5. Larsa–Cassite.

413 220 (060°) × 155 × 2. Larsa–Cassite.

414 125 E × 80 × 1. Neo-Babylonian–Parthian.

415 40 diam. × 1.2. Recent.

416 Qal'a Imnaythir. See figure 28. Qal'a stands on mound 70 diam. × 2. 45 m southwest is a mound 70 NW × 30 × 0.9 with very sparse sherds. Both Recent.

417 70 NW × 40 × 0.4. Late Uruk.

418 Dense sherd accumulation at little more than plain level, 60 m diam. Late Uruk.

419 60 diam. × 1.1. Recent.

420 200 diam. × 3. Parthian.

421 A string of small Recent sites not more than 2 m ht., served by a canal from Qal'a Imnaythir (416). See map for size and distribution.

422 240 N × 120 × 1.5. Debris is sparse, partly sand-covered and partly consisting only of clusters of sherds left after substantial wind erosion of mound surface. One large cluster, possibly representing wasters from an old pottery kiln, forms a prominent knob near north end of site. This may indicate removal by erosion of nearly two meters of deposits. Surface collection illustrated in chapter 8. Possible Jemdet Nasr. Early Dynastic I.

423 200 N × 80 × 0.2. Recent.

424 110 diam. × 0.8. Larsa–Cassite.

425 40 diam. × 0.5. Ur III–Old Babylonian.

426 40 diam. × 1.8. Neo-Babylonian–Achaemenian.

427 250 diam. × 2.7. Cassite–Neo-Babylonian.

428 50 N × 35 × 0.8. Much of sparse debris consists of pottery kiln wasters. Ur III–Larsa.

429 Tell Abla wa Asam. 200 NW × 110 × 7, although only central part of mound rises over 2 m. Pottery very dense on high, central part of mound, although only a very limited number of vessel types, all utilitarian, are represented. This feature, combined with the unusual height of mound for a relatively short occupation, may suggest that a specialized center for ceramic production existed here. Ur III–Larsa.

430 110 NW × 30 × 1.4. Ur III–Larsa.

431 This number applies to the outlying small mounds west of Tell Abla, which also may be considered as having once formed a continuous settlement with it. All elevations 2.5–4 m, pottery sparse, later brick slag noted as common. Ur III–Old Babylonian, with the latter perhaps more common than on Tell Abla itself.

432 Tell Abla. 720 (060°) × 500 × 6. This entire area is elevated, but major summits appear as a group of hills rather than a compact mound. An isolated mound at east end, 160 E × 80 × 6, apparently is composed almost entirely of 36 × 36 (Sassanian?) brick, with walls traced by old, superficial excavations. Pottery is almost entirely absent in this area of what may be a late, limited reoccupation. The remainder of the mound is Ur III–Old Babylonian.

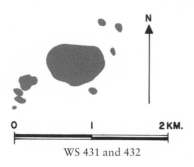

WS 431 and 432

433 At least 300 diam. × 1.5, but limits obscured by surrounding, and partly covering, dunes. Cassite–Parthian.

434 200 diam. × 2. Mainly Parthian, possibly going back to the Neo-Babylonian period.

435 240 diam. × 1.5. Neo-Babylonian–Parthian.

436 480 E × 220 × 1.5. Parthian.

437 A low, vaguely defined site consisting mainly of scattered hummocks. The total area, if indeed it was continuously settled, is about 450 m diam. Near its west side is a low mound 200 (070°) × 140 × 0.3, with a sunken central court (?), and in this area Larsa–Neo-Babylonian pottery predominates. Debris elsewhere is mainly Parthian.

438 190 E × 80 × 0.6. Larsa–Neo-Babylonian.

439 Umm al-Wawīya. 270 diam. × 2. Many brick fragments with stamped inscriptions of Amarsuena and Gungunum (see chapter 8), also baked plano-convex bricks. Late Early Dynastic–Larsa.

440 A sparse Parthian settlement mixed with spoil banks from old watercourse. See map for dimensions of this long, low ridge, which should not be regarded as a large population center in spite of its apparent size. Additional smaller settlements, also with sparse debris, occur farther to the east as shown.

441 A scatter of pottery at plain level, 20 m diam. Parthian.

442 70 diam. × 3. Possible Jemdet Nasr. Early Dynastic I, Recent.

443 Four small, contemporary mounds along old canal line leading to Larsa. North mound 80 diam. × 4, apparently a single building of very large baked brick (34–36 × 34–36 × 10–18). Some of these bricks have triangular impressions like those of Seleucid times, but none of the pottery associated with the mound fits this dating. Second mound 130 E × 80 × 1.9, with a much smaller, lower mound adjoining it immediately to the south. South mound an apparent kiln site with little identifiable pottery. Entire surface collection fits an Ur III–Larsa date.

444 Imām ʿAbbās al-Kurdi. Settlement debris is confined to an area extending 750 m northeast and 200 m southwest of the present shrine, with a maximum width of 220 m and elevation of 1.5 m. A much longer, but essentially sterile, ridge or canal bank continues to both northeast and southwest. Ur III–Old Babylonian, Neo-Babylonian–Achaemenian. Around the present shrine are numerous household articles left there by nomads for safekeeping, but there is no evidence of a Recent occupation.

445 Three adjacent mounds forming an equilateral triangle of settlement 120 m on a side × 2. An outlying mound 140 m NW, 90 diam. × 2, is apparently contemporary, but diagnostic sherd types were extremely rare on both. Probably can be assigned to the Neo-Babylonian–Parthian range.

446 90 NW × 70 × 2. Ur III–Larsa.

447 60 (340°) × 40 × 0.7. Recent.

448 Tell Sifr (Kutallu). Two irregularly shaped, dark-surfaced, saline mounds. The larger, to the northeast, is 600 NW × 400 × 6, with superficial, old excavations and pits. The other, 150 m away, is 280 diam. × 2.6. Collecting conditions were poor, so the full range of occupation is unclear. The few diagnostic sherds that were found were all Old Babylonian (cf. Loftus, "Notes," pp. 263–72).

449 Imām Kamil. 100 NW × 60 × 0.6. Small shrine consists of a conical inner chamber and cubical antechamber, built of mud brick and roofed with reed mats. Numerous individual piles of household articles, including much firewood and many water cans, but also plows, bicycles, and radios, are grouped around the shrine for safekeeping. Surface collection contained no diagnostic types but appeared to belong in the Parthian or Sassanian range.

450 120 E × 105 × 0.6. Saline, dark-surfaced, pottery very sparse. No diagnostic sherds found, but body sherds generally appeared to be of Parthian or Sassanian type.

451 Tell al-Medain, also known as Medina (Bad-Tibira). 2,300 NE × perhaps an average of 500. Individual summits rise to 6 m ht. There are breaks in the main ridge of the site, indicating that it was cut through by contemporary (and surely by later) watercourses, but the profusion of sherds and baked bricks nevertheless indicates a site that was densely and continuously occupied. Early periods are not well attested on surface, although conical cups of Jemdet Nasr or Early Dynastic date occur widely in small numbers. The main occupation would appear to have been in the Ur III–Old Babylonian periods, and it is the latter period which is dominant in the surface debris from all parts of the site. (Cf. Loftus, "Notes," pp. 263–72; V. E. Crawford, "The Location of Bad-Tibira," *Iraq* 22 [1960]: 197–99.

452 Ruqba Medain. See map for outline of this planned, hexagonal city, 900 N × 600 × 3. The outer wall is well preserved. Surface pottery is primarily Sassanian, possibly including some Parthian. There are many Old Babylonian baked bricks, but these can be assumed to have been secondarily transported to site.

453 See figure 11. Main mound 2.5, lesser mound 0.8 ht. Late Uruk–Jemdet Nasr, Larsa–Old Babylonian, Recent.

454 70 NW × 30 × 1.3. Parthian.

455 160 E × 130 × 4. Very saline, sherds extremely sparse. Probably late Early Dynastic. Mainly Akkadian–Larsa.

456 Tell Klāleh. 260 NE × 150 × 1.2. Parthian–Sassanian.

457 Tell Mīzan. A parallelogram 250 m on a side; see

map for orientation. Outer sides of mound are steep, rising to 4 m, and it is low in center; this clearly suggests an enclosing wall. Modern graves are found in the low, central part of the site, many covered with baked bricks 30 × 30 × 7 and 27 × 16 × 7 with triangular or circular, probably Seleucid, impressions. Larsa–Old Babylonian, Parthian. 100 m away (at 200°) is another big Parthian settlement, 350 (340°) × 150 × 1.

458 Tell Ghazilat. 130 diam. × 2, Cassite, Parthian. Same dating applies to a tell 200 NW × 80 × 1 that lies 130 m north of first, although in this case sparse surface debris makes Cassite less certain. A mound occupied only during the Cassite period is 110 m west of the first, and measures 110 N × 50 × 1.1.

459 Tell al-Tawwīl. 550 (280°) × 150–200 × 2. Probably Ubaid III–IV, although these sherds may have been secondarily transported from site 460. Mainly Ur III–Larsa.

460 Tell Awayli. 360 NW × 300 × 4.3. Surface collection illustrated in chapter 8. Ubaid III–IV–Early Uruk. Late Uruk limited to northeast end of site. Northwest half of site is covered with kiln debris of indeterminate date.

461 Imshawwal. 170 NW × 100 × 3.5. Achaemenian–Parthian.

462 190 E × 150 × 0.9. Jemdet Nasr, limited Early Dynastic I, limited Ur III–Larsa.

463 Tell Libbe. 190 diam. × 0.8. Saline, dark-colored, poor collecting conditions. Probable dating late Early Dynastic–Larsa.

464 180 (300°) × 100 × 0.8. Neo-Babylonian–Achaemenian.

465 260 (330°) × 110 × 0.8. Saline, dark-surfaced, sparse pottery. Early Dynastic I, possibly also Jemdet Nasr.

466 120 diam. × 1.7. Saline, dark-surfaced, sparse pottery. Immediately southeast of mound is an area 160 NW × 90 × 0.3, possibly only an extension of site, with more plentiful sherds. Larsa–Old Babylonian, Recent.

Index

INDEX

240

Date Due

| | 5000 | | 4000 | | 3000 | | | 20 |

PERIOD

ERIDU

EARLY
UBAID

EARLY
URUK

JEMDET
NASR

EARLY
DYNASTIC II

AKKAD

HAJJI
MOHAMMED

LATE
UBAID

LATE
URUK

EARLY
DYNAS-
TIC I

EARLY
DYNASTIC III

T
D
T

**SETTLEMENT
HIERARCHY**

Villages

Villages, small and large
towns

Uruk rapidly attains
maximum size. Rural
abandonment begins

Citie
water
of vil
mino

Villages, small towns

Increasing clusters of
villages, small towns;
Uruk approaching
urban size

Numerous walled cities;
smaller settlements
negligible

**SUBSISTENCE
AND LAND USE**

Local enclaves of small-scale
cultivation along minor
stream branches, herding,
fishing, shell-fishing

First detectable canalization

Ir
co
ir
a

Plow
con-
firmed
(used
earlier?)

Development of urban
supporting zones of
intensive cultivation,
complementary herding;
elsewhere sparse herding,
fishing

**POLITICAL
INTEGRATION**

No evidence of
multisettlement territorial
units

Central town,
villages form small
territorial units.
Religious hegemony
of Uruk

Periodically
contending
city-states

Suc
bur
rea

Uruk already a regional
religious center?

Military
dominance,
but limited
ongoing
administrative
control, by
Uruk

Loose ephem
empire